MW00396667

The
MIDDLE-LENGTH TREATISE
on the
STAGES OF THE PATH
TO ENLIGHTENMENT

The

MIDDLE-LENGTH TREATISE

on the

STAGES OF THE PATH TO ENLIGHTENMENT

Tsongkhapa

Translated by Philip Quarcoo

Foreword by His Eminence Ling Rinpoche

Wisdom

Wisdom Publications, Inc.
199 Elm Street
Somerville MA 02144 USA
wisdomexperience.org

Library of Congress Cataloging-in-Publication Data
Names: Tsong-kha-pa Blo-bzang-grags-pa, 1357–1419, author. | Quarcoo, Philip,
    translator. | Yongzin Ling Rinpoche, 1903–1983, author.
Title: The middle-length treatise on the stages of the path to enlightenment /
    Tsongkhapa Losang Drakpa, Philip Quarcoo, Yongzin Ling Rinpoche.
Description: First. | Somerville: Wisdom Publications, 2021. | Includes bibliographical
    references and index.
Identifiers: LCCN 2020040712 (print) | LCCN 2020040713 (ebook) |
    ISBN 9781614294436 (hardcover) | ISBN 9781614294597 (ebook)
Subjects: LCSH: Lam-rim. | Dge-lugs-pa (Sect)—Doctrines. | Meditation—Buddhism. |
    Spiritual life—Buddhism. | Religious life—Buddhism. | Enlightenment (Buddhism)
Classification: LCC BQ7645.L35 T753 2021 (print) | LCC BQ7645.L35 (ebook) |
    DDC 294.3/442—dc23
LC record available at https://lccn.loc.gov/2020040712
LC ebook record available at https://lccn.loc.gov/2020040713

ISBN 978-1-61429-443-6   ebook ISBN 978-1-61429-459-7

25 24 23 22 21
5 4 3 2 1

Cover design by Jess Morphew. Interior design by Gopa & Ted 2.
Typeset by Kristin Goble.
Printed on acid-free paper that meets the guidelines for permanence and durability of the
Production Guidelines for Book Longevity of the Council on Library Resources.

Printed in the United States of America.

Contents

Foreword

BY HIS EMINENCE LING RINPOCHE

IN THE MORE THAN 2,500 years since the peerless Teacher, the incomparable Lord of Sages, came into this world, countless āryas and great masters have appeared and acquired the treasure of his teachings in the noble land of India, in Sri Lanka, in the snowy land of Tibet, in China, and in many other countries in East and Southeast Asia. Through scripture and realizations, they first gathered and propagated the three baskets of scripture teaching the three trainings, which then spread and flourished and were later corrected, summarized, and arranged, thereby becoming known and understood throughout the world up to the present twenty-first century as the way to hoist the banner of the enduring tradition of Lord Buddha.

As for the renowned instructions known as the "stages of the path" (*lamrim*) in particular, the glorious Atiśa, leading scholar of the glorious monastic universities of Nālandā and Vikramalaśīla, wrote *Lamp for the Path to Enlightenment* (*Bodhipathapradīpa*), which is why Lord Tsongkhapa in his *Great Treatise on the Stages of the Path* says that Atiśa is also the author of his own work. In accordance with this statement, *Lamp for the Path* is the root text for the topics presented in the lamrim, and it is said that the stages of the path are a great ocean of eloquent explanations that collects the thousand rivers of excellent texts on the utterly perfect oral instructions taught in accordance with the *Lamp*.

What are called the Great, Middle-Length, and Short Stages of the Path by Lord Tsongkhapa Losang Drakpa are the universally famed *Great Treatise on the Stages of the Path to Enlightenment*; the *Middle-Length Treatise of the Stages of the Path to Enlightenment*, which reduces the number of quotations and the complexity of the refutations and proofs, skillfully summarizing its essence; and the *Core Meaning of the Path*, better known as the *Song of Experience*, born from the realizations in the author's mind and written in the style of a song of spiritual experience (*nyams mgur*). Following the intention of the master himself expressed in the *Great Treatise*, "I hope that the understanding of all the explanations for putting them into practice will endure until the end of existence and serve as protection," the Third Dalai Lama Sönam Gyatso wrote *Essence of Refined Gold* as a commentary on the *Song of Experience*, Panchen Losang Chögyen wrote the direct instruction manual *Easy Path*, the Great Fifth Dalai Lama wrote the *Sacred Words of Mañjuśrī*, Panchen Losang Yeshé wrote the direct instruction manual *Swift Path*, and Gomchen Ngawang Drakpa of Dakpo wrote the *Essence of All Excellent Discourses*. Together these make up the famed eight great guides to the stages of the path. Adding to them the mother of all lamrim texts, the *Lamp* of Atiśa Dīpaṃkara, along with his autocommentary makes a set of ten. According to a traditional explanation taught by the peerless conqueror Tenzin Gyatso, His Holiness the Dalai Lama, the lineage of openly accessible explanations extends to a total of eighteen great commentaries.

As for the actual path referred to by "stages of the path," the *Verse Summary of the Perfection of Wisdom* says, "Every buddha of the past, the future, and the present takes the perfections as their path and no other." In accordance with this, develop bodhicitta and then train in the six perfections, unifying method and wisdom on the path containing the essence of the emptiness and compassion that the Victor, having first manifested it himself, taught to his disciples.

The *Great* and *Middle-Length* treatises say that as you meditate on the lower paths, your desire to reach the higher ones should increase, and when you hear about the higher ones, your desire to accomplish the lower ones should increase. In line with this statement, the important implication of the name "stages of the path" is its emphasis on the need to avoid mixing up the main principles and sequence of the path instructions.

The *Song of Experience* says, "Enormous waves of the merit of teaching and hearing the Dharma arise from even a single session of listening to or reciting this concise instruction that distills the essence of all the scriptures. Therefore contemplate its meaning!" Those who wish to extract the essence of life with its freedoms and endowments should endeavor in this system. We must strive as the great Jé Tsongkhapa advises us to.

With that in mind I commend the English-language publication of the *Middle-Length Treatise on the Stages of the Path* by Wisdom Publications.

By the power of the two collections gathered through everything connected with this endeavor,

> May the marvelous exalted activities of the buddhas and their
>   children
> and the unerring accomplishment of the stages of the path
> grant splendor to the minds of those who desire liberation,
> and may the deeds of the buddhas be long maintained thereby.

I pray that Jé Tsongkhapa's aspiration may be fulfilled and that the holy beings upholding the Dharma throughout the universe, especially the embodiment of the wisdom and compassion of all the buddhas, the one who brings peace and happiness to the world, the unsurpassable exalted lord and great omniscient master with lotus feet, live long. May their aspirations be fulfilled effortlessly, and may the entire world and its inhabitants be free from every harm such as epidemic, war, and conflict so that the glory of joy and happiness may spread.

H. E. the Seventh Yongzin Ling Rinpoche
June 19, 2020

Translation by Philip Quarcoo

ༀ།སྐྱབས་རྗེ་ཕོ་ཆེ།   LING RINPOCHE

།ལམ་རིམ་འབྲིང་པོ་འབྱིན་བསྒྱུར་དཔར་བསྐྲུན་ཁྱད་བརྗོད།

༄༅། །སྟོན་མཆོག་མཉམ་མེད་ཤཱཀྱ་པའི་དབང་པོ་འཇིག་རྟེན་དུ་བྱོན་ནས་མི་ལོ་ཉིས་སྟོང་ལྔ་བརྒྱ་ལྷག་ཕྱིན་
པའི་དུས་ཡུན་རིང་རིང་། རྒྱ་གར་འཕགས་པའི་ཡུལ་དང་། ཞིང་ཁ་ལ། བོད་གངས་ཅན་གྱི་ཡུལ། རྒྱ་ནག་
ཧོར་སོག་ཤར་ཐབ་ནང་དང་། སྟོ་ཤར་ཨེ་ཤེ་ཡའི་ཡུལ་དུ་དར་རྒྱལ་བའི་ལུང་རྟོགས་ཀྱི་བསྟན་པའི་མཛོད་པ་
མཆར་བརྩེ་པའི་སྲིད་མཆོག་བདག་ཉིད་ཆེན་པོ་བྱུང་བ་ལས་འདས་པ་རྗེ་བྟེན་ཚིག་ཙོན། དེ་རྣམས་ཀྱི་
ལུང་དང་རྟོགས་ལས་བསྐུན་པའི་སྲེ་སྟོན་གསུམ་དང་བསྟན་པ་གསུམ་གྱི་བསྐུན་པ་ཐོབ་མར་སྟྱིན་ཡ་
བར་དུ་དར་རྒྱས་སུ་མཛད་པ། ཐ་བར་དག་ཐེར་དང་སྟེང་བསྒྱུར་ལེགས་ཀྲིག་བསས་སྲོ་ནས་རེ་དང་རྒྱུ་ལྷག
ཉིང་གཅིག་པའི་བར་འདིར་སང་རྣ་བསོ་ལུན་འདས་ཀྱི་རིང་ལུགས་ཉིས་ས་ཆེད་པའི་ཉིན་འདིར་གགས་
པའི་བ་དན་སྟྱིང་བར་མཛད་པའི་ཚུལ་ནི་ཀུན་གྱིས་མཐིན་ཞིང་དགོངས་པའི་དི་ལྟར་ལགས་ན།

      ལུག་པར་བྱང་རྒྱལ་ལས་གྱི་རིམ་པ་ཞེས་ཡོངས་སུ་གྲགས་པའི་གདམས་ངག་ནི་དཔལ་ནུ་ལན་ད་དང་
    །བི་ཀྲ་མ་ནེ་ལའི་གཙུག་ལག་ལང་ཀོ་ནས་གི་མཁས་པའི་ཞ་མཆོག་དཔལ་ལྡུན་ཨ་ཏི་ཤ་དང་རྒྱལ་ལས་གྱི་སྲོ
    མི་མཛད་ཅིང་། རྗེ་ཚོང་ཁ་པ་ཆེན་པོས། དེ་མཛད་པ་པོ་ཉིད་འདིའི་ཡང་མཛད་པ་པོརི། ཞེས་ལམ་རིམ་ཆེ་
    བར་བཀའ་སྩལ་བ་ལྟར། ལམ་རིམ་གྱི་བདག་ཏུ་རྒྱའི་གཞུང་དུ་གྱུར་པའི་ལམ་སྟོན་ནས་རྗེ་ལྟར་བསྒྲུན་པའི་
    གདམས་དག་ཡོངས་སུ་རྫོགས་པ་དེ་ལ་གཞུང་བརྒྱད་སྲོང་གི་སོ་འདི་བའི་ལེགས་བཤད་ཀྱི་རྒྱ་མཚོ་ཆེ་པོ
    བྱང་རྒྱལ་ལས་གྱི་རིམ་པ་ཞེས་གསུངས་པ་ཡིན།

      དེ་ལ་ཡོངས་སུ་གྲགས་པའི་བྱང་རྒྱལ་ལམ་རིམ་ཆེན་པོ་དང་། དེ་ལས་ལུང་འབྲིང་དང་དགགས་སྲུབ་ཀྱི་
    སློས་པ་བསྒྲུངས་སྲེ་སྟྱིང་པོ་ལེགས་པར་བསྒྱུས་པ་ལས་རིམ་འབྲིང་པོ། ཚོགས་པ་སྲུགས་རྒྱ་འཐྱུངས་ནས་
    ཉམས་མགུར་གྱི་ཚུལ་དུ་གསུངས་པ་ལམ་རིམ་བསྒྱུས་དོན་ནས་ཡོངས་གགས་ལམ་རིམ་ཉམས་མགུར་བཤས
    རྗེ་ཐབས་ཅད་མཁྱེན་པ་སྟོ་བཟང་གགས་པའི་དཔལ་གྱི་མཛད་པའི་ལམ་རིམ་ཆེ་འབྲིང་རྒྱ་བསྐུམ་དང་
    །བཟང་པ་ཐམས་ཅད་རྣམས་ལེན་དུ་ཁྱེར་ཤེས་པ་སྲིད་མཐར་དུ་སྲུང་ལས་སྲོ་རྒྱ་ནི་བར་བསྒྱུས་ར་དེ་གུང་བ
    ཐྲིགོ། ཞེས་རྗེ་རང་ཉིད་ཀྱིས་ལམ་རིམ་ཆེ་བར་གསུངས་པའི་དགོངས་པ་བཞིན་རྒྱལ་བ་བསྐུན་ནས་རྒྱ་མཆོས
    ལམ་རིམ་ཉམས་མགུར་གྱི་འགྲེལ་བ་ལྱུ་བུར་མཛོང་པ་ལམ་རིམ་གསེར་ཞུན་མ་དང་། བཅ་ཆེན་སྲོ་བཤང་ཆོས
    རྒྱན་གྱིས་དམར་ཁྲིད་པའི་ལམ་དང་། རྒྱལ་དབང་ལྱ་པ་ཆེན་པོས་འཇམ་དཔལ་ཞལ་ལུང་། བཅ་ཆེན་སྲོ་བཟང
    ཡེ་ཤེས་ཀྱི་སྱུར་ལམ་དམར་ཁྲིད། སྟོ་ཆེན་དཀ་དང་དགཀ་སྲས་ལས་མཛད་པའི་ལེགས་གསུང་ཞིང་ང་བཙ

ཡོངས་གྲགས་ལམ་རིམ་ཁྲིད་ཆེན་བརྒྱད་དང་། དེའི་སྟེང་དུ་ལམ་རིམ་གྱི་གཞུང་ཀུན་གྱི་ཕྱི་མོར་གྱུར་པ་དཔལ་
ལྡན་མར་མེ་མཛད་ཀྱི་གསུང་བྱང་ཆུབ་ལམ་སྒྲོན་སོགས་གཞུང་ཆེན་བཅུ་སྟོན་གྱི་རྒྱལ་མཚོག་ཐམས་ཅད་
མཁྱེན་པ་ཆེན་པོ་བསྟན་འཛིན་རྒྱ་མཚོས་གསན་རྒྱལ་རྒྱ་ཆེ་ཁྱིལ་བར་མཛད་པའི་བཞེད་སྲོལ་ཁྲིད་ཆེན་བཅོ་
བརྒྱད་ཅེས་ཡོངས་སུ་གྲགས་པ་སོགས་བཞུགས།

དེ་ཡང་ལམ་རིམ་ཞེས་པའི་ལམ་དངོས་ནི། མངོ་སྦྱང་པ་ལས། རྒྱལ་བ་འདས་དང་མ་བྱོན་ད་ལྟར་གང་
བཞུགས་པ། ཀུན་ལས་པ་རོལ་ཕྱིན་པ་འདི་ཡིན་གནས་མ་ཡིན། ཞེས་གསུངས་པ་ལྟར་བྱང་རྒྱལ་དུ་སེམས་
བསྐྱེད་ནས་སྒྲོ་པ་བྱིན་དྲུག་ལ་བསྒྱབ་རྒྱལ་སྒྲོ་ཞིང་སྟིང་རྗེའི་སྟིང་པོ་ཚན་གྱི་ལམ་ཐབས་ཤེས་ཟུང་འཇུག་
རྒྱལ་བ་རང་ཉིད་ཀྱི་མཛོན་དུ་མཛད་པ་ཇི་བཞིན་དུ་འཁྲལ་བྱ་ལ་གསུངས་པ་དེ་ཡིན།

འདི་ཡང་ལམ་ཟོག་མ་བསྐོམས་ཀྱིན་གོང་མ་ལ་ཕོན་འདོང་ཆེར་འགྲོ་བ་དང་། གོང་མ་མཆན་པ་ན་ཟོག་
མ་ལ་བསྒྱབ་འདོང་ཇི་ཆེར་འགྲོ་ཞིག་དགོས། ཞེས་ལམ་རིམ་ཆེ་འབྲིང་དུ་གསུངས་པའི་དོན་སྒྱུར་ལམ་གྱི་དོ་
པོ་དང་གོ་རིས་མ་འཁྲུགས་པ་དགོས་པ་རྒྱལ་འཛོན་མཛད་དེ་གདམས་ངག་འདིའི་མཚན་ལ་ལམ་གྱི་རིས་པ་
ཞེས་གསུངས་པ་གོ་རྒྱ་ཆེ་བ་ཡིན།

ཉམས་མགྱུར་ལས། ཁབྱུང་རབ་ཀུན་གྱི་སྟིང་པོ་བསྡུ་བསྟུབ། རྒྱལ་འདི་ཐུན་རེ་སྟོན་དང་ཉན་ལས་ཀྱང་
། ངམ་ཆོས་འཆང་དང་ཐོས་པའི་པར་ཡོན་ཚོགས། ཀྲབས་ཆེན་སྒྱང་པར་ངས་པས་དེ་དོན་བསམ། ཞེས་དང་
བའི་རྗེན་ལ་སྟིང་པོ་ཞིན་པར་འདོང་པ་རྣམས་ཀྱིས་རྒྱལ་འདི་ལ་བསྐོན་པར་རིགས་སོ་རྗེ་ཚོང་ལ་པ་ཞིན་པོའི་
རང་ཚག་ལ་གདམས་པར་མཛད་པའི་དོན་བཞིན་ཀུན་ཀྱི་འབད་གལ་ཆེ་བ་ལགས།

རྒྱལ་དེ་ལ་འཆིགས་ཏེ་ད་ལན་Wisdom Publications ནས་ལམ་རིམ་འབྲིང་བ་འཕྱིན་བསྒྱུར་
དཔར་བསྐུན་གནང་བ་ལེགས་སོའི་བསྒྱགས་བརྗོད་ན་ཞིང་། རྒྱལ་འདིའི་འགྱེལ་ཐོགས་ཀུན་ཀྱིས་བསགས་
པའི་ཚོགས་གཉིས་ཀྱི་མཐུ་ལས། ཁྱས་བཅས་རྒྱལ་བའི་རྣམ་བྱུང་ཕྱིན་ལས་ལས། ཁྱགས་གྲུབ་བྱང་རྒྱལ་ལས་
ཀྱི་རིས་པས་ཀྱང་། ཐར་འདོང་རྣམས་ཀྱི་ཡིད་ལ་དཔལ་སྟེར་ཞིང་། རྒྱལ་བའི་མཛད་པ་རིང་དུ་སྐྱོང་གྱུར་ཅིག
ཅེས་རྗེ་བཙུན་བླ་མས་ཐུགས་སྟོན་རྗེ་ལྟར་མཛད་པ་བཞིན་འགྱུབ་པ་དང་། ཕྱོགས་བཅུར་བཞུགས་པའི་བསྒྱན་
འཛིན་གྱི་སྐྱེས་བུ་དམ་པ་ཀུན་དང་། ཁྱད་པར་རྒྱལ་ཀུན་མཁྱེན་བརྒྱེའི་རང་གསུངས་འདིའི་རྗེན་ཞི་བདེའི་
འདྲེན་པ་བླ་ན་མ་མཆིས་པ་༧རྒྱལ་མཚོག་ཐམས་ཅད་མཁྱེན་པ་ཆེན་པོའི་༧ཞབས་པད་བརྟན་ཅིང་གྲུབས་
བཞེད་མཐའ་དག་འབད་མེད་འགྲུབ་པ། སྦྲ་བཅུད་ཀྱི་འཇིག་རྟེན་ཡོངས་ལ་ནན་ཡམས་འཁྲུག་རྩོོ་སོགས་
མི་འདོང་ཞེར་འཚོ་ཞི་ཞིང་བདེ་དགའི་དཔལ་ཡོན་དར་བའི་རྒྱུ་འགྱུར་བའི་སློན་པ་ན།

ཞེས་ཡོངས་འཛིན་སྐྱིང་སྤྲུལ་ཤིང་པ་བསྟན་འཛིན་ལུང་ཆོགས་འཕྲིན་ལས་ཆོས་འཕགས་ཀྱིས་
ཕྱི་ལོ་༢༠༡༠སྦ་༩ཚེས་༡༠ཉིན།

Translator's Preface

WHEN JÉ TSONGKHAPA set about writing his *Middle-Length Treatise on the Stages of the Path to Enlightenment* (*Byang chub lam gyi rim pa chung ba*), or *Middle-Length Lamrim* (*Lam rim 'bring ba*), in 1415, thirteen years had passed since the completion of his *Great Treatise on the Stages of the Path to Enlightenment*, the widely acclaimed *Lamrim Chenmo*, in 1402. Over the course of a fruitful interim he had authored several of his other major works, including the *Great Treatise on the Stages of Tantra*, the *Essence of True Eloquence*, and the *Lamp to Illuminate the Five Stages*. In 1409 he had hosted the first Great Prayer Festival in Lhasa with a view to restoring the most sacred Buddha images of Tibet to their former splendor, thereby performing the third of his four great deeds. Soon after that, he had given up his itinerant life shuttling between monasteries and mountain hermitages and settled down at his newly founded Ganden Monastery, vowing not to leave it for several years. Sadly he had lost his main teacher, Rendawa, in 1412 and only barely defied a prophecy that he himself would not live beyond the age of fifty-seven, falling gravely ill in 1413. After recovering, he resumed writing in the summer of 1414. In 1415 he left Ganden Monastery for the first time since 1410 to honor the invitation of one of his most faithful patrons and gave a series of teachings to hundreds of monastics and laypeople at Tashi Dokha Hermitage. On this occasion Gö Lotsāwa Shönu Pal (1392–1481), the important chronicler on Tibetan Buddhist history, met Tsongkhapa, became his student, and later said the following about him: "When it comes to not confining one's understanding merely to what one has learned but to critically examining the texts through one's own intelligence, and when it comes to everyday conduct, it is for Tsongkhapa alone that I have the deepest admiration" (Jinpa, *Tsongkhapa*, 283).

Soon after his return from the teaching festival at Tashi Dokha, Tsongkhapa wrote his *Middle-Length Treatise*. In the opening verses he intimates that his reason for yet another exposition of the stages of the path is the wish to make the subject matter "easy to access." The fact that he refers to his more elaborate treatise several times throughout the text, inviting readers to deepen their understanding of certain points, clearly shows that he did not intend his earlier work to be superseded. Rather he seems to have felt very keenly that his students required different levels of detail to develop a good grasp of the material.

The topics covered in the present treatise are virtually the same as in the more elaborate earlier exposition. It takes a detailed comparative analysis to work out differences between the two presentations. One major addition to the *Middle-Length Treatise* is a discussion of conventional and ultimate truth. The new chapter is quite substantial, accounting for almost a third of the entire insight section. The *Great Treatise* instead includes a chapter on why insight requires analysis. Another addition in the *Middle-Length Treatise* is found toward the end of the chapter "Accomplishing Śamatha" in a section on "the elimination of doubts" (pp. 326–27). Here the author cautions against mistaking a mere nonconceptual state for a transformative meditation on emptiness. The *Middle-Length Treatise* does not present nearly as many refutations of points raised by philosophical opponents as the elaborate exposition. Tsongkhapa also reduced the number of scriptural quotations considerably.

Overall the *Middle-Length Treatise* is only about 41 percent the size of the *Great Treatise*. Some sections were abridged more than others; the section on insight is less than a third the length of its more extensive predecessor, while the chapters on the preliminaries and the chapter on cultivating śamatha are about half the length.

As for actual textual overlap between the two treatises, just over 30 percent of the lines in the *Middle-Length Treatise* are found verbatim in the *Great Treatise*. It would seem that the text was actually rewritten rather than merely abridged. An analysis of lexical items in the texts also reveals some interesting differences. To name but two, the Tibetan term for bodhisattva, *byang chub sems dpa'*, is the fifteenth most common tetragram in the *Great Treatise*, whereas in the *Middle-Length Treatise* it is only the thirtieth most common one. On the other hand the term *de kho na nyid*, or "suchness," though associated with insight, is found more frequently in the *Middle-Length Treatise*.

I like to think of the *Middle-Length Treatise* as Jé Tsongkhapa's final take on the path to enlightenment. While still detailed and rich in quotations from sūtras and śāstras as well as Tibetan sources, its being less than half the size of the *Great Treatise* makes it far less daunting. This relative concision makes it a handy companion on the path, however far we may go along it.

The gestation for this translation began many years ago, when Cornelia (Conny) Krause, the former interpreter at the Aryatara Institute in Munich, Germany, approached me about a translation project. Lama Zopa Rinpoche and Merry Colony, who was head of the Education Department at the Foundation for the Preservation of the Mahayana Tradition (FPMT) at the time, had asked her to translate the *Middle-Length Lamrim* into English or German. Conny preferred to translate the text into her mother tongue, and since I had been helping interpret for visiting teachers at the Aryatara Institute, she thought I might be willing to work on an English version. In fact I was thrilled at the prospect of studying this text in detail, so I embarked on the project early in 2004.

Our target readership was the students enrolled in the FPMT Basic Program in Pomaia, Italy, and as they worked their way through the material, the pressure was on to produce the next installments of our translation. The students began by using the first volume of the translation of the *Great Treatise* that had recently been published by Snow Lion Publications. As the second volume had not yet come out, Conny and I started working on the great scope, the practices of bodhisattvas. Once we had finished that part, we got some time to rest and gain some perspective. At the time, I was enrolled in a master's program in Tibetan studies at the University of Munich, and since I had done a degree in modern European languages involving a fair amount of translation work, it did not feel right to translate the Tibetan text into English via German. That is why I started translating straight from the Tibetan original. I continued to avail myself of Conny's excellent German translation, but only after I had rendered a section from Tibetan. I also used some of the annotations she inserted based on her frequent discussions with our resident teacher, Geshe Thubten Soepa. The resulting English version turned out to be noticeably different from my earlier output, so I decided to retranslate the bodhisattva section as well. This retranslation was completed in 2007–8 during my work for FPMT Mongolia.

In 2010 the FPMT launched an initiative to harmonize its worldwide translation activities by having affiliated translators agree on key terms to be used in their translations. The idea was to draft a common glossary and then apply it to various texts starting from the *Middle-Length Treatise*, a key work in both the FPMT curriculum and the Geluk tradition as whole. This is what happened over the next couple of years. The present translation is very much a product of this joint effort within FPMT. Obviously, the shared terminology was never meant to be set in stone and leaves some latitude for translators' personal preference; however, it is a step toward harmonization of our translation activities. By far the majority of my departures from the set terminology are found in verse quotations of scripture, where Tibetan syllables are often left out or else inserted for metrical reasons. I have tried to go some way toward rendering the rhythm and tone of the original verse.

Apart from our joint effort at a common terminology, several people have put in a lot of time and hard work reading and editing my translation. First and foremost, Venerable Joan Nicell processed the text for use in the FPMT Basic Program and made countless corrections and improvements. I have the utmost respect for her excellent work and greatly enjoyed my collaboration with her. Many thanks are also owed to Venerable Lhundub Jampa (Alicia Vogel) and Venerable Sangye Khadro (Kathleen McDonald) for their corrections and useful comments. Much further down the road toward publication, Venerable Steve Carlier made numerous suggestions that are also greatly appreciated. Venerable Fedor Stracke of Aryatara Institute offered much useful advice as well as his rather disappointing view that the original Tibetan reads much more fluently than my English. I believe this is no more the case now that the text has gone through meticulous editing by Wisdom Publications. Perhaps his verdict will serve as an encouragement for keen students to master classical Tibetan to the point where they can appreciate the widely acknowledged lucidity of Jé Tsongkhapa's own words. Nevertheless, I very much hope that those who stick with the English version still find the translation useful and inspiring.

I would also like to thank Scott Perry, Karina and Lobsang Chodak, Dolkar Phuntshok, Manfred Keller, and Oona Hassim for their advice on various English and Tibetan expressions.

I am very grateful to Merry Colony, Olga Planken, Tom Truty, and Joona Repo of FPMT for lending their enthusiastic support to the translation project over the years. Many thanks to the latter for proofing the whole text once more toward the end of 2020 and contributing yet another list of very observant and useful comments.

Many thanks also to David Kittelstrom of Wisdom Publications, who has also been involved in this project for more than ten years now. I strongly feel that without his persistence and professionalism, all our work may well have come to nothing but a prefinal draft translation for internal use on FPMT courses. This book also owes a lot to Dechen Rochard, whose experience in publishing Geshe Lhundub Sopa's very extensive commentary on the *Great Treatise* has resulted in many changes and valuable endnotes. Thanks a lot also to Anna Johnson, who suggested plenty of additional changes and notes. More importantly, she did a lot to help break down Jé Tsongkhapa's complex sentences into more manageable chunks of English prose.

For reviewing critical passages in the final stages of the manuscript, I am grateful for the sage interventions of Thupten Jinpa and Gavin Kilty. On Jinpa's recommendation, we have inserted in square brackets throughout the translation the page numbers corresponding to the new critical edition of the collected works of Tsongkhapa and his two principal disciples (Je Yabse Sungbum series, vol. 14, pp. 1–297 [Mundgod: Drepung Loseling Pethub Khangtsen Educational Society, 2019]). That edition can also be consulted to find the sources for all the citations from the Tibetan canon, since it provides for each reference the volume, page, and line numbers from the Pedurma (Dpe bsdur ma) comparative edition of the Kangyur and Tengyur.

Of course my gratitude also goes to the amazing teachers that introduced me to Jé Tsongkhapa's lamrim: Geshe Tashi Tsering as resident teacher at Jamyang Buddhist Centre in London, Geshe Thubten Soepa as resident teacher at Aryatara Institute in Munich, Chöden Rinpoche during the Enlightened Experience Celebration IV in Ulaanbaatar in 2004, and many others.

Lastly, many thanks to my wife, Munkhjargal, and our children, Sarangerel, Temuulen, and Narangerel, for their support serving me countless cups of tea at the computer and their patience excusing me from quite a number of family activities so I could get on with this book.

Despite all these great people's contribution, help, and encouragement, I take full responsibility for the shortcomings of the present translation, and I deeply apologize for any distortions of Jé Tsongkhapa's intended meaning owing to misunderstandings. While I have been frustrated at times that this book did not see the light of day earlier, I am delighted to know that six hundred and six years after its composition, this spiritual classic by the towering figure of Jé Tsongkhapa will now be accessible to English-language readers.

Philip Quarcoo
Munich, January 1, 2021

The
MIDDLE-LENGTH TREATISE
on the
STAGES OF THE PATH
TO ENLIGHTENMENT
TO BE PRACTICED BY THE
THREE TYPES OF PERSONS

༄༅། །སྐྱེས་བུ་གསུམ་གྱི་ཉམས་སུ་བླང་བའི་

བྱང་ཆུབ་ལམ་གྱི་རིམ་པ་ཆུང་བ།།

Tsongkhapa Losang Drakpa

(1357–1419)

Preliminaries

1 | The Greatness of the Author

RESPECTFULLY I PROSTRATE at the feet of those venerable holy beings filled with compassion.

> Blessed One, lord of this Endurance world (*sahā loka*),
> Buddha's regent, Maitreya, lord of the Dharma,
> Mañjughoṣa, sole father of those gone to bliss (*sugata*),
> Nāgārjuna and Asaṅga, foretold by the Victor,
> bowing to you with respect I will here explain
> once more, in a summary fashion, the stages
> of the path of profound view and vast conduct
> for the sake of making them easy to access.

The Dharma to be presented here explains how the fortunate are led to the level of buddhahood through the stages of the path to enlightenment. It summarizes all the points of the Victor's scriptures, follows the tradition of the two great trailblazers Nāgārjuna and Asaṅga, constitutes the Dharma system of supreme beings who progress to the level of omniscience, and contains without omission all the stages to be practiced by the three types of persons.

The scholars of glorious Vikramaśīla Monastery considered it vital to commence with three preliminaries: the greatness of the author of the Dharma teachings, the greatness of the Dharma, and the way to explain and listen to the Dharma. In accordance with that, this guide to the stages of the path to enlightenment has four parts: (1) showing the greatness of the author so as to demonstrate that this Dharma is a pure source, (2) showing the greatness of the Dharma so as to generate respect for the instructions, (3) how the Dharma possessing those two greatnesses should be listened to and explained, and (4) the stages by which a student should be guided through the actual instructions.

SHOWING THE GREATNESS OF THE AUTHOR SO AS TO DEMONSTRATE THAT THIS DHARMA IS A PURE SOURCE

Generally speaking, the present instructions are the ones that the venerable protector Maitreya gives in his *Ornament for Clear Knowledge* (*Abhisamayālaṃkāra*). They are based specifically on *Lamp for the Path to Enlightenment* (*Bodhipathapradīpa*), [2] so that its author is also the author of the present text. Other than under the name of the great master Dīpaṃkara Śrījñāna, he is also widely known as the glorious Atiśa. His greatness is threefold: how he took birth in an excellent family, how he obtained his excellent qualities on that basis, and how he performed deeds for the sake of the teachings after obtaining the excellent qualities.

HOW ATIŚA TOOK BIRTH IN AN EXCELLENT FAMILY

According to the translator's *Praise*:[1]

Due east in the excellent country of Sahor[2]
lies a city of great size—
namely, Vikramaṇipura.

In its midst is the royal court,
an extremely spacious palace
called "the one with golden banners."
Its pleasures, might, and riches
rival those of Chinese emperors.

King of that land is Kalyāṇaśrī,
and his queen is Śrīprabha.
The royal couple has three sons:
Padmagarbha, Candragarbha,
and Śrīgarbha they are called.

Again, Prince Padmagarbha has
five royal consorts and nine sons—
the oldest one, named Puṇyaśrī,
is a great paṇḍita
widely known as Dhanaśrī.

The youngest brother, Śrīgarbha,
is the bhikṣu[3] Vīryacandra.
The middle one is Candragarbha—
he is our exalted guru.

How Atiśa obtained his excellent qualities on that basis

This has two parts: how he obtained the excellent qualities of vast scriptural knowledge and how he obtained the excellent qualities of realization of its correct accomplishment.

How Atiśa obtained the excellent qualities of vast scriptural knowledge

By the age of twenty-one, Atiśa had studied the four areas of knowledge common to Buddhists and non-Buddhists (languages, logical reasoning, crafts, and medicine) and was an excellent scholar. In particular, the great Drolungpa[4] relates how, at the age of fifteen, Atiśa heard Dharmakīrti's *Drop of Reasoning* (*Nyāyabindu*) just once and then defeated in debate a non-Buddhist[5] intellectual renowned for his erudition. This spread Atiśa's fame far and wide.

Then he requested a complete empowerment from the glorious master yogi of the main temple on Black Mountain, the guru Rāhulagupta, who had received direct visions of Hevajra and a prophecy from Vajraḍākinī. [3] He was given the secret name Jñānaguhyavajra. Up to the age of twenty-nine he studied the Vajrayāna under numerous highly realized gurus and thereby became knowledgeable in all the texts and instructions. When the thought "I am the great master of secret mantra" occurred to him, ḍākinīs appeared to him in a dream and showed him several volumes of tantra he had not seen before, which lowered his pride.

Both in his dreams and directly, Atiśa's gurus and personal deities then advised him that vast benefit would accrue for the teachings and many beings if he took the appropriate monastic vows, and upon their encouragement he sought ordination. The great upholder of monastic discipline Śīlarakṣita, an elder of the Mahāsāṃghika tradition who had attained the concentration of single-pointed focus on ultimate reality belonging to the path of preparation, officiated as abbot and gave him the name Dīpaṃkara Śrījñāna.

Up to the age of thirty-one, Atiśa studied the higher and lower baskets of scriptures of the Buddhist dialectical and metaphysical traditions,[6] and in particular, for twelve years, the *Great Detailed Explanation* (*Mahāvibhāṣā*) under Guru Dharmarakṣita in Odantapuri. As he was very well versed in the scriptures of the four original traditions,[7] he had an infallible grasp of the finest details of ways of behavior that should be adopted and discarded according to the different traditions, such as the monastic rules concerning giving and receiving alms.

HOW ATIŚA OBTAINED THE EXCELLENT QUALITIES OF REALIZATION OF ITS CORRECT ACCOMPLISHMENT

Generally speaking, all the scriptural teachings by the Victor are contained in the three precious baskets, so likewise all the realized teachings are contained in the three precious trainings.[8]

ATIŚA'S ACCOMPLISHMENTS IN THE TRAINING IN ETHICS

In this regard the training in ethics is often praised in the scriptures and in the commentaries as the foundation of all excellent qualities, such as the trainings in concentration and wisdom. Therefore it is necessary, first of all, to have qualities of realization that are based on the training in ethics. In this regard there are three kinds.

HOW ATIŚA POSSESSED THE HIGHEST PRĀTIMOKṢA VOWS

Having received the vows of a fully ordained monk, Atiśa guarded them the way a yak guards its tail. A yak is so attached to its tail that it would sooner risk its life to save a strand of tail hair caught on a tree than part with it, even when threatened by a hunter. That is how Atiśa guarded the foundation of the trainings he had undertaken in every detail, to say nothing of the major rules, so that he came to be called the Elder (*sthavira*) who is a great upholder of monastic discipline. [4]

How Atiśa possessed the bodhisattva vows

Atiśa practiced numerous instructions for training in bodhicitta, which is rooted in love and compassion. Especially, following Serlingpa,[9] he trained long in the highest instructions passed on from venerable Maitreya and Mañjughoṣa through Asaṅga and Śāntideva. Thereby bodhicitta, which cherishes others more than oneself, arose in his heart. This aspiring bodhicitta gave rise to engaged bodhicitta, and he never transgressed the rules of the Buddha's offspring on account of his excellent behavior, his engagement in the trainings following his promise to train in the vast conduct of bodhisattvas.

How Atiśa possessed the tantric vows

Owing to the fact that he had gained the concentration of the generation stage in which one's own body is seen as that of a deity and of the completion stage of the indestructible vajra mind, Atiśa became chief among yogis. In particular he guarded his commitments properly without transgressing the prescribed rules.

He not only courageously undertook the trainings in the ethics of the three vows, he also upheld them as promised. He kept the vows without transgressing their respective rules, and even if he transgressed them ever so slightly, he very quickly purified this with a suitable ritual for restoring the given vow.

Atiśa's accomplishments with the training in concentration

His training in concentration has two aspects. As for the common aspect,[10] he achieved the supple mind of śamatha, and as for the uncommon aspect, he gained the utmost stability of the generation stage. Moreover, he trained in the yogic awareness disciplines for three (or perhaps six) years.[11]

ATIŚA'S ACCOMPLISHMENTS WITH THE TRAINING IN WISDOM

His training in wisdom has two aspects. As for the common aspect, he obtained the concentration of special insight, which is the union of śamatha and special insight. As for the uncommon aspect, he obtained the extraordinary concentration of the completion stage.

HOW ATIŚA PERFORMED DEEDS FOR THE SAKE OF THE TEACHINGS AFTER OBTAINING THE EXCELLENT QUALITIES

The deeds he accomplished for the sake of the teachings are of two types: his deeds in India and his deeds in Tibet. [5]

HIS DEEDS IN INDIA

At the temple of great enlightenment in Bodhgāya, Atiśa defeated the misguided proponents of non-Buddhist doctrines three times by means of the Dharma, thereby maintaining the Buddha's teachings. He also eliminated the taints of ignorance, misconception, and doubt with regard to the higher and lower Buddhist systems, whereby he spread the teachings. Thus he was regarded by all schools as a crown jewel free from partiality.

HIS DEEDS IN TIBET

Lha Lama and his nephew[12] sent the two great translators Gya Tsöndrü Sengé and Naktso Tsultrim Gyalwa to India one after the other. Since they took great pains again and again to invite Atiśa, he traveled to Upper Ngari during the reign of Jangchup Ö and was requested to provide a pure form of the Buddha's teachings. Thereupon he spread the teachings by composing *Lamp for the Path to Enlightenment*, a text bringing together all the points of sūtra and tantra and condensing them into applicable stages, as well as other texts. Specifically he spent three years in Ngari, nine years in Nyethang, and five years elsewhere in Central Tibet and Tsang, teaching the fortunate all the scriptures and instructions of sūtra and tantra. He thereby restored the teachings that had declined, caused those that remained to flourish, and corrected those that had been polluted by the errors of misconception, ensuring that the precious teachings were freed from all flaws.

There are three conditions for excellence in the composition of a text clarifying the Sage's intentions: being learned in the five areas of knowledge;[13] having received instructions on how to put into practice the meaning of those texts, which can be traced back to the instructions of the perfectly complete Buddha in an unbroken lineage of exalted masters; and having received the permission to teach through the vision of a personal deity. A text should be composed with at least one of these causes for excellence, and it will turn out all the more excellent if all three are complete. This great master Atiśa possessed all three.

As for help from personal deities, Naktso's *Praise* says:

> From the glorious Hevajra,
> from Trisamayavyūharāja,
> from heroic Lokeśvara,
> from noble reverend Tārā, and others,
> you had visions and permissions.
> Thus in dreams and through direct perception,
> you perpetually listened to teachings
> on the holy, profound, and vast Dharma.

Atiśa held numerous lineages of gurus, such as the lineage of the common vehicle and the lineage of the Mahāyāna, which itself has two—the Pāramitāyāna and the secret Mantrayāna.[14] He held three lineages in the Pāramitāyāna: the lineages of the view and of conduct, with the latter [6] having been passed on in two lineages, one from Maitreya and one from Mañjughoṣa. In the secret Mantrayāna he had received five types of transmission[15] as well as many other lineages, such as the lineage of tenets, the lineage of blessings, and lineages of various instructions. The gurus from whom he heard instructions directly are mentioned in the *Praise*:

> The gurus you always relied on were
> the many who had accomplished siddhis:
> Śāntipa, Serlingpa,
> Bhadrabodhi, and Jñānaśrī.

In particular you held
the profound and vast instructions
that had passed from one to another
all the way from Nāgārjuna.

It is well known that Atiśa had twelve gurus who had attained siddhis and
many others too. It has already been explained that he was learned in the
five areas of knowledge. For all these reasons, this master was able to establish the Victor's intentions skillfully.

Such a master as this had an inconceivable number of students in India,
Kashmir, Oḍḍiyāna, Nepal, and Tibet, though the main ones were the four
great scholars in India who matched the master himself in their exalted
knowledge: Pindo Ācārya, Dharmākaramati, Madhyasiṃha, and Kṣitigarbha. Some add Mitraguhya as a fifth. In Ngari, it was the great translators
Rinchen Sangpo and Naktso as well as the ordained king Jangchup Ö. In
the province of Tsang, it was Gargewa and Gö Khukpa Lhetsé; in Lhodrak,
Chakpa Trichok and Gewa Kyong; in Kham, Naljorpa Chenpo [Jangchup
Rinchen], Gönpawa, Sherab Dorjé, and Chadar Tönpa; and in Central
Tibet, there were the three, Khu, Ngok, and Drom.[16] Among these it was
nevertheless the great lineage holder Dromtönpa Gyalwai Jungné who had
been prophesied by Tārā and who further spread the exalted activities of
his guru.

This is a summary description of the author's greatness. You should come
to understand it more extensively in the great biographies.

2 | The Greatness of the Dharma

SHOWING THE GREATNESS OF THE DHARMA SO AS TO
GENERATE RESPECT FOR THE INSTRUCTIONS

As FOR THE DHARMA, the source text of the present instructions is *Lamp for the Path to Enlightenment*. Although Atiśa[17] composed numerous texts, *Lamp for the Path to Enlightenment* is their culmination, like a root. It indicates all the points of both sūtra and tantra in a condensed manner; thus it is complete in terms of content. It makes the gradual taming of the mind [7] its main topic, so it is easy to put into practice. It is adorned with the instructions of the two masters who were expert in the systems of the two trailblazers,[18] so it is a particularly noble system compared to others.

THE GREATNESS OF UNDERSTANDING ALL TEACHINGS AS WITHOUT CONTRADICTION

The greatness of the instructions of that text has four aspects. The first of these is the greatness of understanding that all the teachings, everything the Victor said, is without contradiction. They all come to be understood as one person's path to buddhahood. That is to say, some are primary points of the path, while others are secondary points.

In this regard the bodhisattva's wish is to work for the welfare of the world. To do this it is necessary to prize all three types of disciples and therefore train in their respective paths. For as Venerable Maitreya explained, the bodhisattvas' goals are accomplished through knowing the paths of the three vehicles.

The Mahāyāna path has both common and uncommon aspects. The former includes those that originate from the Hīnayāna scriptural baskets, except for some peculiarities that are not shared in common, such as the aspiration for individual liberation and certain precepts. In perfectly complete buddhahood, it is not that faults are partially ceased and excellent qualities are partially completed, but rather every kind of fault is eliminated and every excellent quality is completed. Since the Mahāyāna that achieves buddhahood brings about the cessation of all faults and the development of all excellent qualities, the path of the Mahāyāna encompasses all the qualities of elimination and realization of all other vehicles. That is why all the Buddha's teachings are included within the various sections of the Mahāyāna path that leads to perfect buddhahood. For there is no utterance of the Sage that does not cause the cessation of some faults and the development of some virtuous qualities; and there is nothing among all of this that is not to be accomplished by the Mahāyāna practitioner.

Someone may think, "That may be true for the Pāramitāyāna but not for those entering the Vajrayāna." Now although the way you train in the countless delineations of generosity and so forth according to the Pāramitāyāna differs from mantra, both the behavioral basis (the mind generation)[19] and the behavior [8] (the coarse form of the path of training in the six perfections) are nevertheless the same and therefore something shared by them. The *Vajra Peak Tantra* (*Vajraśikharatantra*) says:

> Do not discard the mind of enlightenment
> even for the sake of your life.

And:

> The conduct of the six perfections
> must never be discarded.

This is also taught in numerous other mantra texts. Many authentic sources for the maṇḍala ritual of highest yoga tantra say that both sets of vows must have been taken—the common and the uncommon one—and indeed, the former refers to the bodhisattva vows. The precious Dromtönpa also said, "My guru knows how to carry all the teachings by way of all four corners."[20] This statement is something to be examined in depth.

THE GREATNESS OF SEEING ALL OF THE BUDDHA'S TEACHINGS AS INSTRUCTIONS

Anyone who considers the great scriptures to be expository teachings that do not contain practical instructions, who thinks that guidance on the meaning of the essential points of practice exists separately from them, and who holds that even in the holy Dharma the expository and applied teachings are found in different places will create an obstacle for the arising of deep respect for the immaculate sūtras and tantras as well as the treatises clarifying their intentions. Be aware that the karmic obstruction of abandoning the Dharma is accumulated by despising them, saying that they only outline external knowledge without presenting the inner meaning. For those who want liberation, the infallible supreme instructions are indeed the great scriptures. It is nonetheless possible that, due to poor intelligence and the like, you cannot reach certainty through relying on these scriptures alone as supreme advice. In such a case you should seek certainty with respect to them, thinking, "I will seek certainty with respect to them by relying on excellent oral instructions." But you should never think that the great scriptures do not contain the heart of the matter, thinking they only outline external knowledge while the personal instructions are supreme because they present the inner meaning. [9]

Naljorpa Chenpo Jangchup Rinchen[21] said:

> Someone who has reached certainty about a pithy guidebook cannot be said to have mastered the instructions, whereas this can be said about someone who understands all of the scriptures as instructions.

We need the kind of understanding expressed by Gompa Rinchen Lama, a disciple of Atiśa. He said he had ground his body, speech, and mind to dust in a single meditation session on Atiśa's instructions, and thereby the understanding had now arisen in him that all the scriptures are instructions. In the words of the precious Dromtönpa:

> If after studying the Dharma extensively you feel you need to search elsewhere for a way to apply the Dharma, you are mistaken.

If those who have studied the Dharma extensively over a long period, yet who are completely ignorant as to how to practice it, develop the wish to practice Dharma and think they must search elsewhere for instructions, then they have totally misunderstood this and err in the manner described above. As the *Treasury of Abhidharma* (*Abhidharmakośa*, 8.39) says:

> The Buddha's holy Dharma is twofold:
> its nature is scripture and realization.

In accordance with this statement, there is nothing apart from the scriptural teaching and the realized teaching.

The scriptural teaching is how the Dharma should be practiced and establishes the manner of accomplishment, while the realized teaching is what is thus established. Since you practice in accordance with what is to be established, these two act as cause and effect. To give an analogy, when you have a horse race, you first show the horse the course, and after showing it, the race follows the same course. It would be ridiculous to show it a course and then have the race elsewhere. When it comes to accomplishments, how could it be appropriate to accomplish something after having determined something else through listening and reflecting? This is also expressed in the third *Stages of Meditation* (*Bhāvanākrama*):

> Whatever has been realized by the two types of wisdom arisen
> from listening and reflecting is precisely what should be culti-
> vated by means of the wisdom arisen from meditation. Just like
> a horse runs the course it has been shown.

Thus, through summarizing all the essential points of the paths set forth in the scriptures and their commentaries—starting from how to rely on a spiritual teacher up to śamatha and special insight—[10] they are all condensed into stages of practical application in terms of employing placement meditation where placement meditation is required and analyzing with the wisdom of fine investigation where analytical meditation is required. These instructions guide you so that all the scriptures present themselves to you as personal instructions. The conviction develops that they should be understood as supreme advice, and the misconception that they should be understood as mere background knowledge for the Dharma rather than as actual instructions is completely reversed.

THE GREATNESS OF ALLOWING YOU EASILY TO DISCOVER THE VICTOR'S INTENTION

Although the great texts, the scriptures along with their commentaries, are the best advice, completely uneducated beginners who delve into them cannot find their intention without relying on excellent oral instructions, and even if they find it, it takes them a lot of time and enormous effort. If they rely on a guru's oral instructions and the like, it is easy to understand.

THE GREATNESS OF NATURALLY STOPPING SERIOUS MISDEEDS

As explained in the *Lotus Sūtra* (*Saddharmapuṇḍarīkasūtra*) and the *Satyaka Chapter* (*Satyakaparivarta*), it amounts to abandoning the Dharma if you hold that some of the Buddha's utterances are means of attaining buddhahood while others are obstacles to buddhahood, dividing them into good and bad, appropriate and inappropriate, or Mahāyāna and Hīnayāna, and thereupon holding that a bodhisattva needs to train in some and not in others. This is because you fail to understand that all the Buddha's words directly or indirectly teach the means of attaining buddhahood. The *Gathering All the Threads Sūtra* (*Sarvavaidalyasaṃgrahasūtra*) says that the karmic obstruction accrued by abandoning the Dharma is so subtle that it is hard to recognize.

Concerning the very great faults that ensue if you abandon the Dharma, the *King of Concentrations Sūtra* (*Samādhirājasūtra*) says:

> Say that someone demolishes all the stūpas
> found here in Jambudvīpa;
> the bad actions of someone who abandons the sūtras
> are far more grave.

> Even if someone murders as many arhats
> as there are grains of sand in the Ganges,
> the bad actions of someone who abandons the sūtras
> are far more grave. [11]

Although generally there are many ways in which the Dharma might be abandoned, the one described above appears to be the most significant, which is why we should try hard to give it up. That is to say, since this is reversed simply by gaining certainty about what was indicated above, the misdeed stops naturally. This certainty should be sought by studying the *Satyaka Chapter* as well as the *Lotus Sūtra*. The other ways of abandoning the Dharma should be understood from the *Gathering All the Threads Sūtra*.

3 | Listening to and Explaining the Dharma

HOW THE DHARMA POSSESSING THOSE TWO GREATNESSES SHOULD BE LISTENED TO AND EXPLAINED

THIS HAS THREE POINTS: how to listen, how to explain, and how to conclude the session.

HOW TO LISTEN TO THE DHARMA

This has three points: contemplating the benefits of listening[22] to the Dharma, developing respect for the Dharma and those who teach the Dharma, and the actual way to listen.

CONTEMPLATING THE BENEFITS OF LISTENING TO THE DHARMA

Verses about Listening[23] says:

> Through listening, the Dharma is understood.
> Through listening, bad actions are reversed.
> Through listening, the meaningless is abandoned.
> Through listening, nirvāṇa is achieved.

These four lines say that in reliance upon listening, an understanding of what should be adopted and discarded gradually develops. This knowledge gives rise to the conduct that reverses wrongdoing. Then, once you have turned away from meaningless pursuits, concentration arises, and the mind stays on a virtuous object as long as you wish. Finally, through training in wisdom realizing the suchness[24] that is selflessness, the root of saṃsāra's fetters is cut, and you attain nirvāṇa, or liberation.

Garland of Birth Stories (*Jātakamālā*) also says:

> One who through listening develops a mind of faith
> nurtures a firm rejoicing in that which is excellent.
> Wisdom is born and ignorance vanishes—
> this is well worth paying for with one's own flesh.
> Listening is the lamp that dispels darkest ignorance,
> the greatest wealth no robber can carry away,
> the weapon that conquers the enemy—confusion—
> the best of friends giving guidance in skillful means,
> near and dear whether or not you are poor.
> It is the nontoxic cure for the pains of sorrow,
> the foremost army that destroys a host of faults,
> the greatest treasure, fame, and splendor as well.
> When you meet noble beings, it is the best gift,
> and in assemblies, it is the delight of the wise. [12]

It also says:

> Taking to heart the practice that comes from listening
> you will be freed from the fortress of rebirth with ease.

Keep thinking again and again about these and other benefits of listening, and generate belief from the depths of your heart.

DEVELOPING RESPECT FOR THE DHARMA AND THOSE WHO TEACH THE DHARMA

From the *Kṣitigarbha Sūtra*:

> Listen with one-pointed faith and respect,
> with neither mockery nor disrespect,
> and worship the teachers of the Dharma,
> seeing them as just like buddhas.

As this quote urges, you should view teachers of Dharma as resembling buddhas, offer them service and goods with things like lion thrones, worship them with gifts, and eliminate disrespect. *Bodhisattva Levels* (*Bodhisattvabhūmi*) says that you should be free of arrogance, be free of contempt for the Dharma and those who expound the Dharma, and hold those two in high regard. And *Garland of Birth Stories* says:

> Sit on a seat that is very low,
> fully develop the glory of discipline,
> and look with eyes imbued with joy
> while drinking the nectar of the words.

> Bring forth respect and concentration,
> with a stainless and pure mentality.
> As patients heed a doctor's words,
> respectfully listen to the Dharma.

The actual way to listen

This has two points: giving up the three faults of a vessel and relying on the six perceptions.

Giving up the three faults of a vessel

Even if sent by the gods, rain cannot enter a vessel turned upside down. A vessel that faces upward but is unclean will pollute the rain and render it undrinkable. Or say a vessel is clean but the bottom leaks, then even though the rain goes in and is not spoiled by dirt, it does not stay. In the same way, there is no great need to hear the Dharma if, when you sit in a place where the Dharma is being explained, you do not listen well; or if you listen but take it wrong—with a faulty motivation and the like; or if these other faults are not present, but the words and the meaning you grasped at the time of hearing are not consolidated and get lost through forgetfulness and so forth. Therefore you should be free of these faults. [13] The antidotes to these three are set forth in three phrases in the sūtras: "Listen intently, in the correct way, and keep it in mind!"[25] And in *Bodhisattva Levels* we are told to listen with a desire to understand it all, single-pointedness, a heedful ear, an integrated mentality, and fully focused attention.

RELYING ON THE SIX PERCEPTIONS

This has six points: perceiving oneself as a patient, perceiving the one expounding the Dharma as a doctor, perceiving the instructions as medicine, perceiving persistent practice as the cure, perceiving the Tathāgata as an exalted being, and generating the wish for the Dharma tradition to last long.

PERCEIVING ONESELF AS A PATIENT

Entering the Bodhisattva Way (Bodhicaryāvatāra, 2.54) says:

> Even when stricken with ordinary illness,
> one has to follow the words of a doctor;
> how much more so if a hundred
> ills like desire afflict you perpetually!

Owing to mental afflictions such as attachment, we continually suffer from ills causing lasting and severe suffering that is difficult to cure. Therefore we first need to diagnose them as such. Geshe Kamapa[26] said:

> If we were not sick, then to meditate as if we were would be the wrong procedure. In reality, however, we are stricken with the chronic illness of the three poisons and our illness is very grave, and yet we do not know we are ill at all.

PERCEIVING THE ONE EXPOUNDING THE DHARMA AS A DOCTOR

By way of analogy, if we are stricken with a serious illness such as a wind or bile disease, we look for an expert physician, and upon meeting one we are extremely happy, and we listen to what he says, treat him with respect, and serve him. We should seek out a spiritual guide teaching the Dharma in the same way and, having found him, accomplish what he says, taking it not as a burden but as a treasure, treating him with respect and reverence.

PERCEIVING THE INSTRUCTIONS AS MEDICINE

Third, just as a patient greatly appreciates the medicine dispensed by the doctor, we regard the instructions and precepts taught by someone expounding the Dharma as the most precious things, and then we make an effort [14] to cherish them rather than wasting them through forgetfulness and the like.

PERCEIVING PERSISTENT PRACTICE AS THE CURE

An ill person sees that his illness cannot be alleviated unless he accepts the medicine the doctor has dispensed and takes it. Likewise, once you see that attachment and so forth cannot be eliminated without implementing the advice taught by your Dharma teacher, practice with persistence and do not arrogantly strive to collect numerous presentations without putting them into practice. It does a leper whose hands and feet are falling off no good to ingest a dose of medicine once or twice. Likewise for us who have been stricken since beginningless time with the vicious disease that is the mental afflictions, it is not sufficient to engage the meaning of the instructions only a couple times. This is why we should examine every part of the path in full with the wisdom of fine investigation and be as persistent as a flowing river. As *Praise of Confession* (*Deśanāstava*) says:

> Our minds have utterly and continually been obscured,
> and for long we have perpetuated the disease.
> How can a leper whose hands and feet are falling off
> derive any benefit from only rarely taking his medicine?

The perception of oneself as a patient is key. If it is present, the other perceptions will also arise. However, if the instructions remain mere words, without their meaning being accomplished so as to eliminate the mental afflictions, you will remain a mere listener. The *King of Concentrations Sūtra* says that you will be like a patient who is not cured but, having sought a doctor, seeks out only the medical treatise and does not take the medicine. It also says:

If, after I have explained the excellent Dharma
and you have heard it, you do not apply it well,
you will be like those patients whose pouches are full of medicine
but who still do not cure their own diseases.

And in *Entering the Bodhisattva Way* (5.109):

These should be put into practice physically.
What would be gained by uttering just the words?
Would it be of benefit for the sick
to just read about a medical treatment?

Therefore you should develop the perception that persistence eliminates the disease. *Persistence* (Skt. *prayatna*) in this statement [15] signifies putting into practice the topics of adopting some behaviors and discarding others as advised by the spiritual teacher. Now, to put them into practice you need to know them, and for that you need to hear them. But the point of knowing them through hearing is to do them. Therefore it is crucial that you put the meaning of what you have heard into practice to the best of your ability. Otherwise, at the time of death, you will regret what you failed to accomplish. You will be like someone imitating a professional actor or someone interested in sugar who only eats the husk of the cane. *Exhortation to the Extraordinary Attitude Sūtra* (*Adhyāśayasaṃcodanasūtra*) says:

"My attainments are poor. What should I do now?"
That is how the childish wail while dying.
Not finding the profound, they suffer greatly.
These are the faults of delighting in mere words.

And:

Like someone amid the crowd watching a play
who extols the virtues of another man, the hero,
he is lacking with regard to his own persistence.
These are the faults of delighting in mere words.

And:

The husk of sugar cane has no essence—
the delightful flavor is inside;
someone eating the husk is unable to find
the delicious flavor of molasses.

Similarly, words are like the husk—
the meaning, like the taste, is inside.
Consequently stop delighting in words;
always be conscientious—reflect on their meaning!

PERCEIVING THE TATHĀGATA AS AN EXALTED BEING

The fifth perception consists in bringing to mind the teacher of the Dharma, the Blessed One, and developing respect for him.

GENERATING THE WISH FOR THE DHARMA TRADITION TO LAST LONG

The sixth perception consists in the thought "How wonderful it would be if, from listening to such a Dharma, the Victor's teachings remained in the world for a long time." If, apart from that, you ignore your own mindstream while explaining or listening to the Dharma, the Dharma remaining separate from it, then whatever is being explained will miss the point. Therefore you have to listen with the intention of developing understanding in your mind.

To illustrate this, when you want to see whether there is dirt or some other impurity on your face, you look at yourself in a mirror, and if you find a smudge there, you remove it. Likewise, when you hear the Dharma, your faulty behavior appears in the mirror of Dharma, whereupon [16] you feel anguish, thinking, "That is what my mindstream has come to." Then, as you engage in eliminating faults and attaining excellent qualities, you necessarily train in accordance with the Dharma. It is like in *Garland of Birth Stories* where the son of Sudāsa asks Prince Candra[27] for Dharma teachings:

Seeing the image of my bad behavior
so clearly in the mirror of the Dharma,

anguish strongly arises in me,
and I turn toward the Dharma.

Knowing this to be the thinking of a suitable vessel for hearing the Dharma,
the Bodhisattva gave him teachings.

In short, thinking, "I shall attain buddhahood for the sake of all sentient
beings. To attain that, I need to train in its causes. As it is necessary to listen
to the Dharma for that, I will listen to the Dharma," generate bodhicitta,
contemplate the benefits of listening, and listen with joy, eliminating the
faults of a vessel.

HOW TO EXPLAIN THE DHARMA

This has four points: contemplating the benefits of explaining the Dharma,
generating respect for the teacher and the Dharma, the proper attitude and
behavior with which to explain the Dharma, and differentiating those to
whom the explanations should be given.

CONTEMPLATING THE BENEFITS OF EXPLAINING THE DHARMA

The *Treasury of Abhidharma* (4.125) says:

> Giving Dharma, free of mental afflictions,
> teach according to sūtras and other true texts.

Its *Autocommentary* says:

> Therefore those who explain the Dharma incorrectly, and with
> an afflicted mind that desires material gain, respect, and fame,
> corrupt their own great merit.

Therefore a pure motivation to teach the Dharma is extremely important,
and in accordance with Ngargompa, who said, "I have never explained the
Dharma without meditating upon impermanence before the session," it is
crucial to review it beforehand.

Exhortation to the Extraordinary Attitude sets forth two groups of twenty benefits of giving the gift of Dharma without desire for material things and without concern for gain, respect, and the like. Also, the *Questions of Householder Ugra Sūtra* (*Gṛhapatyugrapariprcchā*) says that the merit of a householder giving immeasurable material things is exceeded by that of an ordained person giving a single verse of Dharma. [17]

GENERATING RESPECT FOR THE TEACHER AND THE DHARMA

When proclaiming the Mother of the Buddhas, the Teacher himself arranged the seat and so on.[28] Accordingly, since the Dharma is a field of veneration even for buddhas, one should bring to mind the excellent qualities and kindness of the Dharma and its Teacher and generate respect for them.

THE PROPER ATTITUDE AND BEHAVIOR WITH WHICH TO EXPLAIN THE DHARMA

This has two points: attitude and behavior.

ATTITUDE

The *Questions of Sāgaramati Sūtra* (*Sāgaramatipariprcchāsūtra*) puts forward five perceptions: generating the perception of oneself as a doctor, of the Dharma as medicine, of the one listening to the Dharma as a patient, of the Tathāgata as a holy being, and of the wish that the Dharma remain for a long time. It also promotes the cultivation of loving-kindness toward those around one.

The jealousy born from anxiety over others becoming superior, the laziness of putting things off, the discouragement of fatigue from explaining things over and over, the praising of oneself and speaking of others' faults, the reluctance to divulge Dharma texts, and the concern for material things such as food and clothing should be abandoned, thinking, "The very merits from teaching for the sake of my own and others' enlightenment are the assurance of my happiness."

BEHAVIOR

Having washed and dressed in immaculate clothes, you sit in a clean and pleasant venue on a cushion placed on a Dharma throne. If you chant a mantra for subjugating demons, then harmful spirits and demonic kinds of gods will not come closer to you than a perimeter of a hundred yojanas,[29] and even if they do come, they will not be able to create any obstacles, as the *Questions of Sāgaramati Sūtra* says. Therefore you should chant that mantra and, with a radiant expression on your face, give your explanations with examples, logical proofs, and quotations, which help ensure your message is understood.

DIFFERENTIATING THOSE TO WHOM THE EXPLANATIONS SHOULD BE GIVEN

The *Vinaya Sūtra* says, "Do not act without being asked to." Accordingly, do not teach without having been asked, and even when someone asks, examine the vessel. However, as the *King of Concentrations Sūtra* says, knowing someone to be a suitable vessel, it is acceptable to teach even without having been asked. Further modes of conduct are set forth in the *Vinaya Sūtra*.

HOW TO CONCLUDE THE SESSION

The roots of virtue of teaching and listening in this way should be sealed[30] by means of pure aspirational prayers, such as the *Prayer of Good Conduct (Bhadracaryāpraṇidhāna)*.

There is no doubt that if the Dharma is explained and [18] listened to in this manner, the benefits stated above will arise in just one session. When the acts of listening and explaining the Dharma have penetrated the heart of the matter, all the karmic obstructions accumulated previously by, for instance, not respecting the Dharma and those who expound it are purified, and all those newly accumulated are cut off.

When such listening arrives at the heart of the matter, the instructions will benefit the mind. Seeing this, all the holy beings of the past pursued it diligently, especially the earlier gurus of this instruction, who persevered in it with utmost diligence.

These are clearly critically important instructions. If you do not gain certainty about them and your attitude does not change, as is often the case, then no matter how much the profound and vast Dharma is explained to you, it will become like a god fallen to the rank of a demon, and that very Dharma will instead fuel your afflictions. They say, "If you miscalculate the first of the month, you will err until the fifteenth," and thus the wise strive to transform their listening and explaining into the path. Accordingly, whenever you have the opportunity to hear or to teach, you must do so in the proper way. For this is the best preliminary for teaching the instructions.

4 | Relying on a Teacher

THE STAGES BY WHICH A STUDENT SHOULD BE GUIDED THROUGH THE ACTUAL INSTRUCTIONS

THIS HAS TWO POINTS: relying on a spiritual teacher, the root of the path; and the stages of training the mind once you have relied on a teacher.

RELYING ON A SPIRITUAL TEACHER, THE ROOT OF THE PATH

This has two points: the somewhat elaborate explanation for generating certainty and the condensed presentation of how to practice.

THE SOMEWHAT ELABORATE EXPLANATION FOR GENERATING CERTAINTY

As all goodness, starting from the development of a single excellent quality and the decrease of a single fault in the mindstream of the disciple, has its root in the sublime friend, it is important to explain the way to rely on him or her at the outset.

This topic has six points: (1) characteristics of the one to be relied on, the virtuous friend, (2) characteristics of the one who relies, the student, (3) the way to rely, (4) the benefits of reliance, (5) the faults of improper reliance, and (6) a summary of the meaning of these points.

CHARACTERISTICS OF THE ONE TO BE RELIED ON, THE VIRTUOUS FRIEND

Generally speaking, a lot is said about this topic in terms of the individual vehicles in the scriptures and their commentaries. But presented here will be the virtuous friend who guides students on the path to buddhahood, the Mahāyāna, by gradually guiding them on the path of the three types of persons. [19]

Ornament for the Mahāyāna Sūtras (*Mahāyānasūtrālaṃkāra*, 17.10) says that students must rely on a spiritual teacher endowed with ten qualities:

> A spiritual teacher with discipline, calm, complete peace,
> superior qualities, diligent, rich in scriptures,
> who has understood suchness, is eloquent,
> loving, and never disheartened—on that one rely!

Furthermore, it says that someone who lacks self-discipline is not in a position to discipline someone else and that therefore a guru who disciplines others must be someone who has first disciplined his or her own mind.

You may wonder, "Well then, how should one discipline it?" It is of no benefit to have done just any practice and then label it an excellent quality of realization within your mindstream. This is why you need a system for disciplining the mind that accords with the general teachings of the victors. That has been ascertained as the three precious trainings, and therefore ethics, concentration, and wisdom have been set forth. In this verse "discipline" refers to the training in ethics. The *Prātimokṣa Sūtra* says:

> In accord with the unruly horse of the mind,
> always straining to run away:
> a bridle studded with a hundred sharp nails—
> that is the prātimokṣa vows.

Someone skilled at breaking in wild horses tames them with a good bridle. Like wild horses, the sense powers pursue wrong objects. Ethics subjugate them when you are drawn to inappropriate activities and makes you engage with much effort in what ought to be done. Someone trained in it has likewise tamed the horse of the mind.

"Calm" means that, having developed the training in concentration in which, based on mindfulness and vigilance with regard to engaging in good behavior and desisting from faulty behavior, the mind abides in a state of inner calm. "Complete peace" means that, based on the śamatha of a supple mind, the training in wisdom has been developed through fine investigation of the meaning of reality.

However, it is not enough merely to have developed, by means of the three trainings, the excellent qualities of realization that act to tame the mind. The excellent quality of scriptural knowledge is also needed, so the text says "rich in scriptures," which means that the three baskets of scripture and so forth have been studied extensively. According to Geshe Dromtönpa:

> For someone to be called a Mahāyāna [20] guru, he must generate boundless understanding when he explains, and at the end of his teaching when he practices, he must demonstrate what is beneficial and directly meaningful.

"One who has understood suchness" refers primarily to someone with special training in wisdom who has realized the selflessness of phenomena or, indeed, perceived the manifest appearance of suchness. However, even if this is not present, it is said that this criterion is also fulfilled when it is realized through scripture and reasoning.

That said, if a teacher has scriptural knowledge and realization but these are inferior or equal to those of the disciple, that is not enough. Someone with "superior qualities" is needed. As *Collection of Indicative Verses* (*Udānavarga*, 25.5–6) says:

> People relying on someone inferior sink,
> those relying on one of their peers stay the same,
> those who rely on the foremost achieve excellence.
> Therefore rely on your superiors.
>
> If you rely on any such masters,
> endowed with ethics, complete peace,
> and extensive superior wisdom,
> you'll even end up ahead of them.

Phuchungwa said, "When I hear the accounts of holy beings, I hold them in esteem," and Thashi said, "I take the old men at Radreng as models."[31] Accordingly, you need someone with more excellent qualities as a model to emulate. Nonetheless, those six qualities are the excellent qualities that you yourself attain.

The remaining ones are excellent qualities for guiding others. As they say:

> The sages do not cleanse bad actions with water,
> they do not remove the suffering of beings by hand,
> they do not graft their realizations on others;
> they liberate by teaching the truth of ultimate reality.

As is expressed here, nothing beyond teaching others the path in an unmistaken manner and taking care of them can be done; one cannot cleanse the bad actions of another with water.

Among the four properties related to this, "eloquent" means experienced in the stages of guidance and skilled at conveying the meaning to the minds of those to be tamed. "Loving" means having a pure motivation to teach the Dharma, [21] teaching out of compassion without regard for material gain or respect. We need someone like Potowa, who said to Chenngawa, "Son of Lima,[32] however many Dharma teachings I have given, not once have I expected appreciation, for there is no sentient being who does not deserve my care." "Diligent" means always delighting in helping others. "Never disheartened" means never tiring of explaining things over and over and rather bearing the hardships of teaching.

Potowa said:

> The three trainings, the realization of suchness, and loving-kindness—these five are essential. My master Shangtsun is not highly or broadly learned, he cannot bear disappointment, and he does not even thank those who have been kind to him. However, since he has the above-mentioned five, whoever is in his presence benefits. Nyentön is by no means eloquent, and each time he dedicates an offering, the only thing he knows is that nobody understands his explanation, but since he has those five, people near him benefit.

Even if it is difficult, in this day and age, to find someone with the complete set of qualities like that, it is said that you should not rely on anyone whose faults predominate or whose faults equal their excellent qualities but on someone whose excellent qualities exceed their faults.

Such a guru who brings about liberation is the root of what you have aspired to for so long. Therefore those wishing to rely on a guru should keep them in mind and make an effort to find someone with the right qualities. Those wishing for students to rely on them should also strive to acquire these characteristics.

CHARACTERISTICS OF THE ONE WHO RELIES, THE STUDENT

From Āryadeva's *Four Hundred Stanzas* (*Catuḥśataka*, 12.1):

> A suitable vessel, a listener, is said to be
> impartial, intelligent, and interested.
> The teacher's qualities do not appear otherwise,
> and nor do those of the person who listens.

As the commentaries say, someone endowed with the three characteristics is a suitable vessel for hearing the teachings. If all three are complete, the excellent qualities of the Dharma teacher appear as excellent qualities and do not appear as faults. Not only that, the excellent qualities of the listener also appear as excellent qualities to himself and do not appear as faults. If the characteristics of a suitable vessel are not complete, the listener, under the power of his or her faults, will classify even a very pure and virtuous Dharma teacher among those who have faults, [22] and they will perceive the teacher's faults as qualities.

In this regard *impartial* means "without bias." If you have a bias, it will obscure your perception, you will not perceive excellent qualities, and therefore you will fail to find the meaning of excellent explanations. It is just as Bhāviveka says in his *Essence of the Middle Way* (*Madhyamakahṛdaya*):

> While the mind is tormented by bias
> one will never realize peace.

To be biased means to be attached to one's own approach and averse to others' approaches. On discovering something like this in your own mind, you should discard it.

Is that in itself sufficient? If someone does not have the *intelligence* to differentiate good ways of explaining from faulty ways of explaining when they seem the same, he is not a suitable vessel, even though impartial. Therefore you need to have the intelligence that understands those two.

Are those two sufficient? Even if one has both impartiality and intelligence, someone who is just like one of those listening to the Dharma in a lifeless painting is not a suitable vessel. Therefore you also need to have strong *interest*. Candrakīrti's commentary[33] states that, first, respect for the Dharma and the expounder of the Dharma and, second, an attentive mind are added, so that five characteristics are set forth. That being so, we can categorize this into four: strong interest in the Dharma, a fully attentive mind while listening, great respect for the Dharma and the expounder of Dharma, and holding to good explanations and rejecting faulty ones. Intelligence is a conducive circumstance for those four, and impartiality is what eliminates adverse circumstances. Examine whether all the qualities that would make you suitable to be guided by a guru are complete, and cultivate joy if they are. If they are not complete, strive to create the causes for their completion before your life is over.

THE WAY TO RELY

Thus someone endowed with the characteristics of a suitable vessel should examine, as explained above, whether a teacher has the necessary characteristics, and if so, receive the kindness of the Dharma from him. As for the way to rely on a spiritual teacher from whom, in general, you receive the kindness of the Dharma and who, in particular, guides your mind well by means of perfectly complete instructions, there are two points: the way to rely in thought and the way to rely through actions.

THE WAY TO RELY IN THOUGHT

This has two points: the root, training in faith, and remembering his kindness so as to generate respect.

The root, training in faith

Jewels' Blaze Dhāraṇī (Ratnolkādhāraṇī) says:

> Faith, a preliminary practice, gives birth like a mother
> to all good qualities, guards them, and makes them increase. [23]

This says that faith gives birth to excellent qualities that have not yet arisen, and once they have come into existence, it maintains and increases them. The *Ten Dharmas Sūtra (Daśadharmakasūtra)* also says:

> Faith is the foremost vehicle
> leading to definite release.
> For that reason the intelligent
> rely on the pursuit of faith.
>
> In those lacking faith,
> virtuous phenomena do not arise,
> just as in seeds burnt by fire,
> no green sprout can germinate.

In terms of what is gained when it is present and what is lost in its absence, faith is said to be the foundation of all excellent qualities. Generally speaking there are many types of faith: in the Three Jewels, in karmic cause and effect, and in the four noble truths; however, here it is faith in the guru.

Furthermore, as for the way to see the guru, the *Tantra Bestowing the Initiation of Vajrapāṇi (Vajrapāṇyabhiṣekamahātantra)* says:

> O Lord of Secrets, how should a student see his master? Just like he would see the Buddha, the Blessed One.

Similar statements can be found in the collection of Mahāyāna sūtras and in the Vinaya. Their meaning is this: If you understand that someone is like a buddha, a mind finding fault with him will not arise and a mind contemplating his excellent qualities will. Likewise, with regard to a guru, eliminate any concept of fault in every respect and train the mind that conceives excellent qualities.

The above tantra also says:

> Apprehend your master's excellent qualities;
> do not ever apprehend his faults!
> Apprehending his qualities will gain you siddhis;
> apprehending his faults will block their attainment.

You should act accordingly. Thus if excellent qualities predominate in your guru but you think about him in terms of the few faults he has, this will become an obstacle to your own siddhis. Even if faults predominate, if you train in faith from the perspective of his excellent qualities without thinking about him in terms of his flaws, this will cause siddhis to arise. When it comes to your own guru, whether his flaws are great or small, contemplate the faults of thinking about him in those terms, repeatedly generate a mind to eliminate this, and make it stop.

If concepts of faults arise due to carelessness, acute afflictions, and so forth, apply yourself to confession and restraint. [24] If you familiarize yourself with these antidotes accordingly, you may see that there are a few faults, but since your mind focuses on excellent qualities, it will not become an obstacle to your faith. For instance, Atiśa upheld the view of the Madhyamaka, while Serlingpa upheld the view of the True Aspectarian Cittamātra, which is why, in terms of view, one guru was higher than the other. However, as Atiśa discovered the general stages of the Mahāyāna path and bodhicitta relying on him, he regarded Serlingpa as peerless among spiritual teachers.

REMEMBERING HIS KINDNESS SO AS TO GENERATE RESPECT

The *Ten Dharmas Sūtra* says:

> He looks for me, who has roamed in cyclic existence for a long time; he awakens me from enduring obscuration and torpor owing to ignorance; he pulls me out as I sink in the ocean of existence; he shows good paths to me, who has entered bad ones; he frees me, who has been bound in the prison of existence; he is a doctor to me, who is long tormented by illness; he is the rain

clouds, drenching me, who has been ablaze with the fires of attachment and the rest.

The *Marvelous Array Sūtra* (*Gaṇḍavyūhasūtra*) also says:

"These are my spiritual friends, expounders of Dharma,
exhaustively teaching the qualities of all phenomena,
thoroughly teaching the conduct of bodhisattvas":
with these thoughts in mind I have come here.

"As they give birth to all of this, they are like my mother.
They pour forth the milk of virtues, hence they are like wet nurses;
they train me thoroughly in the branches of enlightenment.
These spiritual friends completely turn away harm,
like doctors they release from aging and death,
like Lord Indra they shower rains of nectar.
Like the full moon, they enhance the white qualities;
like bright sunlight, they show the way to peace.
Regarding friends and foes, they are stable like mountains,
their minds as undisturbed as the depths of the sea.
They give perfect support, some say 'like boatmen.'"
With this in mind I, Sudhana, have come here.

"These bodhisattvas bring forth my understanding;
they cause the enlightenment of Buddha's children;
these beings, these friends of mine, are praised by the Buddha":
with such virtuous thoughts I have come here.

"As they save the world they are like heroes;
they have become the captains, protectors, and refuge;
they are the eye bestowing happiness on me":
with thoughts like these, I honor my spiritual friends. [25]

Recollect the sentiments expressed here by using a tune to go with the verses, aspiring to take the part of Sudhana yourself.

THE WAY TO RELY THROUGH ACTIONS

Fifty Verses on the Guru (*Gurupañcāśikā*, vv. 46–47) says:

> What need is there for many words here?
> Do everything to make your guru happy;
> abandon everything he is displeased with;
> apply yourself to that, examine that!

> This was said by Vajradhara himself:
> "Spiritual attainments follow the guru."
> Aware of this, use everything there is
> and make your guru absolutely happy.

In brief, try hard to please him and to eliminate whatever he does not like.

The three means of pleasing the guru are offering him material things, serving him and paying him respect with body and speech, and practicing in accord with his advice. In this regard *Ornament for the Mahāyāna Sūtras* (17.11) says:

> Through homage, offerings purely obtained, and service
> and practice, you should rely on a spiritual friend.

As for the first, *Fifty Verses on the Guru* (v. 17) says:

> If through things not [typically] given—your children, your spouse,
> and even your life—you should always rely
> on the master of your commitments,[34]
> then needless to say, you should through fleeting possessions.

And (v. 21):

> Giving [to your guru] amounts to always
> offering gifts to all the buddhas.
> Such offering accumulates merit
> that in turn leads to the highest siddhi.

Second is bathing him, anointing him, massaging him, wrapping him up, cleaning him, nursing him when he is ill, and so forth, and talking about his excellent qualities. The third is the main one, which is practicing without going against his instructions. *Garland of Birth Stories* says:

> The offering to be made in return for his help
> is practice that accords with his instructions.

THE BENEFITS OF RELIANCE

The scriptures say that you will approach the state of a buddha, that the victors will rejoice, that you will not be deprived of virtuous friends, [26] that you will not fall to the lower rebirths, and that you will not easily succumb to bad karma and afflictions. Since you will not transgress the conduct of bodhisattvas, remaining mindful of it, your accumulation of excellent qualities will grow higher and higher, and all your temporary and ultimate goals will be accomplished.

Furthermore, through serving and paying respect to the spiritual teacher, the karma for experiencing the lower rebirths is exhausted directly in this lifetime through only slight harm to body and mind or else through experiences in dreams. It is said that the benefits are enormous, outshining the roots of virtue of making offerings and the like to innumerable buddhas.

THE FAULTS OF IMPROPER RELIANCE

If you take someone as your spiritual teacher and then relinquish your reliance on him, you will be harmed by illnesses and evil spirits in this life, and in future lives you will have to experience the immeasurable sufferings of the lower rebirths. *Fifty Verses on the Guru* (vv. 13–14) says:

> Never agitate the minds
> of any of your masters.
> If you do so out of stupidity,
> you will surely roast in hell.
>
> It was explained authentically
> that all those who disparage their masters

will dwell in the horrific hells
that were taught—like the Avīci.[35]

A passage from the *Commentary on Difficult Points of Kṛṣṇayamāri* (*Kṛṣṇayamāripañjikā*) also says:

> Whoever hears a single verse
> and does not apprehend the guru
> will be born among dogs a hundred times
> and then as someone of low caste.

Aside from that, excellent qualities that have not arisen will not arise, and those that have arisen will deteriorate and vanish.

If you rely on nonvirtuous friends and bad companions, your excellent qualities will also diminish, your faults will increase, and misfortune will befall you. Therefore it was taught that this should be avoided in every way.

SUMMARY OF THE MEANING OF THESE POINTS

The instructions widely known as *guru yoga* should also be understood according to what has been explained above. It will not be enough to perform the visualization in a single meditation session. When you pursue a Dharma practice from the depths of your heart, you should rely on a spiritual teacher who guides you unmistakenly over a long period of time. As Chekawa also said about such an occasion, "When you rely on a guru, you may have doubts and abandon him." Since you will only lose without gaining if you do not know how to rely on him, [27] it becomes evident that the cycles of teachings about relying on a spiritual teacher are more important than any others; they are the root of fulfilling your long-held aspirations.

Owing to our coarse afflictions, we do not know how to rely on a spiritual teacher, or we know how but still do not do it. We have often engaged in many mistaken ways of relying on the guru while listening to the Dharma. It is difficult for us to develop an awareness of that even for the purpose of confession and restraint. However, having understood the benefits and faults as explained above, it is essential to sincerely confess any instances that do not accord with proper reliance and develop many strong resolutions.

If you act in that manner, you will become before long like the bodhi-sattva Sadāprarudita and like the youthful Sudhana, who was insatiable in his quest for a spiritual teacher.

5 | The Meditation Session

THE CONDENSED PRESENTATION OF HOW TO PRACTICE

THIS HAS TWO POINTS: the actual way to practice and the need to employ two kinds of practice.

THE ACTUAL WAY TO PRACTICE

This has two points: what to do during the meditation session itself and what to do in the periods between sessions.

WHAT TO DO DURING THE MEDITATION SESSION ITSELF

This has three points: what to do in preparation, what to do during the actual meditation session, and what to do at the end.

WHAT TO DO IN PREPARATION

Engage in the six preparatory practices presented in the biography of Serlingpa as follows:

First, clean your dwelling and arrange representations of the exalted body, speech, and mind. Second, beautifully arrange offerings honestly acquired. Third, on a comfortable seat straighten your body and assume a suitable lotus or half-lotus posture, making sure that your mind is suffused with refuge and bodhicitta. Fourth, in the space in front of you, imagine the lineage gurus of vast conduct and profound view as well as countless buddhas, ārya[36] bodhisattvas, śrāvakas, and pratyekabuddhas along with those who dwell in the Buddha's words. Thus visualize the merit field.

Fifth, it is exceedingly difficult for paths to arise in your mindstream if the favorable conditions for their arising, the accumulations [of merit and wisdom], have not been collected and their adverse conditions, the obstructions, have not been purified. Therefore, to unite the key points of accumulation and purification, purify your mindstream by means of the seven-limb practice. As for the limb of *prostration*, the prostration combining the three doors is set out in the stanza:[37]

> I bow respectfully with body, speech, and mind
> to all the lions among men without exception,
> in however many worlds there are
> in the ten directions and three times.

This is not prostration to the buddhas in just the world spheres in one direction and of one time. Rather, focusing on all the victors residing in all ten directions past, present, and future, you reverently prostrate body, speech, and mind to them from the depths of your heart.

There are prostrations for each of the three doors individually. [28] Physical prostration is set out in the stanza:

> Owing to the power of prayer for good conduct,
> all the buddhas directly appear to my mind.
> I bow sincerely to all these buddhas
> with as many bodies as there are atoms in the world.

You take all the victors in all directions and times as the objects of your mental focus, as though perceiving them directly. Emanating your own body in manifestations as numerous as fine particles, you prostrate to them. And having generated the power of faith in the excellent conduct of these holy objects, be motivated by that.

Mental prostration is set forth in the stanza:

> On every atom, as many buddhas as there are atoms
> are surrounded by bodhisattvas.
> Every one is absorbed in meditation on suchness.
> I fully venerate all of these accomplished ones.

On top of each minute particle, buddhas as innumerable as dust particles reside encircled by bodhisattvas. Generate the faith that recollects their excellent qualities.

Verbal prostration is set forth in the stanza:

> I extol the good qualities of all the buddhas.
> I praise all of the sugatas
> with the sounds of an ocean of songs
> in voices of inexhaustible seas of praise.

From each of the bodies emanate innumerable heads, and from each of the heads again innumerable tongues singing inexhaustible praises of the objects' excellent qualities to sweet melodies. Here "songs" are praises, and their "voices"—that is, their causes—are the tongues. The word "ocean" conveys a great quantity.

As for the limb of *offering*, surpassable offerings are set forth in the two stanzas:

> I offer these buddhas and bodhisattvas
> fabulous flowers, glorious garlands,
> cymbals, scented balm, precious parasols,
> excellent butter lamps, and superb incense.

> I offer these buddhas and bodhisattvas
> sublime garments, supreme scents,
> sachets of fragrant powder equal to Mount Meru,
> and every wonderful thing in a splendid array.

"Fabulous flowers" are marvelous specimens of divine and human flowers. "Glorious garlands" are many different kinds of flowers strung together. Both together encompass every actual and imaginary flower.

"Cymbals" are the sounds of traditional instruments and the like. "Scented balm" is a mixture of fragrant perfumes. "Precious parasols" are the finest of parasols. "Butter lamps" are fragrant radiant lights from things like incense or butter, as well as glowing jewel lights. "Incense" refers to combinations of fragrant substances and to single ones.

"Sublime garments" are the finest of clothes. A "supreme scent" is water and the like pervaded by a scent that fills the billion world systems with fragrance. The "sachets of powder" are packaged powders of fragrant incense suitable for scattering and burning, or the colored sand powder of a maṇḍala, in multiple layers as wide and as high as Mount Meru. "Array," joined at the end to all the above, means a great quantity, artfully and colorfully arranged.

Unsurpassable offerings are set forth in the stanza:

May all these unsurpassable and vast offerings
appear before all the buddhas and bodhisattvas.
Through the power of faith along with virtuous deeds,
I pay homage and make offerings to all the conquerors.

Since surpassable offerings are those of worldly beings, this here is everything good emanated by powerful beings such as bodhisattvas. [29]

The last two lines are to be joined to all the previous couplets in order to complete them. They indicate the motivation for the prostrations and offerings as well as their object.

The *confession* of bad actions is set forth in the stanza:

I confess each and every one
of the negative actions I have done
with my body, speech, and mind
influenced by desire, hatred, and ignorance.

Depending on the cause (the three poisons) and by means of the three bases (body, speech, and mind), their nature is that I have done them (that is, that I have actually created them), I have made others create them, and I have rejoiced in those created by others, all of which is generally subsumed under "I have done." If through recollecting their faults you regret those done previously and sincerely confess them with the intention to abstain from them in the future, you stop the increase of deeds done in the past and stop committing them in the future.

Rejoicing is set forth in the stanza:

I rejoice in all the merit, whatever it may be,
of all the buddhas of the ten directions,

bodhisattvas, pratyekabuddhas, those with more to learn,
those with no more to learn, and all ordinary beings.

As you recall the benefits of the virtue of the five types of persons, you
cultivate joy.[38]
Requesting to turn the wheel of Dharma is set forth in the stanza:

I implore all the protectors,
lights of the world in the ten directions,
who have reached buddhahood, which is without attachment,
to turn the peerless wheel of the teaching.

Emanating the same number of bodies, you exhort those who have awoken
to complete buddhahood in the fields of the ten directions—those who
have found unobstructed exalted knowledge free of attachment—to teach
the Dharma as soon as possible.
Supplication is set forth in the stanza:

I supplicate, with palms joined in prayer,
those wishing to demonstrate their final nirvāṇa:
please stay as many eons as there are atoms
to benefit and bring happiness to all beings

Supplicate those throughout the ten directions who show how to pass
beyond sorrow to remain, not passing into nirvāṇa for as many eons as the
number of fine dust particles there are in the universe in order to bring
about the benefit and happiness of sentient beings.
The limb of *dedication* is set forth in the stanza:

Whatever little merit I have accumulated
by prostrating, offering, confessing,
rejoicing, requesting, and supplicating,
I dedicate it all to enlightenment.

All the roots of virtue represented by the previous six limbs are made the
common property of all sentient beings and never come to an end, since

they have been dedicated with strong aspiration as causes of complete enlightenment.

If you thus develop an understanding of the meaning of those words and slowly do as was taught without allowing your mind to wander, you will gather immeasurable heaps of merit.

Five of these limbs—prostrating, offering, requesting, supplicating, and rejoicing—belong to the collection of accumulations. [30] Confessing purifies obstructions. One aspect of rejoicing, the cultivation of joy in one's own virtue, multiplies the virtue. By means of dedicating, the virtues of collecting, purifying, and multiplying, however small, are multiplied manifoldly, and what would normally come to an end after producing a temporary effect is made inexhaustible. In brief, there are the three: (1) accumulating, (2) purifying, and (3) multiplying and making inexhaustible.

Sixth, as for the final preparatory practice, with a clear visualization of the objects, offer a maṇḍala, and with strong aspiration, make numerous requests: "Please grant blessings that all erroneous attitudes such as disrespecting the spiritual teacher may cease and that all the nonerroneous attitudes toward the spiritual teacher may come about with ease. I request blessings that all outer and inner obstacles may be pacified."

WHAT TO DO DURING THE ACTUAL MEDITATION SESSION

This has two points: how to practice meditation in general and how to practice this meditation in particular.

HOW TO PRACTICE MEDITATION IN GENERAL

Meditation on a path like the one explained below is to render the mind suitable for attending to a virtuous object just as one wishes. If you jump from object to object to sustain your interest or you pursue a variety of virtuous objects in no particular order, nothing will come of it, and having gone wrong from the beginning, your spiritual practice will continue to be faulty throughout your life. Therefore you should first determine the number and order of objects to be attended to. Then you should unleash a strong resolve that does not permit the advent of thoughts that draw you away from what has been ascertained. Finally you should sustain with mindfulness and vigilance what has been ascertained, without addition or omission.

How to practice this meditation in particular

First contemplate the benefits of reliance and the faults of nonreliance. Then repeatedly resolve to never permit your awareness to get caught up in conceiving faults in the guru, and instead recall the excellent qualities like ethics and concentration that you yourself have perceived in him. Cultivate the faith that has the aspect of mental clarity until it arises. Then contemplate, in accordance with the above quotations from the sūtras, the instances of beneficial kindness that you have received and still receive, and from the depth of your heart, cultivate respect until it arises.

What to do at the end

By means of the *Prayer of Good Conduct* [31] and *Aspiration in Seventy Verses* (*Praṇidhānasaptati*), the virtue accumulated should be dedicated with strong aspiration to the temporary and ultimate aims. You should meditate like this in four sessions—at dawn, in the morning, in the afternoon, and in the evening.

If your sessions are long in the beginning, it is easy to fall under the power of laxity and excitement. Since it is difficult to correct this state of mind once it has become a habit, you should have many short sessions. If you cut the session short when there is still a desire to meditate, you will be drawn to entering meditation subsequently. Otherwise, they say, you will be overcome by nausea at the sight of your meditation seat. Once they have stabilized a bit, prolong the sessions while maintaining them all free from the faults of excessive tension or slackness. If you practice in this way, you will have few obstacles, and exhaustion, laxity, and lethargy will be pacified.

What to do in the periods between sessions

Generally speaking, numerous practices enhance the object between sessions, such as prostrations, circumambulation, and recitation. However, the main point is that if you make an effort in the session itself but then, during the intervals between sessions, you carelessly let go of the causes for maintaining your focus, by not relying on mindfulness and vigilance of the observed object along with its subjective aspect,[39] the outcome will be very little. Therefore, between sessions, you also need to read Dharma texts presenting that object and recall it again and again. Accumulate by various means the conditions that are favorable for the arising of excellent qualities, and purify by various means the adverse conditions, the obstructions. Your determination regarding the vows you have promised to uphold, the basis of everything, should be reaffirmed regularly.

Apart from that, train in the collection of the following four causes for an easy arising of the paths of śamatha and special insight.

RESTRAINING THE SENSE DOORS

When the six consciousnesses arise in dependence upon objects and sense powers, attachment and anger end up arising in the mental consciousness toward the six pleasant and the six unpleasant objects. Restraining the sense doors guards against their arising.[40]

ACTING WITH VIGILANCE

Entering the Bodhisattva Way (5.108) says:

> To examine again and again
> the situation of mind and body—
> exactly that in brief
> is what defines protecting vigilance.

Following this, whenever the body and so forth engage in such and such an action, through understanding whether or not it should be pursued, you behave accordingly.

KNOWING THE RIGHT MEASURE OF FOOD

Knowing the right measure of food means to give up eating too much or too little and to eat only the amount that does not damage your virtuous activities. Furthermore, having meditated upon the faults of craving food, remember what is said in the scriptures about eating, thinking that it should be without mental afflictions, [32] that it should benefit the giver, that while you now gather the microorganisms of your body by means of material things, in the future you will gather them by means of the Dharma, and that you will bring about the welfare of all sentient beings. *Letter to a Friend* (*Suhṛllekha*, v. 38) also says:

> Reasoning that foodstuffs are like medicine,
> depend on them without attachment or hatred.
> They are not meant for you to be sated or haughty
> or fat but just to keep your body going.

PRACTICING EARNESTLY WITHOUT SLEEPING AT THE WRONG TIME, AND BEHAVING WELL WHEN LYING DOWN TO SLEEP

Letter to a Friend (v. 39) says:

> Lord of the lineage, having practiced all day
> and in the first and last periods of the night,
> sleep with mindfulness between those periods,
> so that even your sleeping is not wasted!

The actual sessions of both the entire day and during the first and last part of the night,[41] as well as what should be done between them, have been explained. Whether walking about or seated, completely purify your mind of the five hindrances and thus make whatever you do meaningful.[42]

The act of sleep takes place between sessions and therefore should also not be wasted with no benefit. The physical act consists in lying on your right side during the middle of the three periods of the night, placing the left leg atop the right one, and sleeping like a lion.

As for mindfulness, recollect, until you fall asleep, the predominant virtuous actions that you have cultivated during the day. Therefore, even while asleep, you can maintain whatever spiritual practice, such as concentration, you pursued when you were not asleep.

As for vigilance, if any mental affliction arises while you are cultivating mindfulness, become aware of it and eagerly eliminate it rather than accepting it.

The notion of getting up consists in projecting the thought "I will get up at this and that time."

Apart from the unique aspects of each meditation during the actual yoga, these instructions on what should be done in preparation, during the actual meditation, at the end, and between sessions should be applied to every object and its aspects, from here up to special insight.

THE NEED TO EMPLOY TWO KINDS OF PRACTICE

[33] *Ornament for the Mahāyāna Sūtras* says:

> Here, first of all, proper mental attention arises in reliance upon study, and from proper mental attention, again, arises the wisdom with ultimate reality as its object.

That is to say, from proper mental attention, gained through the arising of wisdom reflecting on the meaning of what has been studied, a direct realization of ultimate reality that comes from meditation arises. *Ornament for Clear Knowledge* (4.53) also says:

> During the stages of definitive analysis[43]
> as well as the paths of seeing and meditation,
> one must repeatedly reflect, assess, and ascertain;
> these are the paths of meditation.

That is to say, repeated reflection, evaluation, and definitive understanding are paths of meditation for Mahāyāna āryas.

The *Compendium of Trainings* (*Śikṣāsamuccaya*) also says:

> Thus you should meditate continuously on all kinds of giving away, guarding, purifying, and increasing your bodies, possessions, and merit.

With regard to the meditations that, according to the statement, should be done on the basis of each of the three (bodies, possessions, and roots of virtue) in connection with all four activities (giving away, guarding, purifying, and increasing), there are both kinds: analytical meditation, which is practiced by analyzing with the wisdom of fine investigation, and placement meditation, in which the mind is placed single-pointedly without analysis.

Now what kind of path is analytical meditation and what kind of path is placement meditation? For meditations such as the cultivation of faith in the spiritual teacher, the preciousness of the freedoms and endowments and how difficult it is to find them, death and impermanence, actions and their effects, the faults of cyclic existence, and the cultivation of bodhicitta, analytical meditation is necessary. Each of them requires an awareness that has great strength and the ability to subdue the mind for a long time, because if those are absent, their counterparts, disrespect and the like, cannot be prevented. Also, the generation of such an awareness depends on nothing but the meditation repeatedly analyzing through fine investigation. For example, just as intense attachment arises when you closely familiarize yourself with an object of attachment, exaggerating its pleasant features, so intense hatred arises when you repeatedly think of the many unpleasant features of an enemy. [34] So in the case of cultivating these paths, no matter whether the image of the object appears clearly, the mind's way of apprehending it must be intense and long-lasting, and this requires analytical meditation. In the context of practicing śamatha, which enables you to place the mind on whatever object you wish, someone whose mind has been unable to stay on one object will not be able to generate śamatha if he keeps analyzing, and placement meditation is required for that.

Some who do not understand this approach may claim that if you are a scholar, you should only do analytical meditation, while if you are a sādhu, you should only do placement meditation. But this is not correct because each of them needs to do both. Scholars also need to achieve śamatha, and sādhus also need to achieve strong faith in the spiritual teacher and the like. Therefore the idea that repeated analysis using the wisdom of fine investigation belongs to the context of study and reflection rather than to the context of practice is incorrect.

The notion that all thought involves apprehending signs and therefore creates obstacles to enlightenment has the fault of not differentiating between improper mental attention apprehending true existence, and proper mental attention thinking of reality.

The idea that you must achieve a nonconceptual concentration that allows you to place the mind on a single object as you wish, and that if you do a lot of analytical meditation beforehand it will prevent the arising of concentration, is contrary to the present instructions. For example, a skillful goldsmith burns gold or silver in the fire and washes it in water again and again, removing all the impurities and making it very pliant, so that it can be made into whatever jewelry one wishes, such as earrings. Likewise, at first you meditate on the afflictions, the secondary afflictions, nonvirtuous actions and their effects in the case of bad conduct, and the faults of cyclic existence, in the order in which they are presented. By meditating with analytical wisdom on such faults again and again, you become completely downhearted or mentally dejected, like burning gold in fire, whereby you turn away from the nonvirtuous side and clear away those defilements. Next you meditate on the excellent qualities of the spiritual friend, the preciousness of the freedoms and endowments, [35] the excellent qualities of the Three Jewels, virtuous actions and their effects, the benefits of bodhicitta, and so on, in the order in which they are presented. By meditating with the wisdom of fine investigation on such excellent qualities again and again, your mind becomes drenched with them, and you develop clarifying faith, like washing gold with water, whereby you turn toward the virtuous side and take delight in it. Thus the mind is saturated with virtuous qualities. When it has been transformed in that way, whether you wish to achieve śamatha or special insight, you will achieve it without difficulty when your mind is focused on it. That is why such an analytical meditation is the best means of achieving a nonconceptual concentration.

That is how Ārya Asaṅga also put it:

> For example, when a smith or his skillful apprentice burns gold or silver in a fire and washes it with water a couple of times in order to remove all impurities and stains, it becomes pliant and malleable for fashioning this or that ornament. Their method is clearly evident. So those with the appropriate mastery of a smith or skillful apprentice can then fashion whatever ornament they wish using a smith's tools. Likewise, a yogi ensures that his mind is not turned toward impurities and stains such as covetousness and cultivates disenchantment, delighting his mind by focusing not on the stresses of the afflicted mind but on the virtuous side instead. That yogi doubtlessly trains his mind in either the side of śamatha or the side of special insight, such that either it is closely applied to this and that or it is resting in its natural state, unmoving and unwavering. It can also be directed for the sake of perfectly achieving whatever purpose he has contemplated.

Furthermore, the main hindrance to the mind abiding on an object continuously is twofold: laxity and excitement. If you have a strong and constant
awareness that sees the excellent qualities of the Three Jewels and so forth,
it is quite easy to overcome laxity, for many valid sources say that its antidote [36] is to uplift the mind by looking at excellent qualities. If you have a
strong and constant awareness that sees the faults of impermanence, suffering, and so forth, it is quite easy to overcome excitement, for excitement is
a distracted mind belonging to the category of attachment and many texts
praise disenchantment as its antidote.

6 | The Freedoms and Endowments of This Life

THE STAGES OF TRAINING THE MIND ONCE YOU HAVE RELIED ON A TEACHER

THIS HAS TWO POINTS: first, an exhortation to take the essence of this life endowed with freedom, and second, the way to take its essence.

AN EXHORTATION TO TAKE THE ESSENCE OF THIS LIFE ENDOWED WITH FREEDOM

This has three points: identifying the freedoms and endowments, contemplating their great value, and contemplating the difficulty in finding them.

IDENTIFYING THE FREEDOMS AND ENDOWMENTS

This has two points: freedoms and endowments.

FREEDOMS

Verse Summary of the Perfection of Wisdom (*Prajñāpāramitāsañcayagāthā*, 32.2) says:

> Through ethical discipline, the characteristics of the numerous
>   animal births
> and the eight unfree states are abandoned; thus you win constant
>   freedom.

So the freedoms consist in freedom from the eight unfree states.

Among the eight unfree states, the four unfree states of humans are
(1) living in a remote and savage land where the four types of followers of
the Buddha do not go, (2) being stupid or dumb, and having incomplete
faculties or missing body parts, such as ears and so forth, (3) holding wrong
views that misconstrue past and future lives, actions and their effects, and
the Three Jewels to be nonexistent, and (4) being born where no buddha has
appeared and therefore being bereft of his teachings. The nonhuman unfree
states are (1–3) those of a hell being, a hungry ghost, and an animal, and (4)
that of a long-lived god. As for the long-lived gods, *Commentary on Letter to
a Friend* (*Vyaktapadāsuhṛllekaṭīkā*) discusses two types: those without perception and those in the formless realm. The former abide in one region of
the fourth dhyāna, Great Result, as if in a hermitage far away from a village.
The latter are ordinary beings born in the formless realms. *Discourse on the
Eight Unfree States* (*Aṣṭākṣaṇakathā*) explains long-lived gods to be gods of
the desire realm who are constantly distracted by activities of desire.

ENDOWMENTS

This has two points, of which the five endowments pertaining to oneself are
said [in *Śrāvaka Levels*] to be:

> Being human, born somewhere central, with unimpaired faculties,
> no inexpiable heinous actions, and faith in the source.

Here "born somewhere central" is to be born in a place where the four types
of followers are active. "Unimpaired faculties" consists of not being stupid or dumb and having fully functioning body parts, eyes, ears, and so
forth. [37] "No inexpiable heinous actions" implies not having committed
or caused others to commit an uninterrupted action. "Faith in the source"
is to have faith in the foundation from which all the mundane and supramundane virtuous dharmas arise—discipline. Here *discipline* should be
understood to encompass all three baskets of scripture.

As those five are brought together in one's own mindstream and constitute circumstances for the accomplishment of the Dharma, they are called
"endowments pertaining to oneself."

The five endowments pertaining to others are said [in *Śrāvaka Levels*]
to be:

The Buddha has come and taught the holy Dharma,
the teachings still remain and are being followed,
there's loving-kindness and compassion for the sake of others.

Here "The buddha has come or arisen" means that after having accumulated the collections [of merit and wisdom] for three countless eons, he manifestly attained complete buddhahood. "Taught the holy Dharma" means that the Buddha or his disciples have taught the Dharma. "The teachings survive" means that from the Buddha coming and teaching the Dharma up to the moment of passing into nirvāṇa, the Dharma attained through seeing the ultimate Dharma has not degenerated. "The teachings survive and are being followed" means that through that very realization of the Dharma, there are those who see that beings have the power to directly perceive the holy Dharma and who then follow the teachings in accordance with that realization. "There is loving-kindness and compassion for the sake of others" means that there are donors and benefactors who provide monastic robes and the like. As these five are present in the mindstreams of others and constitute conditions for accomplishing the Dharma, they are called "endowments pertaining to others."

CONTEMPLATING THEIR GREAT VALUE

If you engage in no practice of pure Dharma at all for the sake of lasting happiness but strive your entire life merely to eliminate your suffering and attain happiness, then you are like an animal despite your fortunate rebirth since animals do the same. You need a physical basis like the one described above in order to practice the Mahāyāna path. *Letter to a Student* (*Śiṣyalekha*, v. 64) says:

> The base of the path of those gone to bliss, the tool for leading
>   beings,
>   is that most powerful mind (bodhicitta), which is gained by human
>   beings.
>   That path is not found by gods or nāgas, nor by asuras,
>   not by garuḍas, knowledge holders, kinnaras, or uragas.

Some gods of the desire realm, with strong predispositions from having previously trained in the path as a human, are suitable as a support for seeing the truth for the first time. But it is impossible to attain the ārya path for the first time on the basis of birth in a realm above that.[44] However, as explained above, the majority of desire-realm gods [38] lack the requisite freedom, so they cannot attain the path for the first time. Again, inhabitants of the continent of Uttarakuru[45] are unsuitable as a support for vows, which is why those beings of the other three continents are praised; and among them, the inhabitants of Jambudvīpa[46] are especially praised.

"Having gained such an excellent basis as this, why would I not make it fruitful? If I do not make it meaningful, could there be any greater self-deception or stupidity? Having passed over and over through the many perilous places that lack freedom such as the lower rebirths, were I to render this unique opportunity for liberation meaningless and go back to those places, I would have lost my mind, as though confused by a magic spell." Thinking in this way, meditate again and again. *Entering the Bodhisattva Way* (1.3) says:

> Having found this kind of freedom,
> if I do not cultivate virtue,
> then no deception could be greater;
> nothing could be more confused than that.

And (1.6–7):

> Having found, by chance, this place,
> so beneficial and hard to find,
> were I now, with understanding,
> to be led away to that hell once again,
>
> as though confused by magic spells,
> I will have utterly lost my mind.
> Even I do not know what so confused me.
> What is it dwelling deep within me?

In that way, think how this physical basis is highly meaningful, not only in terms of the final goal but even temporarily. For with it one can easily accomplish generosity, morality, patience, and so on, the causes of an excellent body, wealth, and all that accompanies a higher status.[47] If with this very meaningful physical basis you do not apply yourself day and night to developing the causes of the two objectives, it would be like returning empty-handed from an island of precious jewels.

CONTEMPLATING THE DIFFICULTY IN FINDING THEM

Chapters of Scriptural Transmission (*Āgamavastu*) says that beings who die and migrate to the lower rebirths, whether from lower or fortunate rebirths, are like the dust of the great earth, while beings who are born in the fortunate rebirths, which are difficult to obtain whether migrating from lower or fortunate rebirths, are like the dust taken up with the tip of a fingernail. [39] If you wonder just why they are so difficult to find, *Four Hundred Stanzas* (7.6) says:

> For the most part, human beings
> cling to the side that is unholy.
> Therefore, generally, ordinary beings
> surely go to the lower rebirths.

Most humans and other beings typically hold on to the side of the ten non-virtues, and consequently they go to the lower rebirths. Furthermore, if you have to spend an eon in the hell of Avīci for each moment of anger toward a bodhisattva and so on, then the bad actions accumulated over many lifetimes, which have neither come to fruition nor been overcome by antidotes, and are present in your own mindstream, will surely cause you to spend many eons in the lower rebirths.

If you definitely purify the causes of lower rebirths accumulated previously and close the door to newly engaging in them, then the fortunate rebirths will not be hard to reach; however, that is very rarely done. If you fail to do so, you go to the lower rebirths; and once you have gone to the lower rebirths, you do not create virtue but continuously commit bad deeds, whereby, as stated in *Entering the Bodhisattva Way*, you do not even hear the name of fortunate rebirths for many eons.

Potowa said:

In Phenpo there was a fortress by the name of Chakar that had been seized by an enemy. For a long time the villagers had been their unfortunate servants. One old man used to wallow in anguish about this fort, and when one day he heard people saying that it had been won back, he grabbed his spear and, not able to walk, dragged himself along saying, "If only the recapture of Chakar Fortress is not dream!" In the same way, having won the freedoms and endowments, you must derive that kind of joy from it and practice Dharma.[48]

As stated here, you should meditate to develop this kind of attitude.

Four states of mind regarding the Dharma are necessary to generate a fully qualified wish to take the essence of this life endowed with freedom:

1. That you need to accomplish the Dharma—because all sentient beings only want happiness and do not want suffering, and accomplishing happiness and eliminating suffering depends solely on the holy Dharma.
2. That you are able to accomplish the Dharma—because you have the external condition, a spiritual teacher, and the internal condition, the freedoms and endowments. [40]
3. That you need to accomplish the Dharma in this very life—because if you do not accomplish it within this life, it will be difficult to obtain the freedoms and endowments for many lives to come.
4. That you need to accomplish the Dharma right now—because the time of death is uncertain.

The third stops the laziness of dismissing it, thinking, "I should practice the Dharma in later lives," and the fourth counteracts the laziness of not entering into it, thinking, "Although I must accomplish it in this life, it is enough to accomplish it later on and not in these immediate years, months, and days." You can also make these points into three, subsuming the last two under the thought "I need to accomplish it soon." Remembering death can also be linked in here, but since that is a lengthy topic, it will be explained below.

The mind becomes more subdued if you contemplate the topic from various points of view, so you should contemplate in the way explained above.

If you cannot manage this much, then subsume those topics under these [three] points: what the nature of this life of freedoms and endowments is, how it is so meaningful in terms of temporary and final goals, and how difficult it is to obtain from the point of view of cause and result. You should take up each of the points explained above in a way that suits you and meditate on them.

Contemplate the difficulty in obtaining the freedoms and endowments from the point of view of the causes. Generally speaking, even to attain a mere fortunate rebirth, you need to cultivate one of the pure virtues such as ethics. In particular, to attain the complete freedoms and endowments, you need to cultivate many roots of virtue such as upholding a foundation with pure ethics, reinforcing it through generosity and so on, and maintaining a connection[49] by means of stainless prayers. Those who accomplish such causes appear to be very few. Therefore, having weighed this up, contemplate how difficult it is, in general and in particular, to obtain the result that is the physical basis of a fortunate rebirth.

Contemplate the difficulty in obtaining the freedoms and endowments from the point of view of the result. Meditate on the fact that, compared to the beings in the lower rebirths different in kind from us, even a mere fortunate rebirth seems beyond the limits of possibility; and compared to the beings in the fortunate rebirths the same in kind as us, those endowed with the fully qualified freedoms[50] are extremely rare. Geshe Dölpa laid great emphasis on this.[51] He said that all other Dharma is brought forth by this understanding. As this is so, you should make an effort accordingly.

7 | The Paths of the Three Types of Persons

THE WAY TO TAKE THE ESSENCE OF THIS LIFE ENDOWED WITH FREEDOM

THIS HAS TWO POINTS: generating certainty with regard to the general presentation of the path, and the actual way of taking its essence.

GENERATING CERTAINTY WITH REGARD TO THE GENERAL PRESENTATION OF THE PATH

This has two points: How all the Buddha's teachings are contained in the paths of the three types of persons, and the reason for gradual guidance from the perspective of the three types of persons.

HOW ALL THE BUDDHA'S TEACHINGS ARE CONTAINED IN THE PATHS OF THE THREE TYPES OF PERSONS

Everything the Buddha did was only for the welfare of sentient beings, from generating the mind of enlightenment in the beginning, [41] through collecting the accumulations in the middle, to manifesting complete buddhahood at the end., Thus all his Dharma teachings too are only for accomplishing the welfare of sentient beings. That being so, the goal to be accomplished is the welfare of sentient beings, which has two levels: the temporary one of higher states and the ultimate one of definite goodness.

All the teachings that pertain to accomplishing the first level are included in the cycle of Dharma teachings for the person of genuine lesser spiritual capacity or that is shared in common with the person of lesser capacity. Special persons of lesser capacity do not act primarily for the rewards of this life. Instead, they pursue the excellence of high rebirth in future lives and try to achieve the causes of that. *Lamp for the Path to Enlightenment* (v. 3) says:

> Whoever pursues by any means,
> the happiness of saṃsāra only,
> just for his own benefit,
> should be known as the least of beings.

There are two kinds of *definite goodness*: (1) the liberation that is a mere release from saṃsāra and (2) omniscience. All the teachings that pertain to the vehicles of śrāvakas and pratyekabuddhas are included in the cycle of Dharma teachings for persons of genuine medium capacity or the teachings that are shared in common with persons of medium capacity. Persons of medium spiritual capacity develop disenchantment with saṃsāra as a whole and make liberation from saṃsāra their goal for their own welfare. Therefore they engage in its method, the three trainings. *Lamp for the Path to Enlightenment* (v. 4) says:

> One who pursues only personal peace—
> turning away from the happiness of saṃsāra
> and desisting from evil deeds—
> is called a "person of medium capacity."

There are two means of attaining omniscience: the great vehicles of the secret Mantrayāna and the Pāramitāyāna. These two are contained in the cycle of Dharma teachings for persons of great capacity. Since persons of great capacity are under the influence of great compassion, they make enlightenment their goal in order to bring all the suffering of sentient beings to an end. Therefore they train in the six perfections, the two stages, and so forth. *Lamp for the Path to Enlightenment* (v. 5) says:

> One who through his own suffering
> yearns to bring to an end completely
> all the suffering of other beings [42]
> is said to be a superior being.

As stated above, the means by which these beings attain enlightenment are twofold: the perfections and secret mantra.

The classification of *three types of persons* is determined in many texts, such as the *Compendium of Ascertainments* (*Viniścayasaṃgrahaṇī*) and the *Treasury of Abhidharma Autocommentary* (*Abhidharmakośabhāṣya*). Although persons of lesser capacity include both those who devote themselves to this life and those who devote themselves to future lives, this is about the latter. One should consider them as engaging in the unmistaken means to higher states.

THE REASON FOR GRADUAL GUIDANCE FROM THE PERSPECTIVE OF THE THREE TYPES OF PERSONS

This has two points: the purpose of guidance in accordance with the paths of the three types of persons, and the reason for such gradual guidance.

THE PURPOSE OF GUIDANCE IN ACCORDANCE WITH THE PATHS OF THE THREE TYPES OF PERSONS

Although this is explained in terms of three types of beings, since the path of persons of great capacity contains within it the paths of the two other types of beings, Master Aśvaghoṣa says that these two are parts of the Mahāyāna path. So here it is not a matter of guidance for the path of persons of lesser capacity who make only the happiness of saṃsāra their goal, nor for the path of persons of medium capacity who make only liberation from saṃsāra for their own sake their goal. Rather, we should consider certain paths common to those two to be preliminary practices leading to the path of persons of great capacity and take them to be part of the training in the path of persons of great capacity.

THE REASON FOR SUCH GRADUAL GUIDANCE

This has two points: the actual reason and the purpose.

THE ACTUAL REASON

The gateway for entering the Mahāyāna is to generate bodhicitta—the mind directed toward supreme enlightenment. Once it has arisen in the mindstream, according to *Entering the Bodhisattva Way* (1.9),

> The instant they give rise to bodhicitta,
> the wretched bound in the prison of cyclic existence
> are declared children of the sugatas.

A person who has gained the title "bodhisattva" is admitted to the ranks of Mahāyāna beings. If their bodhicitta deteriorates, they depart from the Mahāyāna. This being so, those who wish to enter the Mahāyāna must exert themselves in many ways to generate that mind. However, to generate it, they first need to meditate on the benefits of generating that mind, so that delight in those benefits will increase, and do the seven-limb practice together with going for refuge. That is what is taught in the *Compendium of Trainings* and in *Entering the Bodhisattva Way*. [43]

If we summarize the benefits set forth in this way, there are two: temporary and ultimate benefits. The former are twofold: one will not fall to the lower rebirths and one will be born in the fortunate rebirths. Once this mind has arisen, the causes of miserable existences accumulated previously are purified, and the continuity of accumulating them in the future is severed. The causes of fortunate rebirths accumulated previously, being conjoined with it, increase extensively, and the ones newly created, being motivated by it, become unlimited. Eventually the final goals of liberation and omniscience are accomplished with ease through relying on this mind. But if one does not first have an uncontrived wish to gain the temporary and ultimate benefits, then although one may say, "Since those benefits arise from generating bodhicitta, I must make effort to generate that mind," those will be mere words. This is very clear if we examine our own mindstreams.

So to first develop the wish to attain those two benefits, higher states and definite goodness, one must develop the attitudes common to persons of lesser and medium capacity. Once one has developed the wish to gain those two benefits, then to cultivate that beneficial mind one needs to develop its root, love and compassion. When you are thinking about how you yourself are wandering in cyclic existence, deprived of happiness and oppressed by suffering, if the hairs on your body do not rise up and stand on end, then there is no way the inability to bear how other sentient beings are deprived of happiness and oppressed by suffering can come about. *Entering the Bodhisattva Way* (1.24) says:

> If those beings have never before
> felt such an attitude for their own sake,
> not even dreamt of it in their dreams,
> how could it arise for the sake of others?

Therefore, in the training of persons of lesser capacity, you contemplate how the harm of suffering of the lower rebirths befalls you, and in the training of persons of medium capacity, you contemplate how even in higher rebirths there is suffering and no peace or happiness. Then, drawing on your own experience, you contemplate how this applies to sentient beings who have become dear to you. Meditating in this way becomes the cause for love and compassion to arise, from which bodhicitta is born. Therefore training in the contemplations shared with persons of lesser and medium capacity is the means of generating uncontrived bodhicitta.

Likewise, making effort in many means of purification and accumulation—such as contemplating going for refuge, actions and their effects, and so forth, in the context of the two lower levels of training—also constitutes a method for training the mindstream in preliminary practices for bodhicitta. [44] Since they are part of the seven-limb practice along with going for refuge, these contemplations common to persons of lesser and medium capacity should also be understood as methods for generating that mind.

Here the guru indicates how the Dharma teachings of persons of lesser and medium capacity become stages that lead to the arising of bodhicitta, and how the disciple also gains certainty in this regard. Through recalling those points with each practice, thoroughly cherish this training. If you fail to do this, the path of persons of great capacity and the individual paths become disconnected. Since you do not gain certainty with regard to bodhicitta until you reach the actual path of persons of great capacity, this would be an obstacle to the arising of that mind or a deterioration of that great purpose in the meantime. Therefore you should persevere in this.

Training in this way, try to bring about the arising of uncontrived bodhicitta in your mindstream as much as possible. Then, to make that mind stable, go for refuge in the way that is unique to the Mahāyāna and perform the ritual of aspiring bodhicitta. Having taken hold of aspiring bodhicitta by means of the ritual, practice its trainings. Repeatedly develop the wish to train in the bodhisattva conduct—the six perfections, the four ways of gathering disciples, and so forth. Once the desire to train in it has come forth from the depths of your heart, take the pure vow of engaging bodhicitta.

Even at the risk of your life, do not become tainted by a root downfall. Also, try your best not to become sullied by small and medium contaminations or misdeeds either. However, if you still become tainted by one of these, purify it well by means of the countermeasures for infractions as instructed. Then train in the six perfections in general and especially in meditative stabilization, the nature of śamatha, so as to make the mind serviceable for focusing on whatever virtuous object you wish. The statement in *Lamp for the Path to Enlightenment* that you train in śamatha in order to develop clairvoyance is only an example. Atiśa himself stated on other occasions that it also serves to develop special insight. Therefore you should develop śamatha for that purpose too. Then, to cut the fetters of apprehending the two selves, ascertain the meaning of emptiness by means of the view, nurture it by way of flawless meditation, and accomplish special insight, the essence of wisdom.

Accordingly, except for the accomplishment of śamatha and special insight, everything, up to and including training in the vow of engaging bodhicitta, constitutes the training in ethics. *Commentary on the Difficult Points of Lamp for the Path* (*Bodhimārgapradīpapañjikā*) says that śamatha is the training in concentration and special insight is the training in wisdom. [45]

Furthermore, everything up to and including śamatha constitutes the method aspect, the accumulation of merit, the path based on conventional truths, and the stages of the vast path, whereas the generation of the three special types of wisdom constitutes the wisdom aspect, the accumulation of wisdom, that which is based on ultimate truths, and the stages of the profound path. Therefore you need to develop great certainty regarding their order and enumeration, as well as the fact that enlightenment cannot be attained by means of method and wisdom separately.

Having thus trained your mindstream by means of the common paths, you must definitely enter the Mantrayāna, for once you have entered it, you will quickly complete the two accumulations.

If you cannot manage more than the path of the perfections, or owing to having weak potential you do not want to, you should just work on developing these very stages of the path further.

When engaging in the Mantrayāna, since proper reliance on a spiritual teacher is given great emphasis in all the vehicles generally, and particularly in secret mantra, you should make it even more preeminent than before. Then, having ripened your mindstream by means of an empowerment that comes from a pure class of tantra, guard the commitments and vows you obtained at that time even at the cost of your life. Especially if a root downfall occurs, even if you take them again, this will damage your mindstream, and it will become difficult to develop excellent qualities. Therefore make every effort not to become tainted by one. Also do your best to avoid becoming tainted even by a secondary infraction, though if you do, do not be indifferent about it but purify it through confession and restraint. Be guided as appropriate in the yoga with signs in accordance with the lower classes of tantra or in the yoga of the generation stage in accordance with the highest class of tantra. Then based on that, train as appropriate in the yoga without signs in accordance with the lower classes of tantra or in the yoga of the completion stage according to the highest class of tantra.

Such is the structure of the presentation of the path set forth in *Lamp for the Path to Enlightenment*, and the lamrim guides students in the same way.

THE PURPOSE

If the Dharma teachings of persons of lesser and medium capacity are the preliminary practices of persons of great capacity, it should indeed be acceptable to consider them the stages of the path of persons of great capacity. So why use the phrase "the stages of the path *in common with* persons of lesser and medium capacity"?

There are two major purposes for making this division into three levels of beings and guiding them accordingly. First, it undermines the conceit of someone who, without even having given rise to the mental attitudes common to persons of lesser and medium capacity, claims to be a person of great capacity. [46] Second, there is the following great benefit in their threefold categorization as the highest, intermediate, and lowest mental attitudes.

Since the two more advanced beings also need to strive for higher states and for liberation, there is no problem with teaching great or intermediate disciples how to train in those two levels of contemplation because this will give rise to excellent qualities. However, if a lesser being begins training with the more advanced levels, the more advanced attitudes will not arise, and since they have neglected the lower levels, nothing at all will arise. Moreover, some fortunate persons with higher capacity who have been taught the common path and already trained in it, whether in this life or in a previous one, will quickly develop excellent qualities. Having developed the lower ones, they can easily be guided through the higher levels. Thus their path will not be prolonged.

The need to develop the mind gradually is exemplified using the analogy of a skilled jeweler gradually cleaning precious stones, as stated in the *Questions of King Dhāraṇīśvara Sūtra* (*Dhāraṇīśvararājaparipṛcchāsūtra*). The protector Nāgārjuna also taught about leading in stages through the paths of higher states and definite goodness [in *Precious Garland* (*Ratnāvalī*) 1.3]:

> First the qualities of higher states,
> then those of definite goodness come forth.
> Therefore, once you achieve higher states,
> definite goodness will come by stages.

Ārya Asaṅga also said:

> So that the side of virtue may be gradually accomplished in full, a bodhisattva initially gives easy teachings to sentient beings who have immature wisdom and makes them follow simple advice and instructions. Once he knows that they have developed intermediate wisdom, he gives them intermediate teachings and makes them follow intermediate advice and instructions. When he knows that they have developed extensive wisdom, he teaches them the profound Dharma and makes them follow more subtle advice and instructions. His beneficial activities flow down on those sentient beings progressively.

Āryadeva, in his *Lamp That Combines the Practices* (*Caryāmelāpaka-pradīpa*), establishes that having trained in the contemplations of the

Pāramitāyāna, one then needs to gradually engage in the Mantrayāna. [47] Summarizing the meaning of this he says:

> When sentient beings who are beginners
> engage in the ultimate purpose,
> the method, so the Buddha said,
> resembles the steps of a flight of stairs.

THE ACTUAL WAY OF TAKING ITS ESSENCE

This has three points: training the mind in the stages of the path shared in common with persons of lesser capacity, training the mind in the stages of the path shared in common with persons of medium capacity, and training the mind in the stages of the path unique to persons of great capacity.

The Stages Shared with Persons of Lesser Capacity

8 | Death and Future Lives

TRAINING THE MIND IN THE STAGES OF THE PATH SHARED IN COMMON WITH PERSONS OF LESSER CAPACITY

THIS HAS THREE POINTS: the actual training in the attitude of persons of lesser capacity, the measure of that attitude having arisen, and clearing up misconceptions about that.

THE ACTUAL TRAINING IN THE ATTITUDE OF PERSONS OF LESSER CAPACITY

This has two points: generating an attitude of concern for future lives, and relying on the methods for gaining happiness in future lives.

GENERATING AN ATTITUDE OF CONCERN FOR FUTURE LIVES

This has two points: the contemplation recollecting death and that one will not remain in this life for long, and the contemplation of what will happen in future lives in terms of the happiness and suffering of the two types of persons.

THE CONTEMPLATION RECOLLECTING DEATH AND THAT ONE WILL NOT REMAIN IN THIS LIFE FOR LONG

This has four points: the fault of not cultivating mindfulness of death, the benefits of cultivating mindfulness of death, what kind of mindfulness of death should be generated, and how to cultivate mindfulness of death.

THE FAULTS OF NOT CULTIVATING MINDFULNESS OF DEATH

Although we all have the thought that at the end of our life will come our death, each day we think, "I will not die today" and "Today too I will not die." In this way, right up to when we are about to die, our mind holds on to the idea that we are not going to die.

If you do not take to heart an antidote to this, if your mind is obscured by such an idea and you think that you will remain in this life, then you will keep thinking about ways of achieving happiness and eliminating suffering in this life only, thinking, "I need such and such . . ." A mind analyzing meaningful goals such as future lives, liberation, and omniscience will not arise. Thus no opportunity will be created for engaging in Dharma.

Even if you engage in hearing, thinking, and meditating for a hundred years, whatever virtue you do will have little power because it is done for the sake of this life alone. Since you will engage in them in conjunction with faulty behavior, bad actions, and downfalls, it will be rare for them not to be mixed with the causes of lower rebirths.

Even suppose you were to practice with your focus on the next life, you will not be able to stop the laziness of procrastination that thinks, "I will do it later." A great joyous effort at practicing properly will not come about, as you while away your time with drowsiness, pointless chatter, and distractions of food, drink, and the like.

Not only that, through putting great effort into the excellences of this life, [48] the mental afflictions and faulty behavior induced by them increase, and you turn your back on the nectar of Dharma. Since that leads to the lower rebirths, what could be more inappropriate than that? *Four Hundred Stanzas* (1.1) states:

> When someone sleeps as though at ease,
> as though the ruler of three worlds,
> the Lord of Death, did not exist,
> what else could be more awful than that?

And *Entering the Bodhisattva Way* (2.34) says:

Everything must be left behind;
not understanding that this is so,
I did bad actions of all kinds
for the sake of friends and foes.

THE BENEFITS OF CULTIVATING MINDFULNESS OF DEATH

If a genuine mind recollecting death arises, as with most people when they
are convinced they will die in the next few days, then even in those with
only a little understanding of Dharma, upon seeing that they will be unac-
companied by friends and relatives, their craving for them will naturally
be reversed, and they will want to extract the essence of their life by way of
giving and so on; and upon seeing that all efforts made for the sake of such
worldly concerns as material gain, honor, and so on are futile, they will
desist from faulty behavior. In such a way, they will accumulate the good
karmas of going for refuge, ethics, and so forth, by means of which they will
ascend to a holy state and lead sentient beings there too. What is there more
meaningful than this? That is why it is also praised with many analogies.
The *Great Final Nirvāṇa Sūtra* (*Mahāparinirvāṇasūtra*) says:

> Among all plowings of the fields, the plowing in autumn is the best.
> Among all footprints, the elephant's footprints are the best.
> Among all perceptions, those of impermanence and death are the
>   best:
> they eliminate all the desire, ignorance, and pride of the three
>   realms.

Similarly it is praised as, among other things, a hammer that destroys all
mental afflictions and all faulty behaviors at once and as a gateway to the
spontaneous accomplishment of all that is virtuous and excellent.

In brief, the time for accomplishing the goals of beings is only at this
time when we have gained a special human body. We mostly remain in
lower rebirths, and even if we make it to fortunate rebirths just once, they
are predominantly places lacking freedom, [49] so that we do not find an
opportunity to accomplish the Dharma. If we gain a body suited to accomplishing the Dharma and still do not accomplish it properly, it is because

of this thought of "I am not going to die yet." Therefore this mind that holds to the position of not dying is the door to all manner of degeneration, whereas mindfulness of death is the door to all excellence.

Therefore do not think, "This is a practice for those who do not have other profound Dharma to meditate on" or "Although it is something to meditate on, it should be meditated on a bit in the beginning, but is not suitable to be practiced continuously." Meditate on it until you gain certainty from the depths of your heart that it is necessary in the beginning, in the middle, and at the end.

What kind of mindfulness of death should be generated

The fear born from anxiety about separating from relatives and the like is the fear of death of those who are not trained in the path. So this is not what is to be generated here. What kind of fear is to be generated? Every physical form taken up through the power of karma and mental afflictions does not pass beyond death. This is why—even though you may fear it— you cannot prevent death for the time being. Indeed, you should be afraid of death if you have not stopped the causes of lower rebirths or accomplished the causes for higher states and definite goodness. If you consider your fear about this, there is something you can accomplish so as not to be afraid at the time of dying. But if you have not accomplished that goal, then you will be tormented by remorse at the time of death out of fear of not being liberated from the cycle of existence in general and of falling to a lower rebirth in particular.

How to cultivate mindfulness of death

You should meditate on this by way of the three root contemplations, the nine reasons, and the three decisions. Here, the three root contemplations are the contemplation that it is certain that we will die, the contemplation that it is uncertain when we will die, and the contemplation that at the time of death nothing except the Dharma will be of benefit.

THE CONTEMPLATION THAT IT IS CERTAIN THAT WE WILL DIE

This has three points: the contemplation that the Lord of Death will certainly come and there is no way to prevent this, the contemplation that our lifespan cannot be increased but diminishes incessantly, and the contemplation that we die without having had much time to practice Dharma while alive.

THE CONTEMPLATION THAT THE LORD OF DEATH WILL CERTAINLY COME AND THERE IS NO WAY TO PREVENT THIS

The *Collection of Indicative Verses* says that whatever body you have taken up, and wherever you reside, you will be overcome by death at any time. As stated in the *Advice to the King Sūtra* (*Rājāvavādakasūtra*), it will come to pass in that way and cannot be averted by fleeing swiftly away or by force, wealth, material substances, mantras, or medicine. Geshe Kamapa instructed, "You should fear death now, [50] but at the moment of death you must not be apprehensive. We, however, do it the other way round: we are not afraid now, but at the moment of death we dig our fingernails into our chests."

THE CONTEMPLATION THAT OUR LIFESPAN CANNOT BE INCREASED BUT DIMINISHES INCESSANTLY

As the *Descent into the Womb Sūtra* (*Garbhāvakrāntisūtra*) says, attaining a lifespan of a hundred years seems to be the limit of what is possible. However, even if you reach that, the years until then are consumed with the passing of month after month, day after day, day and night. As they too are consumed with the passing of morning and so on, it seems that much of your lifespan has already finished, and the remainder also diminishes incessantly without anything being added. *Entering the Bodhisattva Way* (2.40) says:

> Day and night, without respite,
> this life decreases constantly.

If nothing comes to add to it,
then how could one like me not die?

In addition, you should contemplate this using many analogies, such as a weaver gradually weaving a cloth, animals for slaughter approaching the slaughterhouse step by step, cattle being led without freedom to their destination by a herder, and so forth. This is also taught with numerous analogies in the *Sūtra of Extensive Play* (*Lalitavistarasūtra*):

> The three existences are impermanent, like autumn clouds;
> the birth and death of beings are like a dance performance;
> the course of a being's life is like a flash of lightning;
> it goes fast, like a steep mountain waterfall.

For someone with certainty arising from inner contemplation, there are no external things that do not demonstrate impermanence. Since this is so, as has been taught, certainty arises if we consider it repeatedly from many angles. There is no benefit in thinking we have contemplated something several times but still no certainty has arisen. As Geshe Kamapa said, "You say 'Nothing has come about through my contemplation.' But when did you contemplate? During the day you indulge in distractions; at night you sleep. Don't lie!"

It is not just that death destroys us at the end of our life and we have to go to the next world. Up until then, also, there is not even a moment when we are not proceeding toward it as our life diminishes. Therefore, ever since we entered the womb, we have been going straight toward a future life without remaining still even for a mere instant. This being so, our intervening life also wastes away as we are led toward death by its harbingers, disease and aging. So do not rejoice in the view that while alive [51] you abide without moving toward a future life. Had you just fallen from a high cliff and were tumbling through the sky, it would not be time to rejoice simply because you had yet to crash to the ground. *Commentary on Four Hundred Stanzas* (*Catuḥśatakaṭīkā*) says:

> Hero of humanity, beginning from that first night
> of entering a womb in this world—
> one starts to proceed day by day,
> without pausing a step, toward the Lord of Death.

THE CONTEMPLATION THAT WE DIE WITHOUT HAVING HAD MUCH TIME TO PRACTICE DHARMA WHILE ALIVE

Even if we do live for so long, it is inappropriate to think we have time. As stated in the *Descent into the Womb Sūtra*, in the beginning, during the first ten years of childhood, it does not occur to us to practice the Dharma, and at the end, during the last twenty years of old age, we do not have the energy to practice the Dharma. During the time in between, sleep snatches away one half, while illness and the like also consume a lot of time. So there are only a few occasions remaining to practice the Dharma.

Since it is like this, at the time of death all the excellences of this life will only be an object of recollection—like the recollection of a happy experience in a dream after we wake up. Contemplate: "Why delight in the beguiling pleasures of this life if the enemy—death—will certainly come?" With this thought in mind, resolve that you definitely need to practice the Dharma, and reiterate this innermost resolution many times. From *Garland of Birth Stories*:

> Alas, afflicted worldly beings,
> your stay is not stable, there is no joy.
> Even this water lily's splendor
> will soon be but a memory.

THE CONTEMPLATION THAT IT IS UNCERTAIN WHEN WE WILL DIE

It is certain that death will come sometime between now and a hundred years from now, and within that period it is not certain on which day it will be. Therefore on any day like today, you cannot be certain that you will or will not die. Even so, your mind should be biased toward the idea of death, and you should generate the awareness that thinks, "I will die today." For if the mind is biased toward the idea of *not* dying, giving rise to the thought "I will not die today," then you will constantly prepare for continuing in this life and neglect preparing for future lives. Owing to this, if you are seized by the Lord of Death in the meantime, you will have to die in anguish. But if you prepare to die every day, you will accomplish much that is meaningful for the future—so that even if you do not die, it is good to have done those things, and if you do die, it was all the more necessary. [52]

This topic has three points: the contemplation that the lifespan in this world is uncertain, so the time of death is uncertain; the contemplation that there are many conditions that lead to death and few conditions that promote life; and the contemplation that the body is extremely vulnerable and the time of death therefore uncertain.

THE CONTEMPLATION THAT THE LIFESPAN IN THIS WORLD IS UNCERTAIN, SO THE TIME OF DEATH IS UNCERTAIN

In general the lifespan of the inhabitants of the northern continent (Uttara-kuru) is certain, and that of most inhabitants of the other continents is mainly certain, though whether the full extent of each individual's lifespan is reached is not so certain. But the lifespan of the inhabitants of this world (Jambudvīpa) is extremely uncertain. At the beginning of an eon it reaches an immeasurable number of years, and at the end it reaches a maximum of ten years. However, nowadays it does not seem certain whether death will occur in old age, in youth, or somewhere in between. The *Treasury of Abhidharma* (3.78) says:

> Here it's uncertain; at the end,
> ten years; at the beginning, beyond measure.

You should take to heart the fact that your gurus, friends, and so forth have died from sudden internal or external causes of death before reaching the limit of their lifespans. Think over and over again, "I too am subject to this."

THE CONTEMPLATION THAT THE CAUSES OF DEATH ARE MANY AND THE CAUSES OF LIFE ARE FEW

There are many harmful influences—animate as well as inanimate—that can affect this life. Think deeply about how it is threatened by human beings and nonhuman evil spirits, how certain kinds of animals endanger one's body and life by harming it in many ways, and how both internal illnesses and external elements can cause harm. Furthermore, your body must be formed from the four elements, and since these also harm each other by becoming out of balance if they expand or diminish, they will cause illnesses and deprive you of your life. They exist together with you, so even though your body and life appear to be stable, they cannot be relied on. The *Great Final Nirvāṇa Sūtra* says:

> The discernment of death is that this life, constantly surrounded
> by hostile enemies, deteriorates each moment and that there is
> nothing that increases it.

Precious Garland (4.17) states: [53]

> We live amid the conditions that cause death,
> like a butter lamp in a tumultuous gale.

Apart from that, life itself is involved in the reality of death so that many conditions for life are unreliable. From *Precious Garland* (3.79):

> There are many conditions for death,
> while those for living are only few,
> and even they may well be deadly.
> Therefore always practice the Dharma.

THE CONTEMPLATION THAT THE BODY IS EXTREMELY VULNERABLE, SO THE TIME OF DEATH IS UNCERTAIN

The body is as vulnerable as a water bubble, therefore any little thing, such as a thorn piercing it, may be responsible for destroying life without the need for major harm. In this way, it very easily succumbs to all the causes of death. *Letter to a Friend* (v. 57) says:

> If not even ashes are left behind
> when such bodies as the ground, Mount Meru, and the oceans
> are incinerated by the seven blazing suns,[52]
> then what need to mention extremely vulnerable humans?

Contemplating in this way, reiterate many times your heartfelt resolve to practice the Dharma from this very moment, for it is uncertain when your body and life will be overcome by death, and you cannot assume that you will still have time. As Śrī Jaganmitra Ānanda said in *Letter to King Candra* (*Candrarājalekha*):

> Lord of the Earth! As long as this borrowed body
> stays happy without sickness and without decline,
> take up the essence of this very life.
> Become undaunted by sickness, death, and decline.
> One day when faced with sickness, old age, and decline,
> you may remember, but what can you do then?

Among the three root contemplations, the contemplation about the uncertainty of the time of death is the most important, so you should put effort into it.

THE CONTEMPLATION THAT AT THE TIME OF DEATH NOTHING EXCEPT THE DHARMA WILL BE OF BENEFIT

When you see that you must go to another life, although you may be surrounded by very loving and distressed friends or relatives at that time, you cannot take even one of them with you. Whatever heaps of marvelous riches you have gained, you cannot take along even a tiny particle of them. Indeed, if you have to leave behind even the flesh and bones you were born with, what need to talk of anything else? Now you should contemplate, "There will certainly come a time when all the wonderful things of this life leave me, just as I leave them, and I will proceed to another life. This may even happen today." Repeatedly make the decision to practice the Dharma and avoid falling under the influence of your body, your friends, your possessions, and so forth. Although this decision arises only with great difficulty, try hard to develop it because it is the foundation of the path. In the words of Potowa: [54]

> For me, "exclusion and appearance" consists in this very meditation on impermanence. Dispelling all the appearances of this life—close relationships, possessions, and the like—and aware that I will go to another life alone without anything, I think, "I

must do nothing that is not Dharma," and nonattachment to this life first arises. Until this attitude arises in one's mind, the paths to all the Dharma remain blocked.

And Dölpa said:

> If, incidentally, you accumulate the collections and purify the obstructions, make requests to the deities and your guru, and contemplate insistently with perseverance, then even that which you think will not come about for a hundred years will come about effortlessly, for conditioned things do not remain static.

When someone asked Kamapa about moving on to another topic, he said, "Repeat the previous one!" When asked about the remaining ones, he said, "There is nothing beyond it."

Thus, if you understand the way to practice reliance on a spiritual teacher, the freedoms and endowments, and impermanence in the context of the scriptures and their commentaries, and if you then nurture that understanding, you will easily find the intention of the Victor. In this way you will also understand them in other contexts.

THE CONTEMPLATION OF WHAT WILL HAPPEN IN FUTURE LIVES IN TERMS OF THE HAPPINESS AND SUFFERING OF THE TWO TYPES OF PERSONS

Since it is certain that you will die soon, you have no time to tarry in this life. And after death you will not become nonexistent; you must take rebirth. Since apart from the two there is no other place of birth, you will be born in either the fortunate rebirths or the lower rebirths. In addition, since you are not under your own control but under the control of something else—your karma—you will be reborn according to the virtuous and nonvirtuous karma that impels you.

Contemplate the suffering of the lower rebirths and ask yourself, "What will become of me if I am reborn in the lower rebirths?" Nāgārjuna said [in the *Hundred Verses on Wisdom (Prajñāśataka)*]:

Every day recollect the hells, which are
fiercely hot and bitterly cold.
Remember too the hungry ghosts,
emaciated by hunger and thirst.

Observe the animals and recollect
their numerous sufferings of confusion.
Relinquish their causes,
engage in causes of happiness.

Once you have gained what is hard to gain,
a human body in this world,
endeavor to cut the cause of lower rebirths!

Meditation on the sufferings of cyclic existence in general, and on the sufferings of the lower rebirths in particular, is a crucial point. [55] For if you contemplate how you yourself fall into the ocean of suffering, despair will reverse your pride and arrogance. Seeing that suffering is the result of nonvirtue, you will be very careful to avoid bad actions and downfalls. Since you do not want suffering but want happiness, once you realize that happiness is the result of virtue, you will also enjoy accomplishing virtue. In proportion to your own experience, compassion for others will arise, and out of aversion for cyclic existence, you will strive for liberation. For fear of suffering, you will fervently go for refuge and so forth.

These excellent qualities of suffering that comprise many important points of the practice are stated in *Entering the Bodhisattva Way* in terms of suffering already arisen in one's own mindstream, though they are equally applicable to suffering one is yet to experience.

Contemplating the sufferings of the lower rebirths has three points: contemplating the sufferings of hell beings, of animals, and of hungry ghosts.

CONTEMPLATING THE SUFFERINGS OF HELL BEINGS

This has four points: the great hells of sentient beings, the neighboring hells, the cold hells, and the occasional hells.

THE GREAT HELLS OF SENTIENT BEINGS

Situated thirty-two thousand yojanas[53] below us is the hell of Continual Revival, and below that are seven more hells each separated by four thousand yojanas. In the first of those eight, Continual Revival, the sentient beings gather together and stab each other with various weapons that manifest through the power of their karma. Whenever they faint and collapse on the ground, a voice rings out from the sky, commanding, "You shall revive!" Upon that, they stand up again and start stabbing as before, experiencing immeasurable suffering as a result.

In Black Line, the hell guardians draw black lines in the shape of numerous squares and the like on the bodies of the sentient beings born there. Then the latter experience the pain of being cut into pieces with weapons along those lines.

In Crushing Hell, the guardians round up the sentient beings and pack them in between two goat-faced or similar iron mountains, whereupon they are immediately crushed by those two so that rivers of blood spurt out from all their orifices.

In Howling Hell, the sentient beings, in search of a home, enter an iron house. As soon as they enter, fires blaze up all around them and burn them.

Great Howling Hell [56] is like the previous one except the iron house has another one inside.

In Hot Hell, the hell guardians put the sentient beings into very hot and blazing iron cauldrons several yojanas wide and fry them like fish. They are impaled through their buttocks on blazing iron stakes that emerge at the crown of the heads. Fire blazes out of their mouths, their eye sockets, nostrils, and ears as well as all their pores. They are laid out, on their backs or face down, on the blazing iron foundation and pounded and tormented with blazing iron hammers.

In Very Hot Hell, an iron trident is stuck into the buttocks so that the right and left prongs emerge from the two shoulders and the middle one from the crown of the head. Owing to that, tongues of fire blaze from orifices such as the mouth. Their bodies are wrapped in blazing hot iron sheets and placed headlong into an iron cauldron full of boiling liquid, whereupon they are tossed about, up and down, as they boil. Then, once their skin, flesh, and blood have been cooked away and nothing but the skeleton is left, they are pulled out again and spread out on the iron foundation.

After that, when the skin, flesh, and blood have developed again, they are thrown back in. Apart from that it is like Hot Hell.

In Avīci ("without respite"), the foundation is completely ablaze for hundreds of yojanas from the eastern direction. As it spreads, the force of the fire increases, gradually destroying the skin, flesh, sinews, and bones of the sentient beings to the marrow. Like the wick of a butter lamp, their whole bodies are pervaded by blazing tongues of fire. It is similar from the other three directions. As the fire coming from the four directions mingles, these beings experience incessant sufferings, and only by their pathetic howling can they be recognized as sentient beings. Contained in iron baskets, they are made to jump about on blazing metal. They are made to fall down on the iron foundation and to climb up huge iron mountains. Their tongues are pulled out from their mouths and stretched with a hundred pegs so as to remove folds and creases, as though preparing cow hides. Then again they are placed on the iron foundation on their backs, their mouths are opened with iron tongs, and blazing lumps of iron are inserted into their mouths. Boiling copper is poured into their mouths [57] and burns their mouths, throats, and entrails before issuing from their lower bodies. Apart from that it is like Very Hot Hell.

How long those sufferings are experienced is as stated in *Letter to a Friend* (v. 87):

> Although you endure for billions of years
> such utterly unbearable sufferings,
> you will not relinquish your life
> until that nonvirtue has been exhausted.

Moreover, the *Treasury of Abhidharma* and the *Levels of Yogic Practice* (*Yogacaryābhūmi*) state that fifty human years are one day in the god realm of the Four Great Kings, thirty of those one month, and twelve of those one year. Five hundred such years is the lifespan of the beings of the Four Great Kings. All of that is one single day in Continual Revival, thirty of those a month, twelve of those a year, and five hundred of those a lifespan. Likewise one hundred, two hundred, four hundred, eight hundred and sixteen hundred human years respectively form a day in the other five desire god realms ranging from the Thirty-Three up to Controlling Others' Emanations, and their lifespans can be one thousand, two thousand, four thousand, eight thousand, and sixteen thousand god years. These respectively form a day in Black Line through Hot Hell, and they can reach from one thousand through sixteen thousand of their own years. In Very Hot Hell they can reach half an intermediate eon, and in Avīci one intermediate eon.

THE NEIGHBORING HELLS

Each of the eight great hells has four walls and four gates. They are surrounded by an iron fence, which also has four gates. Outside each of these gates there are the four neighboring hells of sentient beings: the Pit of Burning Embers, the Swamp of Putrid Corpses or the Swamp of Excrement Reeking of Corpses, the Road of Razors and the like, and the River without a Ford.

The first contains hot embers up to the knees. When sentient beings go there looking for a home, as they set their feet down, their skin, flesh, and blood are burned away, and as they lift their legs up, their feet regenerate.

Nearby there is the second one, the Swamp of Excrement Reeking of Corpses. As they cross it in search of a home, sentient beings fall into it and sink up to their heads. In this swamp [58] there are worms called *sharp-beaks* that pierce the skin, flesh, sinews, and bones and dig through them all the way to the marrow.

Near the swamp there is the third one, a path fitted with razor-like teeth. When sentient beings walk along it in search of a home, as they put their feet down, their skin, flesh, and blood are lacerated, and as they lift their legs up, their feet grow back again.

Near that is the Forest of Sword Leaves. As sentient beings wander around in search of a home, making use of its shade and sitting down, swords emerge from the trees and chop up their limbs and other body parts. When they faint, reddish-brown dogs come up, grab them from behind, and eat them.

Near that there is the Forest of Iron-Spiked Trees. Sentient beings wander around there in search of a home and set about climbing the trees. As they climb up, the tips of the thorns point downward, and as they climb down, the tips point upward, chopping up the limbs and other body parts. Birds with iron beaks alight on their shoulders or heads, peck out their eyeballs, and eat them. These places are similar in that the harm is inflicted by sharp weapons, so they should be considered as one.

Near the Forest of Iron-Spiked Trees there is the fourth, River without a Ford, which is filled with seething boiling water. Sentient beings in search of a home fall into it and are cooked as they bob up and down—like peas thrown in a cauldron of water over a great fire. On each bank of the river guardians hold sticks, hooks, and nets and do not let anyone escape. Having pulled them out with the hooks or nets, the guardians place them face upward on the blazing great foundation and ask them what they want. When they say, "I don't know and cannot see anything, but I am hungry and thirsty," the guardians pour molten copper and put fiercely blazing lumps of iron into their mouths.

Levels of Yogic Practice explains that the lifespan in the neighboring and occasional hells is uncertain. However, those sufferings will continue to be experienced as long as the karmic potential for experiencing them has not been exhausted. [59]

THE COLD HELLS

The cold hells are situated outside the eight great hells of sentient beings, each at a distance of ten thousand yojanas. Thirty-two thousand yojanas below here is Blisters, followed by the other seven cold hells each separated by two thousand yojanas from the one above. In Blisters you are hit by strong icy winds and shrink from the cold, while blisters appear all over your body. In Bursting Blisters you shrivel as the blisters burst open. Chattering Teeth, Crying, and Moaning are cold hells named after the sounds uttered in them. In Splitting Apart Like an Utpala Flower, as you are hit by strong icy wind, you turn blue in color and split apart into five or six pieces. In Splitting Apart Like a Lotus you pass beyond blue and turn red, splitting apart into ten or more pieces. In Great Splitting Apart Like a Lotus your skin turns deep red and you split apart into a hundred or even more pieces. All this is explained in *Levels of Yogic Practice*.

As for the lifespan, it is stated that if you were to fill a storage container up to the brim with fifty bushels of sesame seeds from Magadha and take out one sesame seed every hundred years, the lifespan in the hell of Blisters would last far longer than it takes for the sesame seeds to be completely exhausted, and the lifespan in each hell below is twenty times that of the previous one.

THE OCCASIONAL HELLS

The occasional hells adjoin the hot and cold hells. *Levels of Yogic Practice* says that they also exist in the lands of humans, and *Chapters on the Vinaya* (*Vinayavastu*) says that they exist near the shores of great lakes, as depicted in the *Story of Saṅgharakṣita* (*Saṅgharakṣitāvadāna*).[54]

As explained below, it is very easy to create the causes of taking birth there—you accumulate many of them every day. And since those that you accumulated before are also immeasurable, it is unwise to just sit around comfortably. You should think about them and be afraid, for nothing other than your precarious breathing separates you from them. *Entering the Bodhisattva Way* (8.12) says:

> Having created the karma for hell,
> how can you sit there comfortably?

Letter to a Friend (vv. 83–84) also says:

> Evildoers are separated from hell only
> by the time it takes for their breathing to stop.
> Those who hear about the boundless torments of hell
> and are not terrified in a thousand ways are [hard] like vajras.
>
> If seeing, hearing, remembering, and reading
> descriptions of hell and their depictions [60]
> gives rise to fear, then there is no question about
> the experience of the unbearable fully ripened effects.

The intense suffering is also described in *Letter to a Friend* (vv. 85–86):

> Just as the bliss of the extinction of craving
> is supreme among all kinds of bliss,
> likewise among all kinds of sufferings
> those of Avīci are the most unbearable.
>
> The suffering of being brutally stabbed
> in one day by three hundred spears

does not approximate and cannot compare
to even the smallest suffering of hell.

You need to understand that the cause giving rise to such suffering is your
own faulty behavior alone. Strive with all your might not to be tainted by
even the slightest faulty action. The same text says (v. 88):

The seeds of these nonvirtuous effects
are your faulty behavior of body, speech, and mind.
With all your skill make every effort
not to commit even the slightest negative deed.

CONTEMPLATING THE SUFFERINGS OF ANIMALS

The weaker animals are killed by more powerful ones. Having become
the chattel of gods and humans, they are not under their own control
but under the control of others and lack freedom, which is why they are
killed, beaten, and harmed. *Levels of Yogic Practice* explains that since
they occupy the same territory as humans and gods, they have no other
place to stay. The *Treasury of Abhidharma Autocommentary* explains that
their primary abode is the vast ocean and that other species evolved from
there. They are born in darkness in the water, and there they age and
die. Worn out by heavy burdens, they are put to the plow, shorn, driven,
and killed miserably by many different methods of slaughter. They are
tormented by hunger and thirst, sun and wind. They are persecuted by
hunters and the like in many ways and are constantly terrified. So you
should feel saddened and repulsed when thinking of the many ways in
which they suffer.

As for their lifespan, the *Treasury of Abhidharma* (3.83) states that "the
longest animal lifespan is one eon" and explains that the long-lived ones
attain about an eon while the short-lived ones are unspecified. [61]

CONTEMPLATING THE SUFFERINGS OF HUNGRY GHOSTS

Those dominated by miserliness will be born as hungry ghosts. They are
extremely hungry and thirsty. Their skin, flesh, and blood are so parched

that they look like burnt logs. Their faces are covered with hair, their mouths are exceedingly dry, and they keep licking their lips with their tongues.

They may be categorized as three kinds: those with external obstructions to food and drink, those with internal obstructions to food and drink, and those with obstructions within food and drink itself.

THOSE WITH EXTERNAL OBSTRUCTIONS TO FOOD AND DRINK

As for the first kind, when they approach springs, lakes, and ponds, they are stopped externally by sentient beings holding swords, spears, and lances. They also see the water as pus and blood and lose their desire to drink it.

THOSE WITH INTERNAL OBSTRUCTIONS TO FOOD AND DRINK

The second kind have mouths like the mere eye of a needle. Their mouths blaze with fire, and they have goiters and swollen bellies. Even if they end up finding food and drink without others having created obstructions, they themselves are not able to eat and drink.

THOSE WITH OBSTRUCTIONS WITHIN FOOD AND DRINK ITSELF

Among the third kind, the *fire-garlanded ones* get burned because everything they eat and drink catches fire. The *filth-eaters* eat excrement and drink urine. They eat and drink only what is unclean, smelly, harmful, and disgusting. Some cut their own flesh and eat that. They cannot consume food or drink that is clean and wholesome.

The *Treasury of Abhidharma Autocommentary* states that their main abode is situated five hundred yojanas below the city of Rājagṛha in this world (Jambudvīpa), while other hungry ghosts have spread out from there. As for their lifespan, *Levels of Yogic Practice* and the *Treasury of Abhidharma* explain that one human month is a day for them and that they survive for five hundred of their years. *Letter to a Friend* (v. 96) says:

Enduring suffering uninterruptedly,
fettered by the noose of negative deeds,
some embodied beings do not die
for five or even ten thousand years.

The commentary explains that the lifespan of some hungry ghosts is five thousand years and of others ten thousand years.

In all three lower rebirths the body size is indefinite. *Levels of Yogic Practice* says that the power of the nonvirtues gives rise to varying sizes.

Accordingly, when you think about the sufferings of the lower rebirths, you should reflect: "If it would be difficult for me to sit for one day with my hands stuck in embers, or simply to stay in a freezing cave during a winter storm without clothes, [62] or to be deprived of food and drink for a few days, or for my body to be bitten by flies and the like, then how could I bear the sufferings of the hot hells, the cold hells, the hungry ghosts, and the animals that devour one another alive?" You should meditate while evaluating such experiences until a change of heart occurs, giving rise to intense fear and terror. As you think about this now, with your good rebirth, you can purify whatever nonvirtue you have accumulated previously and lessen what you might engage in later on. Your intense aspirational prayers will direct the virtue you accumulated previously, thereby multiplying it, and open up many avenues for engaging in them anew. Every day there will be some new way to make your freedom meaningful. If you do not think about this now, then once you have fallen into the lower rebirths, you will not find a refuge that protects you from those fears even if you look for it. At that time you will lack the power of mind to adopt what should be done and discard what should not be done. This is explained in *Entering the Bodhisattva Way*.

9 | Refuge in the Three Jewels

RELYING ON THE MEANS TO GAIN HAPPINESS IN FUTURE LIVES

THIS HAS TWO POINTS: training in going for refuge, the holy gateway for entering the teachings; and generating the faith of conviction in actions and their effects, the root of all well-being.[55]

TRAINING IN GOING FOR REFUGE, THE HOLY GATEWAY FOR ENTERING THE TEACHINGS

This has four points: the causes of going for refuge; based on those, the objects to which you go to for refuge; the way in which you go for refuge; and the stages of training after having gone for refuge.

THE CAUSES OF GOING FOR REFUGE

Although, in general, there are many causes, here it is the fact, explained above, that we do not stay in this life but soon die and that after death we do not have control over where the force of our karma will send us to be reborn. Regarding karma, *Entering the Bodhisattva Way* (1.5–6) says:

> Just as lightning on a cloudy night
> illuminates the darkness for a moment,
> likewise, through the power of the buddhas,
> a rare wholesome thought appears in the world.
>
> Therefore virtue is perpetually weak,
> while evil is very strong and quite unbearable.

Thinking about how you will fall into the lower rebirths—because the power of wholesome karma is so weak while that of unwholesome karma is extremely strong—will give rise to the two convictions: fear of the lower rebirths and faith that the Three Jewels, so rare and precious,[56] can protect you from them. Consequently, if these two remain but words, going for refuge will be similar. But if they are strong and firm, [63] your going for refuge will come to tame your mind. Therefore put in effort into generating those two causes.

BASED ON THOSE, THE OBJECTS TO WHICH YOU GO FOR REFUGE

This has two points: identifying the objects of refuge and the reasons why they are worthy to be a refuge.

IDENTIFYING THE OBJECTS OF REFUGE

Praise in One Hundred and Fifty Verses (*Śatapañcaśatakastotra*) says:

> The one in whom all faults
> are perpetually completely absent,
> the one in whom, in every way,
> all excellent qualities abide—
> if you have good sense,
> you will go to such a one for refuge.
> It is right to praise and honor him
> and to abide in what he teaches.

Thus if someone has the intelligence to differentiate between a refuge and what is not a refuge, it is appropriate for him or her to go for refuge to the undeceiving protector, the Blessed Buddha. This also characterizes the Dharma Jewel and the Saṅgha Jewel. *Seventy Verses on Going for Refuge* (*Triśaraṇagamanasaptati*) says:

> The Buddha, Dharma, and Saṅgha
> are the refuge of those who want liberation.

THE REASONS WHY THEY ARE WORTHY TO BE A REFUGE

One who is worthy to be a refuge is free of all fear, skilled in the means of liberating others from fear, steeped in great compassion toward everyone without closeness or distance, and works for the welfare of all beings whether they help him or not. As only the Buddha has those qualifications, while Īśvara and the like do not, he is a refuge. For that reason, the Dharma taught by him as well as the Saṅgha of his disciples are also worthy objects of refuge.

That being so, once you have derived certainty with regard to these objects of refuge set forth in the *Compendium*, when you are able to rely on them with a single-pointed mind, it is impossible for you not to be protected. Therefore you should generate certainty from the depths of your heart. Of the two causes for being protected, there is no incompleteness in the external one, our Teacher having established it. However, since the internal cause, taking hold of that refuge trustingly, has not come about, we suffer.

THE WAY IN WHICH YOU GO FOR REFUGE

This has four points: going for refuge by way of understanding their excellent qualities, by way of understanding their distinctions, by way of commitment, and by way of not advocating other ones.

GOING FOR REFUGE BY WAY OF UNDERSTANDING THEIR EXCELLENT QUALITIES

Since this requires recollecting the excellent qualities of the objects of refuge, this has three points: [64] the excellent qualities of the Buddha, the excellent qualities of the Dharma, and the excellent qualities of the Saṅgha.

THE EXCELLENT QUALITIES OF THE BUDDHA

This has four points: the excellent qualities of the Buddha's body, speech, mind, and exalted activities.

THE EXCELLENT QUALITIES OF THE BUDDHA'S BODY

Recollecting the signs and marks of a buddha, *Praise in Analogies* (*Upama-stava*) says:

> Your body is adorned with the signs,
> so beautiful, nectar for the eyes,
> like a cloudless sky in autumn
> ornamented with clusters of stars.
>
> O Sage, endowed with the color of gold,
> so beautiful, dressed in monastic robes,
> like a golden mountaintop
> wrapped in clouds at dusk or dawn.
>
> Protector, the sphere of your face's splendor,
> although unadorned by jewelry,
> is beyond that of the full moon
> in a vast and cloudless sky.
>
> If the lotus of your mouth
> and a lotus in bloom in the sun
> are beheld by a bee, the bee
> will have its doubts about the lotus.
>
> Your face endowed with the color of gold
> is beautified further with your pure white teeth,
> like immaculate autumn moonbeams
> filtering between golden mountains.
>
> Venerable one, your right hand,
> embellished with the mark of the wheel,
> gives breath to the people terrified
> by the cycle of saṃsāric existence.
>
> O Sage, as you walk, your feet
> leave designs on the earth

like resplendent lotuses.
Could Padminī be lovelier?

You should recollect them in accordance with these verses.

THE EXCELLENT QUALITIES OF THE BUDDHA'S SPEECH

Contemplate the marvelous way in which, when many people ask different questions at the same time, the Buddha apprehends them in a single moment of intelligent awareness and answers them all with one utterance, which they understand in their respective languages. The *Satyaka Chapter* says:

> Thus if all beings, simultaneously,
> ask many questions in their specific languages,
> his mind comprehends them in a single moment
> and answers them all with one melodious statement.

> In this way, he who guides the world
> knowingly teaches with his melodious voice. [65]
> He completely turns the wheel of Dharma
> that puts an end to the suffering of gods and men.

Reflect along the lines of these verses.

THE EXCELLENT QUALITIES OF THE BUDDHA'S MIND

This has two points: the excellent qualities of his exalted knowing and the excellent qualities of his loving-kindness.

THE EXCELLENT QUALITIES OF HIS EXALTED KNOWING

Since all objects of knowledge—ultimate and conventional—are engaged by the Sage's unobstructed exalted knowing, like a myrobalan fruit[57] placed in the palm of his hand, the Sage's exalted knowing covers all objects of knowledge. However, others' limited knowing cannot cover the vast extent of objects to be known. Regarding this, *Praise of the One Worthy of Praise (Varṇāhavarṇestotra)* says:

> Only your wisdom
> encompasses all objects of knowledge;
> for everyone else apart from you,
> some objects are yet to be known.

And:

> Blessed One, all phenomena throughout time,
> in every aspect and place of origin,
> are objects of experience of your mind,
> like a myrobalan fruit in the palm of your hand.

> As regards phenomena—static or mobile,
> single or various, each distinct individual—
> your mind is obstructed from none of them,
> like the wind moving across the sky.

Reflect in accordance with these words.

THE EXCELLENT QUALITIES OF HIS LOVING-KINDNESS

Sentient beings are bound by the afflictions without any control. Likewise, the Buddha is bound by great compassion without control because great compassion continuously arises in him when he perceives suffering sentient beings. *Praise in One Hundred and Fifty Verses* says:

> Every one of these sentient beings
> is equally bound by the afflictions.
> You have long been bound by compassion.
> To release them from their afflictions,
> should I first prostrate to you
> or to that which causes you
> to stay in saṃsāra so long, aware
> of its faults—to great compassion?

The *Satyaka Chapter* also says:

> When he observes all beings with minds
> constantly obscured by the darkness of ignorance,
> locked up in the prison of cyclic existence, [66]
> great compassion is born in the holy sage.

Recollect his loving-kindness in accordance with these statements.

THE EXCELLENT QUALITIES OF THE BUDDHA'S EXALTED ACTIVITIES

He benefits all sentient beings through both the spontaneous and the uninterrupted exalted activities of his body, speech, and mind. Insofar as a disciple is fit for guidance, it is impossible for the Sage not to give that trainee what is excellent and pull him or her out of trouble. Thus it is stated that through his actions, he definitely does everything that is necessary.

Potowa said this:

> If you reflect on the Buddha's qualities again and again, your conviction strengthens and your mindstream becomes purer, which gives rise to more blessings. When you have gained certain knowledge about this, you will go for refuge from the depths of your heart. Then, if you merely train in the precepts, whatever you do will become a practice of the Buddhadharma.
>
> We do not value the Buddha's exalted knowing even as much as we value an accurate fortune teller. If an accurate fortune teller tells you, "I know there will be no bad luck for you this year," you walk away happy and comfortable. If she says, "This year there will be great misfortune. Do this. Don't do that!" you will try hard to accomplish it, and if you do not accomplish it, you will think, "I did not accomplish what she told me to do," and your mind will be anxious. If the Buddha says, "Do this and that; accomplish this and that," do you take it on? If you do not accomplish it, does your mind become anxious? To claim "The teachings say that, but owing to present circumstances I cannot do it right now, so I must do this instead" is to

ignore the Buddha's advice and proceed on the basis of your own discernment.

Just as Potowa says here, if we turn our mind inward and examine carefully, we will recognize that it is so true that our normal attitude, one of trusting others' mere words and being content without discernment, is nothing but delusion.

Therefore think about the Buddha's excellent qualities again and again, and try to gain as much certainty as possible. Once that develops, you will have arrived at the main point of going for refuge. For a similar certainty will arise concerning the Dharma received from him and from the Saṅgha of those accomplishing that Dharma. There is no way that going for refuge, or taming the mind, let alone other paths, will occur without it.

The excellent qualities of the Dharma

Out of respect for the Buddha, you should recollect as follows: "The Buddha's limitless excellent qualities arose from his meditating on and actualizing the Dharma of scriptures and realization, true cessations and true paths, the epitome of the elimination of faults and the achievement of excellent qualities." [67] That is the intention of the *Compendium of the Teachings Sūtra* (*Dharmasaṅgītisūtra*).

The excellent qualities of the Saṅgha

This refers mainly to persons who are āryas. Recollecting the excellent qualities of the Dharma, you are mindful of those who accomplish it correctly. That is the intention of the *Compendium of the Teachings Sūtra*.

Going for refuge by way of understanding their distinctions

As is apparent from the *Compendium of Ascertainments*, you go for refuge aware of the distinctions among the Three Jewels.

GOING FOR REFUGE BY WAY OF COMMITMENT

As is apparent from the *Commentary on the Vinaya Sūtra* (*Vinayasūtraṭīkā*), you go for refuge in terms of considering the Buddha to be the one who teaches the refuge; the Dharma to be nirvāṇa, which is the actual refuge; and the Saṅgha to be the companions who help you accomplish the refuge.

GOING FOR REFUGE BY WAY OF NOT ADVOCATING OTHER ONES

Having understood the superiority and inferiority of Buddhist and non-Buddhist teachers, teachings, and students, respectively, you consider the Three Jewels alone to be a refuge and do not consider teachers and so forth who are incompatible with them to be a refuge. As for the difference between the two sets, the difference between the teachers is that the Buddha has eliminated all faults and has completed the excellent qualities while other teachers are the opposite to that. *Praise of the Exalted One* (*Viśeṣastava*) says:

> Having abandoned the other teachers,
> Blessed One, I go to you for refuge.
> If they ask me why, it is because
> you have excellent qualities but no faults.

And:

> The more I think about the other
> non-Buddhist textual traditions,
> the more my faith in you, Protector,
> develops in my mind.

> Their mental states are ruined by faulty tenets
> of those who lack omniscience;
> with ruined thinking, they do not see
> the faultless teachers—not even you.

THE STAGES OF TRAINING AFTER HAVING GONE FOR REFUGE

This has two points: specific precepts relating to the individual objects of refuge and common precepts relating to all three objects of refuge.

SPECIFIC PRECEPTS RELATING TO THE INDIVIDUAL OBJECTS OF REFUGE

This has two points: precepts regarding what is to be stopped and precepts regarding what is to be accomplished.

PRECEPTS REGARDING WHAT IS TO BE STOPPED

The *Great Final Nirvāṇa Sūtra* states:

> One who goes to the three for refuge
> is one who correctly attends to virtue.
> Such a one will never go
> for refuge to some other gods.
>
> One who goes to the Dharma for refuge
> is free from a mind to harm or kill.
> One who goes to the Saṅgha for refuge [68]
> does not mingle with the tīrthikas.

In accordance with this statement, there are three precepts: to not go for refuge to other gods, to abandon causing harm or injury to sentient beings, and to not associate with non-Buddhists.

NOT TO GO FOR REFUGE TO OTHER GODS

If one does not even regard worldly gods—Rudra, Viṣṇu, and the like—as long-term refuge, there is no need to mention nāgas and the local spirits who belong to the hungry ghosts. Yet although one should not rely on them owing to a lack of conviction in the three objects of refuge, it is not inappropriate to seek their assistance for some beneficial temporary objective.

It is analogous to seeking help from a benefactor for financial support or to relying on a doctor for treating an illness.

To abandon causing harm or injury to sentient beings

The second consists in abandoning causing harm or injury to humans, animals, and so forth through thought or actions like beating them, binding them, ensnaring them, piercing their noses, and burdening them unbearably.

Not to associate with non-Buddhists

The third consists in not coming under the influence of those who are not convinced that the Three Jewels are refuges and who denigrate them.

Precepts regarding what is to be accomplished

However excellent or flawed painted pictures of the Buddha's body may be, do not disparage them and do not put them on the ground. Having given up defaming and disrespecting them, as in the case of pawning them and so forth, regard them as fields of veneration like the Teacher himself. *Letter to a Friend* (v. 2) says:

> Just as the wise honor any depiction
> of the Sugata, however fashioned—even those made from wood . . .

Exegesis of the Vinaya (*Vinayavibaṅgha*) states that Mānavakapila abused members of the Saṅgha who were learners and nonlearners in eighteen different ways, saying things like "You elephant heads! How do you know what is Dharma and what is not?" Because of that he was born as a sea monster, a marine creature with eighteen heads, and remained an animal from the time of the teacher Kāśyapa to that of the Śākya king.

Chapters on Finer Points of the Vinaya (*Vinayakṣudrakavastu*) recounts that after the teacher Krakucchanda had passed into nirvāṇa, [69] King Cārumat had a big stūpa built. A hired workman scoffed at it a couple of times, saying, "Who knows when we will ever get such a huge stūpa finished!" Later on, once the stūpa had been completed beautifully, he felt so sorry that he used his wages to have a golden bell made and attached to the stūpa. On account of that, he was born as Well-Sounding One, with an ugly complexion and small body but a very pleasant voice. Therefore do not joke about holy images, saying, "It is like such and such." Also, it is inappropriate to critique a holy image in terms of its size or whether it is made from good materials and to discourage someone from completing it through your disruptive remarks.

Naljorpa Chenpo Jangchup Rinchen showed Atiśa a statue of Mañjuśrī and asked, "What is the quality like? If it is good, I'll take it and offer the four gold coins Rongpa Gargé has given me."

Atiśa replied, "There is nothing that is not excellent about the Venerable One's body. As for the sculptor, he is average." Having said this, he placed the statue on the crown of his head. It is said that he used to do this with every piece of work.

Avoid showing disrespect to even as little as a four-line stanza of the Dharma. Avoid pawning volumes of scripture, trading them, putting them on the bare ground or in dishonorable places, carrying them around together with your shoes, stepping over them, and so forth. Instead treat them respectfully as if they were the Dharma Jewel.

It is said that Geshe Chenngawa used to put his palms together and stand up when he saw scriptures being brought to him. Later on, when he could not stand up any more, he used to simply put his palms together.

It is said that when Atiśa came to Ngari, there was a tantric practitioner who did not listen to the Dharma from him. However, when a scribe smeared plaque from his teeth on a Dharma text, Atiśa saw it and, unable to bear it, exclaimed, "Oh no! Don't do that. Don't do that!" From this, the tantrika gained faith and listened to the Dharma.

Sharawa said, "We play around with the Dharma in all sorts of ways. Disrespect for the Dharma and for Dharma teachers is a cause for distorted wisdom. We are already confused enough now. What are we going to do if we become more confused?"

You should not abuse or despise the Saṅgha or even those who merely bear the signs of ordination. Nor should you look at them as some kind of opponents, having made arbitrary divisions in terms of "your group" and "my group." Instead [70] treat them with respect as if they were the Saṅgha Jewel. *Exhortation to the Extraordinary Attitude* says:

Those who, dwelling in forests, desire excellent qualities
should not look for faults in other people;
they should not produce the attitude
"I'm especially noble, I'm the best."

This haughtiness is the root of all carelessness.
Don't let contempt for lesser monks arise
or else you won't reach liberation for an eon.
This is a training stage in this teaching.

Geshe Dromtönpa and Naljorpa Chenpo, instead of stepping over a piece of yellow material on the ground, would shake it and carry it to a clean place. You should train in accordance with their practice, for others will respect you as much as you respect the Three Jewels. The *King of Concentrations Sūtra* says:

Whatever kinds of actions you have done,
those kinds of effects you will obtain.

COMMON PRECEPTS RELATING TO ALL THREE OBJECTS OF REFUGE

This has six points: (1) by recollecting the distinctions and excellent qualities of the Three Jewels, go for refuge again and again; (2) by recollecting the great kindness of the Three Jewels, always make effort to honor them and offer them the first portion of your food and drink; (3) by recollecting great compassion, establish other beings in this kind of practice; (4) whatever activities you engage in and whatever your purpose, honor the Three Jewels and make requests to them, abandoning all other worldly methods; (5) having understood its benefits, go for refuge three times a day and three times at night; and (6) maintain your refuge and do not forsake the Three Jewels at the cost of your life, not even in jest.

BY RECOLLECTING THE DISTINCTIONS AND EXCELLENT QUALITIES OF THE THREE JEWELS, GO FOR REFUGE AGAIN AND AGAIN

As explained above, think again and again about what distinguishes Buddhist from non-Buddhist teachings as well as about the distinctions among the Three Jewels and their excellent qualities.

BY RECOLLECTING THE GREAT KINDNESS OF THE THREE JEWELS, ALWAYS MAKE EFFORT TO HONOR THEM AND OFFER THEM THE FIRST PORTION OF YOUR FOOD AND DRINK

Recognize all the well-being you experience as the kindness of the Three Jewels and make offerings to them by acknowledging that. Since you constantly need to eat and drink, you will amass a great accumulation of merit with little trouble if you offer the first portion of food and drink each time. Therefore you should offer the first portion of whatever you enjoy, including water, from the depths of your heart. Moreover [71] Sharawa said:

> You shouldn't make offerings of moldy cheese cubes or yellowed leaves. Instead you should offer something good. The first portion of your tea is an offering, not [something you want to get rid of] as if removing a speck of dust.

For example, a sūtra says:

> If seeds are not planted in a fertile field in season, they cannot be established. Accordingly, the holy field from which all present and future well-being springs can be planted continuously with the seeds of well-being throughout all four seasons; may that field of merit be tilled with the plow of faith.

If that which needs to be done does not happen, it will be an extremely heavy loss.

To have less regard for the best of fields [of merit] than you do for an ordinary field is not a good attitude. Therefore always make offerings to the Three Jewels with joyous effort. If you do that, then, through the power of the roots of virtue that grow in the holy field, the power of your intelligence regarding the stages of the path will increase. As long as your intelligence is feeble—whereby you do not retain the words while listening, you do not understand their meaning while reflecting, and nothing arises in your mindstream while meditating—the quintessential instruction is to rely on the power of the holy field.

Also your offering is not determined by the thing offered; it is determined by your faith. As is stated in the scriptures, if you have faith, it is enough to offer mandalas, water, and offerings that nobody cares about. Therefore you should make offerings in this way even if you have no material things to offer. If you have something but you are unable to give it and declare, "I am a wretched pauper without any merit; I have no other possessions to offer,"[58] this would be, in the words of Potowa, like a blind person putting some cheap aromatic plant into a fragrant conch-shell container and trying to fool someone with eyesight by calling it "sandalwood and camphor perfume."

Phuchungwa said:

At first I used to offer a pungent aromatic plant. Then I had the means to offer sweet incense prepared from four substances. Now I offer the most exquisitely fragrant aloe wood, Chinese cypress, and so forth.

In accordance with this statement, if out of contempt for meager offerings you do not give anything, [72] you will go on like that throughout your entire life. However, if you make effort incrementally from the start, you will get better and better. Therefore you should train following Phuchungwa's practice. It is said that he once prepared incense worth twenty-two ounces of gold.

Great bodhisattvas, who have gained control over mundane things, emanate many hundreds of thousands of bodies—and for each body, again, emanate hundreds of thousands of hands and so forth—and they appear in all the buddhafields so as to make offerings to the victors for many eons. But when those who are satisfied with only the semblance of excellent qualities declare, "As for me, I do not hope to reach enlightenment in that way," this is the nonsensical talk of people who know very little about the

Dharma. Instead, you should act according to the instructions given in the *Cloud of Jewels of Sūtra* (*Ratnameghasūtra*):

> Study whatever vast offerings and acts of service are explained in the sūtras and, from the depths of your heart and with the supreme extraordinary attitude, dedicate them to the buddhas and bodhisattvas.

BY RECOLLECTING GREAT COMPASSION, ESTABLISH OTHER BEINGS IN THIS KIND OF PRACTICE

Out of loving-kindness establish other sentient beings in going for refuge as much as you can.

WHATEVER ACTIVITIES YOU ENGAGE IN AND WHATEVER YOUR PURPOSE, HONOR THE THREE JEWELS AND MAKE REQUESTS TO THEM, ABANDONING ALL OTHER WORLDLY METHODS

Whatever activities you engage in and whatever needful purpose you may see, rely on the Three Jewels and do what is in agreement with them, such as making offerings. But it is utterly inappropriate to rely in any way at all on what is not in agreement with them, such as certain practices in the Bön tradition. Consequently, you should trust in the Jewels at all times.

HAVING UNDERSTOOD ITS BENEFITS, GO FOR REFUGE THREE TIMES A DAY AND THREE TIMES AT NIGHT

Here there are eight benefits: (1) it is the measure of being a Buddhist, (2) it is the basis of all vows, (3) the karmic obstructions accumulated previously are reduced and exhausted, (4) one accumulates vast merit, (5) one does not fall into the lower rebirths, (6) one is not harmed by human and nonhuman hindrances, (7) one accomplishes everything one wishes, and (8) one swiftly attains buddhahood.

IT IS THE MEASURE OF BEING A BUDDHIST

Although, generally speaking, there appear to be many ways of positing what constitutes a non-Buddhist and a Buddhist, it is widely known that Atiśa and Śāntipa differentiated them by their going for refuge. Therefore a Buddhist should be understood to be someone who has achieved going for refuge and has not given it up. Hence, as the standard for being a Buddhist, one must consider the Three Jewels to be one's teacher and so forth from the depths of one's heart. Without that, even though you do virtuous deeds, you will not be included among Buddhists.

IT IS THE BASIS OF ALL VOWS

The *Treasury of Abhidharma Autocommentary* says:

> Those who go for refuge gain access to taking all the vows correctly.

[73] And *Seventy Verses on Going for Refuge* also says:

> Upāsakas go for refuge to the three;
> that is the root of the eight vows.

This means that by going for refuge, the thought of passing beyond suffering is stabilized, which gives rise to the vows.

THE KARMIC OBSTRUCTIONS ACCUMULATED PREVIOUSLY ARE REDUCED AND EXHAUSTED

In the context of showing that bad actions are purified by going for refuge, the *Compendium of Trainings* says:

> Here, one must present the edifying story of the pig as an illustration.

A god who was about to be reborn as a pig, by going for refuge, was not born as one.[59] It further states:

Those who have gone for refuge to the Buddha
will not go to the lower rebirths.
They give up their human body
and obtain that of a god.

Something similar is stated regarding the Dharma and the Saṅgha.

ONE ACCUMULATES VAST MERIT

The *Compendium of the Perfections* (*Pāramitāsamāsa*) says:

If the merit of having gone for refuge took shape,
even these three realms would be too small a container.
The water in the great oceans
can never be measured in handfuls.

That is how vast it is.

ONE DOES NOT FALL INTO THE LOWER REBIRTHS

You should understand this from the above.

ONE IS NOT HARMED BY HUMAN AND NONHUMAN HINDRANCES

This is easy to understand.

ONE ACCOMPLISHES EVERYTHING ONE WISHES

Whatever Dharma activity you engage in, if at the beginning you make offerings to the Three Jewels, go for refuge, and supplicate them, it will easily be accomplished.

ONE SWIFTLY ATTAINS BUDDHAHOOD

The *Questions of a Lion Sūtra* (*Siṃhaparipṛcchāsūtra*) says:

Through faith you will abandon the leisureless states.

Accordingly, you will gain the special freedoms and, having found refuge, train in the special path. Thus you will become a buddha without much delay. Recollecting these kinds of benefits, you should go for refuge three times in the day and three times at night.

MAINTAIN YOUR REFUGE AND DO NOT FORSAKE THE THREE JEWELS AT THE COST OF YOUR LIFE, NOT EVEN IN JEST

There is no doubt that we will be separated from this body, life, and possessions. If we give up the Three Jewels for their sake, we will undergo continuous suffering in all successive lives to come. Therefore we should vow not to abandon our refuge, come what may, nor even utter words in jest about giving up our refuge. [74] Earlier masters spoke of a precept that you should train in going for refuge to the tathāgata of whatever direction you are headed in, but I have not seen a source for that. Thus the six common precepts are just as they appear in *Commentary on the Difficult Points of Lamp for the Path*. Regarding the specific precepts, the first three are explained in the sūtra collection, whereas the last three appear in *Six Aspects of Going for Refuge (Ṣaḍaṅgaśaraṇa)*.

As for how transgressing these precepts becomes a cause of degenerating and relinquishing your refuge, it is the transgression of the precept not to forsake your refuge even at the cost of your life that actually constitutes relinquishing it. Similarly, even if you do not forsake the Three Jewels but you uphold both them and another three—teachers and so forth—that are incompatible with them, then you transgress the precept of not advocating another refuge, and by not having faith in your refuge you also relinquish it. I think that if these do not occur, it is a mere transgression of the precepts but not a cause for relinquishing your refuge.

Thus going for refuge is the great gateway to the Buddha's teachings. If your going for refuge is not mere words, you are relying on a superior power. Therefore you will not be thwarted by external or internal hindrances, and various special excellent qualities will arise easily and be hard to diminish, thereby increasing more and more. So it is vital that you uphold your refuge by recollecting the fear and the excellent qualities explained above and that you strive to not transgress its precepts.

10 | Karma and Its Effects

GENERATING THE FAITH OF CONVICTION IN ACTIONS AND THEIR EFFECTS

THIS HAS THREE POINTS: contemplating karma[60] and its effects in general, contemplating karma and its effects in particular, and having contemplated karma and its effects, how to engage in virtue and desist from nonvirtue.

CONTEMPLATING KARMA AND ITS EFFECTS IN GENERAL

This has two points: the actual way to contemplate karma and its effects in general; and contemplating the specific categories.

THE ACTUAL WAY TO CONTEMPLATE KARMA AND ITS EFFECTS IN GENERAL

This has four points: karma is certain, karma greatly increases, you do not meet with karma you have not created, and karma you have created does not dissipate.

KARMA IS CERTAIN

All happiness that is a type of pleasant feeling, whether in ordinary beings or āryas, comes from virtuous karma accumulated previously. This includes even pleasures as small as the pleasure in a sentient being born in hell when a cool breeze springs up. There is no way for happiness to arise from nonvirtuous karma. All suffering that is a type of painful feeling comes from nonvirtuous karma accumulated previously. This includes even pains as small as the pain in the mind of an arhat. [75] There is no way for suffering to arise from virtuous karma. *Precious Garland* (1.21) says:

> From nonvirtue comes all suffering
> and, likewise, every lower rebirth.
> From virtue comes every fortunate rebirth
> and the happiness in all rebirths.

Therefore happiness and suffering do not arise without cause or from an incongruous cause, such as the fundamental nature or Īśvara. Happiness and suffering in general arise, respectively, from virtuous and nonvirtuous karma in general. Also, the various specific instances of happiness and suffering each arise from the various specific instances of the two types of karma without any inconsistency. To gain certainty with regard to actions and their effects being certain and infallible is said to be the correct view of all Buddhists and praised as the foundation of all virtuous phenomena.

KARMA GREATLY INCREASES

Even from a small virtuous action there arises enormous happiness as its effect, while even from a small nonvirtuous action there arises enormous suffering as its effect. There is nothing among external causes and effects that resembles the increase of effects from internal causes. The *Collection of Indicative Verses* (28.25–26) says:

> Even creating a small bad deed
> will result in terrible fear
> and disasters in future lives,
> like having ingested poison.

> Even creating a little merit
> will bring great happiness in future lives
> and accomplish vast objectives,
> like grains that ripen to perfection.

You do not meet with karma you have not created

If you have not accumulated karma that will become the cause for experiencing happiness or suffering, you will never experience the happiness or suffering that is its effect. Also, those who enjoy the effects of the Teacher's accumulation of an incalculable accumulation of merit do not need to accumulate all its causes; however, they need to accumulate one part of them.[61]

Karma you have created does not dissipate

The virtuous and nonvirtuous actions that have been done will bring forth pleasant and unpleasant effects. *Praise of the Exalted One* says:

> Brahmins claim that good and bad deeds
> are transferable like gifts one receives.
> You teach that deeds done are never lost
> and what is not done will not be met.

[76] The *King of Concentrations Sūtra* also says:

> What is done will never not be met.
> What others did you will not experience.

Chapters of Scriptural Transmission says:

> Actions never come to naught,
> even after a hundred eons.
> When the time comes and the conditions are met,
> beings will surely experience their effects.

Contemplating the specific categories

This has two points: the principal teaching of the ten paths of action, and establishing actions and their effects.

THE PRINCIPAL TEACHING OF THE TEN PATHS OF ACTION

So you have first generated certainty concerning the ways of actions and their effects through this understanding that happiness and suffering are certain to occur as effects of their specific causes, that karma increases greatly, that you do not meet with anything you have not created, and that karma does not dissipate. Now which actions should be adopted and which rejected? In general, the doorways for engaging in good conduct and faulty conduct are determined as three. Although not all virtues and nonvirtues of the three doors are included in the ten paths of action, the Blessed One, summing up the essential points, stated the more obvious or coarser virtues and nonvirtues, the main basis of misdeeds being the ten black paths of action. Having seen that, when they are abandoned, the most significant points are also included in those ten, he taught the ten white paths of action.

The *Treasury of Abhidharma* (4.66) says:

> Categorizing the most obvious among them,
> he taught the paths of action as ten:
> virtuous and nonvirtuous, respectively.

Also, *Exegesis of the Vinaya* says:

> Guard your speech, completely restrain your mind,
> and perform no nonvirtuous deeds with the body;
> when you purify these three paths of action,
> you will attain the path taught by the Sage.

Therefore the object praised in the *Ten Grounds Sūtra* (*Daśabhūmikasūtra*) is the ethical discipline of abandoning the ten nonvirtues. This is summarized in *Entering the Middle Way* (*Madhyamakāvatāra*, 2.7):

> For the definite goodness and higher states
> of ordinary beings, those born from his speech,
> those established for self-enlightenment,
> and the victors' children—the cause [77] is none other than ethical
>   conduct.[62]

That being so, if someone who does not rely on restraining the mind again and again, so as to guard even a single ethical discipline, were to claim, "As for me, I am a Mahāyānist," that would be a disgrace. The *Kṣitigarbha Sūtra* says:

> By way of these ten virtuous paths of action, you will become a buddha. On the other hand, if one who does not guard even a single virtuous path of action throughout his life nevertheless says, "I am a Mahāyānist. I seek unsurpassed, perfectly complete enlightenment," that person is an utter hypocrite and a great liar. He is deceiving the world before the eyes of all the blessed ones and propounding nihilism. At the time of death, he will be very confused and fall in the wrong direction.

"Fall in the wrong direction" should be understood as a synonym for the miserable lower rebirths.

ESTABLISHING ACTIONS AND THEIR EFFECTS

This has three points: nonvirtuous actions and their effects, virtuous actions and their effects, and other categories of actions.

NONVIRTUOUS ACTIONS AND THEIR EFFECTS

This has three points: the actual nonvirtuous paths of action, differentiating heavy and light karma, and a presentation of their effects.

THE ACTUAL NONVIRTUOUS PATHS OF ACTION

KILLING

Basis
The basis[63] of killing is another sentient being.

Attitude
This has three points: discernment, mental affliction, and motivation.
  The *discernment* has four possibilities: when the basis is a sentient being,

the discernment of it as a sentient being; when the basis is a sentient being, the discernment of it as not a sentient being; when the basis is not a sentient being, the discernment of it as not a sentient being; and when the basis is not a sentient being, the discernment of it as a sentient being. The first and third discernments are unmistaken, while the second and fourth are mistaken. Here, there may be a particular motivation. For example, if you are thinking to kill only Devadatta, but when it comes to performing the action, you mistakenly kill Yajñadatta, then there is no bad deed in connection with the actual basis. If there were, then an unmistaken discernment would be necessary. However, if at the time of performing the action, you have the general motivation to kill whomever is at hand, then an unmistaken discernment is not necessary. You should understand this rule to apply also to the remaining nine paths of action as appropriate.

The *mental affliction* is any of the three poisons.

The *motivation* consists in the desire to kill.

Performance
This is the same whether you yourself do the killing or whether you cause someone else to do it. The nature of the performance is the act itself, whether done by means of a weapon, poison, mantra, or anything else. [78]

Completion
The completion consists in the death of the other being because of the performance of the action, whether at that time or at some other time before you yourself die.

STEALING

Basis
The basis of stealing is something owned by another.

Attitude
Among the three aspects belonging to the attitude, the *discernment* and the *mental affliction* are as [with killing] above. The *motivation* consists in the desire to take something belonging to someone else away from them without it having been given.

Performance

As for the performance, the agent is as explained above. The nature of the performance is the same whether you take something by force or steal it sneakily. In addition, being deceitful regarding a debt or a trust and using other fraudulent methods also constitute stealing. Also, whether it is done for one's own sake, for someone else's sake, or to harm the owner and so forth, it is stealing.

Completion

The completion consists in the arising of the thought "Now it is mine!" Or, if you have caused someone else to rob or steal, it is enough for that thought to arise in him or her. This is similar to when someone kills someone else because of an order, where when the latter dies, the bad deed of the actual path of action befalls the one who gave the order, even if he does not know the person is dead.

SEXUAL MISCONDUCT

Basis

Among the four bases of sexual misconduct, the first, *inappropriate persons*, is those you should not have sexual intercourse with: your mother and so forth, women under the care of their mothers and so forth, all men, hermaphrodites, and ordained women.

Inappropriate body parts are those other than the entrance to the womb, such as the mouth.

Inappropriate places are in the vicinity of gurus, places with stūpas, and the like.

Inappropriate times are during pregnancy, when you are keeping one-day vows, and so forth.

Attitude

Among the three aspects belonging to the attitude, the *discernment* is explained as follows. The *Compendium of Ascertainments* says "discerning that as that," which indicates that a nonmistaken discernment is necessary. The Vinaya states that in the case of a defeat of impure conduct, it is the same whether the discernment is mistaken or nonmistaken. The *Treasury of Abhidharma Autocommentary* explains that if you approach someone else's wife[64] perceiving her to be yours, this will not constitute the path of action under discussion, and getting involved with someone else's wife while perceiving her to be the wife of yet another person may or may not constitute such a path.

The *mental affliction* can be any of the three poisons.

The *motivation* is the desire for sexual intercourse in a manner that constitutes impure conduct.

Performance
The performance consists in striving for that goal.

Completion
The completion consists in the two joining with each other.

LYING

Basis
Among the two bases of lying, the *expressed basis* refers to the four—that which one has seen, heard, differentiated, or understood—[79] as well as their four opposites.[65] The *object understood* is the meaning understood by the other person.

Attitude
Among the three aspects belonging to the attitude, the *discernment* consists in actions such as taking something one has observed and changing it into something one has not observed. The *mental affliction* is any of the three poisons. The *motivation* is the desire to express that altered discernment.

Performance
The performance consists in indicating a falsehood by speaking, by accepting it through not saying anything, or by signaling with a physical gesture. Moreover, the scriptures state that it amounts to the same whether you say it for your own purposes or for someone else's sake. Here Asaṅga's texts say that the three—lying, divisive speech, and harsh speech—become paths of action for yourself even if you get someone else to perform them. The root text and autocommentary of the *Treasury of Abhidharma* say that all four nonvirtues associated with speech become paths of action when you get

someone else to perform them. The Vinaya states that in order to produce a complete infraction, you yourself must speak.

Completion

The completion consists in it being understood by the other person. The *Treasury of Abhidharma Autocommentary* explains that if it is not understood, it becomes merely idle talk. This is also the same for divisive speech and harsh speech.

DIVISIVE SPEECH

Basis

The basis of divisive speech is sentient beings who are in agreement or in disagreement with each other.

Attitude

Among the three aspects belonging to the attitude, the *discernment* and the *mental affliction* are as above. The *motivation* consists in the desire to divide sentient beings who are in agreement and the desire for those who are in disagreement not to be reconciled.

Performance

The performance consists in making pleasant or unpleasant statements, using true or untrue words, and saying them for either one's own or someone else's sake.

Completion

The completion consists in the divisive words uttered having been understood.

HARSH SPEECH

Basis

The basis of harsh speech is a sentient being who has become the causal basis of a hostile intent arising in you.

Attitude

With respect to the attitude, the *discernment* and the *mental affliction* are as above. The *motivation* is the wish to utter harsh speech.

Performance

The performance consists in speaking unpleasantly, whether truthfully or falsely, about another person's faults associated with his lineage, body, ethics, or behavior.

Completion

The completion consists in the one to whom it was said understanding the meaning.

IDLE TALK

Basis

The basis of idle talk is a meaningless topic.

Attitude

Among the three aspects belonging to the attitude, the *discernment* is stated merely as "discerning that as that." In this context, it is to accurately discern the topic one wants to talk about and then talk about it. There is no need for someone to understand it. The *mental affliction* is any of the three poisons. The *motivation* is the desire to express whatever random thoughts occur.

Performance

The performance consists in starting to utter idle talk.

Completion

The completion is to finish uttering idle talk. [80]

COVETOUSNESS

Basis

The basis of covetousness is the wealth or property of someone else.

Attitude
Among the three aspects belonging to the attitude, the *discernment* consists in an accurate discernment of that basis. The *mental affliction* is any of the three poisons. The *motivation* is the desire to make it one's own.

Performance
The performance consists in striving for the object of that thought.

Completion
The completion is the thought "May this wealth and so forth be mine!"

HARMFUL INTENT

Basis and attitude
The basis, the discernment, and the mental affliction of harmful intent are the same as with harsh speech. The motivation is the desire to hit someone and the like; it is the thought "How nice it would be if this person were to be killed or imprisoned, or if his wealth were ruined by itself or by someone else" and the like.

Performance
The performance consists in actually engaging in this thought.

Completion
The completion consists in the resolve to hit and the like.

WRONG VIEWS

Basis
The basis of wrong views is an object that actually exists.

Attitude
Among the three aspects belonging to the attitude, the *discernment* consists in considering the denial of the object to be true. The *mental affliction* is any of the three poisons. The *motivation* consists in wanting to deny that thing.

Performance
The performance consists in beginning to engage in such thinking. This has four points: *denying causes*, which consists in the view "There is no good conduct and bad conduct"; *denying effects*, which consists in the view "There are no fully ripened effects of those two"; *denying activities*; and *denying existing phenomena*, which consists in the view "Arhats and the like do not exist." The third, denying activities, has three aspects: *denying the activity of planting and holding the seed*, which consists in the view "There is no planting of a seed by the father and no holding of a seed by the mother"; *denying the activity of coming and going*, which consists in the view "There is no coming from a former existence to this one and no going from this one to a future one"; and *denying the activity of being born*, which consists in the view "There is no intermediate state into which sentient beings are miraculously born."[66]

Completion
The completion is to be certain of one's denial. Among these ten, the intentions in the mind are actions but not paths of action. The seven actions of body and speech are actions, and they are also paths of action since they are the basis of carrying out the intentions. The three of covetousness and so on are paths of action but not actions.[67]

DIFFERENTIATING HEAVY AND LIGHT KARMA

This has two points: the heaviness of the ten paths of action, and an ancillary presentation of ways in which karma is strong.

THE HEAVINESS OF THE TEN PATHS OF ACTION

Levels of Yogic Practice states six ways in which they are heavy.

1. Conditioning—this is the strong presence or absence of the three poisons that motivate the action.
2. Habituation—[81] this is having engaged in virtuous or nonvirtuous actions for a long time such that one has become accustomed to them through repetition.
3. Nature—in the case of the seven actions of body and speech, each preceding one is heavier than the subsequent one, whereas with the

three actions of mind, each subsequent one is heavier than the preceding one.

4. Basis—this is what is benefited or harmed, such as the Buddha, the Dharma, the Saṅgha, and the gurus.

5. Singularly adhering to the discordant side—this is spending one's whole life committing nonvirtuous actions with singular conviction and not engaging in even one virtue.

6. Clearing away the discordant side—this is giving up the side of nonvirtue, becoming free from attachment, and training in virtuous actions.

Letter to a Friend (v. 42) also says:

> There are five ways that nonvirtuous and virtuous karma become
>   great:
> persistence, strong adherence, no antidote,
> and a basis with foremost qualities or of primary importance.
> Among these, strive to practice virtue!

There are five because of the division of the basis into two: a basis endowed with foremost qualities, such as the Three Jewels, and a basis of great benefit, such as one's parents.

AN ANCILLARY PRESENTATION OF WAYS IN WHICH KARMA IS STRONG

This has four points: great strength by way of the field, great strength by way of the support, great strength by way of the thing, and great strength by way of the attitude.

GREAT STRENGTH BY WAY OF THE FIELD

In the case of the Three Jewels, gurus, those who are like gurus, one's parents, and so forth, even if one's attitude toward them lacks intensity, and the benefit or harm one does to them is small, any merit or misdeed will be great. The *Application of Mindfulness Sūtra* (*Smṛtyupasthāna-sūtra*) says:

The karma of stealing even a little thing from the Three Jewels is purified if it is returned in the case of the Buddha and the Dharma. However, in the case of the Saṅgha, it is not purified as long as the result is not experienced. If it is a requisite means of providing sustenance for the Saṅgha, one will be born in the great hells, and if something else, then one will be born in the great darkness surrounding Avīci.

Bodhisattvas are an extremely powerful field of virtue and nonvirtue. *Seal Enhancing the Power of Faith Sūtra* (*Śraddhābalādhānāvatāramudrāsūtra*) says that compared to someone who, out of anger, puts all the sentient beings of the ten directions into a dark prison, if someone else, out of anger, turns his back on a bodhisattva, saying, "I will not look upon this horrible person again," he generates an incalculably greater bad deed. [82] Also compared to someone who has destroyed and burned down stūpas as numerous as the sand grains of the Ganges River, if someone else generates anger and harmful intent in his mind toward a bodhisattva and says unpleasant things to him, it is as above. *Seal of Engaging in Certain and Uncertain Destinies Sūtra* (*Niyatāniyatamudrāvatārasūtra*) says that compared to someone who, out of love, restores the eyes of those sentient beings in the ten directions whose eyes were gouged out, and who, after releasing the aforementioned sentient beings from prison, establishes them in the happiness of a universal monarch (*cakravartin*) or of Brahma, if someone else out of trust looks at or out of faith wishes to look at a bodhisattva endowed with Mahāyāna aspiration and sings his praises, he generates incalculably greater merit. Also, the *Magic of the Complete Certainty of Total Peace Sūtra* (*Praśantaviniścayaprātihāryasūtra*) says that compared to killing all the sentient beings of Jambudvīpa or seizing all their possessions, someone who obstructs even as little as the virtue of a bodhisattva's giving a handful of food to an animal generates incalculably greater evil. Therefore you should be very careful with respect to these objects.

GREAT STRENGTH BY WAY OF THE SUPPORT

Just as even a tiny lump of iron sinks whereas a container made from it floats, so likewise the bad actions committed by unskillful people and skillful people are respectively heavy and light. It is said that for those who are skillful, who regret their previous bad actions, restrain themselves in the future, do not keep them secret, and apply their virtuous antidotes, they are light, whereas for those who arrogantly assume they are skillful and do not do this but out of contempt deliberately engage in them, they are heavy.

The *Heap of Jewels Sūtra* (*Ratnarāśisūtra*) also declares that if all the sentient beings of the billion universes were to have entered the Mahāyāna and gained the endowments of universal monarchs, and if each of them were to offer butter lamps in vessels the size of an ocean and with wicks the size of Mount Meru to a stūpa of a buddha, this would not match even one hundredth part of the merit of a bodhisattva who has left his home and who holds up a little bit of wick smeared with butter in front of a stūpa. This makes clear the strength of the support[68] even if there is no difference in the attitude and the field, and even if the thing offered is very different. [83] This reasoning also makes clear that depending on whether one has the support of vows and, if so, whether it is one, two, or three sets of vows, the cultivation of the path will be the more effective the more one has. For example, there is a great difference in the strength of the roots of virtue according to whether a householder, at the time of giving donations and the like, acts on the basis of keeping vows, such as one-day vows, or whether he acts without any vows.

The *Overcoming Faulty Ethical Discipline Sūtra* (*Duḥśīlanigrahasūtra*) says that compared to a human being possessing the ten nonvirtues who, for a hundred years, continuously and uninterruptedly accumulates bad actions, a fully ordained monk who has completely broken his vows of discipline and who for one day, dressed in the victory banner of sages,[69] enjoys that which has been offered in faith to him, accumulates far more bad actions. Again because of the support, the bad actions have greater strength. *Exegesis of the Vinaya* also says:

> It is better that they eat lumps of iron
> blazing with tongues of fire
> than for those with slack or corrupted discipline
> to eat the alms food of the local people.

This has been taught with regard to both corrupted discipline and slackness in training. Dromtönpa's statement—that the sin of engaging in the ten nonvirtues is very small when compared to the sin of having broken one's reliance on the Dharma—appears to be true.

GREAT STRENGTH BY WAY OF THE THING

In the case of giving gifts to sentient beings, giving the Dharma is supreme, and in the case of making offerings to the buddhas, offering one's practice is supreme—each being far superior to gifts and offerings of material things. Using this as an example, understand it to apply in other cases.

GREAT STRENGTH BY WAY OF THE ATTITUDE

The *Heap of Jewels Sūtra* says that if all the sentient beings of the billion universes out of aspiration for self-liberation were each to create a buddha stūpa as massive as Mount Meru, and if they and all those who are objects of respect were to pay respect to them for ten million eons, this would not match the merit generated by a bodhisattva who, never separated from the mind aspiring for omniscience, offers one single flower. Likewise, a difference in attitude—such as aspiring for a higher or lower goal, or focusing on one's own or others' purpose—should be understood also in terms of greater or lesser intensity, and longer or shorter duration. [84] When it comes to faulty conduct, an intense afflicted attitude and long duration also have greater strength.

Also among the mental afflictions, anger is particularly strong. *Entering the Bodhisattva Way* (6.1) says:

> Whatever good conduct has been amassed
> over a thousand eons by giving
> and worshiping those gone to bliss and so on
> is all destroyed by one moment of anger.

Here, anger toward those who perfectly observe their celibacy is very heavy, and anger toward bodhisattvas is heavier still. The *King of Concentrations Sūtra* says:

> If someone harbors harmful intent for another,
> ethical conduct or studying cannot protect him,

nor can meditative concentration or solitude,
nor generosity or worshiping the Buddha.

A PRESENTATION OF THEIR EFFECTS

This has three points: the fully ripened effect, the effect concordant with
the cause, and the dominant or environmental effect.

THE FULLY RIPENED EFFECT

Since each of the ten paths of action depends on whether the basis, the
three poisons, is small, intermediate, or great, the fully ripened effect is also
threefold. *Levels of Yogic Practice* says that through each of the ten great
ones, a great act of killing and so on, you are reborn as a hell being, through
each of the ten intermediate ones you are reborn as a hungry ghost, and
through each of the ten small ones you are reborn as an animal. In the *Ten
Grounds Sūtra* the effects of small and intermediate ones are said to be the
other way around.

THE EFFECT CONCORDANT WITH THE CAUSE

Each of the ten nonvirtuous paths of action also gives rise to an effect concordant with the cause, so that even when you have left the lower rebirths
and taken rebirth as a human being, your life will be short, you will lack
wealth, your partner will leave you, you will be slandered, you will be separated from loved ones, you will hear unpleasant speech, others will not listen to you, and each of the three—attachment, anger, and confusion—will
predominate respectively.

THE DOMINANT OR ENVIRONMENTAL EFFECT

The dominant or environmental effect of killing is that in the surrounding environment, food, drink, medicine, harvests, and the like will have
little potency. The environmental effect of stealing is that there will be
great droughts, torrential rains, poor harvests, and so forth. The environmental effect of sexual misconduct is there will be foul swamps, excessive
filth, unpleasant odors, and so forth. The environmental effect of lying is

that any work, whether in fields or boats and so on, will not succeed. The environmental effect of divisive speech is that the area will be bumpy and uneven, making it difficult to travel, and so on. The environmental effect of harsh speech is that the area will be full of logs, brambles, rocks, pebbles, potsherds, and so forth. The environmental effect of idle talk is that [85] fruit trees will not bear fruit or will bear fruit out of season and so forth. The environmental effect of covetousness is that everything excellent will deteriorate year by year, month by month, and day by day, and so forth. The environmental effect of harmful intent is a multitude of epidemics, injuries, infections, disputes, wars with enemy troops, and so forth. The environmental effect of wrong views is an environment where the best sources of provisions will be exhausted, and so forth.

VIRTUOUS ACTIONS AND THEIR EFFECTS

This has two points: virtuous actions and their effects.

VIRTUOUS ACTIONS

These are the physical acts that, with a virtuous mind cognizing the faults of killing, stealing, and sexual misconduct, correctly refrain from killing, stealing, and sexual misconduct and succeed in having refrained from them. This is to be applied likewise to the four of speech and the three of mind, the difference being that they are called "actions of speech" and "actions of the mind," as stated in *Levels of Yogic Practice*. So this should be applied to the basis, attitude, performance, and completion as appropriate. When applied to the path of action of avoiding killing, the basis is another sentient being, the attitude is the wish to avoid it having seen its faults, the performance is to put effort into completely abstaining from killing, and the completion is the physical act of having successfully refrained from it. The other paths of action should also be understood in this manner.

THE EFFECTS OF VIRTUOUS ACTIONS

From among the three effects of the virtuous paths of action, the fully ripened effect is to be born as a human being, a desire-realm god, or a god of the two upper realms through the force of small, intermediate, or great virtuous action. In the case of the effect concordant with the cause and the dominant or environmental effect, these are the opposite of the respective effects from nonvirtuous actions.

OTHER CATEGORIES OF ACTIONS

This has two points: the difference between propelling and completing actions, and the difference between what will definitely be experienced and what will not necessarily be experienced.

THE DIFFERENCE BETWEEN PROPELLING AND COMPLETING ACTIONS

Propelling actions for a fortunate rebirth are virtuous actions, whereas propelling actions for rebirth in the lower rebirths are nonvirtuous actions. The *completing* ones are undetermined. However, even in the fortunate rebirths, incomplete limbs, minor body parts or sense faculties, hideous looks, a short lifespan, multiple illnesses, poverty, and so forth are caused by nonvirtue. Also, in the case of animals and hungry ghosts, abundant prosperity is caused by virtue. Thus there are four possibilities: that which is propelled by a virtuous propelling action and completed by a virtuous action or by a nonvirtuous completing action, and that which is propelled by a nonvirtuous propelling action [86] and completed by a nonvirtuous action or by a virtuous completing action.

THE DIFFERENCE BETWEEN WHAT WILL DEFINITELY BE EXPERIENCED AND WHAT WILL NOT NECESSARILY BE EXPERIENCED

That which will definitely be experienced is what has been done intentionally and has been accumulated. That which will not necessarily be experienced is what has been done intentionally but has not been accumulated.

The difference between what has been done and what has been accumulated is as follows. What has been done is an intention or is a performance with body or speech following an intention. What has been accumulated are any actions apart from the ten—those done in a dream and so forth—

conversely, what has not been accumulated are the ten types such as those done in a dream.[70]

That which will definitely be experienced has three categories based on when the effect will be experienced: that which will be experienced as a visible phenomenon is an action whose effect will be experienced in this life, that which will be experienced after taking rebirth is an action whose effect will be experienced in the next life, and that which will be experienced at another time is that which will be experienced in the life after that or beyond.

CONTEMPLATING KARMA AND ITS EFFECTS IN PARTICULAR

Through abandoning the ten nonvirtues, you do indeed obtain a good rebirth. But were you to achieve a fully qualified basis for accomplishing omniscience, you would be able to cover the ground in your meditations on the path in an unparalleled manner. Therefore you should try to achieve such a life.

This has two points: the fully ripened excellent qualities and their functions, and the causes of the fully ripened effects.

THE FULLY RIPENED EXCELLENT QUALITIES AND THEIR FUNCTIONS

The first has eight points: excellent lifespan, excellent complexion, excellent lineage, excellent power, respected words, renown for being powerful, male birth, and strength.

Excellent lifespan
The first is to have a long life, propelled by an earlier propelling action, and to live accordingly. On this basis you undertake actions for the purpose of yourself and others, accumulating a lot of virtue over a long period of time.

Excellent complexion
The second is to have a good complexion and attractive physical form, well-proportioned with complete sense powers. Owing to this, disciples gather, just delighted to see you, and listen to your words.

Excellent lineage

The third is to be born into an exalted family that is well known and respected by the world. Owing to this, your commands are accomplished and not transgressed.

Excellent power

The fourth is to have great wealth, many friends, and numerous helpers. Owing to this you gather many beings around you and bring them to spiritual maturity.

Respected words

The fifth is to not deceive others through your verbal or physical actions, so that they trust your words. Due to this you gather sentient beings with the four ways of gathering disciples and bring them to spiritual maturity.

Renown for being powerful

The sixth is to possess excellent qualities such as joyously striving in generosity and so forth, so that you become an object of veneration of great beings. Owing to this, they help you with all activities, acknowledge your deeds, and quickly heed your instructions.

Male birth

The seventh is to be born a male, which allows you to become a receptacle for all excellent qualities and, [87] with aspiration and effort, a receptacle for increasing wisdom. You are not afraid to be in a crowd, and nothing prevents you from traveling together with anyone else or from living in seclusion.

Strength

The eighth is to be naturally healthy and free of adversity, and to have great enthusiasm owing to the present conditions in your life, through the power of previous actions. Owing to that, you do not get overwhelmed by whatever goals you or others may have, and in reliance upon intense diligence, you attain the power of fine investigation, whereby clairvoyance will quickly develop.

THE CAUSES OF THE FULLY RIPENED EFFECTS

This has eight points, the first of which is not to harm any sentient being and to cultivate an attitude of nonharm. Furthermore it says [in the *Discourse Explaining Seven Qualities*]:

> By freeing beings bound for slaughter
> and likewise helping through sustaining life,
> by turning away from harming animals,
> you will obtain longevity.

> Out of caring for the sick as a healer,
> administering medicine,
> and not harming creatures with stones or sticks,
> you will be without illness.

The second is to offer light in the form of butter lamps and so forth, and new clothing. Furthermore it says:

> By relying on having no anger
> and offering jewelry, you will have a good physique.
> The result of having no jealousy
> is said to be good fortune.

The third is to overcome one's pride and, like a servant, to respect gurus and others. The fourth is to give food, clothing, and so forth to those who ask for it, as well as to benefit others without being asked, and to give to those who are suffering as well as to those who are fields of excellent qualities but in need of requisites. The fifth is to cultivate the habit of abandoning the four nonvirtues of speech. The sixth is to make aspirational prayers to accomplish all kinds of excellent qualities in future lives and to make offerings to the Three Jewels, one's parents, śrāvakas and pratyekabuddhas, abbots, masters, and gurus. The seventh is to rejoice in the excellent qualities of being a man, to see the disadvantages of being a woman and not rejoice in them, to oppose the inclinations of those who wish to be born as a female, and to rescue those who are to be castrated. The eighth is to accomplish what others are unable to do, to help them do what they can accomplish with your assistance, and to give food and drink to others. [88] If those eight causes are conjoined with three conditions, their fully ripened effects will be outstanding.

THE FIRST CONDITION: PURE ATTITUDE

There are two kinds of pure attitude: pure attitude related to oneself and pure attitude related to others. Each of these has two aspects.

Pure attitude related to oneself
The two aspects of pure attitude related to oneself are (1) to dedicate the virtues—the causes—to unsurpassed enlightenment without hoping for their maturation in saṃsāra and (2) to accomplish these causes from the depths of one's heart with earnest sincerity.

Pure attitude related to others
The two aspects of pure attitude related to others are (1) to give up jealousy, rivalry, and contempt when you see others practicing the Dharma at a higher, equal, or lower level than you and to instead rejoice, and (2) even if you are not capable of that, to think of it many times a day as the ideal way to act.

THE SECOND CONDITION: PURE APPLICATION

Pure application related to oneself
Pure application related to oneself consists in practicing virtue for a long time, continually, and intensively.

Pure application related to others
Pure application related to others consists in bringing those who are not correctly cultivating virtue to do so, and praising those who are cultivating virtue so that they take delight in it, causing them to continue without interruption and preventing them from abandoning it.

THE THIRD CONDITION: PURE FIELD

This is simply that both attitude and application are like a field in that they produce plenty of good fruit.

HAVING CONTEMPLATED KARMA AND ITS EFFECTS, HOW TO ENGAGE IN VIRTUE AND DESIST FROM NONVIRTUE

This has two points: a general presentation, and in particular, how to purify bad actions by means of the four powers.

A GENERAL PRESENTATION

Entering the Bodhisattva Way (2.63) says:

> "Suffering arises from nonvirtue;
> how can I surely be freed from it?"
> It is appropriate, day and night,
> always to contemplate nothing but this.

And (7.40):

> The Sage taught that resolute faith
> is the root of all virtues.
> And the root of that is to meditate
> continuously on fully ripened effects.

So, once you have come to understand virtuous and nonvirtuous actions and their effects, you should meditate on this over and over again because it is extremely difficult to gain certainty about it, since it is very hidden.

The *King of Concentrations Sūtra* says:

> Even if the moon and stars were to fall,
> the earth were to collapse with its mountains and towns,
> and the heavenly realms were to utterly change,
> still no word you have spoken would be untrue.

You should thus develop conviction in the words of the Tathāgata and maintain it. Unless you have gained uncontrived certainty about them, you will not gain the [89] certainty that pleases the victors about any Dharma teachings. Some profess to have gained certainty about emptiness yet do not have certainty about actions and their effects, nor even care about it. They have arrived at a mistaken understanding of emptiness, for if they understood emptiness, they would see it to be the meaning of dependent arising, which would be helpful for gaining certainty about actions and their effects. From the same sūtra:

> Like an illusion, a bubble, a mirage, or lightning,
> all phenomena are like the moon in water.
> Sentient living beings who after death
> pass to other lives are not perceived.
>
> Yet the actions they have done are not nonexistent,
> for whether virtuous or nonvirtuous, they cause their effects to ripen
>   accordingly.
> This logically consistent approach is excellent,
> though subtle and hard to see; it is the Victor's object of
>   understanding.

Therefore you should generate certainty about cause and effect pertaining to both types of karma and cut yourself off from the lower rebirths by continuously examining the three doors day and night. To start out with little understanding and no skill in differentiating these causes and effects and to remain carefree regarding the three doors only opens the door to the lower rebirths. *Questions of the Nāga King Sāgara Sūtra (Sāgaranāgarājaparipṛcchāsūtra)* says:

> Lord of nāgas, one Dharma of bodhisattvas cuts off falling back down and being born in the lower rebirths. What is that one Dharma? It is to finely investigate with regard to virtuous qualities, thinking, "How am I doing? Am I transgressing or maintaining them day and night?"

Having thought about it in this way, one turns away from faulty conduct, as expressed in the *Satyaka Chapter*:

> O king, do not commit the act of killing.
> Life is very precious for every being.
> Therefore those who wish to keep it long
> should not contemplate killing even deep down.

Like this make a consistent habit of relying on the mind of restraint, your motivation not moving one bit toward misdeeds like the ten nonvirtues.

Khamlungpa said to Phuchungwa, "Geshe Dromtönpa taught that only actions and their effects were of vital importance, [90] but nowadays explaining this, listening to it, and meditating on it are considered worthless. Is this just because it is difficult to practice?"

Phuchungwa said, "It is just so."

Dromtönpa said, "Followers of Atiśa, recklessness is totally inappropriate; this dependent arising is subtle."

Phuchungwa said, "In my old age I am at last turning to the *Sūtra of the Wise and the Foolish (Damamūkasūtra).*"[71]

And Sharawa said, "The Buddha taught that whatever errors and faults come about, they should not be blamed on an inauspicious place or on the construction of some building; it is simply that 'By doing this action in the past, I am born here now.'"

IN PARTICULAR, HOW TO PURIFY BAD ACTIONS BY MEANS OF THE FOUR POWERS

Even though you try to avoid being tainted by faulty conduct, some fault may occur under the influence of carelessness or a multitude of mental afflictions. Do not ignore it. You must make an effort to engage in the means for rectifying it as taught by the compassionate Teacher. Infractions against one's vows should be rectified as is taught according to each of the three types of vows, while bad actions should be rectified by means of the four powers.

THE POWER OF REMORSE

The first of the four powers is the power of remorse, which is to have great regret for the nonvirtuous deeds one has done since beginningless time. For it to arise, one needs to meditate on how the three types of effects, such as fully ripened effects, are produced. When applying this power, use the two confessions: the confession in the *Golden Light Sūtra* (*Suvarṇaprabhāsasūtra*) and the confession to the thirty-five buddhas.

THE POWER OF FULLY APPLYING THE ANTIDOTES

This has six points: relying on the profound sūtras, believing in emptiness, relying on recitation, relying on images, relying on worship, and relying on names.

Relying on the profound sūtras

The first is to hear the words of collections of sūtras like the Perfection of Wisdom Sūtras, retain them, read them, and so forth.

Believing in emptiness

The second is to enter into selfless and luminous reality and to trust in primordial purity.

Relying on recitation

The third is to recite special dhāraṇīs like the hundred-syllable mantra in accordance with the appropriate rituals. *Questions of Subāhu Tantra* (*Subāhuparipṛcchātantra*) says:

> As when the flames of forest fires in spring,
> uncontained, burn all the underbrush,
> so the wind of ethical conduct fans the fires of recitation,
> burning up bad deeds with flames of great joyous effort.
>
> As when the sun's rays strike the snow,
> it cannot withstand the brilliance and melts,
> so when the sunrays of ethical conduct and recitation [91]
> strike the snows of negative actions, they evaporate.

As when lighting a butter lamp in pitch darkness
dispels all the darkness with none remaining,
so the darkness of bad deeds accumulated in a thousand lives
is quickly dispelled by the lamp of recitation.

You should continue this recitation practice until you see signs that your bad deeds have been purified. In the *Dhāraṇī of the Goddess Cundā* (*Cundadevīdhāraṇī*), the signs are said to be dreaming of vomiting black food; drinking and vomiting things like yogurt or milk; seeing the sun and moon; flying in the sky; seeing a burning fire; subduing a buffalo or black-clothed people; seeing a saṅgha of fully ordained monks and nuns; climbing a tree from which milk emerges; seeing an elephant, a bull, a mountain, a lion throne, or a palace; and hearing the Dharma.[72]

Relying on images
The fourth is to create images of the Buddha, having gained faith in him.

Relying on worship
The fifth is to make various types of offerings to the Buddha and his stūpas.

Relying on names
The sixth is to listen to and retain the names of the buddhas and the great bodhisattvas. These are the practices that are explicitly mentioned in the *Compendium of Trainings*, but there are many others.

THE POWER OF TURNING AWAY FROM FURTHER FAULTS

The third of the four powers is the power of turning away from faults in the future, which is to completely resist committing the ten nonvirtues. *Sun Essence Sūtra* (*Sūryagarbhasūtra*) says that this destroys the karma of the three doors accumulated through killing and so on—everything you have done, caused others to do, or rejoiced in being done—as well as the afflictive obstructions and obstructions to the Dharma.[73] The *Commentary on the Vinaya Sūtra* explains that the intention of the question "Will you refrain from them in the future?" asked in the scriptural passage is that a confession without a sincere mind of restraint is nothing but words. Therefore the resolve to refrain from doing it in the future is crucial, though its development also depends on the first power.

THE POWER OF RELIANCE

The fourth of the four powers is the power of reliance, which is to go for refuge and cultivate bodhicitta.

The Victor said that in general there are various ways for beginners to purify bad actions, though the fully complete antidote is the four powers operating together.

THE MANNER OF PURIFICATION

The manner in which bad actions can be purified is as follows. The causes for the arising of great suffering in the lower rebirths are transformed into causes for the arising of minor suffering; or if one is reborn in the lower realms, one does not experience their sufferings; [92] or, having been purified, they result in a mere headache in one's present life. Likewise, something that would need to be experienced for a long time is transformed into something of short duration or that does not need to be experienced at all. There is no categorical certainty here because it also depends on whether the power of the person doing the purification is great or small, and on whether the four opponent powers are complete or incomplete, intense or not intense, of long or short duration, and so on.

The statement in the sūtras and the Vinaya that "actions will never be lost even in a hundred eons" implies "if the antidotes of the four powers are not cultivated." Also, *Commentary on the Perfection of Wisdom in Eight Thousand Lines* (*Aṣṭasāhasrikāprajñāpāramitāvyākhyāna*) says that, if purified in accordance with the explanations, even karma certain to be experienced is purified through the antidote of the four powers. *Blaze of Reasoning* (*Tarkajvālā*) says that once you have thus weakened the potential to bring forth a fully ripened effect by means of confession and the resolve to exercise restraint and the like, the fully ripened effect will not come about even if other conditions are met. Conversely, wrong views and anger can similarly overpower the roots of virtue.

Although through confession and the resolve to exercise restraint you may be able to purify karma so that none at all remains, there is still a big difference between the purity of not being tainted by faults from the beginning and the purity after confession. For example, *Bodhisattva Levels* says that if a root downfall has occurred, it can be restored by taking the bodhisattva vow again, but it will be impossible to reach the first ground in this life. Also, the *Gathering All the Threads Sūtra* says that once the bad action of abandoning the Dharma, which is explained in that sūtra, has occurred, if one confesses it three times every day for seven years, the bad action will be purified, but still it will take ten eons even at the quickest to attain the level of forbearance on the path of preparation. Therefore *purification without remainder* means that the production of unpleasant effects is purified without remainder. However, since the arising of realizations of the path and so forth will be much delayed, you should try not to be tainted from the beginning. Also for that reason it says that āryas do not deliberately engage even in subtle bad actions or infractions even for the sake of their lives. If there were no difference between purifying them through confession and their not arising from the beginning, there would be no need to act like that. In the mundane world, too, if a wounded arm, leg, and so forth heals again, still it will not be the same as if it had never been wounded to begin with. [93]

THE MEASURE OF THAT ATTITUDE HAVING ARISEN

Previously you had an uncontrived interest in this life only, and your interest in future lives was just a vague understanding elicited by the words of others. Once their ranking has been switched so that future lives have become the main interest and this life nothing but a byproduct, the attitude of persons of lesser capacity has developed. As this nevertheless needs to be stabilized, you should strive to train in it even after it has arisen.

CLEARING UP MISCONCEPTIONS ABOUT THAT

The scriptures say that one must turn the mind away from all the advantages of cyclic existence. This has been the basis of some confusion. Some people may think it is improper to strive for a higher rebirth with an excellent body, wealth, and so forth because those are part of cyclic existence.

In terms of what one should strive for, there are both temporary and ultimate goals. Even those who strive for liberation need to temporarily strive for the good things within cyclic existence, such as an excellent body and so forth, since definite goodness is ultimately attained on the basis of a continuous succession of such lives.

Not everything that is an excellent body, wealth, and retinue of a higher state is included in cyclic existence, because the culmination of an excellent body and so forth is the form body of a buddha, the wealth of his field, and his retinue. It is with this intention that *Ornament for the Mahāyāna Sūtras* says the first four perfections accomplish the excellent body, excellent wealth, excellent retinue, and excellent undertakings of a higher state. Many scriptures explain that they accomplish the form body.

This concludes the explanation of training the mind in the stages of the path shared in common with persons of lesser capacity.

The Stages Shared with
Persons of Medium Capacity

11 | Suffering

TRAINING THE MIND IN THE STAGES OF THE PATH SHARED IN COMMON WITH PERSONS OF MEDIUM CAPACITY

THUS, HAVING RECOLLECTED death and contemplated how you fall into the lower rebirths after death, you turn your mind away from this world and strive for fortunate rebirths. Then you give up bad actions through the common refuge practice and through ascertaining virtuous and nonvirtuous actions and their effects. By then putting effort into accomplishing virtue, you will indeed attain the state of the fortunate rebirths. However, that is not considered sufficient here. Rather, after you develop the attitude common to persons of lesser capacity, you develop the attitude common to persons of medium capacity, which counteracts adherence to cyclic existence as a whole. Based on that, you will develop bodhicitta and be led onto the path of persons of great capacity. [94] Therefore train in the attitude common to persons of medium capacity. Even though you attain the state of a god or a human in this manner, you do not pass beyond compositional suffering. Therefore it is a mistake to consider that state to be naturally happy since in reality it is devoid of happiness, and in the end it is bad because you will certainly fall into the lower rebirths again.

HOW TO DEVELOP THE MIND STRIVING FOR LIBERATION

Training the mind in the stages of the path shared in common with persons of medium capacity has four points: the actual training in the attitude, the measure of its development, eliminating misconceptions, and determining the nature of the path leading to liberation.

THE ACTUAL TRAINING IN THE ATTITUDE

This has two points: identifying the mind striving for liberation and the methods for generating it.

IDENTIFYING THE MIND STRIVING FOR LIBERATION

Liberation is freedom from bondage. Karma and the afflictions bind one in cyclic existence. Through the power of these two, the aggregates are reborn in one of the three realms, such as the desire realm, as one of the five or six types of beings, such as gods, and in one of the four birthplaces, such as a womb.[74] This is the meaning of bondage; therefore freedom from this is liberation. The wish to attain that is the mind striving for liberation.

THE METHODS FOR GENERATING THE MIND STRIVING FOR LIBERATION

Developing the wish to pacify the suffering of thirst, for instance, depends on seeing the torment of thirst as undesirable. Likewise, developing the wish to attain the liberation that is the thorough pacification of the suffering of the appropriated aggregates also depends on seeing the faults of the appropriated aggregates and that they have the nature of suffering. Therefore, if you meditate on the faults of cyclic existence but do not produce the intention to reject them, the wish to attain the pacification of suffering will not arise either. *Four Hundred Stanzas* (8.12) says:

> How could one who is not disenchanted here
> have any respect for peace?

This has two points: contemplating the faults of cyclic existence, the truth of suffering; and contemplating the stages of involvement in cyclic existence, the origins.

CONTEMPLATING THE FAULTS OF CYCLIC EXISTENCE, THE TRUTH OF SUFFERING

This has two points: showing why the truth of suffering is taught as the first of the four truths and the actual meditation on suffering.

SHOWING WHY THE TRUTH OF SUFFERING IS TAUGHT AS THE FIRST OF THE FOUR TRUTHS

Someone might ask, "Since origins are causes and the truth of suffering is their effect, origins are earlier and sufferings are later. So why is it that the Blessed One, [95] contrary to that sequence, taught: 'Monks, this is the noble truth of suffering. This is the noble truth of origins'?"

There is no fault in that because the fact that the Teacher stated the cause and the effect in reverse order has great significance for practice.

Someone might reply, "How so?" If the unerring desire for liberation from cyclic existence has not initially arisen in the disciple himself, how should he be guided to liberation while lacking its root? In fact, disciples are initially shrouded in the darkness of ignorance and deceived by the error that apprehends as happiness the advantages of cyclic existence, which are suffering. *Four Hundred Stanzas* (7.1) says:

> Child, if this ocean of suffering
> has no limits in any respect,
> why are you who are drowning in it
> not experiencing fear?

In the same way, many aspects of suffering were taught by saying, "This, in reality, is not happiness but rather suffering." Thus the truth of suffering was taught first because one must develop disenchantment. Then, when you see that you have fallen into the ocean of suffering and want to be liberated from it, you will see the need to counter suffering. When you understand that you will not counter suffering unless you counteract its cause, you come to understand the truth of origins and wonder, "What is the cause?" That is why the truth of origins was taught next. You see that the suffering of cyclic existence is produced by contaminated actions, that those actions are produced by mental afflictions, and that the root of the latter is the apprehension of a self. Then, once such an understanding of the truth of origins has arisen and you see that the apprehension of a self can be countered, you vow to actualize the cessation that puts a stop to suffering. This is why the truth of cessation was taught next.

Someone might think, "Well then, as the wish for liberation arises when the truth of suffering is presented, it would make sense to present the truth of cessation after the truth of suffering." However, there is no fault. Even though at that point the wish for liberation is present in the form of the thought "If only I had achieved cessation, the pacification of suffering...," you have not identified the cause of suffering and do not see that the cause can be countered. Therefore you do not apprehend liberation as something to be attained or think, "I should actualize cessation." In that manner, once you apprehend liberation and think, "I should actualize cessation," you will engage in the truth of the path and wonder, "What is the path leading there?" [96] That is why the truth of the path was stated at the end.

The four truths are taught in this way many times throughout the Mahāyāna and Hīnayāna. They are extremely important for achieving liberation because the Buddha condensed in them the crucial points of entry into cyclic existence and reversal from it. Since it is a major threshold for practice, students need to be guided in this order.[75] If you do not reflect on the truth of suffering and you thus lack any genuine revulsion for cyclic existence, the wish to achieve liberation will become mere words, because whatever you do will become an origin of new suffering. If you do not reflect on the origins and come to a good understanding of karma and the afflictions as the root of cyclic existence, you will miss the crucial point of the path like someone shooting an arrow who does not see the target. You will perceive as the path that which is not the path to freedom from existence, whereupon your hardships will be fruitless. And, if you do not know suffering along with its origins as that which should be abandoned, you will not identify the liberation that is their thorough pacification, whereby your striving for liberation will also end up as nothing but an arrogant presumption.

THE ACTUAL MEDITATION ON SUFFERING

This has two points: contemplating the suffering of cyclic existence in general and contemplating the suffering of the individual realms.

CONTEMPLATING THE SUFFERING OF CYCLIC EXISTENCE IN GENERAL

This has two points: contemplating the eight types of suffering and contemplating the six types of suffering.

Contemplating the Eight Types of Suffering

With regard to practicing the entire cycle of meditations common to persons of medium capacity, here you should also take up the common points explained in the context of persons of lesser capacity. With regard to practicing the ones that are not common to both, if you have the mental strength, you should practice them in meditation as explained here. If your mental strength is small, you should disregard the scriptural citations and just practice the essential meaning of what is described in a given context.

Although these are analytical meditations, you should cease all agitation and so forth, focusing the mind on the object of meditation without allowing it to wander off to other objects, whether virtuous, nonvirtuous, or unspecified. Meditate continuously from within a state of extreme clarity and lucidity, without allowing your mind to fall under the influence of drowsiness or laxity, for it was taught that virtuous activities have minimal results if the mind is distracted toward other things. As *Entering the Bodhisattva Way* (5.16) says:

> Reciting, austerities, and the like
> the Seer taught as meaningless
> if done with the mind distracted elsewhere,
> even if practiced for a long time. [97]

The *Sūtra of Cultivating Faith in the Mahāyāna* (*Mahāyānaprasādaprabhāvanāsūtra*) says:

> Child of the lineage, this enumeration shows that, in this manner, bodhisattvas' faith in the Mahāyāna and anything that springs from the Mahāyāna spring from reflecting correctly

about the meaning and the Dharma with a mind that is utterly undistracted.

Here, "a mind that is utterly undistracted" is a mind that does not stray toward something other than its virtuous object. "The meaning and the Dharma" refers to the meaning and the words. "Reflecting correctly" is to reflect having analyzed with a finely investigating awareness. This shows that both nondistraction and investigation are necessary for every accomplishment of excellent qualities. Therefore it was taught that for every accomplishment of excellent qualities in the three vehicles, two things are necessary: (1) actual śamatha—a single-pointed mind that abides on a virtuous observed object without being distracted—or a similitude of that, and (2) actual special insight, which individually analyzes a virtuous observed object and differentiates the ultimate mode of being from things in their variety, or a similitude of that. In accordance with that, the *Unraveling the Intent Sūtra* (*Saṃdhinirmocanasūtra*) says:

> Maitreya, you should know that all virtuous phenomena are the result of śamatha and special insight, whether mundane or supramundane and whether of śrāvakas, bodhisattvas, or tathāgatas.

Śamatha and special insight must include both actual and a similitude, for it is not certain that all excellent qualities of the three vehicles are effects of actual śamatha and special insight.

THE SUFFERING OF BIRTH

Here, contemplating the suffering of birth, the first of eight types of suffering, has five points.

Birth is suffering because it is painful. Hell beings, perpetually suffering hungry ghosts, [98] beings born from wombs, and beings born from eggs are born with a lot of visceral sensations of pain.

Birth is associated with negative tendencies. Because it is connected with the seeds that produce, sustain, and increase mental afflictions, birth is unsuited to the service of virtue, and it is unsuited to being controlled at will.

Birth is the origin of suffering. The suffering of aging, illness, death, and so forth develop from taking birth in the three realms.

Birth is the origin of the afflictions. Once you have been born into cyclic existence, the three poisons of attachment, hatred, and confusion arise toward objects. Again, because of that, the body and mind are thoroughly unpacified, suffer, and consequently do not abide in happiness. Thus body and mind are tormented in various ways by the mental afflictions.

Birth is suffering because it is in the nature of unwanted separation. It cannot be avoided that the end of all birth is death. This is undesirable and causes beings to experience only suffering.

Think about these points again and again.

The suffering of aging

Contemplation of the suffering of aging has five points.

Your attractive body completely deteriorates such that your spine becomes curved like a bow, your head becomes white like edelweiss, your forehead becomes covered in wrinkles like a cutting board, and so on. Thereby your youth deteriorates and you become ugly.

Power and strength deteriorate such that when you sit down, you look like a sack of soil when the rope holding it is cut. When you get up, you look like tree roots being uprooted. When you speak, you babble incoherently. And when you walk, you hobble, and so on.

The faculties deteriorate such that your eyes and so forth do not clearly perceive forms and so forth any more, and the strength of your memory and so forth diminish as you grow forgetful and so forth.

The enjoyment of sense objects declines. Food and drink become difficult to digest, and you can no longer enjoy other pleasures.

When the lifespan deteriorates completely, you suffer because, your lifespan largely spent, you face death.

Think about these points again and again. Chenngawa said, "The suffering of death is vicious but brief. This aging process is just vicious." Kamapa said, "It is good that old age comes gradually. If it came all at once, it would be unbearable." [99]

THE SUFFERING OF ILLNESS

Contemplation of the suffering of illness has five points.

The nature of the body changes in that the flesh becomes loose, the skin dries up, and so forth.

Suffering and mental unhappiness increase such that you dwell in them most of the time. The bodily constituents, water and so forth, become unbalanced and fluctuate wildly in strength, producing pain in the body. That in turn causes unhappiness in the mind both day and night.

You lack the wish to enjoy pleasant things. You are told that pleasant things are harmful when you are ill, so you are not free to indulge in them as you wish. Thus you cannot do whatever you want.

You must undergo the unpleasant against your will. You must ingest unpleasant medicine, food, drink, and so forth. Likewise, you must rely on rough tests and treatments such as being burned with fire, pierced with sharp instruments, and the like.

You will lose your life. You suffer on seeing that the illness is incurable. Think about these points in detail.

THE SUFFERING OF DEATH

Contemplation of the suffering of death has five points. You are separated from your beloved and excellent possessions, relatives, companions, and body, and at the time of death you experience suffering and intense mental unhappiness. Think about these types of suffering again and again until they produce disenchantment. The way in which the first four become suffering is that you suffer seeing that you will be separated from them.

THE SUFFERING OF MEETING WITH THE UNPLEASANT

The suffering of meeting with the unpleasant has five points. As soon as you meet an enemy, for example, suffering and mental unhappiness arise. You are beset with fear of being punished by him, fear of harsh words, and fear of dying miserably. You also suspect and fear going to a lower rebirth after death because of transgressing the Dharma. Think about these types of suffering.

THE SUFFERING OF SEPARATION FROM THE PLEASANT

The suffering of separation from the pleasant has five points. When you are separated, for example, from a dear relative, sorrow arises in your mind, there is lamentation in your speech, your body is harmed, your mind is tormented by the memory of and desire for the excellent qualities of the object, and you miss the pleasure of it. Think about these types of suffering. [100]

THE SUFFERING OF SEEKING WHAT YOU DESIRE AND NOT GETTING IT

The suffering of seeking what you desire and not getting it has five points that are similar to those associated with separation from the pleasant. Seeking what you desire but not getting it means not getting what you have been hoping for despite your efforts in seeking it, such as doing farm work but not reaping a harvest and doing business but not accruing a profit. This is the suffering of disappointment.

"IN BRIEF, THE FIVE APPROPRIATED AGGREGATES ARE SUFFERING"

Contemplating the meaning of the statement "In brief, the five appropriated aggregates are suffering" has five points. They are a vessel of suffering yet to come; they are a vessel of the suffering already arisen; they are a vessel for the suffering of suffering; they are a vessel for the suffering of change; and they are in the nature of the suffering of conditioning. Think about these points again and again.

Here, the first point is that the sufferings of the next rebirth onward are induced in dependence upon the appropriation of the aggregates. Second, the present aggregates become the basis of illness, aging, and so forth, which depend on them. The aggregates give rise to both the third and fourth types of suffering due to their relationship with the negative tendencies of each. Fifth, by their mere existence, the appropriated aggregates arise in the nature of the suffering of conditioning, because all volitional formations under the control of something other—namely, previous karma and mental afflictions—are the suffering of conditioning. If no genuine disenchantment develops toward cyclic existence, which is of the nature of the appropriated aggregates, there is no way a genuine mind striving for liberation will develop, and great compassion for the sentient beings wandering in cyclic existence cannot develop either. Therefore these contemplations are extremely important whichever vehicle you enter, the Mahāyāna or Hīnayāna.

Contemplating the Six Types of Suffering

Letter to a Friend [in verses 65–76] states the six faults of cyclic existence as lacking certainty, lacking satisfaction, having to discard one's body again and again, being reborn again and again, changing from high to low again and again, and lacking companions. Summarized into three, they are (1) there is nothing reliable in cyclic existence, (2) there is no final point of satisfaction no matter how much of its happiness you enjoy, and (3) you have been in it since beginningless time.

The first has four points: (1) It is inappropriate to rely on the body you have attained; you will discard your body again and again. (2) It is inappropriate to rely on benefit and harm done to you; there is no certainty as to whether your father will become your son, your mother your wife, an enemy someone very dear to you, and the like. (3) It is inappropriate to rely on the excellences you have achieved; [101] you fall from high places to low ones. And (4) it is inappropriate to rely on companions; you have to go on without them in the end.

The third one is that you are reborn again and again; there seems to be no end to the continuity of births. Reflect in this manner again and again.

Furthermore, most of the present happy feelings that increase our attachment are happy mental states that arise with respect to a relief of suffering. There is no intrinsic happiness that is unrelated to the elimination of suffering. For instance, if you suffer because you have walked too much, a happy mind arises due to sitting down: happiness appears to arise gradually, while the great previous suffering gradually ceases. However, it is not intrinsic happiness, for if you sit too much, again, that will produce suffering as before. Just as suffering increases to the same extent as you are subject to the causes of suffering, so too should walking, sitting, lying, eating and drinking, sun and shade, and the like increase your happiness to the same extent that you indulge in them, if those were causes of intrinsic happiness. However, it appears that if these are extended long term, only more suffering is produced.

These points are also set forth in the *Descent into the Womb Sūtra* and the root text of *Four Hundred Stanzas* and its commentary.

CONTEMPLATING THE SUFFERING OF THE INDIVIDUAL REALMS

This has four points: the suffering of the three lower rebirths, the suffering of humans, the suffering of demigods, and the suffering of gods.

THE SUFFERING OF THE THREE LOWER REBIRTHS

This has already been explained.

THE SUFFERING OF HUMANS

This consists in the sufferings of hunger and thirst, the unpleasant contact with heat and cold, frantic activity, and fatigue. In addition, you should understand the seven types of suffering, birth, aging, illness, death, and so forth[76] by means of the previous explanations. Furthermore, the *Discourse on the Collections* (*Sambhāraparikathā*) says:

> All the sufferings of lower rebirths
> also appear to exist for humans.
> They are troubled by suffering like beings in hell,
> are subjects of Yama by their poverty,
> and also have the suffering of animals:
> powerful ones oppress the weak
> by force, inflicting harm on them.
> They are just like raging rivers.

And in *Four Hundred Stanzas* (2.8):

> Higher ones have mental suffering,
> lower ones have physical pain.

> This world is overwhelmed by these
> two types of suffering every day. [102]

Reflect in accordance with these statements.

THE SUFFERING OF DEMIGODS

It is said that the demigods are mentally tormented by jealousy that cannot bear the wealth of the gods. When, based on that, they fight with the gods, they experience many sufferings of having their bodies chopped up, split, and the like. Although they possess intelligence, they have fully ripened obstructions and consequently cannot see the truth while in that body.

THE SUFFERING OF GODS

This has two points: the suffering of desire-realm gods and the suffering of gods of the uppermost realms.

THE SUFFERING OF DESIRE-REALM GODS

This has three points: the sufferings of dying, transmigrating, and falling; the suffering of jealousy; and the sufferings of being chopped up, split, killed, and banished.

THE SUFFERINGS OF DYING, TRANSMIGRATING, AND FALLING

This has two points: the suffering of dying and transmigrating, and the suffering of falling to a lower abode.

THE SUFFERING OF DYING AND TRANSMIGRATING

At the time of dying and transmigrating, when a god has seen the five signs of death, the suffering that springs from this is far greater than the happiness that previously arose from enjoying the delights of gods. The five signs of death are a hideous complexion, dislike for one's seat, wilting of one's flower garlands, one's clothes becoming smelly, and sweat, which until then did not exist, appearing on one's body.

THE SUFFERING OF FALLING TO A LOWER ABODE

In the same way, *Letter to a Friend* (v. 101) says:

> As they transmigrate from the world of the gods,
> in the event that nothing virtuous remains,
> they veer without control into the plights
> of animals, hungry ghosts, and beings of hell.

THE SUFFERING OF JEALOUSY

For the gods with extensive heaps of merit, the most exquisite sense pleasures arise. When the offspring of the gods with little merit see that, they envy them and experience acute suffering and mental unhappiness.

THE SUFFERINGS OF BEING CHOPPED UP, SPLIT, KILLED, AND BANISHED

When the gods fight with the demigods, they experience the suffering of having their limbs and minor body parts chopped off, the suffering of their bodies being split, and the suffering of being killed. If their heads are chopped off, they die, but the remaining limbs and minor body parts that are chopped off or split grow back, and they survive. As for banishment, when there is conflict, the more powerful gods drive the weaker offspring of the gods out of their abodes.

THE SUFFERING OF GODS OF THE UPPERMOST REALMS

Although gods in the two uppermost realms do not have the suffering of suffering, [103] they have mental afflictions and obstructions, and they lack control over their death, their transmigration, and their next state, which is why they suffer through negative tendencies. Furthermore the *Discourse on the Collections* says:

One in the form or formless realms,
having transcended the suffering of suffering,
a master of the bliss of concentration
who stays immovable for eons,
is still not certainly freed at all;
he will still fall from there again.
If he emerges and seems to abide
beyond the whirlpool of pain of lower rebirths,
he won't last long there even with effort.
Like a bird in flight high up,
like an arrow shot by a child,
he also ends up falling;
like butter lamps that blaze for long
while actually perishing moment by moment,
he is completely oppressed by the suffering
called "compositional, thoroughly changing."

12 | Mental Afflictions

THIS HAS THREE POINTS: how the mental afflictions arise, how karma is thereby accumulated, and how you die, transmigrate, and take rebirth.

HOW THE MENTAL AFFLICTIONS ARISE

Although both karma and mental afflictions are necessary as causes that establish cyclic existence, the mental afflictions are primary. This is because if there are no mental afflictions, even though there is karma beyond counting accumulated previously, since the cooperative conditions for karma are absent, the sprout of suffering is not established—just as a sprout is not established from a seed that lacks humidity, soil, and so forth. It is also because if mental afflictions are present, even without any previously accumulated karma, karma is immediately accumulated anew, and future aggregates will be appropriated. That is also how it is set forth in the *Commentary on Compendium of Valid Cognition* (*Pramāṇavārttika*, 2.105–6):

> For those who have passed beyond craving for existences,
> karma cannot impel any more rebirths,
> because the cooperating factors have been exhausted.

And (2.276),

> For if craving is present, they will recur.

Therefore it is crucial that you rely on the antidotes to the mental afflictions, and that depends on knowing the mental afflictions, which is why you should become conversant with them.

This has three points: the actual identification of the mental afflictions, the stages by which they arise, and the faults of the mental afflictions.

THE ACTUAL IDENTIFICATION OF THE MENTAL AFFLICTIONS

This has ten points. The first of those, desire, observes an attractive, pleasant, external or internal object [104] and is subsequently attached to it. To illustrate: just as oil that has penetrated into cloth is hard to remove, it is also difficult to separate desire from its object, as it clings to it and intensifies.

Anger is a hostile attitude. It is an unruly mind that, upon observing a basis of suffering such as sentient beings, suffering, weapons, thorns, and so forth, intends to inflict harm on those objects.

Pride is a puffed-up mind based on the view of the transitory collection. It observes one's external or internal level or qualities and engages them with an aspect of superiority.

Ignorance is afflicted non-knowing owing to a mind that is unclear with regard to the nature of the four truths, actions and their effects, and the Three Jewels.

Doubt is to observe those three objects—the four truths and so forth—and think, "Do they exist or do they not exist? Are they a certain way or are they not?"

The *view of the transitory collection* is an afflicted intelligence that observes the appropriated aggregates and views them as a self or belonging to a self thinking, "I" or "mine." Here *transitory* means impermanent and *collection* means multiple, so the object that it views is a mere impermanent and manifold phenomenon. It is given the name *view of the transitory collection* to indicate that there is no permanent unitary person.

The *view holding to an extreme* is an afflicted intelligence that observes the self as it is apprehended by the view of the transitory collection and views it either as permanent and eternal or as being annihilated without being reborn from this existence to a future one.

The *view holding a bad view to be best* is an afflicted intelligence that observes any of these three—the view of the transitory collection, the view holding to an extreme, or a wrong view—and the aggregates of the person holding the view based on which the view arises, and holds that view to be best.

The *view holding ethics and ascetic practices to be best* is an afflicted intelligence that observes ethics of giving up immorality and ascetic practices that set a certain dress code, manners, and bodily or verbal comportment as well as the aggregates through which the view arises and views them as sufficient for purifying bad actions, liberating from the mental afflictions, and releasing one from cyclic existence.

A *wrong view* is an afflicted intelligence that makes denials, like saying that past and future lives, actions and their effects, and the like do not exist, or that superimposes the apprehension of Īśvara, a fundamental nature, and the like as the cause of sentient beings. [105]

These are the mental afflictions as identified from the perspective that is common to both the higher and lower tenet systems. The Prāsaṅgika Madhyamaka system will be explained below.

THE STAGES BY WHICH THE MENTAL AFFLICTIONS ARISE

If the view of the transitory collection and ignorance are posited as distinct, the stages of how the mental afflictions arise must be understood in the following manner. For instance, once darkness has fallen on a coiled rope, the mind will apprehend it as a snake if the state of the rope is not clear. Likewise, because the darkness of ignorance obscures the clear state of the aggregates, the delusion regarding the aggregates as a self arises, and from that the other mental afflictions arise.

If those two are posited as the same, the view of the transitory collection itself is the root of mental afflictions. In fact, when the view of the transitory collection apprehends a self, a distinction is made between self and other. Once that is made, attachment to one's own side and hatred for the other side arise. Also, conceit arises upon observing that self. That very self is then held to be permanent or subject to annihilation and is viewed as the self and so forth. Then the bad activities connected with it are upheld as supreme. Likewise, wrong views are generated that think, "The Teacher who taught selflessness, the actions and effects he taught, the four truths, the Three Jewels, and so forth do not exist." Or, alternatively, the doubt is generated that thinks, "Do they exist or not? Are they a certain way or are they not?" The *Commentary on Compendium of Valid Cognition* (2.221–22) says:

> When there's a self, there's awareness of other.
> Dividing between them brings grasping and anger.
> Every fault comes into being
> closely connected with those two.

THE FAULTS OF THE MENTAL AFFLICTIONS

Ornament for the Mahāyāna Sūtras (27.25–26) says:

> The mental afflictions destroy you, destroy sentient beings, and
>   destroy your ethics.
> You become lax and poor; guardians and teachers revile you.
> There will be nasty disputes; you will take rebirth elsewhere in
>   unfree states.
> Through the loss of what you had attained or had hoped to attain,
>   there is great mental suffering.

Entering the Bodhisattva Way (4.28–33) says:

> Enemies such as hatred and craving,
> do not have arms, legs, and so on.
> They have no valor either, so why is it
> that they have reduced me to servitude?
>
> While abiding in my mind,
> they happily inflict harm on me. [106]
> The patience that does not get angry at them
> is unsuitable blameworthy patience.
>
> Even if the gods and demigods
> were all to rise as enemies against me,
> they could not lead or put me into
> the fires of the Avīci hell.

The mental afflictions, these powerful foes,
throw me into it in one instant,
where nothing met with, not even Mount Meru,
is left behind—not even ashes.

Compared to my foes, the mental afflictions—
protracted, with neither beginning nor end—
not one of all my other enemies
could possibly endure so long.

While everyone helps you and makes you happy
when you act harmoniously and with reverence,
if you attend to mental afflictions,
they inflict suffering and harm in return.

Reflect on the faults stated here. Gönpawa said:

> To eliminate the mental afflictions, you must know their faults,
> their definitions, their antidotes, and the causes for their arising.
> Once you have understood their faults, you should see them as
> faults and apprehend them as enemies. If you do not understand
> their faults, you will not understand them to be enemies. There-
> fore you should contemplate them along the lines of the state-
> ments from *Ornament for the Mahāyāna Sūtras* and *Entering
> the Bodhisattva Way*.

And:

> In order to know the definitions of the mental afflictions, you
> should also study the Abhidharma, at least *Explanation of the Five
> Aggregates* (*Pañcaskandhaprakaraṇa*). Once you have become
> acquainted with the root and secondary afflictions, you will iden-
> tify attachment, anger, and so forth, whatever it is, as soon as they
> arise in your mindstream, thinking, "This is that. Oh no! It has
> arisen," and you will then fight the mental afflictions.

This kind of understanding is necessary.

13 | Cyclic Existence and Liberation

How karma is thereby accumulated

THIS HAS TWO POINTS: identifying the karma that is accumulated, and how karma is accumulated.

Identifying the karma that is accumulated

Mental karma is the karma that is intention, the mental factor that makes its concomitant mind move and urges it toward objects.

First, the Vaibhāṣikas divide the karma of body and speech that is motivated by that intention into the perceptible and the imperceptible and posit them as only being form. Master Vasubandhu refutes that and maintains that karma of body and speech is the intention that operates together with the perceptible physical and verbal actions, whereby he explains both types of karma to also be intention. [107] In this regard, nonvirtuous karma is *nonmeritorious* karma. *Meritorious* karma is virtuous karma included in the level of the desire realm. *Immovable* karma is contaminated virtuous karma included in the levels of the form and formless realms.[77]

How karma is accumulated

Once you have directly realized selflessness, you can still be reborn in cyclic existence under the power of karma and mental afflictions. However, you do not newly accumulate any propelling karma. Therefore those who accumulate the karma that propels one into cyclic existence are all ordinary beings up to and including those abiding on the great level of supreme worldly dharma on the Mahāyāna path of preparation. If, with that body, you create nonvirtuous actions by means of the three doors—for instance, killing—you will accumulate nonmeritorious karma. If you create virtuous actions, such as giving gifts and guarding ethics, you will accumulate meritorious karma. If you cultivate the śamatha and the like included in the [form-realm] dhyānas and the levels of the formless realm, you will accumulate immovable karma.

HOW YOU DIE AND ARE REBORN

This has five points: conditions for death, the minds of death, from where the heat withdraws, how the intermediate state is reached after death, and how you take rebirth in an incarnation.

CONDITIONS FOR DEATH

To die from the exhaustion of one's lifespan is to die when the time has come, when one's entire lifespan propelled by previous karma is exhausted. To die following the exhaustion of one's merit is, for example, to die from a lack of basic requirements. To die by failing to avoid dangers includes the nine causes and conditions for death, such as overeating, taught in the sūtras.[78]

THE MINDS OF DEATH

Both virtuous minds such as faith and nonvirtuous minds such as attachment arise in the mind as long as coarse compositional factors operate depending either on one's own actions or on being made to recall them by others. To die with an unspecified mind implies that one did not recall virtuous or nonvirtuous minds by oneself nor was one reminded of them by others. For those who have cultivated virtue, death is like going from thick darkness into light. At the time of death, various pleasant dream-like forms appear to them. They die happily, and even the end-of-life agony is of very minor severity. For those who have cultivated nonvirtue, it is like going from light into thick darkness. At the time of death, various dream-like repulsive forms appear to them, intense feelings of pain arise, and the end-of-life agony is also severe. In all birthplaces except for gods and hell beings, there is end-of-life agony.[79] [108]

Neither happiness nor suffering, as explained above, arise in those who have an unspecified mind. At the time of death, whichever mind is most familiar becomes manifest, virtuous or nonvirtuous, and other minds do not subsequently operate. If they are equally familiar, that which is recalled first will become manifest, and others do not subsequently operate. At the time when the mind becomes subtle, virtuous and nonvirtuous minds come to a stop and become unspecified minds. At the time of death, the attachment to a self that they have long been familiar with befalls everyone until perception becomes unclear. After that, you take joy in a body under the influence of attachment to a self and think, "I am becoming nonexistent." That is the cause for reaching the intermediate state. While attachment to a self also arises in stream enterers and once returners, they analyze it with wisdom and eliminate it rather than acquiescing to it, just like, for instance, a strong person beating someone weak. That attachment to a self does not arise in nonreturners.

FROM WHERE THE HEAT WITHDRAWS

In those who have cultivated nonvirtue, the heat first withdraws from the upper part of the corpse and dissipates down to the heart. In those who have cultivated virtue, the heat first withdraws from the lower part of the corpse and dissipates up to the heart. In both cases the consciousness transfers from the heart. The place where the consciousness first enters into the semen and blood becomes the heart, and where it eventually exits is that very place it first entered.

HOW THE INTERMEDIATE STATE IS REACHED AFTER DEATH

Death and the intermediate state are reached from the place the consciousness exits, as explained above, without a break, just like the swing on the armature of a scale. A being in the intermediate state has complete sense powers, such as eyes, and has the body of whatever it will become in the following birth. Its vision is flawless like the divine eye until it takes rebirth, and its body is also unobstructed as though possessed of magical powers.[80] It is seen by intermediate-state beings of similar type and by the flawless divine eye arisen from meditation. It is set forth in the *Treasury of Abhidharma* that once any being has reached the intermediate state, there is no diverting it into some other rebirth; however, the *Compendium of Abhidharma* (*Abhidharmasamuccaya*) also explains reversals.

The intermediate existence of those who have cultivated nonvirtue appears like black cloth or like a dark night, [109] and the intermediate existence of those who have cultivated virtue appears like a white blanket or a moonlit night. It sees intermediate-state beings of similar type as well as their and its own birthplaces. The *Descent into the Womb Sūtra* states that the intermediate state of hell beings is like the color of a burnt log, the intermediate state of animals is like smoke, the intermediate state of hungry ghosts is like water, the intermediate state of desire-realm gods and humans is like gold, and the intermediate state of form-realm gods is white.

If you are reborn from the formless realm into the two lower rebirths, there is an intermediate state. However, if you are born from those two realms into the formless realm, the aggregates of the formless realm are obtained wherever you die, and there is no intermediate state. It is taught that the intermediate-state being of a god travels upward, that of a human travels straight ahead, and that of someone who has done faulty actions travels downward with the eyes cast downward. For the three lower rebirths the same meaning is intended.

As for its lifespan, if it does not find the conditions for rebirth, it abides for as many as seven days. If it finds them, the number of days is uncertain. If it does not find them, it changes bodies and abides up to seven times seven days. However, it does not abide any longer than that, since it will certainly find the conditions for rebirth by then. After seven days in the intermediate state, a god might die and transfer into, for example, another intermediate state of a god or an intermediate state of a human being, and so forth. This is because the seeds of the intermediate state change through the changing activity of other karma. It is the same for other intermediate states.

How you take rebirth in an incarnation

The *Many Levels* (*Bahubhumika*) teaches that when you are born in a womb, an erroneous vision arises with regard to the semen and blood of your father and mother. In that moment, like an illusion, you see your parents having intercourse even though they are not, and you develop attachment to them. The *Treasury of Abhidharma Autocommentary*, however, explains that you see your parents actually having intercourse. Furthermore, if you are to be born female, you want to get rid of the woman and you become attached to the man and want to sleep with him. If you are to be born male, you want to get rid of the man and you become attached to the woman and want to sleep with her. Once this kind of desire has arisen, the closer you approach, the other limbs of that man and woman no longer appear, and you only see the male and female sexual organs. After becoming angry at that, the intermediate-state being dies, transfers, and is reborn.[81]

Furthermore, intense attachment between father and mother concludes with the emission of a thick fluid. After that, two drops of semen and blood invariably emerge from the two. Once the two substances have united in the woman's womb, [110] they turn into something like, for instance, the skin on boiled milk that has cooled. At that point, the intermediate existence ceases. At the exact same time that ceases, by the power of the consciousness that connects with the new birth, another combination of semen and blood arises, one that accords with a fusion of the subtle elements that are a basis for the sense powers. Along with that, the consciousness that enters at that time is posited as the foundational consciousness by those who accept a foundational consciousness. Those who do not accept a foundational consciousness assert that it is the mental consciousness that takes rebirth.

If it has no desire to go to a birthplace, the intermediate-state being will not go there, and if it does not go there, it will not be born there. Therefore the intermediate-state being of someone devoted to wrongdoing who has committed and accumulated an action for rebirth in hell, such as killing sheep or trading in poultry or pigs and the like, will see, as if in a dream, sheep and so forth at his birthplace and will rush there with the delight of previous familiarity.[82] He will then become angry at the sight of his birthplace, the intermediate existence will end, and he will be born there. Similar to this are rebirths as hell beings, hungry ghosts with goiters, and so forth.

Levels of Yogic Practice says that if you are born as an animal, hungry ghost, or human being or as a god in the desire and form realms, you will see delightful beings of similar type to yourself at your birthplace. Then, having generated delight in and desire for that, you will go there. As you get angry at your birthplace, the intermediate existence ceases and you are born there. The way in which someone other than those, one who is devoted to wrongdoing and trades in poultry, pigs, and the like, is born in hell is similar to this.

In the *Treasury of Abhidharma*, the line "Others strongly desire odors and an abode" (3.15) means that if you are born from heat and moisture, you are born upon desiring odors, and if you are born miraculously, you are born upon desiring an abode. Moreover, the commentary explains that if you are born in the hot hells, you go to the intermediate state upon desiring heat, whereas if you are born in the cold hells, you go to the intermediate state upon desiring coolness. The *Treasury of Abhidharma Autocommentary* explains birth from an egg to be similar to birth from a womb.

THE MEASURE OF ITS DEVELOPMENT

When you have come to understand the characteristics of cyclic existence in detail from the point of view of sufferings and their origins, the desire to eliminate them and the desire to attain their complete pacification arises. While this is indeed the attitude of renunciation, it is not sufficient by itself. Therefore you should generate that mind to the same extent as the mind that does not want to be stuck in a house ablaze with fire or stay locked up in prison and to the same extent that it desires liberation from them. [111] It will then still be necessary to increase it.

As Sharawa taught, if this attitude is no more than mediocre, like flour thrown into sour milk, the view that rejects the causes of cyclic existence, the origins, will also not become more than that. Accordingly, one's striving for liberation, the cessation that is the ceasing of sufferings and origins, will be the same. Because of that, the desire to accomplish the path of liberation will be mere words, and also, there will be no basis for the compassion that cannot bear the suffering of other beings who wander in cyclic existence. Since unsurpassed uncontrived bodhicitta, which has the power to arouse the mind, will not arise, you become a Mahāyānist only in the way your understanding follows from words. For that reason you should cultivate that attitude again and again.

ELIMINATING MISCONCEPTIONS

You may think, "It is explained in the *Sūtra Teaching the Tathāgata's Inconceivable Secret (Tathāgatācintyaguhyanirdeśasūtra)* that if you cultivate extreme revulsion and disenchantment with cyclic existence, you will fall into the extreme of peace like the śrāvakas because of your disgust for reentering cyclic existence. Therefore it is excellent for Hīnayānists but unreasonable for bodhisattvas to cultivate disenchantment."

The meaning of the statement "Thus a bodhisattva should not be terrified by cyclic existence" is not to point out that he should not be repulsed by the sufferings of birth, aging, illness, death, and so on of wandering in existence under the power of karma and the mental afflictions. Rather, it is that, owing to his bodhicitta, he should not be afraid of taking rebirth in existence for the benefit of sentient beings under the power of aspirational prayers and compassion.

In fact, as we wander in existence under the power of karma and the mental afflictions, we are oppressed by many sufferings and cannot even bring about our own welfare, let alone anyone else's. Since that is the door to all degeneration, we need to block it. We must develop extreme disenchantment, even more than the Hīnayānists, and enjoy taking rebirth in existence under the power of aspirational prayers and compassion. In accordance with that, the same sūtra also says:

> Bodhisattvas, having taken care of ripening sentient beings, view cyclic existence to be beneficial, unlike the great passage to peace.

It is set forth in *Bodhisattva Levels* that if someone with bodhisattva vows expresses himself in the above manner and fails to differentiate the two, he commits an afflicted misdeed. [112] The intention of *Four Hundred Stanzas*, clearly set forth by the great master Candrakīrti in his commentary on that text, is to see those sentient beings as one's relatives and thus generate bodhicitta after developing revulsion for cyclic existence.

DETERMINING THE NATURE OF THE PATH LEADING TO LIBERATION

Through meditation on the faults of existence as explained above, an intense desire to renounce cyclic existence and, owing to that, the need to avert cyclic existence arise. Therefore two points are made in this regard: the kind of life through which cyclic existence is averted and the kind of path to cultivate to avert it.

THE KIND OF LIFE THROUGH WHICH CYCLIC EXISTENCE IS AVERTED

Letter to a Friend (v. 64) states:

> Now that you have obtained a birth of freedom
> beyond the so-called defective eight unfree states,
> make an effort to avert rebirth.

As is set forth here, you need to avert cyclic existence at this time when you have the freedoms and endowments, for it has already been explained that in the unfree states there is no opportunity to avert it. Naljorpa Chenpo Jangchup Rinchen said, "Now is the time to distinguish ourselves from cattle." Potowa also said, "Since it has not yet stopped by itself while we were roaming about so long, it will also not now stop by itself. Therefore we must avert it. However, the time to avert it is now that we have obtained the freedoms and endowments."

Even more than that, lay people have many obstacles to accomplishing the Dharma and have the disadvantage of numerous faults. Since those who are ordained avert them, the ordained have the best life for averting cyclic existence. That is why the wise should delight in ordination. The *Questions of Householder Ugra Sūtra* says that lay bodhisattvas should aspire to ordination. This mainly refers to aspiring to full ordination. *Ornament for the Mahāyāna Sūtras* (20.5) also says:

> Those on the side of the ordained
> have limitless excellent qualities.
> Thus those exerting themselves in vows
> excel over householder bodhisattvas.

Thus ordination is not only praised for the attainment of the complete release that is liberation from cyclic existence but is also presented as the best basis for the accomplishment of omniscience by way of the perfections and mantra. [113] Among the three vows, the vows of ordination are those of prātimokṣa. That is why you should respect the prātimokṣa vows as the root of the teachings.

THE KIND OF PATH TO CULTIVATE TO AVERT CYCLIC EXISTENCE

Letter to a Friend (vv. 104–5) says:

> Even if your head or clothes caught fire,
> give up fighting it; simply make an effort
> to destroy the occurrence of future rebirths.
> There is no purpose better than that.
>
> Through pure ethics, wisdom, and concentration,
> attain nirvāṇa, the peaceful, immaculate, tamed state,
> which is ageless, deathless, and limitless,
> free from earth, fire, water, wind, sun, and moon.

Train in the three types of precious trainings of the path as set forth in this statement.

If this were an independent commentary on the path of persons of medium capacity, an extensive commentary on the three trainings would be necessary here. However, since this is not the case, the training in wisdom, special insight, and the training of the mind for generating śamatha will be explained in the context of persons of great capacity. Therefore here I will only briefly state the way to train in ethics.

In this regard, initially contemplate the benefits of ethics again and again, and increase your heartfelt enthusiasm for it. *Letter to a Friend* (v. 7) says:

> It is said the rules are the basis, the ground of all excellent qualities,
> just like the earth is the basis for the animate and the inanimate.

And in the *Questions of Subāhu Tantra*:

> Just as crops grow faultlessly depending on the soil,
> the most superior virtuous phenomena grow
> depending on someone's ethics,
> moistened by the water of compassion.

Contemplate this according to these statements.

Just as guarding the ethics you have undertaken brings enormous benefits, likewise there are great faults to not guarding them. You should contemplate the faults of not guarding them again and again as taught in the scriptures. The *Sūtra on Cherishing Monks* (*Bhikṣuparejusūtra*) says:

> Ethics are happiness for certain people;
> ethics are suffering for others.
> They are happiness for those who have them;
> they are suffering for those who breach them.

The *Root Tantra of Mañjuśrī* (*Mañjuśrīmūlatantra*) says:

> If ethics decline in those who recite, [114]
> there will be no highest attainments,
> nor will there be middling attainments;
> even the least ones will remain absent.
>
> The King of Sages did not teach
> mantra attainments for those of loose ethics,
> nor is that the place or direction
> to go to the city of nirvāṇa.
>
> How could there be in such bad children
> any attainments of mantra at all?
> How could there be fortunate rebirths
> for those beings who disregard ethics?
>
> If they do not take high rebirths
> nor partake of highest bliss,
> what need mention their accomplishing
> the mantras that the Victor taught?

The *King of Concentrations Sūtra* says:

> The trainings that I taught to those
> who wear the laity's gray apparel—

even monks who are fully ordained
will not have those trainings then.

According to this statement, striving in the trainings is special and has more effect at this time when it is said that even fully ordained monks do not completely guard the five basic trainings taught to lay vow-holders. Therefore you should make effort in this. The same sūtra says:

> At the time when the Dharma decays and the Sugata's teachings are coming to an end,
> the merit of those who practice a single training just one day and night
> will extraordinarily exceed the one who for millions of eons, as many as there are sand grains in the Ganges,
> and with a clear mind honors billions of trillions of buddhas with food, drink, parasols, banners, and garlands of light.

Among the four causes for infractions, the antidote to *not knowing* is to study and know the trainings.

The antidote to *carelessness* is the mindfulness that does not forget the objects and aspects of what to adopt and what to discard; the vigilance that individually analyzes the three doors at every moment and brings to mind the good or faulty actions you engage in; the shame that shuns faults from the perspective of oneself or the Dharma; the embarrassment that shuns faults, thinking that others will criticize you; [115] and the intimidation that fears the fully ripened effects of faulty conduct. Train in these and others.

As an antidote to a *lack of respect*, be respectful toward the Teacher, his formulated rules, and those whose conduct accords with purity.

As an antidote to *many mental afflictions* you should examine your mindstream and try to apply the antidote to whatever mental affliction predominates.

If you do not put effort into this and commit even a minor transgression and then think, "It is a small mistake," this engagement in carelessness with respect to the formulated rules will only cause you to suffer, because as *Exegesis of the Discipline* says:

Those who are unconcerned with regard to the teachings
of the compassionate Teacher and slightly transgress them
will from that come under the power of suffering,
like mango groves that are spoiled through cutting bamboo.

Though some can transgress the royal decrees of the king
and, if it's infrequent, not get punished at all,
if they transgress the Buddha's words improperly,
they will migrate to the beasts like the nāga Elāpatra.[83]

Therefore put effort into not being stained by faults and infractions. If you are nevertheless stained by them, do not leave it at that indifferently but put effort into undoing the downfall or bad action as has been taught.

If this method of guarding morality is for those who hold the prātimokṣa vows, it is also similar in the case of mantra, because the *Questions of Subāhu Tantra* states:

Among all pure ethics from the prātimokṣa
and the Vinaya that I, the Victor, taught,
lay people practicing mantra should abandon
the signs and rituals and practice the rest.

Lay practitioners of mantra should behave as set forth in the Vinaya except for the trappings of ordination and some parts of the ritual actions. So what need is there to mention ordained practitioners of mantra?

Khamlungpa also said:

When a famine breaks out, everything depends on barley. Likewise everything hinges on ethics; therefore earnestly apply yourself to it. Pure ethics also do not come about in someone who has not reflected on actions and their effects. Therefore it is an essential instruction to reflect on them. [116]

Sharawa also said:

Generally, whatever happens, good or bad, depends on the Dharma. Within that, if you rely on what is suggested in the

Vinaya, you need not change anything. You will become sincere, withstand investigation, enjoy practice, and have a good end.

And Geshe Dromtönpa also said:

Many people rely on the Vinaya and reject mantra or rely on mantra and reject the Vinaya. Only in my guru's tradition does the Vinaya become the companion of mantra and mantra the companion of the Vinaya.

Atiśa said:

With us in India, whenever an important matter or unprecedented activity arose, those who upheld the scriptural baskets convened to determine whether it was repudiated by or in contradiction to the three scriptural baskets, and a decision was made based on that. We from Vikramaśīla then had the task to examine whether it was rejected by or in contradiction to bodhisattva behavior, and the decision was upheld by the entire ordained community.

That concludes the explanation of training the mind in the stages of the path common to persons of medium capacity.

The Stages of Persons
of Great Capacity

14 | Entering the Great Vehicle

HOW TO TRAIN THE MIND IN THE STAGES OF THE PATH OF PERSONS OF GREAT CAPACITY

THROUGH MEDITATING in this manner on the faults of cyclic existence from different perspectives over a long time, you will see all existence as a pit of blazing fire. Your mind will be thoroughly overcome by the desire to attain the liberation that completely pacifies suffering. If, because of that, you train in the three trainings, you will attain liberation that is freedom from cyclic existence, and that will not even be reversible, unlike the splendors of high rebirths. Nonetheless, extinguishing one's own faults and achieving excellent qualities will be limited, and your own welfare will not be complete. For that very reason, you will temporarily neglect the welfare of others. In the end, you will be urged by the buddhas and have to enter the Mahāyāna. Therefore the intelligent enter the Mahāyāna from the start. [117] The *Compendium of the Perfections* (6.65) says:

> Those whose nature is of one taste with altruism
> abandon forever those two vehicles
> that have no power to bring about all the world's aims
> and enter the vehicle that the Victorious Sage taught out of
> compassion.

The happiness, magnificence, and capacity of beings is to take responsibility for the welfare of others, because to observe only one's own welfare is something even animals do. Therefore the natural disposition of great beings is to categorically strive for the benefit and happiness of others. *Letter to a Student* (vv. 100–101) says:

When cattle see a mouthful of grass that is easy to get, they eat it
    themselves;
when they are greatly tormented by thirst and find some water, they
    drink it with relish.
Here, whoever makes efforts to bring about the welfare of other
    beings
is magnificent and excels in the skills of great happy individuals.

Traveling, riding across the sky, the powerful sun illuminates all;
regardless of the burden, the earth supports the world with every-
    thing in it.
Those without the least self-interest, equal in nature to great beings,
totally strive for that singular taste of benefit and joy for the world.

That being so, those who see how sentient beings everywhere are tormented
by suffering and who toil for their welfare are called persons of great capacity, or the wise. The same text says (v. 102):

Those who have seen sentient beings confused by dense gray clouds
    of worldly ignorance
as they fall without control into the blazing fire of suffering,
and who mentally toil and exert themselves for them as if fire
were blazing overhead, now they are great beings; they also are the
    wise.

There exists an entrance way to the Mahāyāna that possesses the great
skillful means such that by working for the welfare of others, you accomplish your own welfare without any incompleteness. The Mahāyāna is the
source of all your own and others' excellence, the medicine removing all
degeneration, and the great path traveled by all wise beings that nurtures
and nourishes all beings through seeing, hearing, remembering, and touching. Engage in this best of vehicles with whatever ability of a great being you
have, and think, "Oh, I have found exactly what I was looking for!" [118]
    There are three points concerning the training of the mind in the states
of the path of persons of great capacity: how generating the mind [of
enlightenment] is the only gateway to the Mahāyāna, how to generate that
mind, and how to train in the conduct after generating the mind.

How generating the mind [of enlightenment] is the only gateway to the Mahāyāna

As it is necessary to enter the Mahāyāna, think about how it is to be entered. There is no Great Vehicle apart from the Pāramitāyāna and Mantrayāna taught by the Victor. Whichever of the two you may enter, the only gateway is bodhicitta. Whenever this has arisen in the mind, even though nothing else has arisen, one is considered a Mahāyānist, whereas whenever one is separated from it, whatever excellent qualities one may have, such as the realization of emptiness and so forth, one will fall to the level of a śrāvaka and the like and fall from the Mahāyāna. This is taught in numerous texts of the Mahāyāna and is also established by reasoning. Therefore whether one is a Mahāyānist is determined by whether one has this mind.

Thus *Entering the Bodhisattva Way* (1.9 and 3.26) says that as soon as this mind has arisen, you become a child of the Victors. Likewise, the *Life of Maitreya* (*Maitreyavimokṣa*) says:

> Child of the lineage, it is like this. For example, even a broken precious diamond outshines all gold jewelry, however refined; it does not lose its name "diamond" and still averts all poverty. Child of the lineage, likewise the precious diamond that is the mind generation for omniscience, even without effort, outshines all the gold jewelry that is the excellent qualities of the śrāvakas and pratyekabuddhas; the name "bodhisattva" is not lost, and all the misfortunes of cyclic existence are averted.

If that mind exists even in someone untrained in bodhisattva conduct, he is said to be a bodhisattva. Therefore it is not sufficient for the Dharma to be Mahāyāna Dharma, but rather it is important that the person has entered the Mahāyāna. Whether you become a Mahāyānist depends on bodhicitta itself. If that mind is no more than an intellectual understanding, your being a Mahāyānist is the same. On the other hand, if you have fully qualified bodhicitta, you will also become a completely pure Mahāyānist. Therefore you should make an effort.

With respect to this, the *Marvelous Array Sūtra* says: [119]

Child of the lineage, bodhicitta is like the seed of all the Dharma of the Buddha.

This will be explained because it is necessary to gain certainty about it. Since water, manure, heat, soil, and so forth act as causes for a rice sprout when combined with a rice grain and as causes for sprouts of wheat, pulses, and so forth when combined with their respective seeds, they are common causes. Since a barley seed is not suitable as a cause of a rice sprout and so forth even if the conditions are gathered together, it is the uncommon cause of a barley sprout, while the water, manure, and so forth that cooperate with it are the common causes of the barley sprout. Similarly, among the causes for a buddha sprout, the mind of unsurpassed enlightenment, like the seed, is the uncommon cause, whereas the wisdom realizing emptiness, like the water, manure, and so forth, is the common cause of the three types of enlightenment.[84] That is why the *Sublime Continuum* (*Uttaratantra*, 1.34) says:

> Conviction in the supreme vehicle is the seed;
> wisdom is the mother that gives birth to the qualities of
> enlightenment.

This means that conviction in the Supreme Vehicle is like the father's seed and the wisdom realizing selflessness is like the mother. For instance, since a Tibetan father cannot have a child who is Indian, Chinese, or Mongolian, the father is the cause that determines the lineage. On the other hand, a Tibetan mother is like the common cause, since she can give birth to all kinds of children.

In his *Praise to the Perfection of Wisdom* (*Prajñāpāramitāstotra*, v. 17), Nāgārjuna also says that śrāvakas and pratyekabuddhas equally rely on it:

> Buddhas, pratyekabuddhas, and śrāvakas
> definitely rely on you,
> singular path to liberation;
> it is true to say there is no other.

That is why the perfection of wisdom is also known as the mother. Since it is the mother of the sons of both the Mahāyāna and the Hīnayāna, it is not the wisdom realizing emptiness that differentiates the Mahāyāna and the Hīnayāna. Rather bodhicitta and vast conduct differentiate them. In *Precious Garland* (4.90) they are also taught to be differentiated not by view but by conduct:

> The Śrāvaka Vehicle does not explain
> the bodhisattvas' aspiration,
> conduct, or complete dedications.
> How could they become bodhisattvas? [120]

Therefore, if even the wisdom realizing emptiness is not a path unique to the Mahāyāna, what need is there to mention other paths? For that reason, it is necessary to train in bodhicitta, having made instructions on it one's main concern.

How to generate the mind of bodhicitta

This has three points: the stages of training in bodhicitta, the measure of it having arisen, and the way to adopt it by means of a ritual.

The stages of training in bodhicitta

This has two variations: the sevenfold cause-and-effect instruction transmitted from Atiśa, and the training based on texts by the bodhisattva Śāntideva.

15 | The Sevenfold Instruction for Training in Bodhicitta

THE SEVENFOLD CAUSE-AND-EFFECT INSTRUCTION TRANSMITTED FROM ATIŚA

THE SEVENFOLD CAUSE-AND-EFFECT instruction is this: a complete buddha is born from bodhicitta; this mind from the extraordinary attitude; this attitude from compassion; compassion from love; love from the wish to repay the kindness; the wish to repay the kindness from remembering the kindness; and remembering the kindness from seeing beings as one's mother. There are two points: generating certainty concerning the stages and the actual gradual training.

GENERATING CERTAINTY CONCERNING THE STAGES

This has two points: the way compassion is the root of the Mahāyāna, and the way the other causes and effects become causes and effects of that compassion.

THE WAY COMPASSION IS THE ROOT OF THE MAHĀYĀNA

The first has three points: the importance of compassion at the beginning, the importance of compassion in the middle, and the importance of compassion at the end.

THE IMPORTANCE OF COMPASSION AT THE BEGINNING

If your mind is moved by great compassion, you will certainly resolve to free sentient beings from cyclic existence. However, if your compassion is inferior, such deeds will not come about. Therefore whether you take responsibility for liberating all beings without exception depends on that compassion, and if you do not take that responsibility, you do not enter the Mahāyāna. That is why compassion is important at the beginning. The *Teachings of Akṣayamati Sūtra (Akṣayamatinirdeśasūtra)* says:

> Venerable Śaradvatīputra, the great compassion of the bodhisattvas is inexhaustible. Why is that? It is because it is a preliminary. Venerable Śaradvatīputra, it is like this. By way of analogy, just as the inward and outward flow of the breath is a preliminary for our human life-force faculty, likewise the great compassion of the bodhisattvas is a preliminary for perfectly accomplishing the Mahāyāna.

The *Gayāśīrṣa Hill Sūtra (Gayāśīrṣasūtra)* says:

> "Mañjuśrī, what initiates the conduct of bodhisattvas? What is its object?"
> Mañjuśrī replied, "Divine child, what initiates the conduct of bodhisattvas [121] is great compassion. Its object is sentient beings."

THE IMPORTANCE OF COMPASSION IN THE MIDDLE

Although you enter the Mahāyāna when a mind like this has arisen once, when you see the great number and bad actions of sentient beings and the great difficulty, boundlessness, and limitless time required of the trainings, you may become discouraged and fall into the Hīnayāna. However, by familiarizing yourself increasingly with great compassion rather than generating it just once, you will become unconcerned with your own happiness and suffering and will not despair over the welfare of others, whereby you will easily complete all the accumulations.

THE IMPORTANCE OF COMPASSION AT THE END

Even when the buddhas have achieved their result, they do not dwell in peace like the Hīnayānists but bring about the welfare of however many sentient beings there are throughout space. This is also due to the power of great compassion, for without it, they would become like śrāvakas.

Glorious Candrakīrti [in *Entering the Middle Way* (1.2)] said that for a harvest, what is important in the beginning is the seed, in the middle the water, and in the end its ripening. Likewise, for the harvest of buddhahood, what is important in the beginning, the end, and in the middle is compassion.

Shang Nachung Tönpa said, "Although I asked the Elder for instructions, nothing more came of it than 'Let go of your worldly thoughts. Cultivate bodhicitta.'" Geshe Dromtönpa laughed at him and said, "You got the central point of the Elder's instructions! He knew the key point of the teachings, the Dharma."

Since it is difficult to gain certainty about this, you must gather the accumulations and purify again and again, study the scriptures such as the *Marvelous Array Sūtra* as well as their commentaries, and seek firm certainty. It is as the glorious Aśvaghoṣa says, referring to the Buddha:[85]

> Your mind, Heroic One, is precious,
> the seed of complete enlightenment;
> only you know it as the essence;
> other beings do not guess that.

THE WAY THE OTHER CAUSES AND EFFECTS BECOME CAUSES AND EFFECTS OF THAT COMPASSION

This has two points: the way four of the sevenfold instructions, from *understanding as mothers* through *love*, are causes, and the way the extraordinary attitude and bodhicitta[86] are their effects.

THE WAY FOUR OF THE SEVENFOLD INSTRUCTIONS, FROM "UNDERSTANDING AS MOTHERS" THROUGH "LOVE," ARE CAUSES

If you reflect again and again on the suffering of a sentient being, this will generally give rise to the mere wish that it be free from suffering. [122] However, for this mind to arise easily and for it to arise very strong and stable, its object must first be a sentient being who has the aspect of being likable and valuable. When someone close to us meets with suffering, we cannot bear it. When our enemies meet with suffering, we enjoy it. When someone who is neither a friend nor an enemy meets with suffering, mainly a neglectful equanimity arises.

In this regard, since our mind finds the first ones are likable, the more we cherish them, the more their suffering becomes unbearable to us, and the more compassion arises for them. If we cherish them a little or moderately, our inability to bear their suffering will also be relatively small. But if we cherish someone very much, we find it unbearable when that person meets with only minor suffering. When we see our enemies suffering, not only does the wish that they be free from it fail to arise, but also the thought occurs to us "May their suffering increase and may they not be free from it." That is our reaction to someone we find unlikable. Moreover, our joy at their suffering will also be greater or smaller depending on how much aversion they induce in us. With respect to the suffering of those who are neither friend nor enemy, we find it neither unbearable nor enjoyable. That is our reaction when someone is neither likable nor unlikable.

Given this is so, meditating on sentient beings as our relatives is to make them attractive to us. Since our closest relation is our mother, others are established as dear and likable to us through meditating on them as having been our mother, remembering their kindness, and wishing to repay this kindness. The effect of these three steps is a love that cherishes sentient beings like one's only child. They produce compassion.

With respect to compassion and the love that wishes that others meet with happiness, there does not seem to be any certainty as to which one is the cause and which one is the effect.

These meditations on sentient beings as our relatives have been explained by the master Candrakīrti, the venerable Candragomin, and the master Kamalaśīla as the cause for bodhicitta to arise.

THE WAY THE EXTRAORDINARY ATTITUDE AND BODHICITTA ARE THEIR EFFECTS

It should be sufficient to say that compassion arises based on such a gradual training of the mind and the desire to attain enlightenment for the welfare of all sentient beings arises after that. Why is the extraordinary attitude inserted between them? Śrāvakas and pratyekabuddhas also have immeasurable compassion and the love that thinks, "If only sentient beings were to meet with happiness and if only they were free from suffering!" Yet those who are not Mahāyānists do not take on the responsibility to accomplish happiness and eliminate suffering for every sentient being. Therefore it is necessary to generate the extraordinary attitude, which is the special attitude of those with brave hearts. [123] This is understood from a quotation from the *Questions of Sāgaramati Sūtra* in the commentary on the *Sublime Continuum.*[87]

After the mind to free sentient beings has arisen in this manner, you are still unable to complete even the welfare of one sentient being owing to your current situation. Not only that, even if you were to attain the states of the two kinds of arhats, you would only be able to complete the welfare of very few beings, and their welfare would be to merely accomplish liberation. They cannot establish them in omniscience, so who can complete the temporary and final welfare of limitless beings? If you reflect in this vein, you will come to understand that only a buddha is able to do this, and you will generate the wish to attain buddhahood for the welfare of sentient beings.

THE ACTUAL GRADUAL TRAINING

The second, the actual training, has three points: training in the mind that strives for the welfare of others, training in the mind that strives for enlightenment, and identifying the bodhicitta that is the result of that training.

TRAINING IN THE MIND THAT STRIVES FOR THE WELFARE OF OTHERS

The first has two points: laying the foundation for that mind to arise and the actual generation of that mind.

LAYING THE FOUNDATION FOR THAT MIND TO ARISE

This has two points: achieving an equanimous mind toward sentient beings and establishing that they all have a likable aspect.

ACHIEVING AN EQUANIMOUS MIND TOWARD SENTIENT BEINGS

The preliminary steps and the like, as explained above in the context of persons of lesser and medium capacity, should be adopted and maintained here as well. To start with, if you do not accomplish an equanimous mind, then having stopped the bias of attachment toward some sentient beings and hatred toward others, any love and compassion that arise will arise with partiality. As they do not arise if you observe them without impartiality, you should cultivate equanimity. The two types of equanimous mind that have been taught are that which has the appearance of lacking mental afflictions such as attachment, anger, and so forth in sentient beings and that in which there is no attachment or anger toward sentient beings. Here, it refers to the latter of these two.

This is the order of meditation by which it will easily arise. Initially, take as your object of attention a neutral person who has neither helped nor harmed you and develop an equanimous mind through eliminating attachment and anger. When an equanimous mind toward that person has developed, you then need to develop an equanimous mind toward friends and relatives. A mind that lacks equanimity toward them is either biased owing to attachment and hatred, or lacks equanimity owing to a lesser or greater degree of attachment. Once you are equanimous toward friends, you should then cultivate an equanimous mind toward enemies. The lack of equanimity toward enemies [124] derives from hatred that sees them as totally incompatible with yourself. After you have become equanimous toward them, you should cultivate an equanimous mind toward all sentient beings.

Moreover, Kamalaśīla's second *Stages of Meditation* teaches you to think, "Since from their side all sentient beings are the same in wanting happiness and not wanting suffering, it would be unreasonable for me to benefit some whom I consider close and harm or fail to benefit others whom I consider distant," and "Since from my own side there is not a single sentient being who in beginningless cyclic existence has not been my companion hundreds of times, who should I have attachment for and who should I have hatred for?" Also with regard to attachment to our relatives, the *Questions of the Daughter Candrottara Sūtra* (*Candrottaradārikāparipṛcchāsūtra*) says:

In former times I killed each one of you;
I, too, was slashed and cut into pieces by you.
We all have been foes and murderers of each other.
How can a mind of attachment arise in you?

Think about the way in which friends and enemies quickly change as it was explained above in the context of the fault of uncertainty. This will avert both anger and attachment.

We need to distinguish friends from enemies by apprehending them to be the basis of their respective attributes. What is to be ceased is the mind that is biased owing to attachment and anger on account of someone being a friend or enemy; the notion of friend and enemy itself does not need to be averted.

ESTABLISHING THAT THEY ALL HAVE A LIKABLE ASPECT

This has three points: meditating on them as one's mother, remembering their kindness, and meditating on repaying their kindness.

MEDITATING ON THEM AS ONE'S MOTHER

In the sūtras it is taught that, since cyclic existence is beginningless, our births are also beginningless. Therefore we have been born and we have died incessantly, so that there is no body in cyclic existence that we have not taken, no place where we have not been born, and also no one who has not been a relative such as our mother.

Moreover, not only have they been our mother in the past, they will also be so in the future. Therefore, reflecting in that way, try to gain firm certainty that they have been your mother, for once that certainty arises, it will be easy to remember their kindness and so forth. On the other hand, if it does not arise, you will have no basis for remembering their kindness and so forth.

REMEMBERING THEIR KINDNESS

Meditate according to Geshe Potowa, who maintained that the memory of their kindness will arise quickly after meditating on all sentient beings as your mothers if you initially meditate on your mother of this life. [125] Visualize your mother in front of you in a clear aspect and repeatedly reflect, "She has been my mother not only now but countless times previously in the beginningless rounds of existence." In that way, when she was your mother, she protected you from all harm and accomplished all happiness and benefit for you.

In particular, even in this life she initially carried you in her womb for a long time. Then, after she gave birth to you, she pressed your yellow tousled hair against the heat of her body, swung you on her ten fingers, nursed you with her milk, fed you and wiped away your snot with her mouth, cleaned your feces with her hands, and cared for you untiringly in many different ways. In addition, she gave you food and drink when you were hungry or thirsty. She gave you clothing when you were cold. In times of need, she gave you her possessions that she would not spend on herself. When everyday necessities were hard to come by, she bore great hardship and spared herself no bad action, suffering, or bad talk to get them and give them to you.

Whenever her child suffered from a disease and so forth, she wished from the depths of her heart to die rather than for her child to die, for herself to be ill rather than for her child to be ill, and so forth. With effort, she did whatever she could to eliminate her child's suffering. To summarize, by whatever degree of knowledge and whatever degree of ability she had, she thought single-pointedly about ways to bring about your happiness and benefit and to remove any harm and suffering from you.

If, by meditating in this way, a mind remembering her kindness that is not just words arises, then meditate on recognizing other friends and relatives, your father and so forth, as also having been your mothers. Then you meditate on recognizing neutral persons as having been your mothers. When a similar mind arises toward them as that toward your friends and relatives, you should also meditate on recognizing your enemies as having been your mothers. When a similar mind arises toward them as that toward your mother, proceed to recognize all beings as having been your mothers and meditate, gradually extending it more and more.

MEDITATING ON REPAYING THEIR KINDNESS

There is nothing more shameful than carelessly neglecting your kind, suffering, protectorless mothers just because you do not recognize them anymore owing to birth, death, and transmigration and to being preoccupied with freeing yourself from cyclic existence. *Letter to a Student* (v. 95) says:

> My kin are drowning in the ocean of cyclic existence
> and seem to have fallen into an abyss. If I neglect them,
> unrecognized owing to birth and death and transmigration,
> and seek liberation alone, nothing is more shameful. [126]

Thus you should take the responsibility to reciprocate their kindness, thinking, "If neglecting such kind beings is inappropriate even for the ill-mannered, how can I reconcile it with my own ways?"

You may wonder, "Well then, how should I repay the benefit?" Whatever pleasures and riches of cyclic existence your mothers obtain, they are misled by all of them. Thus you should repay the benefit, thinking, "In the past, under the power of the evil spirits that are the mental afflictions which possessed me, I produced all kinds of additional sufferings in those who were already suffering by nature, like pouring salt in the wounds of those severely injured. I will establish all those who out of love have benefited me in the happiness of liberation, nirvāṇa."

In brief, your own kind mother is restless and insane, blind and without anyone to guide her, and is stumbling with each step as she approaches a fearsome abyss. If she cannot put her hope in her child, who can she count on? If it is not for the child to free the mother from fear, who else should do it? Likewise, owing to the evil spirits of the mental afflictions, the minds of sentient beings who have been our mothers are agitated rather than in the natural state. They are insane and without control over their consciousness, lack eyes to see the path to higher states and definite goodness, and lack a true friend, a guide for the blind. In each instant they stumble from being distracted by faulty behavior and wander toward the abyss of cyclic existence in general and the lower rebirths in particular. As you see them, you should reflect that these mothers necessarily put their hopes in their child, and that it is also for the child to get their mother out of there. You should repay their kindness by definitely getting them out of cyclic existence. The *Compendium of Trainings* says:

> Insane with afflictions, blinded by ignorance,
> on a path with many abysses,
> stumbling with every step, myself
> and others are always subject to sorrow.
> Beings are the same in suffering.

In view of this, although it is indeed said to be inappropriate to look for faults in others and you should marvel at the slightest positive quality [127] when you see it, here it is appropriate to focus on misery.

ACTUAL GENERATION OF THAT MIND THAT STRIVES FOR THE WELFARE OF OTHERS

This has three points: meditating on love, meditating on compassion, and meditating on the extraordinary attitude.

MEDITATING ON LOVE

The object of love is sentient beings who do not possess happiness. Its expressions are the thoughts "How wonderful it would be if they were to meet with happiness!" "May they meet with happiness!" and "I will make them meet with happiness!"

As regards the benefits, the *King of Concentrations Sūtra* says:

> Many kinds of offerings without measure
> in myriad neighboring pure fields
> constantly offered to the most excellent beings
> do not equal a fraction of the mind of love.

This is to say, the merit is much greater than that of constantly making incredibly vast offerings to the field that is the highest object. Also, *Array of Qualities in Mañjuśrī's Buddhafield* (*Mañjuśrībuddhakṣetraguṇavyūha*) explains:

In the land called Ornamented by a Thousand of the great king Buddheśvara, in the northeastern quarter, sentient beings possess a happiness similar to the happiness of fully ordained monks who have entered cessation. If a mind of love toward all sentient beings generated in this land for as little as the duration of a finger snap produces far more merit than someone celibate practicing pure conduct there for a trillion years, what need is there to mention that of abiding in that mind day and night?

Nāgārjuna's *Precious Garland* (3.83–85) states:

> Giving three hundred pots of food
> three times daily does not equal
> the merit of love maintained
> for the duration of just one moment.

> You will be loved by gods and humans,
> they will protect you, and you will have
> mental happiness and much pleasure.
> Poison and weapons will no longer harm you.

> You will achieve your goals without effort
> and will be born in the Brahma worlds.
> Even if you do not reach liberation,
> you will win the eight qualities of love.

If you have love, gods and human beings will love you and naturally gather around you. Since the Victor [128] defeated the hosts of Māra by the force of love, it is the best of protections and so forth.

The stages of meditation on love are to meditate initially on love for your friends and relatives, then for neutral persons, then for your enemies, and then for all sentient beings. The way to meditate on love is as follows. Just as compassion arises when you reflect again and again on how sentient beings have the suffering of suffering, likewise you should reflect again and again on how sentient beings are devoid of happiness, in that they lack both contaminated and uncontaminated happiness. Once you have familiarized yourself with this, the wish for them to encounter happiness will arise naturally. In addition, having contemplated the various kinds of happiness, offer them to sentient beings.

MEDITATING ON COMPASSION

The observed objects of compassion are sentient beings who suffer owing to any of the three kinds of suffering. Its expression is the thoughts "If only they were free from these sufferings," "May they be free from them," and "I will free them from them." The sequence of the meditations is to meditate on compassion for your friends and relatives first, then for neutral persons, then for your enemies, and then for all the sentient beings of the ten directions.

This gradual meditation on equanimity, love, and compassion in which you differentiate their objects was developed by the master Kamalaśīla following the *Abhidharma Sūtra*. This is a very important point, because if from the start you train in observing sentient beings in general without dividing them into specific categories, it will seem as if equanimity and so forth have arisen, but when you then think about friends and so forth one by one, it will appear that they have not arisen for any of them. On the other hand, if you experience a change in your mentality toward them one by one as explained above, and then extend that to many, finally focusing on them in general and sustaining it, those feelings will arise purely regardless of who is observed, whether a group or each one singly. The way to meditate is in terms of the sufferings that were explained when contemplating how the sentient beings who have been our mothers have fallen into existence and are experiencing the general and specific sufferings.

The measure of the arising of compassion is taught in the first *Stages of Meditation*:

> Compassion is complete at the point where it expresses itself as a constant desire to remove the suffering of all beings as if your beloved child were unhappy and operates naturally in you spontaneously and in accordance with your nature. Thereby it obtains the name *great compassion*.

Thus if compassion toward all sentient beings naturally arises to the extent that it arises in a mother when the child she loves with all her heart suffers,

[129] it is known as fully qualified great compassion. It should be known that this is also the measure of the arising of great love.

Meditating on the extraordinary attitude

After meditating on love and compassion in this manner, finally, you will think, "Alas! If these sentient beings who are pleasant and dear to me are thus deprived of happiness and tormented by suffering, how can I give them happiness and how can I free them from suffering?" In taking upon yourself the responsibility to liberate them, you train the mind at least through the mere words.

Although this was mentioned briefly in the context of repaying kindness, it is shown here that the love and compassion that think "How wonderful it would be if they were to meet with happiness" and "How wonderful it would be if they were free from suffering" are not sufficient. This is because you need to generate the love and compassion that is capable of inducing the thought "I myself will accomplish the happiness and benefit of sentient beings." As is taught in the first *Stages of Meditation*, you should practice it continuously and recollect it during all your activities, after sessions, and so forth, not just during meditation sessions.

Training in the mind striving for enlightenment

Once you are encouraged by the steps explained so far and realize that enlightenment is necessary for the welfare of others, you will also develop the desire to attain it. However, that in itself is not sufficient. At the beginning you must increase your faith through thinking about the excellent qualities of the exalted body, exalted speech, exalted mind, and enlightened activities as they were explained above in the context of going for refuge. Then, since that faith is said to act as the basis for your aspiration, you generate the wish to attain those qualities from the depths of your heart. That will induce certainty that the achievement of omniscience is indispensable also for your own welfare.

IDENTIFYING THE BODHICITTA THAT IS THE RESULT OF THAT TRAINING

The general definition is taught in *Ornament for Clear Knowledge* (1.18): "Bodhicitta is the desire for perfect complete enlightenment for the welfare of others."

It is classified into two, aspiring and engaging bodhicitta, as taught in *Entering the Bodhisattva Way* (1.15), which follows the *Marvelous Array Sūtra*. It says:

> Just as one understands the difference between
> the wish to go and actually going,
> so the wise should understand
> the difference between those two accordingly. [130]

Although there are many disagreements about this, the first *Stages of Meditation* says that aspiring bodhicitta is the mind that thinks, "May I become a buddha for the welfare of sentient beings," and the engaging bodhicitta is that mind after the vow has been taken.

16 | Equalizing and Exchanging Oneself and Others

THE TRAINING BASED ON TEXTS BY THE BODHISATTVA ŚĀNTIDEVA

THE TRAINING BASED ON texts by Śāntideva has three points: contemplating the benefits of exchanging and the faults of not exchanging oneself and others, demonstrating that you can generate this mind if you familiarize yourself with it, and the stages of meditation on how to exchange oneself and others.

CONTEMPLATING THE BENEFITS OF EXCHANGING AND THE FAULTS OF NOT EXCHANGING ONESELF AND OTHERS

Entering the Bodhisattva Way (8.120) says:

> Whoever wishes to protect
> himself and others rapidly
> should practice the secret instructions that
> consist in exchanging oneself and others.

And (8.129–31):

> All happiness that exists in the world
> arises from wanting happiness for others.
> All suffering that exists in the world
> arises from wanting one's own happiness.
>
> What need is there to say any more?
> The childish work for their own welfare,

the sages for the welfare of others.
Look at the difference between the two!

If one fails to correctly exchange
one's own happiness with others' suffering,
one will not reach buddhahood
or even be happy in cyclic existence.

Just as it is expressed here, think of cherishing yourself as the door to all degeneration and cherishing others as the basis of all excellence.

DEMONSTRATING THAT YOU CAN GENERATE THIS MIND IF YOU FAMILIARIZE YOURSELF WITH IT

Fear used to arise in you even at hearing your enemy's name, but later on, you reconciled and became friends and were very sad if he were absent. Likewise, from the mind following habits, you can learn to see yourself as like someone else and others as like yourself. The same text says (8.119):

Do not avoid things because they are difficult.
By the strength of familiarization,
you become sad at the absence of someone
whose name was once frightful to hear.

And (8.112):

It is not all that hard to posit
my body as belonging to others. [131]

One might think, "Since someone else's body is not my own body, how could it be appropriate to generate the same attitude of 'mine' toward it?" This body was also created from the semen and blood of our parents, and even though it was created from parts of others' bodies, we hold it to be "I" by the power of previous familiarization. Likewise, this mind will arise if we familiarize ourselves with cherishing others' bodies as if they were our own. The same text says (8.111):

Thus you apprehend drops
of someone else's blood and semen
as yourself; like that
get used to it regarding others!

A strong enthusiasm for this meditation will arise from the depths of the heart through thorough reflection on the benefits and faults along these lines. If you familiarize yourself with this, you will see that you can generate this attitude.

THE STAGES OF MEDITATION ON HOW TO EXCHANGE ONESELF AND OTHERS

This has two points: removing obstacles and the actual way to meditate.

REMOVING OBSTACLES

What is called "exchanging oneself and others" and "making oneself into the other and making others into oneself" does not mean training in the mind that thinks, "The other person is me" and "His eyes and so forth are my eyes and so forth." Rather, it is to exchange the perspective of the mind that cherishes oneself and the mind that neglects others—to generate the mind that cherishes others like we cherish ourselves and neglects ourselves like we neglect others. That is also why it was taught that one's own happiness and the suffering of others should be exchanged. When we perceive self-cherishing as our enemy, we stop making our own happiness our priority. When we perceive cherishing others as an excellent quality and stop neglecting the suffering of others, we make it our priority to eliminate it. In short, we will act for the sake of eliminating the suffering of others without concern for our own happiness.

When training in this mind, there are two obstacles. We separate the two, oneself and others—the basis of one's own and others' happiness and suffering—into distinct natures, like blue and yellow, and hold them to be established in that way. Then, with respect to the happiness and suffering based on them, we think, "Since it is mine, it should be accomplished or removed. [132] Since it is someone else's, it is to be neglected." Therefore the antidote to this is to think that myself and others are not distinct entities by nature. Rather, as we look at one another, the mind "other" arises in me, whereas the mind "I" arises in the other person. Thus it is like "the mountain over here" and "the mountain over there." For instance, although from this perspective the mind "the mountain over there" arises with respect to the mountain over there, when you go to the mountain over there, the mind "the mountain over here" arises. Therefore this is not the same as the fact that a mind of just blue will arise in whoever looks at the color blue and a mind of another color will not arise.

In this manner, the *Compendium of Trainings* also teaches that self and other are not inherently established but merely posited in dependence on the following point of view:

> Through familiarity with the equality
> of other and self, bodhicitta grows firm.
> *Self* and *other* are relational and
> just as false as *that side* and *this side.*
>
> The slope is not *that side* by itself;
> depending on the perspective, it's *this side.*
> The *self* in itself is not established;
> depending on the perspective, it's *other.*

You must remove the obstacle of thinking "Since the suffering of others does not harm me, I need not make an effort to remove it." If this were the case, there would be no need to accumulate wealth when young out of concern for the sufferings of old age, since the sufferings of the elderly person would not harm the youth. It was also said that the hand would likewise not eliminate the sufferings of the foot because they are other.[88] This is a mere illustration and should also be applied to the sufferings of the morning and those of the evening, and so forth.

Someone might think, "Self and other are not the same as these, since the elderly person and the youth are the same continuum and the hand and the foot are the same collection." A *continuum* and a *collection* are imputed to many instants and a combination of many parts; they lack an autonomous nature. Since your own self and the self of others must be posited on a continuum or a collection, self and other are not inherently established apart from mere relation. Yet your own suffering is unbearable owing to the power of familiarization with self-cherishing from beginningless time. Therefore, if you familiarize yourself with cherishing others, their suffering will also become unbearable. [133]

THE ACTUAL WAY TO MEDITATE

By the power of attachment to the self, this self-cherishing has produced much that is undesirable from beginningless time up to now. Despite the fact that you have wanted to create excellence for yourself, you have relied on unsuitable means, contemplating your own welfare as paramount. Owing to this, neither your own welfare nor that of others has been accomplished despite the passing of countless eons. Not only have you failed to accomplish that, you have only been tormented by suffering. If you had shifted the concern for your own welfare to that of others, you would have become a buddha a long time ago, and both your own and others' welfare would have become excellent without a doubt. But since you did not do that, the time has been spent in meaningless exertion.

Think, "Now that I have understood this, I will rely on the mindfulness and vigilance that this self-cherishing is my worst enemy, and make much effort so that the self-cherishing that has not arisen does not arise and that which has arisen does not last long." Having made this certainty firm, familiarize yourself with it many times. By thinking about the benefits of cherishing others again and again in this way, you will generate strong enthusiasm to do so from the depths of your heart. Then you will not generate new mental states that are neglectful of others, and any that have arisen will not last long. By giving rise, to whatever degree you can, to the thought that others are dear, pleasant, and likable, generate the mind cherishing others just as you previously cherished yourself.

Atiśa said, "The Tibetans celebrate 'bodhisattvas' who do not know how to train in love and compassion." He was then asked, "Well then, how do you do that?" and he replied, "You must train sequentially from the beginning."

Langri Thangpa said, "Shawopa and I have eighteen human methods and one horse method, nineteen altogether. The human methods are to generate the mind set on supreme enlightenment and train in doing whatever one does for the welfare of sentient beings. As for the horse method, since it is our self-cherishing that prevents any bodhicitta that has been born from surviving, we adopt a sideways stance [like a warrior] and then confront it and train in whatever we can to harm it. With sentient beings, we cherish them and train in whatever we can to help them."

Khamlungpa said, "Since we act deviously toward precious sentient beings, they will also do the same to us."

It is good if a habit develops that constantly checks to what extent this mind has been generated, because everything stems from it: whether the root of the Mahāyāna has been planted and whether one is included among Mahāyānists. [134] If it does not arise, do not leave it at that but rely on a virtuous friend who teaches it. Always keep company with the companion that is mind training. Read the scriptures of the Teacher and their commentaries. As its cause, accumulate the collections and purify your obstructions. Since it is certain that if you train your mind in this way, the seed will be fully planted, these actions are of no little importance and a reason for joy. It is as Atiśa said [in his *Concise Method for Accomplishing the Mahāyāna Path* (*Mahāyānapathasādhanavarṇasaṃgraha*)]:

> For those who wish to enter the gate of
> Mahāyāna Dharma, it's worth an eon of effort
> for bodhicitta to grow, which like the sun and moon
> eliminates darkness and pacifies scorching heat.

THE MEASURE OF IT HAVING ARISEN

That should be understood from what was already explained above.

The Ritual for Adopting Bodhicitta

THE WAY TO ADOPT IT BY MEANS OF A RITUAL

This has three points: receiving that which has not yet been received, guarding that which has been received without it degenerating, and the method for restoring it if it has degenerated.

RECEIVING THAT WHICH HAS NOT YET BEEN RECEIVED

This has three points: the object from whom it is taken, the person who takes it, and the ritual by which it is taken.

THE OBJECT FROM WHOM IT IS TAKEN

The assertions of the earlier masters accord with Master Jetari, who said that it is not enough for the preceptor to possess the vow of aspiring bodhicitta and to be abiding in the trainings; he must possess the vow of engaging bodhicitta.

THE PERSON WHO TAKES IT

All gods, nāgas, and so forth who are physically and mentally suitable to generate aspiring bodhicitta are also a suitable basis for it. *Commentary on Difficult Points of Lamp for the Path* says:

> Repulsed by cyclic existence, mindful of death, with wisdom and great compassion.

Thus the vow taker should be someone who has gained a little experience of transforming his mentality into bodhicitta by training the mind in the stages of the path as explained above.

THE RITUAL BY WHICH IT IS TAKEN

This has three points: the preparatory ritual, the actual ritual, and the concluding ritual.

THE PREPARATORY RITUAL

This has three points: special going for refuge, accumulating the accumulations, and training in the attitude.

SPECIAL GOING FOR REFUGE

This is divided into three points: decorating the place, displaying representations, and setting up offering substances; making a request and going for refuge; and stating the trainings of having gone for refuge.

DECORATING THE PLACE, DISPLAYING REPRESENTATIONS, AND SETTING UP OFFERING SUBSTANCES

Clean an isolated place, smear it with the five cow substances, anoint it with exquisite perfumed water such as sandalwood water, [135] and scatter fragrant flowers.[89] Set out representations of the Three Jewels—metal statues and so forth, texts and so forth, and images of bodhisattvas—on a throne, a table, or a raised platform. Do the preparatory ritual with items such as canopies and flowers that are as valuable as possible, as well as music, food, and so forth. Arrange a throne for the teacher and also adorn it with flowers. The accumulation of merit is done by paying respect to past masters and the Saṅgha and by giving a *torma* offering cake to the elemental spirits.

If you do not have any offerings at all, as described in the *Good Eon Sūtra* (*Bhadrakalpikasūtra*), it can be done even by offering scraps of cloth. If you do have offerings, they should have been obtained through great effort, without deceit, and should be arrayed in such a way that your friends cannot help marveling. When Atiśa was asked to confer the mind generation by Tibetan teachers in Mangyul and Samyé, he reportedly said that it did not arise through inferior offerings. He also said that a consecrated statue of the main master of the teachings was imperative as a representation, and at least the *Verse Summary of the Perfection of Wisdom* should be used as a text.

Then the assembly of āryas is invoked. The student, washed and well dressed, with his hands joined, is encouraged by the guru to generate clear faith in the excellent qualities of the merit field from the depths of his heart. He should then slowly do the seven-limb practice and imagine that he is in front of the buddhas and bodhisattvas.

MAKING A REQUEST AND GOING FOR REFUGE

Then the student generates the perception of his guru as the Teacher, prostrates to him and makes offerings to him, including a maṇḍala. With his right knee on the floor and palms joined, he makes a request for generating bodhicitta:

> Just as the tathāgatas, arhats, and perfectly complete buddhas, as well as the great bodhisattvas abiding on the great grounds, first generated the mind of unsurpassed, perfectly complete enlightenment, likewise I, whose name is _____, request the master to generate the mind of unsurpassed, perfectly complete enlightenment.

Repeat this three times.

Then the student goes for refuge, with the behavior explained above, to the objects—the Buddha, the Dharma (the true paths that mainly bring about the cessations), and the Saṅgha [136] (the irreversible ārya bodhisattvas). The student thinks, "From now until I achieve enlightenment, in order to protect all sentient beings, I go for refuge to the Buddha, the teacher of refuge; I go for refuge to the Dharma, the actual refuge; I go for refuge to the Saṅgha, whom I ask to be my companions in practicing refuge." Then, with the general and special attitude, the student makes the strong aspiration: "I will never turn away from this attitude at any time."

> Master, please grant me your attention. I, whose name is _____, from now until I reach the quintessence of enlightenment, go for refuge to the best of humans, the blessed buddhas.
>
> Master, please grant me your attention. I, whose name is _____, from now until I reach the quintessence of enlightenment, go for refuge to the best of Dharmas, the Dharma that is peace, free from attachment.
>
> Master, please grant me your attention. I, whose name is _____, from now until I reach the quintessence of enlightenment, go for refuge to the best of assemblies, the Saṅgha of irreversible ārya bodhisattvas.

Repeat this three times. The request for attention when going for refuge to each of the Jewels and the unusual words of going for refuge to the Dharma accord with the ritual composed by Atiśa.

STATING THE TRAININGS OF HAVING GONE FOR REFUGE

Here too the master should mention the trainings that were explained above in the context of persons of lesser capacity.

ACCUMULATING THE ACCUMULATIONS

As before, the seven-limb practice should be done in the presence of the direct and lineage gurus and the merit field explained above.

TRAINING IN THE ATTITUDE

The observed objects and aspects of love and compassion should be visualized as explained above.

THE ACTUAL RITUAL

In front of the master, the student should kneel down on his right knee; sitting in a crouching position is also appropriate. With palms joined, he should generate bodhicitta. Mind generation here is not the mere mind generation that thinks, "I will attain buddhahood for the welfare of others." Rather, one focuses on that mind that has been generated and makes the promise, "I will not give it up as long as I have not attained enlightenment." Thus generate that attitude in reliance upon ritual.

If you are unable to train in the precepts of aspiring bodhicitta, you should not make this promise. However, everyone may ritually generate the mere thought "I will become a buddha for the welfare of all sentient beings," [137] regardless of whether they are able to train in the trainings of mind generation. These two approaches may be appropriate for aspiring bodhicitta, but it is inappropriate to ritually take on engaged bodhicitta without training in the precepts. Therefore it is incorrect to claim that there are differences among the many vow rituals passed down by Nāgārjuna and Asaṅga in terms of whether or not it is appropriate.[90] The *Advice to the King*

Sūtra says that if one cannot train in the precepts of generosity and so forth, a great amount of merit is accomplished in mere mind generation.[91] Taking this as its source, the first *Stages of Meditation* says:

> Those who cannot train in the perfections fully in all their aspects should still generate bodhicitta thoroughly conjoined with method because the results will be great.

Thus it is clear that it is appropriate for someone incapable of training in the precepts of generosity and so forth to adopt the mind generation but inappropriate to take the vow.

The ritual for adopting bodhicitta is as follows:

> All buddhas and bodhisattvas residing in the ten directions, please grant me your attention. Master, please grant me your attention. I, whose name is _____, by means of the roots of virtue of the nature of generosity, the nature of ethics, and the nature of meditation that I have created, caused to be created, and rejoiced in the creation of in this life and in previous lives, just as the previous tathāgatas, arhats, perfectly complete buddhas and great bodhisattvas thoroughly abiding on the great grounds generated the mind of unsurpassed perfectly complete enlightenment, in the same way also I, whose name is _____, from now until I reach the quintessence of enlightenment, will generate the mind of unsurpassed, perfectly complete, great enlightenment, I will liberate the beings who are not liberated, free those who are not free, give relief to those without relief, and cause those who have not completely passed beyond sorrow to completely pass beyond sorrow. [138]

Say this three times. Even though it is not clearly mentioned, it is necessary to repeat these words after the master in the refuge ceremony and in this ritual.

This is the manner of adopting bodhicitta in the presence of a master. Atiśa's *Mind Generation Ritual* says what to do if we cannot find a master:

> The ritual for generating bodhicitta oneself in the absence of

a master is as follows. Having brought to mind the Tathāgata Śākyamuni and all the tathāgatas of the ten directions, prostrate to them and do the rite of offerings and so forth. Then, as with the previous order, make the request and go for refuge, but leave out the word "Master" and so forth.

The concluding ritual

The master should proclaim the precepts of the aspiring mind to the student.

17 | Guarding One's Bodhicitta

GUARDING THAT WHICH HAS BEEN RECEIVED WITHOUT IT DEGENERATING

THIS HAS TWO POINTS: training in the cause of bodhicitta not degenerating in this life and training in the cause of not being separated from bodhicitta again in future lives.

TRAINING IN THE CAUSE OF BODHICITTA NOT DEGENERATING IN THIS LIFE

This has four points: training in remembering the benefits so that the strength of one's delight in bodhicitta increases, training in generating it six times so that actual bodhicitta increases, training in not mentally abandoning any sentient being for whose welfare bodhicitta has been generated, and training in accumulating the collections of merit and wisdom.

TRAINING IN REMEMBERING THE BENEFITS SO THAT THE STRENGTH OF ONE'S DELIGHT IN BODHICITTA INCREASES

Contemplate the benefits of bodhicitta by studying the sūtras or hearing them from your guru. Since they have been taught extensively in the *Marvelous Array Sūtra*, they should be studied there. As quoted above,[92] it says, "Bodhicitta is like the seed of all the Dharma of the Buddha," and all the conduct and aspirations of the bodhisattvas are summarized in it. Therefore it is said to be like a brief presentation, since although the extensive explanation of the elements is boundless, the brief presentation contains everything and distills the essential points of all bodhisattva paths.

Because the benefits taught in Asaṅga's *Bodhisattva Levels* concern aspiring bodhicitta, the two benefits of generating stable bodhicitta are mentioned first. You become a holy field and thoroughly endowed with the merit of nonharm.

YOU BECOME A HOLY FIELD

As stated, "The world with its gods and human beings will bow to you."[93] [139] As soon as you generate this mind, you become an object of veneration for all sentient beings. As stated in the scriptures, you outshine all the great arhats by way of your lineage as soon as you generate this mind; you become a superior or an exalted being. You become a field of merit by yielding limitless effects even through minor meritorious acts. You become like a father of all beings in accordance with the statement "Supporting the whole world, you are like the earth."

YOU BECOME THOROUGHLY ENDOWED WITH THE MERIT OF NONHARM

Since you are guarded by twice as many protectors as protect a universal monarch, yakṣas and nonhuman primordial local guardians cannot harm you even when you are asleep, intoxicated, or careless.

You pacify calamities, harm, and infectious diseases with the words of secret mantra and knowledge mantra. If even things that cannot be accomplished in the hands of sentient beings will be accomplished when they come into your hands, what need is there to mention that other things will be accomplished? Owing to this, the activities of pacification and so forth are shown to be easily accomplished in reliance upon bodhicitta.[94] Therefore, if you have that, you will also quickly accomplish the common siddhis.

Fear, famine, and harm from nonhuman beings will not occur in those places in which they have not occurred, and you will experience little harm, be without illness, and so forth after transmigrating.

Because you are endowed with patience and a gentle disposition, you will bear harm that is done to you and will not return harm and the like. Also it will be difficult for you to be reborn in the lower rebirths and, if it happens, you will quickly be freed. While there, you will have little suffering and as a result become extremely disenchanted with cyclic existence. Compassion for those sentient beings will also arise.

If the merit of bodhicitta were to become form, it could not be contained in space itself. Making offerings of material things to the buddhas does not compare to it even partially. The *Questions of the Householder Vīradatta Sūtra (Vīradattagṛhapatiparipṛcchāsūtra)* says:

If the merit of bodhicitta
were to take physical form,
it would fill the entire realm
of space and then even surpass it.

Someone might offer buddhafields [140]
filled with jewels as numerous as
the sand grains of the river Ganges
to the protector of the world,

but to join the palms and bow
to bodhicitta is distinctly
superior to that offering made.
As for this, it has no limit.

Once Atiśa was circumambulating the Vajra Seat [in Bodhgaya] and contemplating how to attain complete enlightenment quickly. Then the smaller statues stood up and asked the bigger ones, "What should those who want to quickly become a buddha train in?" The latter replied, "They should train in bodhicitta." In the sky above the main temple, a young woman questioned an older woman, and the latter made a similar reply. It is said that his mind became very certain about bodhicitta from hearing this.[95]

In that way, you should understand bodhicitta as the condensed essential point of all the Mahāyāna instructions, the great treasure among all siddhis, the distinctive feature that differentiates the Mahāyāna from the Hīnayāna, and the supreme basis that exhorts one to the vast conduct of the victors' children. Increase the strength of your delight in meditating on it, like someone thirsty hearing of water. This is because the buddhas and their children analyzed the paths for many eons and with increasing subtlety with their marvelous exalted knowledge and saw it to be the supreme method for attaining buddhahood. Thus *Entering the Bodhisattva Way* (1.7) says:

Having reflected thoroughly for many eons,
the lords of sages saw this as of foremost benefit.

TRAINING IN GENERATING IT SIX TIMES SO THAT ACTUAL BODHICITTA INCREASES

This has two points: training in not giving up aspiring bodhicitta and training in increasing it.

TRAINING IN NOT GIVING UP ASPIRING BODHICITTA

The *Verse Summary of the Perfection of Wisdom* teaches that it is a sin worse than a defeat of prātimokṣa to vow to liberate sentient beings who have not been liberated and so forth in the presence of the buddhas, bodhisattvas, and your spiritual teacher as witnesses but then lay down the burden of bodhicitta because of discouragement from seeing the enormous number of sentient beings and their bad actions; the long time, many eons, you need to exert yourself; or the necessity of training in the two limitless accumulations and difficult practices. [141] *Entering the Bodhisattva Way* says that if you give up the mind you have undertaken, you will have to wander in the lower rebirths for a long time. That same text also says (3.27):

> Just as a blind man finds a jewel
> in a heap of dust
> by chance, bodhicitta
> has arisen within me.

Like this, think, "What I have found is absolutely amazing" and "I will not give it up under any circumstances." Observing this, reinforce your heart's decision not to give it up even for an instant.

TRAINING IN INCREASING ASPIRING BODHICITTA

Since it is not enough to merely not give it up, you should reinforce it three times a day and three times at night with great effort. If you can accomplish the extensive ritual explained above, you should do it according to that. If you cannot accomplish it, train in love and compassion, having visualized the merit field and made offerings. You should do this six times a day. The ritual for that is to say the following three times in the day and three times at night:

> I go for refuge until I am enlightened
> to the Buddha, the Dharma, the Highest Assembly.
> Through practicing generosity and the rest,
> may I attain buddhahood for the benefit of beings.

TRAINING IN NOT MENTALLY ABANDONING ANY SENTIENT BEING FOR WHOSE WELFARE BODHICITTA HAS BEEN GENERATED

The measure of mentally abandoning a sentient being is the occurrence of the thought "I will not work for his welfare now or ever after" depending on some condition—for example, that he has done something unacceptable.

TRAINING IN ACCUMULATING THE COLLECTIONS OF MERIT AND WISDOM

Having adopted aspiring bodhicitta through a ritual, you should put effort into the accumulations through daily offerings to the Jewels and so forth as the cause for increasing bodhicitta.

TRAINING IN THE CAUSE OF NOT BEING SEPARATED FROM BODHICITTA AGAIN IN FUTURE LIVES

This has two points: training in abandoning the four nonvirtuous practices that cause it to degenerate, and training in adopting the four virtuous practices that do not allow it to degenerate.

TRAINING IN ABANDONING THE FOUR NONVIRTUOUS PRACTICES THAT CAUSE IT TO DEGENERATE

Among the four nonvirtuous practices, the first is deceiving one's abbot, master, guru, or those worthy of offerings. The objects are one's abbot and master, which is easy to understand, your guru, who is someone who wishes to benefit you, and those worthy of offerings are those endowed with excellent qualities, even though they do not belong to the two preceding categories.

Someone might wonder, what action becomes a nonvirtuous practice when it is done to [one's abbot and so on]? It is a nonvirtuous practice to knowingly cheat him, whatever the means. [142] However, as the deceit and shiftiness that are not lies are indicated below, here it must refer specifically to cheating through lying. This is because the *Compendium of Trainings* teaches that abandoning a nonvirtuous practice constitutes a virtuous practice and because the antidote of this nonvirtuous practice is the first of the four virtuous practices [listed below].

The second is to cause others to regret virtues that they do not regret. Here, the object is another person who does not regret a virtue that he has done. The action toward that person is to express regret for that which is not an object of regret with the intention of making him regret it. Whether or not the person is deceived and whether or not the person has regrets, it is the same.

The third is to say something uncomplimentary and the like about a sentient being who has entered the Mahāyāna. The object here is someone who has generated bodhicitta and possesses it. The action toward them is to say something unpleasant motivated by hatred. In this case, the object to whom it was said must understand the meaning. It is easy for this to occur, and it is also a very great fault. This was already mentioned above in brief. Furthermore, the *Magic of the Complete Certainty of Total Peace Sūtra* teaches that if a bodhisattva generates a mind of contempt toward a bodhisattva, he must remain in hell for an eon and that there is nothing apart from deprecating another bodhisattva that can make a bodhisattva fall into the lower rebirths. The *Verse Summary of the Perfection of Wisdom* also says that if a bodhisattva who has not yet obtained a prophecy argues out of anger with a bodhisattva who has obtained a prophecy, he will have to spend as many eons longer on the path as there were moments of a mind of anger. Because of that, the same text also teaches that you must put an end to anger in all its aspects and put effort into confessing it and restraining it immediately whenever it arises.

The fourth is an action done out of deceit and shiftiness but without the extraordinary attitude. Here, the object is any other sentient being. The action done toward them is to act with deceit and shiftiness. Deceit and shiftiness are explained here in terms of deceiving with respect to measures and weights and so forth and like Gyalwa Yechung's actions, for example. In order to send someone off to Rakma, Gyalwa Yechung sent him first just to Tölung so that he would then be willing to go all the way to Rakma. According to the *Compendium of Trainings*, *deceit* is to feign qualities one does not possess, [143] and *shiftiness* is to take measures to hide one's faults.

TRAINING IN ADOPTING THE FOUR VIRTUOUS PRACTICES THAT DO NOT ALLOW IT TO DEGENERATE

The object of the first virtuous practice is all sentient beings. The action is to eliminate knowingly lying to them even for the sake of one's life or for as little as a joke. If you act in this way, you will be sure not to cheat special objects such as your abbot, master, and so forth through lies.

The object of the second virtuous practice is all sentient beings. The action is to abide with the extraordinary attitude toward them without deceit or shiftiness—that is, to abide with an honest attitude. It is the antidote to the fourth nonvirtuous practice.

The object of the third virtuous practice is all bodhisattvas. The action is to generate the perception of them as resembling the Teacher and to proclaim truthful praise about them in the four directions. Sharawa said that although we have created a little bit of something like virtue, there is no sign of its increase and many signs of its exhaustion. Virtue is exhausted through hatred, disdain, and offense toward bodhisattvas and our companions. Therefore, if we are able to eliminate offending our companions and bodhisattvas, we will no longer experience what is referred to in the *Compendium of Trainings* as "harm based on persons." Since we do not know in whom bodhicitta is present, we act from the perspective of training in pure appearances, generating the perception of all sentient beings as the Teacher in accordance with the *Kāśyapa Chapter* (*Kāśyapaparivarta*). If there is an audience and an opportunity to express their excellent qualities, do so. However, if you do not go to all four directions and proclaim them, this is not a fault. This virtuous practice is the antidote to the third nonvirtuous practice.

The objects of the fourth virtuous practice are the sentient beings who are ripened by you. The action is to cause them to hold to complete enlightenment without wishing for a temporary vehicle. Moreover, while from your side you should cause your disciple to make a connection with it, if that thought does not arise in the disciple, it does not become a fault because you were unable to accomplish it. By means of this virtuous practice, you abandon the second nonvirtuous practice, for if you wish from the depths of your heart to establish others in the ultimate of all types of happiness, you would not do something to cause them to give rise to mental unhappiness so that they give rise to regret that is, itself, mental unhappiness. [144]

The *Questions of a Lion Sūtra* says:

> "By what means is bodhicitta
> not given up in all one's lives,
> not even in one's dreams,
> much less while one is not asleep?"

> He spoke: "In cities or in villages
> in the countries where you live,
> guide others correctly to enlightenment.
> Through that, bodhicitta will not be abandoned."

Furthermore, *Array of Qualities in Mañjuśrī's Buddhafield* teaches that the aspiration is not abandoned if one possesses four qualities: having abandoned pride, having abandoned jealousy, having abandoned miserliness, and being mentally joyful when seeing others' wealth. The *Cloud of Jewels of Sūtra* clearly teaches that if you train in bodhicitta in all behaviors and generate bodhicitta before starting any virtuous activity, you will not be separated from this precious mind in other lives either. As it is said, "If a person investigates time and time again . . ."

THE METHOD FOR RESTORING IT IF IT HAS DEGENERATED

If you transgress the precepts other than giving up the aspiring mind and mentally giving up sentient beings, there is no infraction from the point of view of a bodhisattva as long as you do not have bodhisattva vows. However, since it transgresses the precept of promising virtue in the interim, it becomes faulty conduct and therefore should be confessed by means of the four powers.

How to train in the conduct after generating the mind

This has three points: the reason it is necessary to train in the precepts after generating bodhicitta, demonstrating that buddhahood is not achieved by training in method or wisdom alone, and explaining the actual stages of training in the precepts.

The reason it is necessary to train in the precepts after generating bodhicitta

According to the above scriptural passage from the *Life of Maitreya*, even if you do not train in the precepts of generosity and so forth after generating aspiring bodhicitta in this manner, it will still be of great benefit. However, if you do not make the bodhisattva precepts your essential practice, it will be impossible to become a buddha. Therefore you should train in the conduct. The *King of Concentrations Sūtra* says:

> One should make it the essential practice. Why? Because, oh youthful one, it will not be difficult for one who makes it his essential practice to obtain unsurpassed perfectly complete enlightenment. [145]

Also, Kamalaśīla says in the first *Stages of Meditation*:

> A bodhisattva who has generated the mind understands that he cannot tame others without taming himself and thoroughly applies himself to the practice of generosity and so forth. Without the practice he cannot achieve enlightenment.

Once the vow has been taken, you must practice training in those very precepts associated with it.

Demonstrating that buddhahood is not achieved by training in method or wisdom alone

The second *Stages of Meditation* says:

One who engages in the method for accomplishing buddhahood needs an unmistaken method, for however hard you try, a mistaken path will not bring about the desired result, like yanking a cow's horn to get milk. If it is faultless but incomplete, the result will not come about despite your effort, just as a sprout will not grow if the seed, water, earth, or the like is missing.

Well then, what are the complete and unmistaken causes and conditions? *Vairocana's Manifest Enlightenment* (*Vairocanābhisaṃbodhi*) says:

O Lord of Secrets, the wisdom of omniscience arises from the root that is compassion. It arises from the cause that is bodhicitta. It is concluded by method.

In this regard "compassion" has already been explained. "Bodhicitta" is both conventional bodhicitta and ultimate bodhicitta. "Method" is thoroughly complete generosity and so forth. This was explained by the great trailblazer Kamalaśīla.

One erroneous conception regarding the path is upheld by the Chinese Heshang and others, who say, "As long as they are discursive thoughts— even if they are good conceptions, to say nothing of bad conceptions—they bind us in cyclic existence. Therefore their effects do not transcend cyclic existence, just as one can be bound with fetters of gold or ropes, just as both white and black clouds obscure the sky, and just as pain is produced whether one is bitten by a white or a black dog. That is why just equipoise without conceptions about anything is the path to buddhahood. Generosity, ethics, and so forth were taught for the sake of immature beings incapable of meditating on this definitive meaning. Therefore, having found the definitive meaning, to engage in that conduct is like a king becoming a commoner or like tracking an elephant's footprints after you have found the elephant." [146]

Heshang substantiates his position by quoting eighty passages from sūtras that praise nonconceptuality. His statement that all the factors of method are not a genuine path to buddhahood is an enormous denigration, and by negating engagement in the essence of the Victor's teachings— selflessness—with a fine investigative wisdom, it abandons the ultimate meaning, straying far away from it. Kamalaśīla has negated this well with stainless scriptures and reasonings and has presented in detail the good path that pleases the victors. Yet there are still some who scorn the side of conduct such as guarding and restraint and who discard them while cultivating the paths and act as has been described above. It appears that some not only denigrate the factor of method but also discard the way of understanding the view, while others discard the search for the view of suchness by means of fine investigative wisdom and then cleverly assert the Chinese meditation of not thinking about anything.

They do not approach meditation on emptiness either. Even if it were accepted as meditation on emptiness, the statement "Those who meditate well on the meaning of emptiness should meditate on emptiness alone and need not cultivate a subject that has a conventionality as its object in the domain of conduct" contradicts all the scriptures and simply seems to leave behind the path of reason. The object to be achieved by Mahāyānists is nonabiding nirvāṇa. For that, *nonabiding in cyclic existence* is achieved through what is called the wisdom realizing suchness, the stages of the path based on the ultimate, the path of the profound, and what is called the accumulation of wisdom and the factor of wisdom. *Nonabiding in nirvāṇa or peace* is necessarily achieved through what is called the wisdom that knows things in their variety, the stages of the path based on conventional truths, the vast path, the accumulation of method, and the factor of merit.

The following words are taken from the *Sūtra Teaching the Tathāgata's Inconceivable Secret*:

> The accumulation of wisdom is what eliminates all mental afflictions. The accumulation of merit is what fully nurtures all sentient beings. Blessed One, since this is so, the bodhisattva great beings [147] put joyous effort into the accumulation of merit and wisdom.

Also, the *Teaching of Vimalakīrti Sūtra* (*Vimalakīrtinirdeśasūtra*) says:

> In response to the questions "What is the bondage of bodhisattvas?" and "What is their liberation?":
> Wisdom not conjoined with method is bondage.
> Wisdom conjoined with method is liberation.

Method not conjoined with wisdom is bondage.
Method conjoined with wisdom is liberation.

And in the *Gayāśīrṣa Hill Sūtra*:

The bodhisattva path, in brief, is made up of two. What are the
two? They are method and wisdom.

Their significance is also clearly taught in *Lamp for the Path to Enlightenment* (vv. 41–43):

The obstructions will not be exhausted
without engaging in perfect wisdom.

Therefore, in order to eliminate
all afflictive and cognitive obstructions,
the yoga of the perfection of wisdom
should always be practiced combined with method.

That is why method divorced from wisdom
as well as wisdom divorced from method
are referred to as "bondage." Therefore
you should not abandon either.

And (vv. 45–47):

The victors explained method as
all the accumulations of virtue,
the perfections of generosity and so forth,
except for the perfection of wisdom.

Great beings who cultivate the wisdom aspect
through familiarity with the methods
thereby quickly achieve enlightenment,
not by meditating on selflessness alone.

Wisdom is thoroughly explained as
knowing the emptiness of inherent existence,
which is to realize that aggregates, elements,
and sources are not produced.

The *Questions of Ratnacūḍa Sūtra* (*Ratnacūḍaparipṛcchāsūtra*) teaches that it is necessary to meditate on the emptiness that possesses all supreme aspects—complete in all the method factors of generosity and the rest.

The *Gathering All the Threads Sūtra* says:

> Foolish people seek to repudiate the bodhisattvas' [148] practice of the six perfections for the sake of enlightenment, saying, "You should train in the perfection of wisdom alone. What is the use of training in anything else?"

And:

> Foolish people also say, "One becomes enlightened by only one approach, the approach of emptiness." However, they do not have completely pure conduct.

One may claim, "Training in the conduct of generosity and so forth is necessary if one does not have a stable realization of emptiness, but if one has that, it is sufficient." If this were so, conduct would not be necessary for the victors' children who have attained the first ground and so forth, nor especially for the victors' children on the eighth ground who have achieved power over nonconceptual wisdom. However, this is incorrect, for the *Ten Grounds Sūtra* teaches that on each of the ten grounds, one perfection such as generosity becomes paramount, but that does not mean that the remaining ones are not practiced. Therefore, on each of the grounds, all six or all ten perfections are said to be practiced.

In particular, on the eighth ground when the bodhisattva has exhausted all mental afflictions and therefore abides in the ultimate with all elaborations pacified, the buddhas exhort him and say, "Buddhahood cannot be achieved through this mere realization of emptiness; this realization is achieved even by śrāvakas and pratyekabuddhas. Look at my immeasurable bodies, wisdom, buddhafields, and so forth. You do not have my powers and the like. Therefore set about it with joyous effort. Think of the unpacified sentient beings agitated by various mental afflictions. Do not give up patience either." If the buddhas are so emphatic in explaining to eighth-ground bodhisattvas the need to train in bodhisattva conduct, this obviously applies even more so to others. Although there are indeed differences in the context of the high paths of unsurpassed mantra, it was already explained above that both the Mantrayāna and Pāramitāyāna are the same by and large in sharing the structure of the path of the two types of bodhicitta and training in the six perfections.

The opponent might respond, "We do not assert that generosity and so forth are unnecessary but that they are complete in the mind with no thoughts [149] because nonapprehending generosity is complete by nonadherence to the recipient, to the act of giving, and to the substance given. The remaining perfections are likewise complete in this way. This is also because the sūtras say that the six perfections are contained in each one of them." If all the perfections were complete simply through this, they would also be complete in the śamatha of a tīrthika's single-pointed mind at the time of meditative equipoise since there is no adherence to those three in that way. In particular, as the *Ten Grounds Sūtra* says, śrāvakas and pratyekabuddhas who have a nonconceptual wisdom of reality would become Mahāyānists during meditative equipoise because the entire bodhisattva conduct would be complete.

If you assert that this alone is sufficient because it is taught that all six are included in each perfection, then it would also be appropriate just to offer a mandala with the verse "Giving cow dung together with water . . ." since it is said that all six are present in it.

The following analogy is given in order to illustrate conduct conjoined with the view and wisdom conjoined with method. When a mother tormented by sorrow at the death of her beloved child engages in conversations with other people and the like, no matter what mental states arise, she does not give up her sorrow because it is so powerful, even though not all her mental states are those of sorrow. Similarly, if the wisdom realizing emptiness is very powerful, then even though the mental states that observe your generosity, prostrations, circumambulations, and so forth do not realize emptiness, this does not contradict the fact that they operate with the power of that wisdom. If you start off with the intense power of bodhicitta, as you do at the beginning of a meditation session, although bodhicitta is not manifest during the concentration of emptiness, that does not mean it is not influenced by it. The way in which wisdom and method are not separate is also like that.

Do not be misled by the statement that, for example, the body, wealth, and long life you enjoy in cyclic existence are results of the accumulation of merit. When method is divorced from wisdom, this is indeed the case. However, if they are conjoined, merit is altogether suitable to be the cause of liberation and omniscience. There are infinite scriptural passages for this, like in Nāgārjuna's *Precious Garland* (3.12):

> In brief, Your Highness, the form body [of a buddha] [150]
> is born from the accumulation of merit.

Moreover, you [the opponent] sometimes expound that the faulty conduct and all the mental afflictions that become the causes of the lower rebirths can also become causes of buddhahood, and sometimes you seem to say that the virtues of generosity, ethics, and so forth that lead to higher states are causes of cyclic existence rather than causes of enlightenment. You should settle your mind before talking!

Do not misconstrue these statements from the sūtras:

> Adherence to the six, generosity and so forth, is the action of Māra.

The *Three Heaps Sūtra* (*Triskandhakasūtra*) also explains:

> Making offerings while falling into objectification, guarding one's ethics while considering ethics to be supreme, and so forth should be confessed individually.

Also the *Questions of Brahma Sūtra* (*Brahmaparipṛcchāsūtra*) says:

> Conduct in all its varieties is conceptual. Thorough nonconceptuality is enlightenment.

The meaning of the first is that generosity and so on motivated by erroneous clinging in terms of the two selves is explained as an action of Māra because it is impure. However, generosity and so forth are not presented as the actions of Māra. Otherwise, you would have to say, "Giving gifts should be confessed in general" without the need for it to have fallen into fixation, saying, "Bestowing gifts having fallen into fixation." Therefore it follows that it was not taught in this manner. In the third *Stages of Meditation*, it becomes a very crucial point for Kamalaśīla to give this kind of answer, for if you misunderstand this, you will apprehend signs of a self of persons or a self of phenomena and assert the entire side of conduct to be qualified by signs.

If the mind of giving that thinks "I will give away this substance," the mind of restraint that thinks "I will restrain myself from this faulty conduct," and all such virtuous conceptions were apprehensions of a self of phenomena apprehending the three spheres, it would make sense for those who have found the view of selflessness of phenomena to stop them in every way, just like hatred, pride, and so forth, [151] and it would be inappropriate to rely on them for that purpose. If any conception that thinks "This is this" were considered to be an apprehension of a self of phenomena that apprehends the three spheres, then thinking about the excellent qualities of a spiritual teacher, the great significance of the freedoms and endowments, and so forth, remembering death, thinking about the sufferings of the lower rebirths, going for refuge, contemplating that from this action arises that effect, training in love, compassion, and bodhicitta, and training in the trainings of engaged bodhicitta would be thoughts that think "This is this," "From this that arises," and "This has these excellent qualities and those faults." Since those necessarily induce certainty, the apprehension of a self of phenomena would increase more and more as certainty with respect to those above-mentioned topics increases. Moreover, certainty about those paths would decrease as certainty about the selflessness of phenomena is nurtured more and more. Thereby, the side of conduct and the side of the view would come to contradict each other like hot and cold, and a strong and enduring mind of certainty about both could not be generated.

At the time of the result, both the truth body and the form body are construed as the object to be obtained, and these are not contradictory. Accordingly, at the time of the path, these following two must also not be contradictory: a mind of certainty induced with respect to the total freedom from even the merest particle of elaborations of a referent object that is apprehended as having signs of the two selves, and a mind of certainty induced with respect to "From this, that arises" and "This has that fault or quality."

That depends, in fact, on how the view of the two truths is established in the context of the ground. The valid cognition thoroughly positing the ultimate determines the mode of subsistence or the manner of being of all the phenomena of cyclic existence and nirvāṇa as being without the merest particle of inherent existence. The valid cognition of conventions thoroughly positing causes and effects individually determines phenomena that are causes and effects without the slightest confusion. Once you gain certainty, by way of scriptures and reasonings, that these two do not harm each other in the least but rather assist each other, then you will realize the meaning of the two truths and you will come to count yourself among "those who have found the intention of the Victor."

The meaning of the third scriptural passage is explained in the third *Stages of Meditation*. The context for this line of the sūtra is an analysis of production and so forth in order to teach that generosity and so forth are not really produced, so the term "conceptuality" [152] is used to teach that they are merely imputed by conceptuality. However, they are not taught to be objects to be discarded and not relied upon. The *Compendium of the Sūtras* (*Sūtrasamuccaya*) also clearly sets forth that a one-sided path is not enough:

> Bodhisattvas who lack skillful means should not make strong effort in the profound Dharma.

The *Sūtra Teaching the Tathāgata's Inconceivable Secret* says:

> Child of the lineage, it is like this. A fire burns because it has a cause; if the cause is absent, it subsides. Likewise, a mind blazes due to an observed object; if the observed object is absent, the mind subsides.
>
> Therefore the bodhisattva skilled in means knows how to completely extinguish observed objects by means of the thoroughly pure perfection of wisdom, but he does not completely extinguish observed objects with respect to the roots of virtue. He does not allow the observed objects for mental afflictions to arise but places the mind on the observed objects of the

perfections. He also individually analyzes the observed object that is emptiness but looks upon the observed object that is all sentient beings with great compassion.

You must differentiate between statements that there is an observed object and statements that there is no observed object. The bonds of the mental afflictions and apprehending signs need to be loosened, whereas the ropes of the trainings need to be tightened. The two misdeeds must be destroyed, whereas virtuous actions need not be destroyed. Therefore being restrained by the trainings and being bound by the apprehension of signs are not the same, nor is loosening one's guarding and restraint the same as loosening the bonds of apprehending a self. Therefore the meaning of *destruction* and *self-liberation* and so forth need to be examined well.

When Master Kamalaśīla negates mental inattention, he does not negate the meditation where the mind is placed within the view that has determined the meaning of the ultimate mode of being and settled single-pointedly on that without attending to anything else. However, he does negate that meditation on emptiness consists of a mere stabilization in which the mind is left without conceiving anything, without placing it on the meaning determined by the view, the ultimate mode of being. [153] This is the same for the Mantrayāna and Pāramitāyāna. What similarities and differences exist between the two systems with regard to analyzing with the wisdom of fine investigation and maintaining one's meditation will be explained below.

18 | Training in the Perfections and Gathering Disciples

THIS HAS TWO POINTS: how to train in the Mahāyāna in general and how to train in the Vajrayāna in particular.

HOW TO TRAIN IN THE MAHĀYĀNA IN GENERAL

This has three points: developing the wish to train in the precepts of bodhisattvas, taking the vows of the victors' children after developing the wish, and training in the vows after taking them.

DEVELOPING THE WISH TO TRAIN IN THE PRECEPTS OF BODHISATTVAS

It is inappropriate to study the precepts of the Vinaya and tantra without taking the respective vows, but these present precepts are different. First, you come to understand the precepts so that your mindstream is purified. Then, if you feel enthusiasm for holding them, the vows are imparted on you. They will be very stable if you bring them to mind as an object after having understood the precepts, develop a heartfelt desire to train in them, and then take the vows. That is why this is a good method.

TAKING THE VOWS OF THE VICTORS' CHILDREN AFTER DEVELOPING THE WISH

In my commentary on the ethics chapter of Asaṅga's *Bodhisattva Levels*, I already extensively determined how to first take the vows, how to then guard against the root downfalls and infractions that are misdeeds, and how to restore the vows if they have degenerated.[96] Therefore, since the vows certainly need to be looked into before they are taken, consult that source to understand these points.

TRAINING IN THE VOWS AFTER TAKING THEM

This has three points: the foundation of the precepts, how the precepts are contained in it, and the stages of training.

THE FOUNDATION OF THE PRECEPTS

Although there are infinite clear divisions, when grouped together by type, all the precepts of bodhisattvas are contained in the six perfections. Therefore the six perfections constitute the great synopsis that condenses all the essential points of the bodhisattva path.

HOW THE PRECEPTS ARE CONTAINED IN IT

This has two points: the main topic, which is the specific number of perfections, and a secondary discussion of their specific order.

THE MAIN TOPIC: THE SPECIFIC NUMBER OF PERFECTIONS

The Blessed One made just a synopsis of the six perfections, whereas Maitreya, the holy regent of the victors, established certainty in them by elucidating, as they had been intended, the essential points among the reasons for their formulation. They account for how their number was specified. Therefore, when you find certainty about this in a way that captivates the mind, you will hold the practice of the six perfections as supreme instructions. The number of the perfections is specified as six from the points of view of: high status, the accomplishment of the two welfares, the complete accomplishment of the welfare of others in all aspects, [154] their comprising the entire Mahāyāna, their influencing all aspects of the path or method, and the three trainings.

THE NUMBER AS SPECIFIED FROM THE POINT OF VIEW OF HIGH STATUS

To bring the vast conduct of a bodhisattva to completion, you need many consecutive lives, and to progress along the path in them, you need a life totally complete in all excellent characteristics. Without it, even if you practice with something that merely has some excellent aspects like our current life, there will be no progress whatsoever. Thus a life that is excellent in all its aspects is necessary. To elaborate, you need a life that is endowed with the four excellences: wealth at your disposal, a body with which to practice, companions with whom to practice, and the ability to complete the actions you undertake.[97]

However, many things become conditions for the mental afflictions simply because they are excellent. Thus it is also necessary not to come under the power of the mental afflictions. But that is not enough either; you must differentiate well the objects that are to be unmistakenly engaged in and turned away from with respect to what should be adopted and what should be discarded. Otherwise, the excellences will destroy you, just like bamboo and plantain trees are destroyed by bearing fruit and like a young molly mule is destroyed by pregnancy. The wise will understand that the excellences are the effects of previous good actions and will strive for their causes again so that they will increase. The unwise will use the effects previously accumulated and thereby exhaust them. If you do not develop them anew, they will engender suffering in future lives. Hence, in future lives, those six perfections will not emerge causelessly nor from a nonconcordant cause. Like their respective corresponding causes, the perfections are specified as six.

The wealth and so forth at the time of the path are temporary higher states, while those in ultimate higher states such as an excellent body and so forth exist on the buddha ground. Similarly, *Ornament for the Mahāyāna Sūtras* (16.2) states:

> Excellent wealth, body, companions,
> and effort are higher states [of the first four perfections].
> To not be controlled by mental afflictions
> and to be unmistaken regarding activities [are results of the final two].

THE NUMBER AS SPECIFIED FROM THE POINT OF VIEW OF THE ACCOMPLISHMENT OF THE TWO WELFARES

When you train in bodhisattva conduct with such a life, there are only two types of bodhisattva activities: [155] those that accomplish one's own welfare and those that accomplish the welfare of others.

Specifically, in order to accomplish the welfare of others it is necessary to first benefit them with material gifts. Since generosity accompanied by harm to sentient beings leads to nothing, it is itself of great benefit to others to completely turn away from actions that harm others, together with their bases. Therefore ethics are necessary. However, those pure ethics cannot come about if you are unable to bear being harmed and you retaliate once or twice. So to perfect ethics, it is necessary to have the patience that in the face of harm thinks, "It does not matter." Since your patience prevents you from retaliating, you then prevent others from accumulating a lot of bad actions. Inspired by that, they will then apply themselves to virtue. Thus it is of great benefit to others.

If your own welfare is to attain the happiness of liberation through the power of wisdom, this will not come with a distracted mind, and so you must place your mind in equipoise by means of meditative stabilization. Thus it is necessary to achieve the suppleness of a mind that abides on the observed object for as long as you wish. Since this does not arise in the lazy, you need to set about it with joyous effort, not relenting day or night. This is the basis of the other perfections. Therefore, in order to bring about the two welfares, the perfections are specified as six. *Ornament for the Mahāyāna Sūtras* (16.3) says:

> Great effort for the welfare of beings
> is made by giving, not harming, and patience.
> Abiding and liberation, together with their bases,
> enact your own welfare in all aspects.

These components do not exhaust the means of securing the welfare of others in its entirety.[98]

In the statement "Abiding and liberation," the *mind abiding* on the observed object is said to be the work of meditative stabilization, and *liberation* from cyclic existence is said to be the work of wisdom. When these two are differentiated, śamatha will not be mistaken for special insight.

THE NUMBER AS SPECIFIED FROM THE POINT OF VIEW OF THE COMPLETE ACCOMPLISHMENT OF THE WELFARE OF OTHERS IN ALL ASPECTS

At the outset, eliminate their poverty through material things. Following that, do not harm any sentient beings whatsoever. Not only that, be patient when harmed. Since you are their companion, act with undaunted joyous effort. Relying on meditative stabilization, fulfill their wishes through magical emanations and so forth. When they have become suitable vessels, offer them good explanations in reliance upon wisdom, so that you liberate them by clearing up their doubt. This is why the perfections are specified as six. [*Ornament for the Mahāyāna Sūtras* (16.4) says:]

> The welfare of others is also your own welfare
> when you are unstinting, cause no harm at all,
> are patient when harmed, are not thwarted by what is to be done,
> and are joyful and well-spoken. [156]

THE NUMBER AS SPECIFIED FROM THE POINT OF VIEW OF THEIR COMPRISING THE ENTIRE MAHĀYĀNA

You will not be attached to wealth you have acquired, and you will not view wealth that you have not acquired with interest. When that is present, you will be able to guard the trainings, whereby you will take up ethics and respect them. You will not be discouraged because you have patience with sufferings caused by sentient beings and nonsentient phenomena. You will apply yourself to and delight in any kind of virtuous activities, and so you will not be discouraged by them. You will cultivate the nonconceptual yoga of śamatha and special insight. These six encompass all Mahāyāna practices, which you arrive at through these six. They are sequentially accomplished through the six perfections, and nothing more than those six is necessary. *Ornament for the Mahāyāna Sūtras* (16.5) says:

> All Mahāyāna is merely this:
> taking no joy in wealth, having highest respect [for ethics],
> not being discouraged regarding the two,[99]
> and nonconceptual yoga.

THE NUMBER AS SPECIFIED FROM THE POINT OF VIEW
OF THEIR INFLUENCING ALL ASPECTS OF THE PATH OR
METHOD

Generosity is the path or the method of nonattachment to wealth, or objects you have acquired, because you become free from attachment to them by getting used to giving them away. Ethics is the method for avoiding the distraction of trying to acquire objects not yet acquired, because the vows of a fully ordained monk prevent all the distractions of earning a living. Patience is the method for not giving up on sentient beings, because one is not depressed by all the sufferings caused by their harm. The method for increasing virtue is joyous effort, because it increases through undertaking virtue with joyous effort. The last two perfections are the methods for completely purifying the obstructions, because the mental afflictions are completely purified by meditative stabilization and the obstructions to omniscience are completely purified by wisdom. That is why the perfections are specified as six. *Ornament for the Mahāyāna Sūtras* (16.6) says:

> One path is nonattachment to objects.
> The others are restraint from the distraction of obtaining them,
> not giving up on sentient beings, increasing virtues,
> and purifying obstructions.

THE NUMBER AS SPECIFIED FROM THE POINT OF VIEW OF
THE THREE TRAININGS

The nature of training in ethics is ethics. Moreover, since it is adopted when you have the generosity that is indifferent to wealth, the accumulation of ethics is that generosity. Also, when ethics are adopted, patience follows, because it is protected by the patience that does not return abuse for abuse. [157] Meditative stabilization is training of the mind [in concentration, the second training], whereas wisdom is training in wisdom. Joyous effort is included in all three trainings. This is why the perfections are specified as six. *Ornament for the Mahāyāna Sūtras* (16.7) says:

> The Victor perfectly explained the six perfections
> from the perspective of the three trainings:

the first training includes the first three perfections,
the other two are aspects of the last two perfections,
and one perfection is included in all three trainings.

Thus one thoroughly completes either one's own or others' welfare by means of a certain excellent physical basis, through the variety of methods one possesses depending on one's vehicle. The perfections should thus be known as six because they are completely perfected and subsumed by the basis that accomplishes a given practice, the welfare, the Mahāyāna, the method, and the trainings. You should think about this until you gain great certainty that they are the sum of all the essential points of the bodhisattva practices.

A SECONDARY DISCUSSION OF THEIR SPECIFIC ORDER

This has three points: the order in which they arise, the order in terms of superiority, and the order in terms of subtlety.

THE ORDER IN WHICH THEY ARISE

If you have generosity that is indifferent and not attached to wealth, you will adopt ethics. If you possess ethics that restrain faulty behavior, you will be patient with regard to harm. If you have patience that does not despair with respect to hardships, adverse circumstances will be few, so you will be able to act with joyous effort. As you act with joyous effort day and night, the concentration that is able to establish the mind in virtue will arise. When the mind is in meditative equipoise, you will realize reality just as it is.

THE ORDER IN TERMS OF SUPERIORITY

The earlier are inferior and the latter are superior.

THE ORDER IN TERMS OF SUBTLETY

Since the earlier are easier to engage in and perform than the latter, they are coarser. Since the latter are more difficult to engage in and perform than the earlier, they are more subtle. *Ornament for the Mahāyāna Sūtras* (16.14) says:

> The latter grow based on the earlier ones;
> they were taught in stages like that
> because they abide as inferior and superior
> and they are coarser and more subtle.

THE STAGES OF TRAINING

This has two points: how to train in the conduct in general and how to train in the last two perfections in particular.

HOW TO TRAIN IN THE CONDUCT IN GENERAL

This has two points: training in the perfections that ripen one's own buddha qualities and training in the four ways of gathering disciples that ripen the minds of others. [158]

TRAINING IN THE PERFECTIONS THAT RIPEN ONE'S OWN BUDDHA QUALITIES

This has six points: how to train in generosity, ethics, patience, joyous effort, meditative stabilization, and wisdom.

Generosity

HOW TO TRAIN IN GENEROSITY

This has three points: the nature of generosity, its subdivisions, and how to generate generosity in one's mind.

THE NATURE OF GENEROSITY

The nature of generosity is a virtuous intention to give and the actions of body and speech motivated by it. It is the intention at the time the body and speech engage in generosity. The completion of the perfection of generosity does not depend on having eliminated the poverty of sentient beings by giving things to them. Rather, generosity is perfected when one's miserly grasping is destroyed and when one has become completely familiarized with the mind of giving to others along with its effects.

ITS SUBDIVISIONS

This has two points: subdivisions from the point of view of individual bases and subdivisions of the nature of generosity itself.

SUBDIVISIONS FROM THE POINT OF VIEW OF INDIVIDUAL BASES

The *Bodhisattva Prātimokṣa* teaches that generosity of material things is generally practiced by lay bodhisattvas, whereas ordained bodhisattvas should practice the generosity of the Dharma rather than generosity of material gifts. Moreover, the *Compendium of Trainings* says that it is prohibited for the ordained to give gifts after working for material things, considering that it interrupts studies and so forth. However, they should give material things if they obtain them in great quantities through the power of previous merit without harm to their virtuous activities. Sharawa also said, "I will not talk to you about the benefits of giving; I will talk instead about the faults of grasping." This is the talk of one who was not pleased that the ordained were giving gifts, having toiled to obtain and accumulate wealth and often damaged their ethics.

SUBDIVISIONS OF THE NATURE OF GENEROSITY ITSELF

The *generosity of the Dharma* is to unmistakenly teach the holy Dharma, to teach the worldly aims of actions such as crafts and so forth in a way that is logical and free from wrongdoing, and to make others engage in upholding the basis of the trainings. The *generosity of fearlessness* is to thoroughly protect others from fear of humans such as kings, bandits, and so forth, fear of nonhumans such as lions, tigers, and so forth, and fear of the elements such as water, fire, and so forth. The *generosity of material things* is to give material things to others.

HOW TO GENERATE GENEROSITY IN ONE'S MIND

Generosity is not perfected by merely destroying all miserliness toward one's body and wealth, [159] because the two types of Hīnayāna arhats without exception have also abandoned that along with all its seeds, given that miserliness is included in the factor of attachment. It is necessary not only to eliminate the obstacle to giving, which is miserliness or clinging to all things, but rather to generate from the depths of one's heart the thought of giving away all one's possessions to others. For that, it is necessary to meditate both on the faults of clinging to things and on the benefits of giving.

As taught in the *Moon Lamp Sūtra* (*Candrapradīpasūtra*), the former [the faults of grasping] are that the body is unclean, the life force fluctuates like water gushing down a steep mountain, and both body and life force are under the power of karma, thus lacking an independent self. Therefore you should see things to be false, like a dream or a mirage, and cease your attachment to them. If you do not counter your attachment, you will come under its power, accumulate great faulty conduct, and go to the lower rebirths.

The second, the benefits of giving, are as taught in the *Compendium of Trainings*:

> In this way, my body and mind
> pass away in every instant.
> If I attain permanent
> untainted enlightenment
> with this tainted impermanent body,
> is it not obtained for free?

Entering the Bodhisattva Way (3.10) describes how generosity should actually be generated:

> I give away with no sense of loss
> my body as well as my possessions
> and all my virtues of the three times
> to accomplish the welfare of all sentient beings.

Like that, taking body, wealth, and roots of virtue as your object, familiarize yourself again and again with the thought of giving them away to all sentient beings.

Since your current determination is immature and of little strength, you should not actually give away your flesh and so forth, even though you have already mentally given away your body to sentient beings. Nonetheless, the *Compendium of Trainings* says that if we do not train in the thought of giving away our body and life now, we will also not be able to do so in the future owing to a lack of familiarity with it. Therefore it is necessary to train in that thought from now on.

Thus it is an afflicted infraction when out of craving you use food, clothing, and so forth that you have sincerely given away to sentient beings, having forgotten the thought "I will use these for the welfare of others" and instead using them for your own welfare. [160] It is a nonafflicted infraction if, without this craving, you forget the perception that includes all sentient beings or if you are attached to those things for the sake of another sentient being. It is stealing if you use for your own sake those things dedicated to others, knowing they are someone else's property. If those things are valuable, it becomes a defeat of the prātimokṣa vow. On the other hand, there is no fault if you use them thinking, "I will use this sentient being's wealth for his own welfare." This is mentioned in the *Compendium of Trainings*.

It becomes a defeat when you have dedicated something with a sincere thought to a sentient being who is a human and he is aware of it and also holds it to be his. The factors for it to become a defeat are present if you take it for your own welfare, aware that it belongs to someone else, and if it is of some value. That is the intention here. Apart from that, *Bodhisattva Levels* teaches that merit increases immeasurably and with little effort through training in the determination to emanate immeasurable varieties of offerings and to give them with clarity to sentient beings from the depths of one's heart. That is the generosity of the wise bodhisattva.

Training in the perfection of generosity will be very powerful if, at the time it occurs, it is endowed with the six perfections. Specifically, the six are made complete if there is, at that time, the ethics that restrain the mental attention of śrāvakas and pratyekabuddhas; the determination and patience derived from aspiring to the qualities of omniscience, and patience when abused by others; the joyous effort that generates the aspiration for increasing that more and more; the meditative stabilization that is a single-pointed mind not mixed with the Hīnayāna and that dedicates that virtue to complete enlightenment; and the wisdom that understands the object given, the act of giving, and the recipient to be like illusions.

Ethics

HOW TO TRAIN IN ETHICS

This has three points: the nature of ethics, its subdivisions, and how to generate ethics in one's mind.

THE NATURE OF ETHICS

Ethics is the mind of abandonment—a mentality turned away from harming others—together with its basis. This is mainly from the point of view of the ethics of restraint. Ethics is perfected through thoroughly completing one's familiarity with this mind more and more. It is not that you externally establish all sentient beings in freedom from all harm without exception. *Entering the Bodhisattva Way* (5.11) says:

> The perfection of ethics is taught as
> achieving the mind of abandonment. [161]

ITS SUBDIVISIONS

This has three points: the ethics of restraint, the ethics of gathering virtuous qualities, and the ethics of bringing about the welfare of sentient beings.

THE ETHICS OF RESTRAINT

From the point of view of being accompanied by a motivation, the ethics of restraint is the ten abandonments that abandon the ten nonvirtues. From the point of view of its nature, it is the seven abandonments of body and speech that abandon the seven nonvirtues. This is the intention of the statement in *Bodhisattva Levels* that the ethics of restraint in the mind of a bodhisattva is the seven types of prātimokṣa vows. When those who possess the prātimokṣa vows possess the bodhisattva vows, the ethics of restraint is the actual lay or monastic prātimokṣa vows and the abandonments and vows common to them in their minds. When those who are unsuitable as bases for the prātimokṣa vows possess bodhisattva vows, the ethics of restraint is the abandonments and restraints of abandoning either the natural misdeeds or the proscribed misdeeds that are common to prātimokṣa.[100] Although the prātimokṣa vows in the mind of a bodhisattva are ethical vows, they are not actual bodhisattva vows, whereas the other vows share a basis with the bodhisattva vows.

THE ETHICS OF GATHERING VIRTUOUS QUALITIES

The ethics of gathering virtuous qualities is to observe virtues such as the six perfections and to generate those that have not yet arisen in one's own mind, to not degenerate those that have arisen, and to increase them more and more.

THE ETHICS OF BRINGING ABOUT THE WELFARE OF SENTIENT BEINGS

The ethics of bringing about the welfare of sentient beings is to accomplish appropriately the welfare of sentient beings in this and future lives through ethics free of misdeeds.

HOW TO GENERATE ETHICS IN ONE'S MIND

Pure ethics depend on practicing what should be engaged in and avoided according to the formulated rules of the Buddha. Furthermore, they follow the strong and firm wish to guard one's ethics. For them to arise, you must meditate for a long time on the faults of not guarding them and the benefits of guarding them. This was explained above in the context of persons of medium capacity.

The *Compendium of the Perfections* (2.48) also says:

> You cannot attain your own welfare with degenerate ethics,
> so where would you get the power for the welfare of others?
> Therefore it's wrong for those who make good effort
> for others' welfare to loosen their respect for ethics.

And (2.60–61):

> As for these ethics, the path of special attainment, [162]
> they make one equal to the naturally compassionate.
> They are of the excellent nature of pure wisdom;
> free from errors, they're called "the best of ornaments."
>
> They are a salve not at odds with ordination,
> a pleasant fragrance that permeates all three realms.
> Those who have ethics will be nobles among humans
> even if they look the same on the outside.

This means that in reliance upon ethics, your mindstream improves more and more, you become similar in training to the great beings who are naturally compassionate, and you attain the pure wisdom that has abandoned all seeds of faulty conduct. Although other ornaments do not beautify the very young or very old, the ornament of ethics is the supreme ornament for whoever possesses it, whether young, old, or in between, since it pleases everyone. Although other fine fragrances are one-sided, only spreading in the direction of the wind, the scent of ethics' fame spreads in all directions. Although the ordained are prohibited from using ointments such as sandalwood, which cool the torment of heat, the ointment that protects from the torment of the heat of the afflictions is suitable and not prohibited for them. Even though the same in possessing the signs of ordination, those who possess the jewel of ethics are more outstanding than anyone else.

Again from the same text (2.62–64):

Without expressing a word, without much effort,
resources and services needed for practice gather.
The whole world bows low without intimidation;
power and wealth are gained without effort and work.

All beings, including the ones he never knew,
bow to a being endowed with ethical discipline,
even if his lineage may be unworthy of mention
and even if he did not help or benefit them personally.

Even the dust made auspicious by his feet
is raised to the head for its sanctity. Gods and humans
prostrate so it touches their heads and carry it everywhere.

Thus one should think about the benefits as expressed here.

Although there are three kinds of ethics, in the beginning it is important for bodhisattvas to have the ethics of restraint, which is to practice what to engage in and avoid according to the formulated prātimokṣa rules or what is common with them. If this is guarded, the others will also be guarded; [163] if it is not guarded, the others will not be guarded either. Therefore the *Compendium of Ascertainments* says that if the ethics of the bodhisattva vows degenerate, all the vows degenerate. Whoever thinks that the prātimokṣa vows are for śrāvakas and rejects their formulated rules of engagement and avoidance, saying, "I must train in the other bodhisattva trainings," has thus not grasped the essential point of the training in bodhisattva ethics, for it is taught many times that the ethics of restraint is the basis and domain of the two subsequent sets of vows.

The main ethic of restraint is to abandon the natural misdeeds. The synthesized essential points of the great faults of the natural misdeeds are that one should abandon the ten nonvirtues. Therefore you should repeatedly generate the mind of restraint that is not even tempted toward them. The *Compendium of the Perfections* (2.8–9) says:

The path to the bliss of high birth and liberation
is to not violate these ten paths of action.
Abiding in them, you will have as a special effect
the intention to benefit sentient beings.

"Completely restraining one's speech, body, and mind,
in summary, is ethics," said the Victor.
This is the basis comprising all ethical conduct,
without exception, so thoroughly train in it.

In brief, the practice of ethics is to take this [restraint from the ten non-virtues] as the basis and repeatedly train in the mind of restraint that trains in the precepts of whatever ethics one has undertaken.

Ethics are made to possess the six perfections like this: generosity is to abide in ethics oneself and establish others in them, and the remaining perfections are as above [in the presentation of generosity].

Patience

HOW TO TRAIN IN PATIENCE

This has three points: the nature of patience, its subdivisions, and how to generate patience in one's mindstream.

THE NATURE OF PATIENCE

The nature of patience is the mind abiding at ease without being overwhelmed by harm and suffering, as well as a very staunch belief in the Dharma. Its opposites are hatred, disheartenment, lack of belief, and dislike. The completion of the perfection of patience is just to fully cultivate the mind that ceases one's anger and so forth; it does not depend on getting rid of unruly sentient beings.

ITS SUBDIVISIONS

There is the patience of disregarding harm done by others, [164] the patience of accepting the suffering that arises in one's own mindstream, and the patience of a mind certain about the Dharma.

HOW TO GENERATE PATIENCE IN ONE'S MINDSTREAM

It is necessary to meditate on the benefits of patience and the faults of impatience. Think about how later on you will have few enemies, you will not be separated from dear ones, you will experience much happiness and mental ease, you will die without regret, and you will be reborn among the gods after this body has perished. The *Compendium of the Perfections* (3.3–5) says:

> For those with a mind that neglects the welfare of others
> it was taught that "the best of ways is patience."
> Patience protects that which is good and excellent
> in the world from the faults of anger.
>
> It is the best of ornaments for the strong,
> the peak of power for those embracing austerities,
> a torrent of water for grassland fires of malice.
> All harm is removed by patience in this life and others.
>
> The arrows of words of unruly beings are wrecked
> against the armor of patience of excellent beings.
> Thereby they turn into excellent flowers of praise
> and become attractive garlands of fame.

And (3.8):

> Patience is also the workshop where bodies are made
> with beautiful qualities and adorned with the signs [of a buddha].

Meditate on the benefits as taught here until you reach a strong and stable certainty about them.

Second, *Entering the Bodhisattva Way* (6.1) says:

> An instant of anger destroys everything
> that has been gathered in a thousand eons—

256 | THE MIDDLE-LENGTH STAGES OF THE PATH

all those good deeds, whatever they are,
like generosity and honoring sugatas.

This appears to have been composed in accordance with Āryaśūra's *Compendium of the Perfections*. The *Play of Mañjuśrī Sūtra* (*Mañjuśrīvikrīḍitasūtra*) says that it destroys the virtue accumulated over a hundred eons.

Some explain that the object of that anger must be a bodhisattva, whereas others assert that it is any object in general. The former accords with *Entering the Middle Way* (3.6):

Therefore, through anger toward a child of the victors,
the virtue from giving and ethics one has amassed
over a hundred eons is crushed in an instant. [165]

As regards the person in whom anger arises, even bodhisattvas destroy their roots of virtue if they get angry, so needless to mention this is the case for one who is not a bodhisattva and who gets angry at a bodhisattva. The *Entering the Middle Way Autocommentary* says that whether or not it is certain that the object is a bodhisattva and whether or not the reason for the anger, seeing faults, is true, the destruction of virtue is similar to how it was explained above. In general, anger does not need to be directed at a bodhisattva in order for it to destroy roots of virtue. A passage quoted from the Sarvāstivādin scriptures in the *Compendium of Trainings* says:

If a fully ordained monk prostrates with extended limbs and a clear mind to a stūpa of hair and nail relics, he will come to enjoy as many thousands of universal monarch kingdoms as there are particles of dust that cover the ground all the way down to the golden foundation.[101]

And:

Even those roots of virtue will be destroyed if he injures or disparages one of pure conduct. Therefore, if one should abandon even anger at a charred log, how much more so at a body endowed with consciousness!

Some scholars say that "destruction of roots of virtue" means that the potential of earlier virtue to quickly bring about its effect is destroyed, and the emergence of its effect is delayed, so that the effects of hatred and so forth emerge first. Their respective effects do emerge, however, if they eventually meet with suitable conditions, for no mundane path whatsoever can eliminate the seeds that are to be eliminated, so it is impossible for seeds to be eliminated by the mental afflictions.

This is not a reliable reason. Even though ordinary beings purifying nonvirtues by means of the four opponent powers do not eliminate their seeds, it is impossible for the fully ripened effects to emerge even if the conditions are met later on. Once the peak and forbearance levels of the path of preparation have been attained, although wrong views and the seeds of nonvirtues that become the causes of lower rebirths have not been abandoned, wrong views and rebirths in the lower rebirths are impossible even if these seeds meet with their conditions.

Vasubandhu states in the *Treasury of Abhidharma Autocommentary*, "As for the karma that produces cyclic existence, some is heavy."[102] [166] Accordingly, either a virtuous or a nonvirtuous karma, by ripening sooner, can temporarily block the occasion for another karma to ripen. However, it cannot be posited nor has it been taught that it can destroy virtuous or nonvirtuous karma. "Destruction of roots of virtue" does not mean the mere temporary postponement of its ripening. Otherwise it would have been necessary to teach that all strong nonvirtues destroy the roots of virtue. Therefore, with respect to this, as Master Bhāviveka has said [in his *Blaze of Reasoning*] and as was explained above,[103] neither nonvirtues that have been purified by the four powers nor roots of virtue that have been destroyed by wrong views or harmful intent can bring about their effects even if later on they meet with the conditions, just as a seed that has been damaged cannot produce a sprout even though the conditions are met.

Moreover, even though accumulated bad actions are cleared away by purifying them with the four powers as described above, this does not contradict the fact that they delay the arising of higher paths. Thus, in some people, the effects of giving gifts and guarding ethics, such as the arising of excellent wealth and bodies, are destroyed. However, owing to the effect corresponding to the cause, familiarization with giving and the mind of abandonment, the roots of virtue of generosity and ethics arise again easily and cannot be destroyed. In others the arising of the effect corresponding to the cause as a continuum of similar type—inner ethics and so forth—is destroyed, but the arising of an excellent body, wealth, and so forth is not destroyed. Again others, as described above, will have some realizations of the path that enable them to completely traverse it within one eon unless anger toward a bodhisattva who has obtained his prophecy arises in their minds. If one thought of anger arises, their traversal of the path within one eon will be delayed although the path that exists in their mindstream is not relinquished. In brief, I think that when it comes to purifying nonvirtue, not all its efficacy is necessarily purified; isn't it likewise the case that when it comes to the destruction of virtue, not all its efficacy is necessarily destroyed?

Nonetheless this is an important point, and since it seems necessary to analyze it in reliance upon the Buddha's [167] unique scriptures and the reasonings based on them, you should look at the Buddha's excellent teachings and analyze.

Thus the *invisible* faults of anger are that it propels very unpleasant fully ripened effects and prevents the emergence of other very pleasant fully ripened effects. The *evident* faults of anger are taught in *Entering the Bodhisattva Way*: you do not experience peace of mind and certainty, previous joy and happiness are ruined and not achieved later on, sleep does not come, and the mind does not remain at ease. If your hatred is strong, even those you nurtured with kindness forget about your kindness and kill you, even friends and relatives get irritated and abandon you, even those you gather through generosity do not stay, and so forth. *Entering the Bodhisattva Way* (6.2) says:

> There's no bad action equal to hatred;
> there's no austerity equal to patience.
> Therefore patience should be practiced
> earnestly and in various ways.

Thus you should contemplate the benefits and faults and make an effort to develop patience in many ways.

It should be understood from the *Compendium of Trainings* that hatred is not the only faulty conduct that accumulates both major fully ripened effects and the destruction of roots of virtue. There are also holding wrong views that deny reality, abandoning the holy Dharma, despising and being arrogant toward beings such as bodhisattvas and gurus, and so forth.

How to cultivate the patience that is unconcerned with respect to harm

If you investigate whether someone who harmed you was free not to harm you, you will find that he did not harm you while in control; he generated the desire to harm you out of causes and conditions such as the seeds of mental afflictions from previous habituation and improper attention. Also owing to them, he engaged in activities that inflicted harm and thereby produced suffering in others, for under the power of another—the mental afflictions—he had become as if their slave.

Anger is also unreasonable when someone harms you under the influence of something else without control. For instance, someone possessed by an evil spirit might under its power wish to harm you while you are trying to help him get rid of it. Were he to strike you, [168] you would not get even the slightest bit angry at him, and instead you would think, "He is acting like this now because the evil spirit has robbed him of his freedom." You would put effort into doing whatever you could to free him from the evil spirit. A bodhisattva should also act like that. *Four Hundred Stanzas* (5.9) says:

> Just as a doctor is not disturbed
> by one who is gripped by a spirit and angry,
> the Sage beholds the mental afflictions
> and not the person afflicted by them.

Master Candrakīrti also says [in his commentary]:

> "This is no fault of sentient beings;
> it is a fault of the mental afflictions."
> The wise who have analyzed this in detail
> are not disturbed by sentient beings.

Moreover, the experience of suffering produced by the one who harms you is the experience of the effect of a negative action accumulated by you yourself in the past, and the action is thereby exhausted. If you cultivate patience toward it, you will not newly accumulate causes for experiencing suffering later on, whereas if you get angry, you will have to experience even greater suffering. It is therefore quite appropriate to bear minor suffering in order to turn away greater suffering, like when one is patient with blood-letting, burning, and so forth as methods for curing a serious illness.

How to cultivate the patience that accepts suffering

If the suffering that has arisen is curable, aversion is unnecessary. If it cannot be cured, again, aversion to it is useless because it is without benefit and is even a fault. This is because even tiny suffering becomes extremely hard to bear if you are very intolerant, whereas even great suffering is bearable if your intolerance is subdued.

The way to mentally accept suffering is to repeatedly train the mind by thinking, "If there were no such suffering, the desire to renounce cyclic existence would not arise. Therefore it has the excellent quality of exhorting my mind to liberation. It has the excellent quality of eliminating my arrogance since, when I am beset with suffering, my conceited superiority is destroyed. It has the excellent quality of making me shun bad actions because when I experience an intense feeling of suffering, since it arises from nonvirtue, I must turn away from its cause if I do not want this effect. It has the excellent quality of making me delight in accomplishing virtue since, owing to the torment of suffering, I wish for happiness, and to get that I must accomplish virtue. [169] And having understood that compassion is generated for the beings of cyclic existence, I think, 'In proportion to my own experience, others also suffer,' and so this suffering fulfills my wishes."

Furthermore *Entering the Bodhisattva Way* (6.14) says:

> Nothing does not get easier
> as you get used to it.
> Therefore bear even major harm
> by first getting used to minor harm.

Thus your strength to accept suffering will grow if you don the armor of the intention to accept suffering and expose yourself to suffering in small steps.

The way to cultivate the patience that is dedication to a mind of certainty regarding the Dharma is to train in dedication to being unbiased regarding the following: the objects of clear faith, the Three Jewels; the objects to be actualized, the two selflessnesses; the object of desire, the great power of the buddhas and bodhisattvas; the objects to be adopted and discarded, the causes that are excellent conduct and faulty conduct as well as their effects; the object of meditation, enlightenment, which is the aim to be achieved; the method for attaining that, the path of the bodhisattva trainings; the objects of study and contemplation, the holy Dharma of the twelve types of scripture; and so forth.

Joyous Effort

HOW TO TRAIN IN JOYOUS EFFORT

This has three points: the nature of joyous effort, its subdivisions, and how to generate it in one's mindstream.

THE NATURE OF JOYOUS EFFORT

Bodhisattva Levels explains joyous effort as a mind that is truly delighted to gather virtue and work for the welfare of sentient beings, as well as the actions of body, speech, and mind motivated by such a mind.

ITS SUBDIVISIONS

Among the three, the first is *armor-like joyous effort.* When bodhisattvas undertake joyous effort, they don the armor of mental delight as a preliminary attitude before applying themselves to something. That is, even if to attain buddhahood to eliminate the suffering of one single being, they must abide exclusively in the hells for a hundred thousand times ten million rounds of three immeasurable eons, they delight in it. Also with respect to their joyous effort at attaining complete enlightenment, they wear the armor of the attitude "If I will not give up engaging in joyous effort for that length of time, what need is there to mention that I will not give it up if the duration and suffering are less?" The *joyous effort of gathering virtuous phenomena* is to apply oneself to them for the sake of accomplishing the six perfections. The *joyous effort of working for the welfare of sentient beings* is similar to the above. [170]

HOW TO GENERATE IT IN ONE'S MINDSTREAM

The benefits of undertaking joyous effort are as described in *Ornament for the Mahāyāna Sūtras* (16.65–66):

> Joyous effort is best among virtue's accumulations.
> By relying on it, one attains the rest.
> Through joyous effort, one immediately gains
> the best source of happiness, including mundane and transcendental
>   attainments.
>
> Through joyous effort, one gains the worldly wealth one desires.
> Through joyous effort, one becomes totally pure.
> Through joyous effort, one is liberated,
>   passing beyond the transitory collection.
> Through joyous effort, one wakes to supreme enlightenment.

The *Compendium of the Perfections* (4.2) also says:

> There is nothing that can't be attained, that can't be accomplished,
> for those who have great joyous effort and do not dismay.

And (4.41–42):

> All nonhumans like to benefit him.
> He achieves all manners of concentration.
>
> He passes days and nights experiencing results.
> Through masses of excellent qualities, he won't decline.
> Through aims more noble than concerns of humans,
> he will flourish like an utpala flower.

The faults of not undertaking joyous effort are described in the *Questions of Sāgaramati Sūtra*:

> For the lazy, enlightenment is in all ways very far. In the lazy, generosity and so forth up to wisdom do not exist. For the lazy, the welfare of others does not exist.

The *Application of Mindfulness Sūtra* also says:

> The one foundation of mental afflictions
> is laziness, no matter in whom.
> He who has only laziness
> does not have any Dharma at all.

You should think like this.

There are two adverse conditions for joyous effort: seeing that one is able to accomplish virtuous Dharma but not engaging in it, and the discouragement that thinks, "How could I ever accomplish anything like that?"

SEEING THAT ONE IS ABLE TO ACCOMPLISH VIRTUOUS DHARMA BUT NOT ENGAGING IN IT

This has two points: one postpones things thinking "There is still time," or else one is overcome by attachment to bad activities. The antidote to the first is to meditate on these three thoughts: this body that you have obtained will quickly disintegrate, after death [171] you will fall into the lower rebirths, and it will be difficult to find such a good life once again. This was already taught above. The antidotes to attachment to bad activities are that you stop them by seeing that the holy Dharma is the cause for the arising of boundless joy in this and future lives, by seeing that meaningless idle chatter and the distractions of excitement and so forth degenerate the great aim in this life, and by seeing that it is the source that generates manifold suffering in future lives.

THE DISCOURAGEMENT THAT THINKS, "HOW COULD I EVER ACCOMPLISH ANYTHING LIKE THAT?"

This discouragement is also of three types. There is the discouragement that thinks, "Since the objects to be attained, the excellent qualities of a buddha, are limitless, I cannot attain them." There is the discouragement that thinks, "Since the method, giving away my arms, legs, and the like, is immensely difficult, I cannot accomplish it." And there is the discouragement that thinks, "Since it is necessary to return to this place, taking infinite rebirths in cyclic existence, during that time I will be harmed by the sufferings of cyclic existence."

There are also three antidotes. The antidote to the first is the thought "Even the buddhas did not already attain high paths right from the start. Rather, they were like me and became buddhas by going on to increasingly higher paths. Since the Blessed One also said that even those who are greatly inferior to me will attain buddhahood, why should I not attain it too unless I fail to put in joyous effort?"

The antidote to the second is to think, "As long as the perception arises that it is difficult to give away my body and so forth, I will not give it away. However, when the time to give it away arrives, it will not be difficult but will be like giving away vegetables."

The antidote to the third is to stop discouragement, thinking, "Because a bodhisattva abandons bad actions, their effects, suffering feelings, do not arise. Owing to his stable realization that cyclic existence lacks inherent existence, like an illusion, there is no suffering in his mind. If he thrives with physical and mental bliss even while remaining in cyclic existence, despair is pointless."

Relying on favorable conditions for joyous effort has four types. The power of *aspiration* is to meditate on causes and effects so as to generate the aspiration to discard and adopt. The power of *fortitude* is to not pursue anything impulsively without first investigating it but, having investigated it, to engage in it until you complete it. The power of *joy* makes your undertaking of joyous effort uninterrupted and insatiable, like a child engaged in a game. The power of *suspension* is to rest when your body and your mind are worn out owing to your joyous effort. [172] As soon as you have recovered, you start again.

In this way, in reliance upon stopping adverse conditions and relying on favorable conditions, undertake joyous effort until your body and your mind become light like a piece of cotton carried by the wind.

When you train in joyous effort, do so in such a way that possesses the six perfections. The generosity of joyous effort is to abide in joyous effort yourself and to establish others in it. The remaining are as above.

Meditative Stabilization

HOW TO TRAIN IN CONCENTRATION

This has three points: the nature of meditative stabilization, its subdivisions, and how to generate it in one's mindstream.

THE NATURE OF MEDITATIVE STABILIZATION

The nature of meditative stabilization is a mind that abides single-pointedly on any suitable virtuous object.

ITS SUBDIVISIONS

Its nature is twofold: mundane and supramundane.

Its orientation is threefold: śamatha, special insight, and a union of the two.

Its functions are threefold: the meditative stabilization that causes one to abide in physical and mental happiness in this life, the meditative stabilization that accomplishes excellent qualities, and the meditative stabilization that secures the welfare of sentient beings. The first is the meditative stabilization that generates physical and mental pliancy as one places the mind in meditative equipoise. The second is a meditative stabilization that accomplishes the excellent qualities shared with śrāvakas, such as the clairvoyances, liberations, totalities, and masteries.[104] The third is the meditative stabilization that accomplishes the welfare in eleven ways by means of meditative stabilization.[105]

HOW TO GENERATE IT IN ONE'S MINDSTREAM

The thoughts regarding the benefits of cultivating meditative stabilization and the faults of not cultivating it will be explained in the chapter on śamatha.

The generosity of training in meditative stabilization possessing the six perfections is to abide in meditative stabilization oneself and establish others in it. The remaining are as above.

Wisdom

HOW TO TRAIN IN WISDOM

This has three points: the nature of wisdom, its subdivisions, and how to generate wisdom in one's mindstream.

THE NATURE OF WISDOM

In general, wisdom is that which very thoroughly differentiates qualities in the thing that is being investigated. Here it is the wisdom that is skilled in the five areas of knowledge and so forth.

ITS SUBDIVISIONS

There are three: the wisdom realizing the ultimate, the wisdom realizing conventionalities, and the wisdom realizing the welfare of sentient beings. The first is the wisdom comprehending the suchness that is selflessness by means of a generic image [173] and the wisdom comprehending the suchness that is selflessness by means of something manifest. The second is the wisdom that is skilled in the five areas of knowledge. The third consists in knowing how to accomplish, without misdeeds, the welfare of sentient beings in this and future lives.

How to generate wisdom in one's mindstream

The third is to think about the benefits of generating wisdom and the faults of not generating it. First, the *Hundred Verses on Wisdom* says:

> The root of all the excellent qualities,
> the seen and the unseen, is wisdom.
> Thus wisdom should be fully embraced
> in order to accomplish both.

The complete purity of the first five perfections, generosity and so forth, depends on wisdom. Although a bodhisattva gives his own flesh to someone who asks him for it, like offering a leaf from a medicinal plant, he does not do it with the discursive thoughts of pride, discouragement, and so forth; rather he does it out of the suchness manifested by wisdom. When he practices ethics for the welfare of others, he purifies his ethics with the wisdom that sees the flaws of both cyclic existence and the peace of nirvāṇa. His mind is subdued by means of the wisdom realizing the faults of impatience and the excellent qualities of patience, and so he is not consumed by offense and suffering. By means of wisdom, he understands well the basis for undertaking joyous effort and exerts himself in that, whereby there is great progress on the path. By means of the wisdom relying on a process of reasoning, he achieves the supreme joyful bliss of the meditative stabilization that abides in the meaning of suchness.

Those endowed with wisdom can accomplish without any contradiction two excellent qualities that appear to be opposed. Were a bodhisattva to become a universal monarch with power over the four continents, the minister of wisdom would prevent his succumbing to the sway of desirable objects. Likewise, although his love that sees sentient beings as likable is very strong, it is not even slightly mixed with attachment. Although he has lasting and intense compassion that cannot bear the suffering of sentient beings, he is without the laziness that is oppressed by sorrow and that does not delight in virtue. Although he possesses immeasurable joy, he is without the restlessness that distracts the mind from a focal object. Although he possesses great and continuous equanimity, he does not neglect the welfare of beings even for an instant. This is all owing to wisdom, because wisdom eliminates the obstacles to accomplishing a balanced strength. [174]

Praise of the One Worthy of Praise says:

> They accord with conventionalities
> without discarding ultimate reality.

Thus there is no need to discard ultimate reality, the great certainty one has gained that not even a mere particle of the referent object whose signs are being apprehended is established. That is not contradictory to, but in agreement with, the fact that conventionalities are found through a profound certainty that individual effects arise from their individual inner and outer causes and conditions. Although these are grossly contradictory for those without a sharp mind, for those who possess wisdom they are compatible and not contradictory.

The same text also says:

> Regarding permissions and prohibitions,
> some of your words are definitive
> whereas others are not. Still
> there is no contradiction among them.

Thus there are many contradictory permissions and prohibitions in the higher and lower vehicles and in sūtra and tantra, and at the same time, they are to be practiced by a single person. Those without a sharp mind who seek the meaning of the countless scriptures see these two as contradictory whereas the skilled do not. This too is owing to wisdom.

Separated from wisdom, the other five—generosity and so forth—and the view will not be pure. The *Compendium of the Perfections* (6.5) says:

> In those who strive for results in the absence of wisdom,
> their giving does not purify. It was taught
> that the best generosity is to benefit others.
> The rest only serves to increase wealth.

And (6.11):

If wisdom's light does not dispel the darkness,
one will not come to possess pure ethics.
In the absence of wisdom, that discipline
will mostly be disturbed by afflictions through flawed
understanding.

And (6.13):

Excellent qualities of patience will not remain in one's mind
if it is disturbed by faults of distorted wisdom.
Nor will fame remain for a king without excellent qualities,
who hates to examine what is good and what is faulty.

And (6.16):

It is extolled as sublime for the learned. [175]
There is nothing more subtle and deep.
Without wisdom, the mind will not take the straight path,
completely unobscured by the fault of desire.

And (6.18):

Some believe wisdom's way does not involve effort;
their view will not become completely pure.

As for a king's fame here, a king who lacks excellent qualities may find fame once, but it will degenerate and pass.

Therefore it is necessary to generate wisdom. Its cause, hearing completely pure scriptures in accordance with one's mental capacity, is set out in the *Compendium of the Perfections* (6.48):

One who studies little is blind and doesn't know how to meditate.
Without that, what understanding would someone reflect on?
So from the cause of putting effort into studying
arises vast wisdom through meditation with reflection.

Venerable Maitreya also says in his *Sublime Continuum* (5.14–15):

> Conceptualization of the three spheres
> is posited as the obstruction to omniscience.
> Conceptualizations like miserliness
> are posited as afflictive obstructions.
>
> There is no cause apart from wisdom
> that eliminates these, and therefore
> wisdom is supreme. Since study
> is its basis, study is supreme.

And the *Compendium of Trainings in Verse* (v. 22) says:

> You should be patient. You should pursue study.
> Then you should retreat to a forest.
> Strive at equipoise meditation!

The holy beings of the past also said to first gather together in your mind the Dharma you have studied. Then reflect on it repeatedly, appraise it, and investigate it. Training merely to focus the mind is of no help if you allow yourself to forget the Dharma. The highest teachings are suitable for excellent meditators, and intermediate teachings are suitable for intermediate meditators. One's knowledge of the Dharma should grow to the same extent as one meditates. Once this certainty has grown firm through such contemplations, you will no longer listen to the words of bad companions who say, "All virtuous and nonvirtuous thoughts are to be abandoned because they are conceptuality." Rather, you will think, "The Dharma does not teach anything like that, [176] and my teacher also does not assert that," and you will not listen to them. Lacking that, someone who has a little bit of faith but no wisdom will burst into tears when he sees a crying face and will burst into laughter when he sees someone who is laughing. Considering true whatever people say, like a river he will go wherever he is led.

When you train in wisdom, make it possess the six perfections. The generosity of wisdom is to abide in the state of wisdom oneself and to establish it in others. The remaining ones are as above.

The Four Ways of Gathering Disciples

TRAINING IN THE FOUR WAYS OF GATHERING DISCIPLES THAT RIPEN THE MINDS OF OTHERS

Generosity is the same as explained in the context of the perfections. *Pleasant speech* is to teach the perfections to disciples. *Meaningful conduct* is to encourage disciples to engage in the meanings they were taught or to induce them to correctly adopt them. To *act in accord with the meaning* is to abide in the meanings one has introduced to others and train accordingly.

Ornament for the Mahāyāna Sūtras (16.73) says:

> Generosity is as before, while teaching it,
> making others adopt it, and engaging in it oneself
> are asserted, respectively, to be pleasant speech,
> meaningful conduct, and accord with the meaning.

Why are the means of gathering disciples specified as four? In order to gather a retinue for the sake of introducing them to virtue, they first need to be joyful. For this purpose, (1) give them gifts of material things and benefit their bodies. Once they have become joyful in that way, in order for them to engage in the path, they first need to know how. For that, (2) explain the Dharma to them by speaking pleasantly, so that they eliminate ignorance and doubts, and make them understand the meaning unmistakenly. When they understand that, (3) cause them to engage in accomplishing virtue through meaningful conduct. Furthermore, if you do not practice that yourself but merely explain to others, "This is how you should engage and desist," they will say, "Why do you tell others to practice it if you do not practice it yourself? You too still need to be corrected by others," and they will not listen to what is to be practiced. However, if you practice that yourself, they will also think, "Since he himself abides in the virtue in which he guides me, there will definitely be benefit and happiness for me if I accomplish it," and they will enter the path. Also, those who are already on the path will not turn away from it and will grow firm. Therefore you should (4) act in accordance with the meaning. [177]

Since the buddhas taught that the four ways of gathering disciples accomplish all the welfare of all disciples and that they are a good method, those who gather followers should rely on them. *Ornament for the Mahāyāna Sūtras* (16.78) says:

> Those who gather followers
> perfectly rely on this method.
> It accomplishes all the aims of everyone
> and is extolled as an excellent method.

The Great Elder, Atiśa, taught the way to accomplish [the six perfections] during meditative equipoise and post-meditation [in his *Heart Summary (Hṛdayanikṣepa)*]:

> Bodhisattva conduct includes
> the vast six perfections and so forth.
> The yogi arising from meditative equipoise
> steadfastly accomplishes the path of accumulation.

In this way, the beginner bodhisattva who has taken the vows of the victors' children and abides on the path of accumulation never passes beyond the six perfections, whether in meditative equipoise or in post-meditation. Therefore some of the six perfections are maintained in meditative equipoise and some in post-meditation. Meditative stabilization, which is śamatha, and the perfection of wisdom, which is special insight, are partially cultivated in meditative equipoise. The first three perfections and some elements of meditative stabilization and wisdom are maintained in post-meditation. Joyous effort occurs both in meditative equipoise and in post-meditation. One type of patience—some mental states of certainty regarding the profound Dharma—also occur during meditative equipoise.

The Great Elder, Atiśa, said [in his *Concise Method for Accomplishing the Mahāyāna Path*]:

> Each time you rise from meditative equipoise
> cultivate a view of all phenomena
> as like illusions, such as the eight similes.[106]

In post-meditation purify conceptuality
and emphasize the training in method.
At the time of meditative equipoise,
balance śamatha and special insight
and cultivate them continuously.

For those whose minds are untrained, to hear about such wonderful but difficult conduct produces anguish. Although even bodhisattvas are unable to take it as a practice right from the start, if you come to understand it and acquaint yourself with it as something to aspire to, later on you will naturally engage in it without effort. That is why familiarization is important, for if you see it as impossible and refuse to familiarize yourself with training your mind in it, [178] you will be extremely far from the completely pure paths. *Praise of Infinite Qualities (Guṇāparyantastotra)* says:

Practices that distress worldly beings to even just hear about them,
and that even you have never practiced for an extended time,
will become natural to you through gradual familiarization with
those practices.
Hence it is hard to increase excellent qualities without familiarity.

Therefore those who have taken bodhisattva vows must train in the conduct, but even those who have not taken up engaged bodhicitta by means of a ritual should try to develop the desire to train in it. The vows will be very stable if they are taken after enhancing one's delight in the training. Therefore you should put effort into this.

This concludes the explanation of training in aspiring bodhicitta and the stages of the path of training in the conduct of the victors' children in general within the stages of the path of persons of great capacity.

Meditative Stabilization
and Wisdom

19 | Śamatha and Special Insight

HOW TO TRAIN IN THE LAST TWO PERFECTIONS IN PARTICULAR

TRAINING IN THE last two perfections in particular consists in methods for cultivating śamatha and special insight because those two are included, respectively, in the perfections of meditative stabilization and wisdom. This has six points: the benefits of cultivating śamatha and special insight, demonstrating that these two include all concentrations, the nature of śamatha and special insight, the reason both need to be cultivated, how their order is definite, and how to train in each of them.

THE BENEFITS OF CULTIVATING ŚAMATHA AND SPECIAL INSIGHT

The *Unraveling the Intent Sūtra* teaches that all the mundane and supramundane excellent qualities of the Mahāyāna and Hīnayāna are results of śamatha and special insight. Someone might wonder, "Aren't śamatha and special insight excellent qualities of a mind that has attained a meditative state? How is it possible that all those excellent qualities result from those two?" Actual śamatha and special insight are indeed excellent qualities of the mind that has attained a meditative state, as explained below. Therefore not all the excellent qualities of the Mahāyāna and Hīnayāna are results of the two. Nevertheless, all the concentrations that include a single-pointed mind placed on a virtuous object are included in the category of śamatha, and all the virtuous wisdom minds that individually distinguish the ultimate mode of being from things in their variety are included in the category of special insight. It is with that intended meaning [179] that all the

278 | THE MIDDLE-LENGTH STAGES OF THE PATH

excellent qualities of the three vehicles are said to be results of śamatha and special insight. Hence there is no contradiction.

The *Unraveling the Intent Sūtra* also says:

> After beings have cultivated
> special insight and śamatha,
> they gain complete liberation from
> the bondage of negative tendencies and signs.

The meaning of this verse is that "negative tendencies" are the imprints that remain in the mindstream and are capable of generating increasingly erroneous subjective states, while "signs" activate the imprints for perpetual attachments to erroneous objects. *Instructions on the Perfection of Wisdom* (*Prajñāpāramitopadeśa*) explains that the former are eliminated through special insight and the latter through śamatha. Although those are the benefits of what are known as *śamatha* and *special insight*, statements on the benefits of meditative stabilization and wisdom should also be understood as the benefits of these two. They have the same meaning even though they are not called *śamatha* and *special insight*.

DEMONSTRATING THAT THESE TWO INCLUDE ALL CONCENTRATIONS

The *Unraveling the Intent Sūtra* says that all the limitless concentrations proclaimed in the Mahāyāna and the Hīnayāna are subsumed under śamatha and special insight. Therefore, since those who strive in concentration cannot investigate all its limitless manifestations, they should thoroughly investigate how to practice the epitome of all concentrations, śamatha and special insight.

THE NATURE OF ŚAMATHA AND SPECIAL INSIGHT

The nature of śamatha is set forth in the *Unraveling the Intent Sūtra*:

> Dwelling alone in solitude, you settle the mind within and attend
> to those very phenomena you have been reflecting on just as they
> are. Whatever mind it may be, since that mind of attention is

continuously directed inward, it is called *attention*. Repeatedly placing it in this way, it becomes stable, and when physical and mental pliancy arise, this is called *śamatha*.

The meaning of this is that if the mind attends to it continuously without distraction and stays on the object by itself so that the bliss and joy of physical and mental pliancy arises, the concentration becomes śamatha. This will arise from merely keeping the mind inwardly focused on its object of visualization without distraction; it does not depend on comprehending ultimate reality. [180]

The nature of special insight is set forth in the same sūtra:

> After achieving physical and mental pliancy, you abide in that state and eliminate other aspects of mind. With strong resolution you finely investigate the very phenomena you have been reflecting on just as they are, the object of concentration being an internal image. Thus, with regard to the images that are the objects of your concentration, any differentiation of the meaning of those objects to be known, any thorough differentiation, full investigation, full analysis, forbearance, acceptance, classification, viewing, and conceptualization is called *special insight*. In that way the bodhisattva is skilled in special insight.

Here, "differentiation" is a differentiation of things in their variety, and "thorough differentiation" is a differentiation of the ultimate mode of being. "Investigation" is a coarse investigation, and "analysis" is a subtle analysis. The *Cloud of Jewels of Sūtra* says:

> Śamatha is a one-pointed mind;
> special insight is fine investigation.

Venerable Maitreya also says [in *Ornament for the Mahāyāna Sūtras* 14.8]:

> Distilling words about phenomena[107]
> should be known as the path of śamatha,
> while a full analysis of their meanings
> should be known as the path of special insight.

And (18.66):

> In reliance on proper stability,
> śamatha and special insight
> serve to place the mind on mind
> and thoroughly differentiate phenomena.

This says that placing the mind in reliance on correct concentration is known as *śamatha*, and the wisdom thoroughly differentiating phenomena is known as *special insight. Bodhisattva Levels* presents it just like that, and the second *Stages of Meditation* also says:

> Once distraction toward external things has been pacified, resting with joy and pliancy within the mind itself, continuously and naturally engaging its internal object, is called *śamatha*. At the time of abiding in that śamatha, any thorough analysis of suchness is known as *special insight*. [181]

Instructions on the Perfection of Wisdom explains this in the same way.

According to *Bodhisattva Levels* and *Instructions on the Perfection of Wisdom*, śamatha and special insight can each have both the ultimate mode of being and things in their variety as its object. Therefore śamatha and special insight are not differentiated by way of their objects. There is śamatha that realizes emptiness, and there is also special insight that does not realize emptiness. Also, when the scattering to external objects has been pacified and the mind abides on an internal object, this is called *śamatha*, whereas seeing something special or superior is called *special insight*.

Some claim that the mind abiding nonconceptually without a vibrant clarity of cognition is śamatha whereas if it does have a vibrant clarity it is special insight. But this is not correct because it contradicts everything explained above and because this distinction is merely the distinction between concentration with or without laxity. This is also because every concentration of śamatha must definitely be free of laxity, and in every concentration that is free from laxity, clarity of the mind will definitely arise.

Thus to identify whether a mind is a concentration or a wisdom that observes emptiness, you must check whether that mind realizes either of the two selflessnesses. This is because there are countless nonconceptual concentrations of bliss and clarity in which the mind is not directed at the ultimate nature of an object. It is established by direct perception that it is possible for a mind to apprehend without discursive thought but not find the view that realizes the ultimate mode of being. Therefore there is not the slightest contradiction in the arising of nonconceptual concentrations that do not understand emptiness. From that point of view, when the mind is held for a long time, the power of the mind being so held gives rise to serviceable winds. Bliss at that time is not precluded because when the serviceable winds arise, it is natural for bliss and joy to arise in the body and the mind. Once that has arisen, the power of one's clear sensation of bliss and joy produces clarity in the mind. Therefore you cannot posit that all blissful, clear, nonconceptual concentrations realize suchness. Consequently, since bliss, clarity, and nonconceptuality arise in concentrations that do realize emptiness, and since there are also many concentrations in which the mind is not directed at emptiness and yet do have bliss, clarity, and nonconceptuality, one must distinguish between the two. [182]

THE REASON BOTH NEED TO BE CULTIVATED

Why is it not enough to cultivate either śamatha or special insight? Why must one cultivate both? To illustrate, when you light a butter lamp at night in order to look at murals, if the butter lamp is both very bright and does not flicker due to wind, you will see the painted figures very clearly. However, if the butter lamp is not bright or is bright but flickers in the wind, you will not see the forms clearly. Likewise, with respect to viewing the profound meaning, you will see suchness clearly if you have both the wisdom that ascertains the meaning of suchness without error and the imperturbability of a mind that stays on its object at will. However, if you do not have the wisdom that realizes the ultimate mode of being, you will not penetrate the ultimate mode of being no matter how much you familiarize yourself with concentration, even if you have nonconceptual concentration and your mind remains unscattered. On the other hand, if you have the view that comprehends selflessness but you lack the firm concentration in which the mind remains single-pointed, you will be unable to see the meaning of the ultimate mode of being clearly. Therefore both śamatha and special insight are necessary.

The second *Stages of Meditation* says:

With special insight alone without śamatha, the yogi's mind is distracted to other objects, and it will be unstable like a butter lamp in the wind. Consequently, the light of exalted wisdom will not shine forth brightly, which is why you should rely on both equally.

And:

A mind with the power of śamatha will not be moved by the winds of conceptualization, like a butter lamp secluded from the wind. Through special insight you eliminate the snares of all inferior views so that others no longer lead you astray. As the *Moon Lamp Sūtra* describes it:

Through śamatha's power, you will be immovable;
through special insight, you will be like a mountain.

You will know the meaning of reality if you analyze with wisdom that is conjoined with the meditative equipoise of śamatha that is not unbalanced by laxity or mental excitement. With that intention the *Compendium of the Dharma* says: [183]

When your mind is in meditative equipoise, you will know reality as it is.

The first *Stages of Meditation* says:

Since the mind is unsteady like water, there is no abiding without the basis of śamatha. A mind that is not in meditative equipoise cannot know reality as it is. The Blessed One said, "A mind in meditative equipoise fully knows reality as it is."

When you accomplish śamatha, it not only eliminates the fault of your wisdom consciousness wandering off while correctly analyzing selflessness; it also eliminates the fault of distraction during all analytical meditations that you do with fine investigative wisdom: on impermanence, actions and their effects, the faults of cyclic existence, love, compassion, training in bodhicitta, and so forth. As a result, everything virtuous you do is powerful because when you focus on each individual object, whatever it may be, you are never pulled away to something else. Until you obtain śamatha, any virtuous practice you do will be weak owing to a predominance of distraction. It is as *Entering the Bodhisattva Way* (8.1) says:

> A person with a distracted mind
> is in the fangs of the mental afflictions.

And (5.16):

> The Sage taught that recitation,
> ascetic practices, and so forth,
> even if you pursue them at length,
> are pointless with a distracted mind.

How their order is definite

Entering the Bodhisattva Way (8.4) says:

> Having understood that special insight
> conjoined with śamatha destroys the afflictions,
> first seek śamatha . . .

As this says, you first accomplish śamatha and then cultivate special insight based on it.

With regard to that you may wonder the following. The first *Stages of Meditation* says that the object observed in śamatha is unspecified when it says, "Its object of observation is unspecified." And as explained above, the objects of śamatha can include both conditioned phenomena and ultimate reality. [184] Therefore it should actually be possible to first understand the meaning of selflessness and then, by focusing and meditating on that, to simultaneously generate both śamatha, a mind not distracted, and special insight observing emptiness. So why first seek śamatha and then cultivate special insight?

This is how śamatha precedes special insight. Prior śamatha is not necessary to induce an understanding of the view that realizes selflessness, because the view is also seen to arise in the absence of śamatha. Prior śamatha is also unnecessary to induce an experience of mental transformation concerning that view, because even without śamatha there is nothing contradictory in an experience of mental transformation arising through repeatedly cultivating analysis by means of fine investigative wisdom. If it were contradictory, it would absurdly follow from the same reason that the experience of mental transformation arising with respect to impermanence, the faults of cyclic existence, or training in bodhicitta would also depend on śamatha.

In what way, then, does śamatha precede special insight? Here the context for the generation of special insight is that of ordinary beings with no prior realization arisen from meditation who newly generate it. In this regard, there is a method of meditation on selflessness with a special awareness that realizes emptiness. Its peculiarities will be explained below. Apart from that, analytical meditation is necessary in the vehicle of the perfections and in the three lower classes of tantra because special insight, which is a realization born from meditation, does not arise unless you have examined the meaning of selflessness by means of fine investigative wisdom and then engaged in analytical meditation upon it. If you seek an understanding of selflessness and repeatedly analyze its meaning prior to accomplishing śamatha, you will be unable to accomplish śamatha in reliance upon that because you have not accomplished śamatha. If you perform nonanalytical placement meditation, however, you can accomplish śamatha in reliance upon it, but this will only be a method for accessing śamatha, and you will need a method for accessing special insight distinct from that. Therefore you seek special insight afterward. That is why you do not deviate from the order of seeking śamatha first and then cultivating special insight in reliance upon it. If the method for generating special insight in this system did not require the generation of pliancy by means of the analytical meditation of fine investigation, there would be no particular reason to seek śamatha first and then cultivate special insight in reliance upon it.[108] [185]

It is completely unreasonable to not meditate in accordance with that order. The *Unraveling the Intent Sūtra* says that you cultivate special insight in reliance upon the attainment of śamatha, as mentioned above. Furthermore, the line "The latter grow based on the earlier ones"[109] refers to the sequence of meditative stabilization and wisdom within the six perfections. In particular, the arising of the higher training in wisdom in reliance upon the higher training in concentration is an order in which you first cultivate śamatha before special insight is cultivated. *Bodhisattva Levels* and *Śrāvaka Levels* (*Śrāvakabhūmi*) also say that special insight is cultivated in reliance upon śamatha. *Essence of the Middle Way, Entering the Bodhisattva Way*, and the three volumes of *Stages of Meditation*, as well as Jñānakīrti and Śāntipa, set forth that you seek śamatha and then cultivate special insight. Therefore the assertions of some Indian masters that you start out by generating special insight through analysis with fine investigative wisdom without seeking śamatha separately are in contradiction to the texts of the great trailblazers. Therefore it is inappropriate for the intelligent to rely on them.

This is the order of śamatha and special insight when you newly generate them. Later on the order is unspecified, because you continue to cultivate śamatha after you have cultivated special insight.

Someone might say, "Well, the *Compendium of Abhidharma* says:

> Some have attained special insight but have not attained śamatha.
> They strive for śamatha in reliance upon special insight.

Why is that?" We would respond that this does not refer to those who have failed to attain the śamatha included in the preliminary stage of the first dhyāna but to those who have failed to attain the śamatha of the actual first dhyāna and above.[110] Śamatha of the first dhyāna and above are in fact attained in reliance upon direct realization of the four truths. This is because, as stated in *Levels of Yogic Practice*:

> Furthermore, you can fully understand as they really are the four truths, from suffering up to the path without having attained the first dhyāna and so forth. As soon as you understand them, you place the mind and do not perform any thorough differentiation. In reliance upon just that superior wisdom, you apply yourself to superior states of mind.

In general, [186] to put it simply, the nine mental states are known as *śamatha*, while the four investigations of thorough differentiation and so forth[111] are known as *special insight*. However, actual śamatha and special insight, as explained here, must be posited as occurring after pliancy has arisen.

How to train in each of them

This has three points: how to train in śamatha, how to train in special insight, and how śamatha and special insight unite.

20 | The Practice of Śamatha

HOW TO TRAIN IN ŚAMATHA

THIS HAS THREE POINTS: attending to the prerequisites of śamatha, how to cultivate śamatha in reliance upon them, and the measure for the accomplishment of śamatha through meditation.

ATTENDING TO THE PREREQUISITES OF ŚAMATHA

This has six points: staying in a favorable location, having few desires, contentment, completely abandoning one's many activities, pure ethics, and completely eliminating one's conceptualization of desire.

As regards *staying in a favorable location*, the five excellent qualities of a location are: (1) good access, in that food, clothing, and so forth can be easily obtained, (2) a good site, in that predators and other wild beasts as well as enemies and the like do not live there, (3) good ground, in that it does not produce diseases, (4) good company, in that one has companions of equal ethics and views, and (5) good attributes, in that during the day there are few people around and at night there is little noise. *Ornament for the Mahāyāna Sūtras* (8.7) says:

> Locations for wise people's attainments
> have good access, a good site, and
> good ground, as well as good companions
> and conveniences for yoga.

Having few desires means not being excessively attached to good or numerous robes and so forth. *Contentment* means always being content with merely adequate robes and the like. *Completely abandoning one's many activities* is to completely abandon inferior activities such as business, excessive socializing with lay or ordained people, one's medical practice, astrological calculations, and so forth. *Pure ethics* means, with regard to prātimokṣa and bodhisattva vows, not damaging the basis of the trainings through natural or proscribed misdeeds, and even if it is damaged owing to carelessness, it is quickly restored through regret in accordance with the Dharma. *Completely eliminating one's conceptualization of desire* and the like means you eliminate all conceptualization of desire by meditating on its faults in this life, such as getting killed or arrested, and in future lives, such as birth in the lower realms. Or you should meditate thinking, "All the pleasant and unpleasant things of cyclic existence [187] are impermanent and subject to destruction. As I will definitely be separated from all of them before long, why do I get overly attached and so on?"

Lamp for the Path to Enlightenment (v. 39) says:

> Even if you put in great effort
> for a thousand years,
> concentration will not be accomplished
> if the limbs of śamatha are impaired.

For those with the heartfelt desire to accomplish the concentration of śamatha and special insight, it is therefore essential to put effort into the thirteen prerequisites and the like set forth in *Śrāvaka Levels*.[112]

HOW TO CULTIVATE ŚAMATHA IN RELIANCE UPON THEM

This has two points: the preparation and the actual practice.

THE PREPARATION

You should long cultivate the six preparatory practices explained above as well as bodhicitta and, as part of that, also train in the core meditation topics shared with persons of lesser and medium capacity.

THE ACTUAL PRACTICE

This has two points: the physical posture for meditation and explanation of the stages of meditation.

THE PHYSICAL POSTURE FOR MEDITATION

According to *Stages of Meditation*, you should sit on a very soft and comfortable seat and adopt a physical posture with the following eight characteristics. The legs may be fully crossed or half crossed. The eyes are directed over the tip of the nose, neither too open nor too closed. You should sit with your body straight and erect, rather than too bent or crooked, and with your mindfulness placed inward. Your shoulders should be straight and even. The head is held not too high nor too low and without tilting to one side; you should keep yourself erect from the nose down to the navel. The teeth and lips should remain natural, just as they are. The tongue should be placed near the upper teeth. As for the breath, your exhalations and inhalations should not be audible, forceful, or uncontrolled. Rather, their coming and going should by all means proceed imperceptibly, leisurely, and effortlessly. Thus you should first accomplish the eightfold posture and especially gentle breathing as explained. [188]

EXPLANATION OF THE STAGES OF MEDITATION

Most expositions of the stages of the path say that śamatha is accomplished by way of the eight factors set forth in *Distinguishing the Middle from the Extremes* (*Madhyāntavibhāga*) that eliminate the five faults.[113] The instructions from Geshe Laksorwa's lineage explain that on top of that, the six powers, the four attentions, and the nine states of attentional development explained in *Śrāvaka Levels* must be accomplished. In his *Ornament for the Mahāyāna Sūtras* and *Distinguishing the Middle from the Extremes*, the venerable Maitreya also sets forth the nine states of attentional development for mental abiding and the eight factors for eliminating the faults. Following them, Indian scholars such as Haribhadra, Kamalaśīla, and Śāntipa also set forth many stages of accomplishing concentration. In the Mantrayāna you also need to know them. Within the scriptures, the sūtra collection in particular presents extensively the faults of concentration such as the five faults and the way to eliminate them.

This has two parts: the way to generate flawless concentration and the stages of śamatha that arise in reliance upon it.

THE WAY TO GENERATE FLAWLESS CONCENTRATION

This has three points: what to do before focusing the mind on the object, what to do while focusing the mind on the object, and what to do after focusing the mind on the object.

WHAT TO DO BEFORE FOCUSING THE MIND ON THE OBJECT

If you cannot put an end to laziness, which delights not in cultivating concentration but rather in the opposite, it will prevent you from engaging in concentration all along, and even if you achieve it once, it cannot possibly be durable and will therefore deteriorate quickly. For this reason it is of great importance to put an end to laziness from the start.

Now if you achieve pliancy and your body and mind expand with bliss, you will not weary, day or night, in applying yourself to virtue, and laziness will thereby be stopped. To generate it, you must be able to continuously maintain joyous effort for concentration, the cause for generating pliancy. To generate that, you need the intense, sustained aspiration of striving for concentration. To engender that, you need the firm faith of captivation from seeing the excellent qualities of concentration. Therefore you should cultivate that faith by repeatedly reflecting on the excellent qualities of concentration.

Distinguishing the Middle from the Extremes (4.5) says:

> The basis, that which is based on it,
> the cause, the effect . . .

Here "the basis" is aspiration, which is the basis of effort. "That which is based on it" is effort or joyous effort. [189] The "cause" of aspiration is the faith of conviction with regard to the excellent qualities. The "effect" of effort is pliancy.

The excellent qualities of the concentration to be cultivated here are as follows. Once concentration has been accomplished, mental happiness and physical comfort greatly increase, so that you are always happy in this lifetime. From acquiring physical and mental pliancy, the mind is fit to be placed on any virtuous object at will. Since uncontrolled distraction toward mistaken objects has subsided, you rarely commit faulty conduct, and whatever virtue you perform has great strength. In reliance upon śamatha, you can achieve excellent qualities, such as clairvoyance and miraculous powers, and in particular, the realization of special insight that realizes emptiness so that the root of cyclic existence can be cut quickly. If you contemplate any of these and other excellent qualities, the power of your enthusiasm for cultivating concentration will increase. You should get to know them and meditate on them. Once this has arisen, it will constantly compel you from within to cultivate concentration so that you will easily attain it, and since you engage in the meditation again and again, it will be very difficult for it to degenerate after you attain it.

WHAT TO DO WHILE FOCUSING THE MIND ON THE OBJECT

This has two points: how to identify the focal object that is the basis for the mind and how to direct the mind toward it.

HOW TO IDENTIFY THE FOCAL OBJECT THAT IS THE BASIS FOR THE MIND

This has two points: general presentation of objects and identification of objects for specific situations.

GENERAL PRESENTATION OF OBJECTS

This has two points: indicating the actual objects and indicating what person should meditate on which object.

INDICATING THE ACTUAL OBJECTS

Among the four types of objects the Blessed One taught for yogis, the first, *pervasive objects*, is fourfold: the ones you place the mind on without analyzing; those that are objects of analysis; the limits of phenomena, the ultimate mode of being and things in their variety; and the accomplishment of a purpose, which is to achieve transformation through meditation by means of the previous two meditation methods that observe the ultimate mode of being and things in their variety.

As for *objects that purify conduct*, five meditation objects serve as antidotes to one's predominant conduct in previous lives. The repulsive, love, dependent arising, the divisions of the elements, and one's breath, respectively, are the five objects that are antidotes to attachment, hatred, ignorance, pride, and conceptualization.

The *objects for the skillful* are also fivefold: objects of skill with regard to the aggregates, the elements, the sense fields, and the twelve links of dependent arising, as well as the established and the unestablished. [190]

There are two *objects that purify mental afflictions*: the relative peacefulness of higher levels compared to lower levels, and the sixteen aspects of the four truths—impermanence and so forth.[114]

In this regard, the objects that purify conduct are special objects in that the attachment and so forth of those who act predominantly from attachment and so forth are easily stopped and concentration is easily achieved in reliance upon them. The objects for the skillful are good objects for śamatha because they negate a self of persons apart from those phenomena and are therefore in harmony with the arising of the special insight that realizes selflessness. The objects that purify mental afflictions are of great significance in that they become general antidotes to mental afflictions. There are no pervasive objects apart from the objects listed above. Therefore concentration should be accomplished in reliance upon the objects of śamatha with their special purposes. Those who practice concentration with a pebble, a piece of wood, and the like as the object of attention clearly do not know the presentation of objects of meditation.

INDICATING WHAT PERSON SHOULD MEDITATE ON WHICH OBJECT

In accordance with what is set forth in the *Questions of Revata Sūtra*, it is taught that persons with a predominant affliction, ranging from those in whom attachment predominates to those in whom discursive thought predominates, should rely on the individual objects of attention specified, ranging from the repulsive to one's breath, respectively.[115]

Those with balanced conduct and those with slight mental afflictions may concentrate on any one object explained above that they are happy with; they do not need a specific one. In this regard, predominance of one of the five mental afflictions of attachment and so forth means that through habituation to attachment and so forth in previous lives, long-term attachment and so forth arise toward small objects of attachment and so forth. Those with balanced conduct have not been habituated to attachment and so forth in previous lives, but they still do not see them as faulty. Therefore, even though predominant long-term attachment and so forth do not arise toward their respective objects, it is not that they do not occur at all. Those with slight mental afflictions have not been habituated to attachment and so forth in previous lives, and owing to the fact that, among other things, they do see them as faulty, attachment and so forth only arise slowly toward strong and abundant objects of attachment and so forth. They do not arise toward medium or small objects. [191]

Moreover, those with predominant attachment or another one of the five take long to accomplish śamatha, those with balanced behavior not that long, and those with slight mental afflictions accomplish it quickly.

IDENTIFICATION OF OBJECTS FOR SPECIFIC SITUATIONS

On which object is śamatha accomplished here? In general, the meditation objects for individual people are just as explained above. In particular, it is important that those with predominant discursive thought meditate on the breath. Alternatively, the second and third *Stages of Meditation* follow the *Sūtra on the Concentration That Perceives the Buddha of the Present Face to Face* (*Pratyutpannabuddhasaṃmukhāvasthitasamādhisūtra*) and the *King of Concentrations Sūtra* in teaching the accomplishment of concentration observing the Tathāgata's body. *Commentary on Difficult Points of Lamp for the Path* also quotes statements by Master Bodhibhadra that concentration is accomplished observing the Tathāgata's body.

In the concentration on the Buddha's body, limitless merit arises through recollecting the Buddha. If your image of that body is clear and stable, it makes a great difference to your visualization of the field for accumulating merit through prostrations, offerings, prayers, and so forth, as well as the field for purifying obstructions through confession, restraint, and so forth. Its great advantage is also revealed by the excellent benefit that your recollection of the Buddha does not deteriorate at the time of death, by the great difference it makes to deity yoga when you cultivate the path of mantra, and so forth. The *King of Concentrations Sūtra* says:

> With his body like the color of gold,
> the Lord of the World is exceedingly beautiful.
> The bodhisattva whose mind is engaged in this object
> is said to be in equipoise meditation.

You should make something like that your object of attention.

Moreover, between the two types of visualization, one that sees the object as freshly contrived by the mind and one that sees the object as naturally present, the latter has the great distinction of generating faith, and as it also accords with the teachings of both [sūtra and tantra] vehicles, you should proceed in the latter way.

As you investigate the object of attention, the basis for the mind to focus on, first find a good painted image, statue, or the like of the Teacher's body, look at it repeatedly, capture the features, and familiarize yourself with its appearance as an object of the mind. Or else reflect on the meaning of a description by a guru that you have heard, make it appear to your mind, and pursue this as your object of attention. However, rather than making the object of attention appear like a painted image, [192] statue, or something like that, train for it to appear in the aspect of the actual Buddha.

It makes perfect sense that Master Yeshé Dé[116] refutes the practice of some people who set up an image in front of them, look at it with their eyes, and meditate by staring at it. This is because concentration is not accomplished with a sensory consciousness but rather with the mental consciousness; the actual object of concentration is a direct object of the mental consciousness, so you must focus on that. Also, in accordance with what was explained above, it is taught that you must focus on the idea of the meditation object or the image of it that appears to your mind.

Elsewhere it says that although the image has both rough features and finer details, you should first focus on the rough features and afterward, when your meditation on that has stabilized, observe the details. Based on experience, the rough features should appear very easily, so attend to the focal object starting from the rough outline of its image. In particular, when you practice, as long as you have not accomplished fully qualified concentration, it is inappropriate to move among many different objects. If you practice concentration while moving among many dissimilar objects, it will become a great obstacle to your accomplishment of śamatha. Āryaśūra says [in *Compendium of the Perfections* 5.12):

> Stabilize the thoughts of the mind
> by settling it on one object.
> Cycling through a lot of objects
> disturbs the mind with mental afflictions.

And *Lamp for the Path to Enlightenment* (v. 40) also says it with the specification "on any one":

> Place the mind on something virtuous,
> on any one suitable object.

That being so, the measure of first rendering the object of attention that the mind focuses on is as follows. When you visualize the head, two arms, torso, and two legs successively a couple of times and then attend to the whole body at the end of that, if merely half the limbs and features appear to the mind, be satisfied with that and focus on it, even if there is no brilliant clarity. If you are not satisfied with that alone and do not focus on it but rather seek more clarity [193] and repeatedly visualize, the object will become clearer, but not only will you fail to acquire stable concentration, this will become an obstacle to its acquisition. So even though the object is not precise, you will acquire concentration more quickly if you focus on just that mere partial object. Then, owing to its benefit for clarity, the clarity aspect will also be accomplished easily. This appears in Master Yeshé Dé's advice and is essential.

You should focus on the whole body to the best of your abilities, and if some parts of the body appear clearly, focus on those. If they become unclear again, focus on the whole once more.

At that time, a color, shape, number, or size might appear that was not ascertained earlier; for example, you want to meditate on something yellow and something red appears, you want to meditate on a sitting figure and a standing one appears, you want to meditate on one and two appear, or you want to meditate on something big and something small appears. If this happens, it is inappropriate to pursue them; just make your original object, whatever it is, the object of attention.

In practicing the deity yoga of secret mantra, you need to achieve a clear appearance of the deity, and so until that appears, you need to try to generate it by various means. However, if it is difficult and the deity's aspect does not appear, you may also accomplish concentration by placing the mind and focusing on any one of the objects presented above that is suitable or within the view ascertaining suchness, for the main purpose is to accomplish śamatha.

HOW TO DIRECT THE MIND TOWARD IT

This has three points: the faultless approach, eliminating faulty approaches, and determining the length of sessions.

THE FAULTLESS APPROACH

The concentration to be accomplished here has two features: the factor of vibrant clarity of an extremely clear mind and the factor of nonconceptual stability of a mind abiding single-pointedly on its object. Here some add bliss and make it three features, while others add limpidity and make it four. However, the limpidity has two aspects: the limpidity of one's awareness feels more limpid than even an immaculate crystal bowl full of immaculate water being hit by sunlight on a cloudless day. And when objects such as pillars appear, a limpidity arises that feels as if one could count even their finest particles. [194] These two aspects nevertheless arise from the vibrant clarity that is generated and maintained once subtle laxity has been eliminated. Therefore it is unnecessary to mention them separately in the beginning. And although joy and bliss in the form of pleasurable sensations arise as an effect of the concentration accomplished here, they do not arise in association with all the concentrations included in the preliminary stage of the first dhyāna and therefore are not counted here.

The emergence of such vibrancy of the clarity is impeded by laxity, and single-pointed nonconceptuality is impeded by excitement. Precisely that is the reason why laxity and excitement are the main obstacles to the accomplishment of pure concentration. That is why, if you do not know how to identify subtle and coarse laxity and excitement, and if you do not know an impeccable method for maintaining concentration that stops both of them, even śamatha cannot arise, to say nothing of special insight. Therefore the intelligent who strive for concentration should become skilled in this way. That is to say, laxity and excitement are adverse conditions to the accomplishment of śamatha. The identification of adverse conditions and the methods for stopping them are taught below. Here I will describe how to generate concentration in a manner that is conducive to śamatha.

Concentration (*samādhi*) is the factor of the mind single-pointedly abiding on its object; it stays on the object continuously. There are two requirements for that: a method for not letting the mind get distracted from its original object and a precise awareness of whether it is actually distracted. The first is mindfulness (*smṛti*), and the second is vigilance (*samprajanya*). The *Commentary on Ornament for the Mahāyāna Sūtras* (*Mahāyānasūtrālaṃkārabhāṣya*) says:

> Mindfulness and vigilance focus it, for one prevents the mind from scattering away from its object, and the second is fully aware of the mind scattering away.

When mindfulness deteriorates and you forget the object, there is distraction, and you lose the object immediately. Therefore mindfulness that does not forget the object is the root.

This is how to direct the mind toward its object. As explained above, visualize the focal object. Then, once it appears at least minimally, generate a forceful apprehension of the object with your consciousness. Having placed the mind firmly, [195] keep it there without newly analyzing anything.

The *Compendium of Abhidharma* says that mindfulness has three features:

> What is mindfulness? A mind that is not forgetful, that has a familiar object, and that functions without distraction.

The *objective aspect* is that it "has a familiar object," since mindfulness does not arise with respect to a hitherto unfamiliar object. In this context, it is the appearance of an object of attention that was previously ascertained.

The *subjective aspect*, its apprehension, is "a mind that is not forgetful," a mind that does not forget the object; in this context, it does not forget the focal object. The way the mind does not forget is not the mere ability to remember, when others inquire and you are made to think about it, that your guru taught "The object of attention is like this. . . ." Rather, it is the way the mind tied to the object is directly mindful of it and is not distracted even in the slightest. When there is distraction, mindfulness is lost through its mere occurrence. Hence, after you have placed the mind on the basis of observation, you generate the thought "In this way, it is tied to the object." Then, without renewing conceptual thought, you sustain the force of this very mind continuously, without interruption. That is the real point of the instruction on how to practice mindfulness.

The *functional aspect* is to not let the mind get distracted from its object.

Tying the mind to an object so as to tame it is taught through the analogy of taming an elephant. In this analogy, a wild elephant is tied to a firm tree trunk or pillar with many thick ropes, and if it follows the instructions of the elephant tamer, all is well. If it does not, it is repeatedly prodded into submission with a sharp hook and thus tamed. Likewise the mind, which resembles an untamed elephant, is tied to a firm pillar, the focal object explained above, with the rope of mindfulness. If it cannot stay there, it is pricked with the hook of vigilance and gradually brought under control. *Essence of the Middle Way* says:

> The errant elephant of the mind
> is firmly tied with the rope of mindfulness
> to a stable pillar, the focal object, and [196]
> gradually ruled with the hook of wisdom.

And the second *Stages of Meditation* says:

> With the ropes of mindfulness and vigilance, tie the elephant of
> the mind to that very tree trunk of the focal object.

It is said that concentration is accomplished in reliance upon mindfulness and that, like a rope, mindfulness continuously ties the mind to the object. Therefore the principal method for fostering the accomplishment of concentration is that of maintaining mindfulness. Yet mindfulness apprehends its objects with an aspect of certainty. So if you maintain concentration and place the mind without a firm mind of certainty, you may gain the clarity of mental limpidity, but the clarity associated with the vibrancy of the mind of certainty does not emerge. As a result, powerful mindfulness does not arise, and since subtle laxity is not stopped either, the concentration becomes faulty.

Even someone who maintains mere nonconceptuality of the mind, without placing it on any other object of attention such as a deity's body, should remind himself "I will place the mind without conceiving of any object whatsoever" and then prevent the mind from scattering and being distracted. Since this *nondistraction* is also synonymous with *mindfulness that does not forget the object*, he does not deviate from the above method of maintaining mindfulness. Therefore someone who meditates in this manner applies a mindfulness powerful enough to produce an ascertaining consciousness.

Eliminating faulty approaches

One encounters the following type of misconception. Some say, "When the mind is roused as explained above, held firmly, and placed on the object nonconceptually, there is no laxity but there is a tendency toward excitement. I can see that I will not be able to gain continuous stability as a result. However, with my aroused mind relaxed by loosening my tight grip on it, I see the stability factor rise quickly. This is an excellent method." A lot of people think so and expound it as "the best meditation during the best relaxation."

However, this position fails to distinguish laxity from meditation. As explained above, faultless concentration requires two features; stability of the nonconceptual mind is not in itself sufficient. If you think, "When the mind has become confused and there is darkness, this is laxity, [197] but otherwise it is faultless concentration, because the clarity of mental limpidity is present," you clearly fail to distinguish lethargy from laxity. These will be elaborated below.

Therefore, whenever your mind is held overly tight and made vibrant, clarity is present but excitement predominates so that it is difficult for stability to arise. On the other hand, whenever you relax it a lot while maintaining your meditation, stability is present but laxity predominates so that vibrant clarity is absent. It is difficult to maintain just the right amount of tightness and relaxation, and therefore it is difficult for concentration free from laxity and excitement to arise. Thinking of that, Candragomin says [in his *Praise of Confession*]:

> When I apply exertion, excitement arises;
> sinking occurs when I abandon it.
> By this it is hard to get balanced engagement,
> so what should I do with my agitated mind?

And:

> When I focus with effort, excitement arises;
> however, when I relax it, sinking occurs.
> It is hard to find a practice midway between these,
> so what should I do with my agitated mind?

He is saying that when you try hard to hold your mind tight, thus making an effort, there is excitement. On the other hand, when you notice this, relax your mind that is trying hard to get involved in its object, and abandon the exertion, the laxity of sinking arises within the mind. Therefore it is hard to find the middle ground free from the two extremes of laxity and excitement, a balanced engagement in which the mind abides evenly. If he were presenting relaxation as best, there would be no reason for any difficulties. Yet since he is saying that it produces laxity, it is incorrect to practice concentration that way.

As for the point where tightness and relaxation are balanced, investigate this for yourself. You should be more relaxed than the mind state where you think, "If I tighten it this much, excitement will surely arise," and you should also place it above that mind state where you think, "If I place it only here, laxity will easily arise." In the context of the first and second mental states,[117] the noble Asaṅga also says, "That is to say, when placement and continuous placement are performed, there is a mental attention that holds the object tight as it engages in it."[118] The first *Stages of Meditation* also instructs, "Eliminate laxity and hold the object tight." [198] If you maintain your meditation without knowing the above method for applying mindfulness, then however much you meditate, you will acquire only a host of faults: great forgetfulness, a dulling of your wisdom that distinguishes among phenomena, and so forth.

Someone might wonder, "Well then, while mindfulness ties the mind to the object, is it appropriate to generate conceptual thought that observes whether the object is being held well?" The second *Stages of Meditation* says that this is indeed what needs to be done. Specifically, it is not that you first release your concentration and then observe in this way. Rather, from within your placement in concentration, you merely observe whether the mind is still on the original focal object like before, and if not, whether it has become excited or lax. Once your mind is placed in concentration, you should observe it now and then, at intervals neither too short nor too long. If you do this before the force of the previous mind has been exhausted, it has the value that the mind will become vibrant again, that its vibrancy will last for a long time, and that laxity and excitement will be recognized quickly.

Maintaining the meditation like that, periodically recalling the original focal object, is also necessary as a cause for powerful continuous mindfulness. That is why this method for maintaining mindfulness is set forth in *Śrāvaka Levels* and why it says the following in *Explanation of Distinguishing the Middle from the Extremes* (*Madhyāntavibhāgaṭīkā*):

> The statement "Mindfulness is not forgetting the object" means for the mind to exhibit the instructions on placing the mind.

One applies mindfulness in order to stop being distracted from the object and forgetting it. Therefore not forgetting the object is to mentally exhibit the object and mentally attend to it again and again. It is like when you are afraid that you might forget something you know: you recall it again and again, making it hard to forget.

DETERMINING THE LENGTH OF SESSIONS

Someone might ask, "Now, is there an established length of meditation sessions, specified in terms of 'Tie the mind to the object and place it for just this long'?" Major texts such as *Śrāvaka Levels* do not seem to clearly uphold an established length. However, the third *Stages of Meditation* says:

> Doing these practices in this order, [199] sit for twenty-four min-
> utes, an hour and a half, three hours, or as long as you can.[119]

This appears to have been set forth in the context of establishing the length
of meditation sessions for cultivating special insight after śamatha has
already been accomplished, but it is evidently similar in the context of initially practicing śamatha.

If you recollect the object and observe your practice periodically, the
method for maintaining mindfulness and vigilance explained above is
indeed faultless even for long sessions. However, for most beginners, forgetfulness arises if the sessions are long. They become distracted and mentally wander off, and although laxity and excitement occur in the process,
they do not identify them quickly but recognize them only after much
time has elapsed. Alternatively, even if they do not lose their mindfulness, they easily fall under the power of laxity and excitement and do not
identify them quickly. It is difficult to cut through laxity and excitement,
because the former of these two impedes the arising of strong mindfulness
whereas the latter impedes the arising of strong vigilance. Specifically, it
is a lot worse to forget the meditation object, become distracted, and then
fail to notice laxity and excitement than it is to not identify laxity and
excitement quickly but still remember the meditation object. Therefore
the method of maintaining mindfulness explained above is very important as the antidote that counteracts distraction and the deterioration of
mindfulness.

Short sessions are needed in the event of great forgetfulness, or the mind
getting distracted and wandering off a lot, when the vigilance that quickly
identifies laxity and excitement is weak. On the other hand, if forgetfulness
rarely arises and it seems that laxity and excitement are being recognized
quickly, there is nothing wrong with slightly longer sessions either. It is
with an awareness of this that the duration is not specified as twenty-four
minutes and so on. In brief, it says "as long as you can," because the length
must accord with one's mental abilities.

Apart from that, you should rest in meditative equipoise unless you suffer some temporary physical or mental harm. If that happens, do not continue meditating but rather eliminate the obstacles to your physical and
mental constitution first and then meditate. That is the opinion of experts,
so you should know that doing that factors into the length of sessions.

WHAT TO DO AFTER FOCUSING THE MIND ON THE OBJECT

This has two points: what to do when excitement or laxity occur, and what to do while free from laxity and excitement.

WHAT TO DO WHEN EXCITEMENT OR LAXITY OCCUR

This has two points: applying the antidote for failure to notice laxity and excitement, and applying the antidote for not trying to eliminate them even though they have been noticed. [200]

APPLYING THE ANTIDOTE FOR FAILURE TO NOTICE LAXITY AND EXCITEMENT

This has two points: defining laxity and excitement, and the method for generating vigilance that recognizes laxity and excitement during meditation.

DEFINING LAXITY AND EXCITEMENT

Excitement is just as stated in the *Compendium of Abhidharma*: "What is excitement? It is a very unpeaceful mind, a form of attachment that pursues pleasant signs. It has the function of disrupting śamatha." It has three features. Its *object* is something attractive and pleasant. Its *aspect* is the mind being unpeaceful and scattered outward, and because it is a form of attachment, it engages its object through craving. Its *function* is to disrupt the mind placed on its object.

While tied to an inner object, the mind is drawn without control through the excitement of attachment to forms such as sounds and becomes distracted. It is just as stated in *Praise of Confession*:

> Right when you are focused on śamatha,
> directing your mind at an object again and again,
> your attention is drawn away by the noose of the mental afflictions
> without control, by the rope of attachment to objects.

In many translations laxity is also rendered as *sinking*. Some people claim that laxity is when the mind does not scatter to other objects but is lethargic and lacks clarity and limpidity. However, that is incorrect, because the second *Stages of Meditation* and the *Unraveling the Intent Sūtra* say that laxity arises from lethargy. In the *Compendium of Abhidharma* laxity is indeed explained in the context of the secondary affliction of distraction. However, when there is distraction as explained there, virtue may also arise, so it is not necessarily afflicted.[120]

Consequently, in the *Compendium of Abhidharma* and in the *Treasury of Abhidharma Autocommentary*, lethargy is said to be a heaviness, an unserviceability of the body and the mind that forms part of ignorance. With laxity, the way the mind holds its object is slack, and the object is not held clearly or tightly. Therefore, even if limpidity is present, when the way the object is held lacks clarity, there is laxity. The second *Stages of Meditation* says, "You should know that at times when [201] the mind does not see the object clearly, like someone blind or someone entering darkness or someone closing his eyes, there is laxity." I have not seen a clear definition of laxity in the other great texts. Laxity is either virtuous or neutral, whereas lethargy is only a nonvirtuous or neutral obstruction[121] and part of ignorance.

The great texts say that in order to eliminate laxity, you should uplift the mind by meditating on a joyful object such as a Buddha image or light. You thereby prevent lack of clarity in the object, which is like darkness having fallen on the mind, and prevent decline in the way the mind holds it. Then you need to both clarify the object and tighten how you hold it.

Excitement is easy to recognize, but laxity is difficult to understand because it is not clearly identified in the great texts. Yet such an understanding is essential because this is a major ground for mistaking one's concentration to be faultless. Therefore you should investigate and identify it well with mental subtlety based on your experience and in accordance with the statements in *Stages of Meditation*.

THE METHOD FOR GENERATING VIGILANCE THAT RECOGNIZES LAXITY AND EXCITEMENT DURING MEDITATION

It is not enough to merely have an understanding of laxity and excitement. Rather, you need to be able to generate vigilance that knows precisely whether laxity or excitement have arisen during your meditation. In fact, in your cultivation of powerful vigilance, you not only need the vigilance that identifies laxity and excitement as soon as they arise, you also need the vigilance that knows them when they are just about to arise but have not actually arisen. As it says in the second and third *Stages of Meditation*, "If you notice laxity in the mind or suspect it might arise . . ." and "Noticing excitement in the mind or suspecting it might arise . . ." Until you generate this kind of vigilance, you cannot identify laxity or excitement if they arise. You might assert that from this point to that point there was flawless meditation without laxity or excitement, but that would be unsubstantiated, because without that powerful vigilance, you could not be certain. In accordance with that, *Distinguishing the Middle from the Extremes*, when it says, "Once laxity and excitement are realized. . . ," teaches that you need vigilance to notice laxity and excitement. [202] Therefore, if the vigilance that cannot fail to know laxity and excitement has not arisen, you could meditate for a long time and even spend years with subtle laxity and excitement without noticing that they are occurring.

Well then, how do you generate vigilance? One very essential cause is the method for maintaining mindfulness presented above. If you can generate continuous mindfulness in that manner, you will be able to stop forgetting the object and mentally wandering off. You will thereby reverse long-term insensitivity to the arising of laxity and excitement and come to recognize laxity and excitement easily. This is very clear when, from the perspective of your own experience, you compare the amount of time it takes you to know laxity and excitement when mindfulness has deteriorated with the amount of time it takes you when it has not. With this understanding *Entering the Bodhisattva Way* (5.33) says:

> When mindfulness is there to stay
> at the gate of the mind to guard it,
> at that point vigilance will come.

Explanation of Distinguishing the Middle from the Extremes also explains mindfulness as the cause of vigilance.

One such cause is to focus the mind on the apprehended object, such as an image of the deity's body and the like, or on the apprehending subject, such as the experience of mere awareness or mere clarity. Then apply mindfulness as explained above, focus the mind, and continuously observe whether it is scattering. This should be understood as the essential point for maintaining vigilance. In accordance with that, *Entering the Bodhisattva Way* (5.108) also says:

> Investigating again and again
> the state of body and mind, in brief,
> just that alone is the definition
> of the guarding of vigilance.

By doing this, you therefore generate vigilance that is aware of any laxity and excitement when they are about to arise. By means of applying mindfulness on the other hand, the forgetfulness of your mind being distracted and wandering off is stopped so that you observe well. You need to distinguish between them.

APPLYING THE ANTIDOTE FOR NOT TRYING TO ELIMINATE LAXITY AND EXCITEMENT EVEN THOUGH THEY HAVE BEEN NOTICED

Through properly applying the method for maintaining mindfulness and vigilance as explained above, strong mindfulness will arise. Then even subtle laxity and excitement can be recognized by means of that vigilance, [203] and the fault of not noticing laxity and excitement will not be there. However, when you fail to cultivate the effort to stop the two as soon as they arise, that complacent lack of effort or nonapplication is a big problem for concentration. That is why you should cultivate the intention referred to as *application* or *effort* as its antidote.

This has two points: identifying intention and the way it stops laxity and excitement, and identifying the causes that give rise to laxity and excitement.

IDENTIFYING INTENTION AND THE WAY IT STOPS LAXITY AND EXCITEMENT

The *Compendium of Abhidharma* asks, "What is intention? It is the mind creating karmic formations, the activity of the mind that causes the mind to get involved in virtue, nonvirtue, or something neutral." That means intention is the mental factor that moves the mind and impels it to something virtuous, nonvirtuous, or neutral, like iron moving without control under the power of a magnet. Here you should understand it as the intention that motivates the mind to eliminate either laxity or excitement when they occur.

Now how do you stop laxity and excitement? A mind that is lax has withdrawn inward too much and lost its apprehension of the object. For that reason the first *Stages of Meditation* says that you should attend to a cause for the mind to move outward again, an uplifting phenomenon. Specifically, it should be something like the Buddha's body rather than something arousing that gives rise to mental afflictions. Alternatively, if you clear away the laxity by focusing on a sign of light, such as sunshine, that should immediately tighten the way you apprehend the object and maintain it. In this situation, do not meditate on a disenchanting object, because disenchantment is a cause for the mind to withdraw inward. However, if you analyze any object you wish to analyze with fine investigative wisdom and feel enthusiasm, this will reverse laxity. The *Compendium of the Perfections* (5.13) says:

> When there is sinking, uplift the mind through the
> power of effort in special insight.

Now, this laxity or sinking is *lax* because the apprehension of the object has diminished, and it is *sinking* because it has withdrawn inward too much. Therefore it is counteracted by the enthusiasm upon uplifting the mind of apprehension and expanding the object. [204] *Essence of the Middle Way* says:

> When it sinks, expand the mind through
> meditation on spacious objects.

And:

> When it sinks, uplift it by seeing
> the benefits of joyous effort.

The most important antidote for stopping laxity is as follows. When you contemplate the benefits of the Three Jewels and bodhicitta as well as the excellent qualities of the precious freedoms you have gained and the like, it should be as effective for refreshing your awareness as cold water splashed in the face of someone asleep. This depends on the experience you have gained through your analytical meditation of fine investigation on beneficial topics.

When you apply the antidote meditation on light to the causes that reinforce the development of laxity—lethargy, sleepiness, and mental states with an aspect of darkness that induce those two—the laxity that depends on them does not arise, and that which has already arisen is reversed.

Śrāvaka Levels also talks about going for a walk; taking to mind the characteristics of light and familiarizing oneself with them again and again; uplifting the mind with any of the six recollections—of the Three Jewels, ethics, generosity, and deities—or other objects for greater clarity, as well as reciting Dharma teachings on the faults of lethargy and sleepiness; looking in various directions or at the moon and the stars; splashing one's face with water; and so forth.

Furthermore, if the mental laxity is only slight and does not occur more than once in a while, tighten the mind's apprehension as you meditate. However, when dense laxity recurs repeatedly, suspend the meditation, apply the antidotes as appropriate, and continue to meditate once the laxity has been cleared away. If the focal object becomes unclear and the mind takes on an aspect, slight or dense, of something like darkness, take up the characteristics of lights such as a butter lamp, fire, and sunshine as an antidote to that. If you familiarize yourself with them again and again, a great limpidity of mind will arise.

When it comes to excitement, the mind runs after forms, sounds, and other objects owing to attachment. [205] For that you should attend to something disenchanting, a cause for the mind to withdraw inward. However, as soon as the excitement has subsided because of that, rest in equipoise. *Essence of the Middle Way* says:

> Pacify excitement by
> attending, for instance, to impermanence.

And:

You should collect the distracted mind
by seeing the faults of the signs of distraction.

When intense or prolonged excitement occurs, collecting the mind inward
and placing it every time it scatters is not effective. It is more effective to let
go of the meditation for a while and meditate on something disenchanting.
However, when the excitement is not that strong, you should collect the
distracted mind inward and tie it to the object. *Compendium of the Perfections* (5.13) says:

> Whenever your mind becomes excited,
> avert this by means of śamatha.

With an excited mind, you should not attend to inspiring or delightful
objects, for they cause the mind to be distracted outward.

IDENTIFYING THE CAUSES THAT GIVE RISE TO LAXITY AND EXCITEMENT

The common causes of both laxity and excitement are not guarding one's
sense doors, not eating the right amount, not putting effort into practice
without sleeping during the first and last parts of the night, and lacking
vigilance.

The causes of laxity are great sleepiness, the mind being excessively loose
in its hold on the object, not balancing śamatha and special insight but
relying on śamatha too much, the mind remaining as though in darkness,
and not taking joy in directing the mind toward the object.

The causes of excitement are said to be insufficient disenchantment,
excessive tightness with respect to the focal object, unfamiliarity with
effort, and being distracted by thoughts of family and the like.

Therefore you need, through vigilance, to know even subtle aspects of
laxity and excitement and completely stop them all. If you give up and
think, "I cut through subtle excitement, distraction, and the like in the
beginning, but they were never terminated, so I will not cut through them
any longer," or if you think, "Unless they are intense or come for excessively
long stretches, there is no need to cut through them; no karma will be accumulated if they are brief and weak," you do not know how to accomplish

pure concentration. [206] That is because you depart from the methods to accomplish concentration established by the venerable Maitreya and others.

Therefore summon your mind from its wandering and excitement so that it is tied to the object within, and seek stability. Whenever there is stability, beware of laxity and bring forth intense clarity. Accomplish faultless concentration by alternating between those two. Do not trust a mere limpidity that lacks clarity together with intense apprehension.

WHAT TO DO WHILE FREE FROM LAXITY AND EXCITEMENT

It is a problem for your concentration if you apply yourself or make effort after subtle laxity and excitement have been terminated as explained above and the mind has entered into equanimity without the imbalances of becoming either lax or excited through the meditation. So as the antidote to that, you should cultivate equanimity. Application and effort become problems at the point when you grow confident that laxity and excitement will not arise in every session because you draw the mind inward and uplift it whenever it is lax. At that stage, it is a mistake to be as cautious of laxity and excitement as you were in the beginning. If you were, your mind would become distracted, so you need to know to loosen up at that time. That means to loosen the effort rather than letting go of the vibrancy of your apprehension. Therefore this cultivation of equanimity is not performed at all times that laxity and excitement are absent but rather after laxity and excitement have been largely destroyed. This is because there is no equanimity until you have largely destroyed laxity and excitement.

Well then, what is this equanimity? Among the three types of equanimity—a neutral feeling, immeasurable equanimity, and equanimity of application—it is the last one. Its nature is the mind resting evenly and at ease upon its object associated with either śamatha or special insight, operating naturally, and achieving suppleness, just as explained in *Śrāvaka Levels*. When you have achieved equanimity like this as you cultivate concentration free from laxity and excitement, you should let that equanimity be fully manifest as you place the mind without strong effort. This is in accordance with what is set forth in *Distinguishing the Middle from the Extremes*:

Staying with that, there is suppleness
and achievement of all aims.
It springs from the causes to rely on:
the eight factors removing five faults.

Laziness, [207] forgetting the instructions,
laxity and excitement,
nonapplication, and application
are asserted to be the five faults.

[The eight factors are:]
The basis, that which is based on it,
the cause, the effect,[122]
not forgetting the observed object,
noticing excitement and laxity,
application to remove them, and
resting naturally when they are calmed.

Here "staying with that" means staying with joyous effort in order to eliminate unfavorable conditions. Concentration characterized by mental suppleness arises from that. Furthermore, since it is the foundation or basis of miraculous powers such as clairvoyance that bring about all goals, it achieves those goals. Such concentration arises from eliminating the five faults and relying on the eight factors.

The five faults are as follows. At the time of application, laziness is a fault because you will not apply yourself to concentration. When you put effort into concentration, forgetting the instructions is a fault, for if you forget the object, there will be no meditative equipoise of the mind on the object. Laxity and excitement are faults because they prevent mental suppleness in meditative equipoise. When laxity and excitement occur, it is a fault not to make effort, for the two are thereby not pacified. When there is no more laxity and excitement, the intention to apply yourself becomes a fault. *Stages of Meditation* says that there are five faults if you count laxity and excitement together and six if you count them separately.

Among their antidotes, the eight factors for eliminating them, laziness has four. They are faith, aspiration, effort, and pliancy. The antidotes for forgetfulness, laxity and excitement, nonapplication, and application are, respectively, mindfulness, vigilance, the intention to apply yourself, and the equanimity of placing the mind naturally. They have already been explained above.

This freeing of the single-pointed concentration of the mind from laxity and excitement by means of mindfulness and vigilance is common to all the instructions on how to practice. Therefore you should not consider it a specific detail of the Lakṣaṇayāna[123] that is unnecessary in mantra. It is also taught in many highest yoga tantras. [208]

21 | Accomplishing Śamatha

THE STAGES OF ŚAMATHA THAT ARISE IN RELIANCE UPON IT

THIS HAS THREE POINTS: the actual stages of śamatha that arise, the method for accomplishing them by means of the six powers, and how they involve the four types of attention.

THE ACTUAL STAGES OF ŚAMATHA THAT ARISE

The first has nine points. *Placing the mind* on something is to draw the mind away from all external objects and direct it toward the object within. *Ornament for the Mahāyāna Sūtras* says:

> Having directed the mind toward the object,[124]

In *continuous placement*, the directed mind is continuously placed on the object over a period of time without it being distracted to anything else.

> Continuously prevent it from getting distracted.

In *patchy placement*, if you get distracted because of forgetfulness so that you are pulled away to external things, you realize it and tie your mind to the object once again.

> Realizing distraction quickly,
> you should patch it up again.

Close placement is explained in *Instructions on the Perfection of Wisdom* as enhancing placement by repeatedly drawing in and refining the mind, which is expansive by nature. This accords with the statement:

> Intelligent people should more and more
> draw their minds inside.

Taming is to reflect on and rejoice in the excellent qualities of concentration.

> Then, as you see the excellent qualities,
> the mind is tamed in concentration.

Pacification is to view distraction as a fault and pacify dislike for concentration.

> By seeing distraction as a fault, you
> pacify dislike for the meditation.

Complete pacification is to completely pacify whatever mental states of attachment, unhappiness, lethargy, sleepiness, and so forth occur.

> Attachment, unhappiness, and the like
> should be pacified as they arise.

Single-pointedness is to make an effort for the sake of effortless engagement. [209]

> Then, by means of restraint and effort,
> with full attention of the mind,
> you get it to come about naturally.

Even placement is said in *Stages of Meditation* to be the equanimity when the mind has become balanced. In *Instructions on the Perfection of Wisdom* it is said to be spontaneous, natural engagement and the attainment of control owing to the habit of unifying the mindstream. In accordance with that, *Ornament for the Mahāyāna Sūtras* also says:

Since it's habitual, there's no application.

The names of these nine mental states are as quoted in sources such as the first *Stages of Meditation*, which says:

This path of śamatha is explained in the Perfection of Wisdom Sūtras and so on.

You should act in accordance with quotations like these.

THE METHOD FOR ACCOMPLISHING THEM BY MEANS OF THE SIX POWERS

The six powers are those of hearing, thinking, mindfulness, vigilance, joyous effort, and thorough acquaintance.

The mental state of placement is accomplished through the power of hearing, for it is merely first tying the mind to the object and following just the instructions you have heard from someone on how to place the mind on an object. It is not something that you have become familiar with through repeated reflections.

The mental state of continuous placement is accomplished through the power of thinking, for you keep thinking about the continuation of that first bond with the object and maintain it. From that you will initially achieve the capacity for a somewhat connected continuity.

The two mental states of patchy placement and close placement are accomplished through the power of mindfulness, for when the mind is distracted from the object, you are mindful of the earlier object and collect the mind back within. You generate the power of mindfulness from the start and do not let your mind get distracted from the object.

The two mental states of taming and pacification are accomplished through the power of vigilance, for through recognizing with vigilance the faults of scattering toward conceptualization and toward the signs of the secondary afflictions, and through viewing them as faults, you do not allow your mind to scatter toward those two.

You accomplish the two mental states of complete pacification and single-pointedness through the power of joyous effort, for you eliminate even subtle occurrences of conceptualization and secondary afflictions

[210] with effort and do not respond to them. By doing this, laxity, excitement, and so forth cannot obstruct your concentration, and concentration that arises continuously is accomplished.

You accomplish the mental state of even placement through the power of thorough acquaintance, for concentration that operates naturally without effort arises from the power of intense familiarization with the previous power.

These points accord with the intended meaning of *Śrāvaka Levels,* so do not rely on other explanations.

The attainment of the ninth mental state is illustrated by an analogy: When you are very used to reciting a text or something like that, then whenever the motivation to recite it first arises and you begin reciting it, the recitation itself continues uninterruptedly without effort, even if your mind is distracted by something else in the meantime. Likewise, when you have placed your mind in equipoise once through the mindfulness of having initially directed it toward the object, then you become capable of entering concentration continuously over a long period without being interrupted by scattering, even though mindfulness and vigilance are not applied continuously. There is no need for the effort of application when mindfulness and vigilance are continuous, and that is called *without application or effort.*

For that to arise, first, whenever mindfulness and vigilance are each applied with effort, a long-lasting concentration that cannot be obstructed by unfavorable conditions such as laxity and excitement has to arise. That is the eighth mental state. That and the ninth one are the same in that conditions unfavorable to concentration such as laxity and excitement cannot disrupt them. Yet since it is necessary here to apply mindfulness and vigilance uninterruptedly, it is said to be connected with application or effort. For that to arise, it is necessary to stop even subtle laxity, excitement, and so forth as soon as they arise, without responding to them. Therefore the seventh mental state is necessary. For that to arise, powerful vigilance is needed to notice that there is no scattering toward conceptual thought and secondary afflictions, because distraction by them is understood to be a fault. Therefore you need the fifth and sixth mental states because those two are accomplished with powerful vigilance. For something like that to arise, however, requires both the mindfulness that quickly recalls the object even if the mind has been distracted from it and the mindfulness that does not allow any distraction from the object in the first place. Therefore the third and fourth mental states [211] are necessary because they are accomplished by those two types of mindfulness. For these to arise, however, the mind must first of all be bound to the object, and the continuity of that bond must be undistracted. Therefore the first and second mental states arise first.

Thus, to summarize, you should first follow the instructions you have heard and correctly perform the method for placing the mind in equipoise. Then repeatedly think about that manner of placement and maintain its continuity by piecing short periods together. Then, if mindfulness deteriorates and you get distracted, quickly collect your mind and quickly be mindful of the object you have forgotten. Then generate even stronger mindfulness and generate a power of mindfulness such that you do not get distracted from the object in the first place. You should generate intense vigilance to watch over the mind by accomplishing powerful mindfulness and by seeing the faults of laxity, excitement, and so forth, where your mind gets distracted from the object to something else. Then generate strong effort so that, when there is distraction through even subtle forgetfulness, it is recognized immediately and eliminated, and once it has been eliminated, the periods without obstruction by unfavorable conditions are lengthened. Once that has arisen, you put in effort, you perfect your familiarization through meditation, and you accomplish the ninth mental state that enters concentration without effort. In fact before the ninth mental state has been achieved, the yogi needs effort to place the mind in concentration. But when the ninth mental state has been attained, even though you do not exert effort to place the mind in meditative equipoise deliberately, your mind completely goes into concentration.

If, despite having achieved the ninth mental state, you have not achieved pliancy, you still cannot say you have achieved śamatha, let alone the achievement of special insight. This is explained below.

HOW THEY INVOLVE THE FOUR TYPES OF ATTENTION

Śrāvaka Levels explains that the nine stages of śamatha involve four types of attention. In accordance with that, it is explained that there is *tight engagement* at the time of the first and second mental states because the mind must be tightened with effort. Then, during the next five mental states, laxity and excitement interrupt you and you cannot maintain long meditation sessions, so at that time there is *interrupted engagement*. Then, during the eighth mental state, laxity and excitement cannot cause interruptions, and you can thereby maintain meditation sessions for long stretches, and so there is *uninterrupted engagement* at that time. Then, for the ninth mental state, there is no interruption, and it is not necessary to rely on constant effort, so you settle into the attention of *engagement without effort*. [212]

Someone might ask, "Well, there is interrupted engagement at the time of the first and second mental states, and there is also a need to tighten the mind at the time of the five intermediate mental states. Why is it that the first and second are not said to have the attention of interrupted engagement and that the five in between are not said to have the attention of tight engagement?"

With the first and second mental states, the mind is in and out of concentration, but the latter is more prolonged. With the five intermediate ones, the mind abides far longer in concentration. Therefore the latter and not the former has been labeled as having interrupted concentration. So although the two sets are indeed the same in having tight engagement, the presence and absence of interruptions and engagement over time is what makes them distinct. Therefore those five intermediate mental states are not posited as attentions that have tight engagement.

The *Compendium of the Perfections* (5.10–11) says:

> Through uninterrupted yoga strive
> for meditative stabilization.
>
> Just as you will not get fire through friction
> if you take breaks again and again,
> the method of yoga is similar.
> Go on till you gain the distinctive state!

You should accomplish it in accordance with that statement.

THE MEASURE FOR THE ACCOMPLISHMENT OF ŚAMATHA THROUGH MEDITATION

This has three points: indicating the dividing line between accomplishing and not accomplishing śamatha, indicating how to traverse the path in reliance on śamatha generally, and indicating how to traverse the mundane path in particular.

INDICATING THE DIVIDING LINE BETWEEN ACCOMPLISHING AND NOT ACCOMPLISHING ŚAMATHA

This has two points: first the main topic, and second the signs of possessing attention and an elimination of doubts.

THE MAIN TOPIC

This has two points: indicating whether śamatha has been achieved based on whether pliancy has been completely achieved, and the way śamatha is accomplished once pliancy has been achieved.

INDICATING WHETHER ŚAMATHA HAS BEEN ACHIEVED BASED ON WHETHER PLIANCY HAS BEEN COMPLETELY ACHIEVED

Has śamatha been achieved when you can maintain the ninth mental state free from subtle laxity and excitement throughout prolonged meditation sessions as explained above, and when you attain concentration that operates spontaneously, independent of the effort of continuously applying mindfulness and vigilance? When this concentration has been achieved, there is a twofold division based on whether pliancy has been achieved. If pliancy has not been achieved, it is a similitude of śamatha rather than actual śamatha. The *Unraveling the Intent Sūtra* says:

> "Blessed One, what is that attention called when the bodhisattva [213] directs his attention inward, his mind observing the mind, before physical pliancy and mental pliancy have been achieved?"

"Maitreya, it is not śamatha. It should be described as a type of attention that is similar to śamatha."

Ornament for the Mahāyāna Sūtras (14.15) also says:

> Since it's habitual, there's no application.
> Then his body and mind attain
> extreme overwhelming pliancy;
> afterward he is said to have attention.

"Attention" here means śamatha. The second *Stages of Meditation* also clearly says:

> When the body and the mind of the one who has thus familiarized himself with śamatha become extremely pliable, and when his mind becomes fully tractable with regard to objects observed at will, at that time he should know that śamatha has been accomplished.

And *Instructions on the Perfection of Wisdom* says:

> Here the bodhisattva dwelling alone in seclusion should attend to his intended object. He should eliminate his mental conversation and attend many times to the mind itself as it appears. Until physical and mental pliancy arise, it is a mental attention that approximates śamatha. After they have arisen, it is śamatha.

Now, which realm does concentration fall within before pliancy is attained? It falls within the desire realm. Although it has such single-pointedness of mind, it is a state of nonequipoise and is not posited as a state of equipoise.[125] The reason explained in *Levels of Yogic Practice* is that its accomplishment is not achieved with nonregret, supreme joyful bliss, and pliancy. Thus before pliancy is attained, there is a concentration that does not rely on constant mindfulness, in which the mind goes into nonconceptuality of its own accord, and that appears as though it could be combined with any physical activity—traveling, walking, lying, and [214] sitting. This concentration is called single-pointed mind of the desire realm, and it is not actual śamatha.

THE WAY ŚAMATHA IS ACCOMPLISHED ONCE PLIANCY HAS BEEN ACHIEVED

How then is pliancy achieved? And once it is achieved, how does one proceed to śamatha? This is what the *Compendium of Abhidharma* says with respect to pliancy:

> What is pliancy? It is the suppleness of the body and the mind from having cut the continuity of negative physical and mental tendencies. Its function is to eliminate all obstructions.

"Negative physical and mental tendencies" mean that the body and the mind are unfit to be employed for any virtuous activity at will. The antidote, physical and mental pliancy, is a consummate suppleness of body and mind for virtuous activities owing to a freedom from negative physical and mental tendencies. Physical pliancy is the lightness that comes from being free from physical intractability, such as a sense of heaviness and so on, while trying to eliminate afflictions, which are negative physical tendencies included in the affliction category and which prevent the joy of eliminating afflictions. Likewise, mental pliancy is for the mind to unobstructedly engage in the object, free from the inability to delight in directing the mind toward a virtuous object, while trying to eliminate afflictions, which are mental negative states in the affliction category and which prevent the joy of eliminating afflictions. In accordance with that Master Sthiramati says [in his *Commentary on Thirty Verses (Triṃśikābhāṣya)*]:

> In this regard, suppleness of the body is the source of buoyancy and lightness in physical activities. Suppleness of the mind, which arises when engaging in pure attention, is a different quality, a mental factor that is the cause of the mind becoming fresh and happy. When you are endowed with it, you engage in the object with no resistance, which is why it is called suppleness of the mind.

In brief, if pliancy is attained, the body and mind become easy to use after having reversed the intractability of the body and mind in which a sense of resistance makes it difficult to engage, like having to do unpleasant work. [215] *Śrāvaka Levels* says that such perfectly complete suppleness of the body and the mind arises in small portions from right when you first obtain concentration, and it increases from there, eventually becoming pliancy and single-pointed śamatha. It is subtle and therefore hard to recognize at first, but later on it becomes easy to recognize.

An early sign of the arising of such fully qualified and easily discernible pliancy is when the person striving to cultivate concentration experiences a feeling of heaviness at the top of the head, but not an uncomfortable heaviness. As soon as it arises, you are freed from negative mental tendencies that obstruct the enjoyment of eliminating afflictions. The antidote to those negative tendencies, mental pliancy, arises just prior to them.[126] *Śrāvaka Levels* says:

> An early sign that coarse single-pointedness of mind, which is easy to discern, as well as mental and physical pliancy will soon arise is a heavy feeling at the top of the head. This symptom is not harmful. As soon as it arises, one eliminates any negative mental tendencies within the affliction category that obstruct the enjoyment of eliminating them, and their antidotes, mental suppleness and mental pliancy, arise.

Then, in reliance upon the force of the pliancy of mental suppleness that has arisen, the winds that produce physical pliancy circulate within the body. When those winds circulate in your body parts and pervade them, you are freed from negative physical tendencies, and physical pliancy, which is the antidote to negative tendencies, arises. Moreover, after they have spread throughout the body, it is as though one is filled with the power of supple winds. *Śrāvaka Levels* says:

> Because it arises, the winds of the great elements that are conducive to the arising of physical pliancy circulate within the body. As they circulate, one is freed from negative physical tendencies within the affliction category that obstruct the joy of eliminat-

ing them. Their antidote, physical pliancy, spreads throughout
the body [216] and appears to fill it.

In this regard, physical pliancy is an extremely pleasant sensation within
the body; it is not a mental factor. Master Sthiramati says [in his *Commentary on Thirty Verses*]:

> If a distinctive physical sensation is conjoined with joy, you
> should know it as physical pliancy because the sūtras say that
> when the mind is joyful, the body becomes pliant.

Thus, when physical pliancy first arises, through the power of the winds, a
great experience of bliss arises within the body. In reliance upon that, a very
exquisite experience of joyful bliss is also produced in the mind.

After that, the power of that initial pliancy gradually diminishes. In fact,
it is not that pliancy has been exhausted and goes away. Rather, that coarse
pliancy agitates the mind excessively, so when it neutralizes, an unshakable
pliancy that is delicate like a shadow and compatible with concentration
arises. When the joy has disappeared, the mind remains firmly on its object
and achieves śamatha free from the restlessness of agitation caused by great
joy. *Śrāvaka Levels* says:

> When that first arises, the mind is joyful, greatly at ease, focused
> on supreme happiness, and appears manifestly endowed with
> joy. Then, gradually, all the power of the initial pliancy turns
> extremely subtle, and the body gains a shadow-like pliancy.
> Any mental joy is eliminated, and through śamatha, the mind
> engages the object in a way that is completely firm and utterly
> peaceful.

Śrāvaka Levels explains that if that happens, then through attaining the
attention and śamatha included in the preliminary stage of the first meditative stabilization (*dhyāna*), one attains the lowest type of attention of the
stage of meditative equipoise.

THE SIGNS OF POSSESSING ATTENTION AND AN ELIMINATION OF DOUBTS

This has two points: the actual signs of possessing attention and the elimination of doubts. [217]

THE ACTUAL SIGNS OF POSSESSING ATTENTION

Śrāvaka Levels teaches the signs that indicate you or someone else has achieved attention. Through attaining that, a set of four is achieved in small measure: a mind included in the form realm, physical pliancy, mental pliancy, and single-pointedness. Also, you are able to purify mental afflictions by means of peaceful and coarse paths[127] or paths associated with aspects of the four noble truths; physical and mental pliancy arise very quickly when the mind is in inward equipoise; the five hindrances—aspiration for sensual pleasures, sleepiness, and so forth—have largely disappeared; and when you rise from equipoise, you are still imbued with some physical and mental pliancy.

Once attention with these signs is achieved, it is easy for the path of śamatha to become pure.[128] After meditative equipoise of the mind in single-pointed śamatha, physical and mental pliancy can quickly be induced so that pliancy increases. *Śrāvaka Levels* explains that the more pliancy increases, the more śamatha also increases, whereby they mutually enhance each other. In brief, when the mind is supple, the winds become supple. At that time extraordinary physical pliancy occurs, and upon its occurrence, extraordinary concentration arises. Through that, again, an extraordinary suppleness of winds is accomplished, whereby physical and mental pliancy is induced.

Furthermore, *Śrāvaka Levels* says:

> To turn away from all the signs and to prevent distraction, focusing at the start, engage with no thought and without any mentation.

This explains that when at the outset the mind is placed in single-pointedness, it is done so with no other thought or any other mentation whatsoever. When you have cultivated that, according to *Śrāvaka Levels*:

Progressively focus on single-pointedness itself and on the mind's internal śamatha. Through that, place your mind in just this way on the mindstream and on the entire continuity of the mind becoming free from signs, free from conceptualization, and absolutely calm.

When you have achieved the mind of śamatha in that manner, if signs and conceptualization arise because of forgetfulness and unfamiliarity, if appearances arise because of secondary mental afflictions, or if holes start showing [218] and they become your object, then because you have already seen their faults, do not pursue thoughts about such occurrences nor attend to them.

In this way, with no thoughts about them and no attending to them, those objects completely disintegrate, and when they have been completely eliminated, the mind is placed on the very absence of appearances.

Sir, this object is subtle and hard to comprehend; therefore aspire and make a strong effort in order to comprehend it.

That is how concentration is said to arise.

The section up to "absolutely calm"[129] shows how freedom from signs, freedom from conceptualization, and absolute calm arise gradually from maintaining the meditation as before.

Then, the section up to "do not pursue thoughts about such occurrences" explains that whenever signs and so forth appear in the mind when śamatha has been accomplished but there is no great familiarity with it and so forth, you should remember the faults of the mind coming under their power, not pursue them, and place the mind without thinking of anything.

Then, the section up to "absence of appearances" explains that through familiarizing yourself in this manner, whichever of the three signs and so forth arises,[130] through the force of familiarity with relinquishing all thoughts about them, it will subside by itself independently of deliberately focusing the mind. The section explains that thereafter you abide in the nonappearance of the three, and you are not carried away by them.

The remainder of the passage points out that this śamatha is subtle and that explanations of it are difficult to comprehend.

In this regard, the signs are explained as ten: signs of the five objects (forms, sounds, smells, tastes, and tactile objects), of the three poisons, and of male and female. As for the manner in which they vanish, first a multiplicity of signs of forms and so forth appear, and as soon as they appear, they subside by themselves and are purified. Finally, when you settle in meditative equipoise, the signs of forms, sounds, and so forth do not appear; the only things that appear are the mind, which is aware and clear, and vibrant happiness.

Then the following is how conceptual thoughts disappear. As you place your mind as before, without recollecting them and without attending to them, conceptual thoughts that arise do not proliferate greatly or compound; [219] they subside naturally, like bubbles emerging from water one after another. Then, through maintaining the meditation as explained above, your experiential awareness and the sense of bliss, without being stopped deliberately but just unable to withstand the focus, again subside by themselves and are purified as soon as they arise, like the shedding of an old skin. Bliss and experiential awareness become more subtle. At that time, when you are in meditative equipoise, you will have no awareness of your own body, and you will feel as if your mind has become indistinguishable from space. When you rise from this meditation, you will feel as if your body has suddenly appeared. Afterward, even afflicted conceptual thoughts of hatred and the like that arise are different from before or originally; they are weak and unable to compound over long periods of time.

These periods are periods of what is called *complete pacification*. The experience of clarity is great, and you feel you can count the minute particles of pillars and walls of a house. Because of the intense stability, when it is time to sleep, your sleep is unlike it was before you achieved concentration; it seems mixed with concentration, and you have many pure dream appearances and the like.

THE ELIMINATION OF DOUBTS

Someone might ask, "When the kind of concentration explained above is achieved, where does it fall in the context of the five paths?" If it is the concentration explained above that is cultivated after the view of selflessness has been unmistakenly ascertained and the mind has been placed within that view,[131] it can fall within a path of liberation of ordinary beings. However, if it is not a meditation like that, *Śrāvaka Levels* says that this concentration can also cause the accomplishment of even mundane paths that view peaceful and coarse aspects to accomplish the actual first dhyāna. Therefore non-Buddhist sages who free themselves from attachment by means of mundane paths up to nothingness also need it to progress to higher paths.[132] So it is a concentration common to both non-Buddhists and Buddhists.

Furthermore, it becomes a path of liberation if it is conjoined with detachment from cyclic existence owing to the view that realizes selflessness without error and to a realization of the faults of existence, and if it is conjoined with an attitude of revulsion that strives for liberation. [220] If it is conjoined with bodhicitta, it even becomes a Mahāyāna path. Likewise, for example, if the generosity of giving a morsel of food to an animal and the guarding of even one kind of ethics is conjoined with that attitude, they become accumulations, respectively, of the paths of liberation and omniscience.

However, here what is being analyzed is not whether it becomes a path of liberation or omniscience when conjoined with another factor of the path. Rather, what is being analyzed is which path it becomes by that concentration's nature. The states of meditation free of thought and mentation, referred to as *unfabricated by the mind* and *subjectless* and endowed with bliss, clarity, and nondiscursiveness, are of two types: one that is a genuine emptiness meditation with the mind in equipoise on the meaning of suchness and one that is not. Therefore it is extremely important to differentiate them well, for otherwise you put yourself at great risk of mistakenly believing that you have had a realization of suchness when you have not. If you do not differentiate them as explained above, you might even take concentration, which is common to Buddhist and non-Buddhist Dharma, to be the main point of completion stage highest yoga tantra. So you should investigate this in detail.

INDICATING HOW TO TRAVERSE THE PATH IN RELIANCE UPON ŚAMATHA GENERALLY

Someone might ask, "Should someone who has thus achieved attention, the nonconceptual concentration explained above, maintain only that nonconceptuality endowed with bliss, clarity, and nondiscursiveness?" One generates such concentration in the mindstream in order to generate special insight that destroys the mental afflictions. If special insight does not arise in reliance upon it, however much you familiarize yourself with concentration, you will not be able to eliminate even the mental afflictions of the desire realm, let alone mental afflictions as a whole. That is why you must cultivate special insight.

In fact there are two: the special insight that progresses along mundane paths and eliminates manifest afflictions, and the special insight that progresses along supramundane paths and eliminates the seeds of afflictions from the root. The former is a meditation with the coarse and peaceful aspects, viewing lower levels as coarser and higher ones as more peaceful; the latter is a meditation of the view with the sixteen aspects— impermanence and so forth—of the four noble truths. Both are set forth in *Śrāvaka Levels*, the principal one being the view that realizes the selflessness of persons.[133] [221]

That being so, the śamatha explained above is required as the basis for eliminating afflictions for both non-Buddhist and Buddhist yogis. It is for anyone: non-Buddhists who eliminate manifest afflictions by cultivating the path with coarse and peaceful aspects and Buddhists who eliminate afflictions from the root by meditating on the meaning of selflessness. Not only that, but any Mahāyāna or Hīnayāna yogi must accomplish that concentration. As for Mahāyānists, all yogis of the vehicles of both the perfections and mantra must accomplish that śamatha. Therefore this śamatha is crucial as the basis of progress on the paths of all yogis. For Buddhists it is not unacceptable to lack the former of those two special insights, but it is unacceptable to lack the latter special insight that realizes selflessness.

In fact, if you attain the śamatha explained above that is included in the preliminary access stage of the first dhyāna, then you can attain in reliance upon it the liberation that is freedom from all bonds of cyclic existence by cultivating special insight even without having achieved the śamatha of higher [form-realm] concentrations or formlessness. On the other hand, if you do not realize the nature of selflessness and fail to meditate on it, you will not free yourself from cyclic existence even if you eliminate all manifest afflictions up to nothingness and thus attain the mind of the peak of existence by means of the śamatha explained above and the mundane special insight dependent on it. As *Praise of the One Worthy of Praise* says:

> Beings who fail to turn to your Dharma,
> who are blinded by their ignorance,

having gone to the peak of existence,
maintain existence and suffer again.

Followers of your teachings who don't gain
the basis of meditative stabilization
still turn away from existences
while under the gaze of Māra's eye.

It follows that with respect to highest yoga tantra too, even though such a yogi does not develop śamatha and special insight by focusing on the variety of saṃsāric states, he still needs to cultivate śamatha, and the point where śamatha arises is on the generation stage.

INDICATING HOW TO TRAVERSE THE MUNDANE PATH IN PARTICULAR

Here *Śrāvaka Levels* explains that from the ninth mental state on, you are a beginner in attention until you achieve attention, [222] and you are a beginner in purifying afflictions if you have achieved attention and, out of a desire to purify mental afflictions, cultivate the attention that knows the characteristics.[134] If you do not correctly ascertain this point explained in *Śrāvaka Levels*, you will mistakenly think that the lowest of the paths of dhyāna and formlessness is the preliminary stage of the first dhyāna, and that the first mental state that arises in the preliminary stage is knowledge of characteristics because knowledge of characteristics is the first of six attentions that are discussed in that regard.[135]

It is illogical to claim this because there is no way for the preliminary stage of the first dhyāna to arise like that without śamatha having been achieved, and if that preliminary stage has not been achieved, śamatha is not achieved. Also, since knowledge of characteristics is an analytical meditation, śamatha that has not been achieved before cannot be newly accomplished by means of that meditation. Therefore the first of six attentions of the preliminary stage is the beginning of cultivating the special insight included in the preliminary stage. However, it is not immediately at the beginning of the first preliminary stage, for the śamatha included in the preliminary stage must precede it. All the concentrations prior to the achievement of the concentration included in the first preliminary stage are single-pointed mental states of the desire realm. That is why there seem to be very few who achieve even śamatha according to the great texts.

Fearing excessive wordiness, I will not write here about how to free oneself from attachment to the desire realm by means of the six attentions of the preliminary stage.

22 | The Practice of Special Insight

HOW TO TRAIN IN SPECIAL INSIGHT

THIS HAS FOUR POINTS: relying on the prerequisites of special insight, divisions of special insight, how to cultivate special insight, and the measure of having accomplished special insight through meditation.

RELYING ON THE PREREQUISITES OF SPECIAL INSIGHT

This has two points: a general presentation of how to rely on the prerequisites of special insight and how to determine the view in particular.

A GENERAL PRESENTATION ON HOW TO RELY ON THE PREREQUISITES OF SPECIAL INSIGHT

The second *Stages of Meditation* sets forth three prerequisites for special insight: relying on holy beings, seeking to study the Dharma with them, and reflecting on it properly. [223] It is an indispensable causal prerequisite of special insight to study the stainless texts with experts who unmistakenly know the essential points of the scriptures and then to develop the view that realizes suchness by means of the wisdoms of studying and reflecting. This is because if you lack the *view* that has discerned the ultimate mode of being, the *realization* of special insight that realizes things as they are cannot arise.

Again, such a view must be sought by one who is relying not on the interpretable meaning but on the definitive meaning. Therefore you need to know the difference between interpretable and definitive meanings and to comprehend the meaning of the scriptures of definitive meaning. Again, with this, if you do not rely on a treatise by one of the great, valid, trailblazing founders that elucidates the Buddha's intentions, you will be like a blind person without a guide wandering off in a treacherous direction. Therefore you should rely on a commentary without errors. Who should you rely on? Rely on Ārya Nāgārjuna, widely renowned on the three levels,[136] whom the Blessed One himself prophesied very clearly in numerous sūtras and tantras as elucidating the essence of his teachings, the profound meaning free from all extremes of existence and nonexistence. You should seek the view that realizes emptiness relying on his texts.

Since the great Mādhyamikas such as the masters Buddhapālita, Bhāviveka, Candrakīrti, and Śāntarakṣita consider Āryadeva to be as reliable as his master, both the father and his spiritual son are sources for the other Mādhyamikas. Therefore earlier generations designated those two as "Mādhyamikas of the original texts" and the others as "partisan Mādhyamikas." Some spiritual teachers of earlier generations say that there are two kinds of Mādhyamikas named from the point of view of how they posit conventionalities: Sautrāntika-Mādhyamikas, who assert that external objects conventionally exist, and Yogācāra-Mādhyamikas who assert that, conventionally, external objects do not exist.

There are also two names applied from the point of view of how the ultimate is asserted: *proponents of illusions established by reasoning* are those who assert ultimate truth to be the composite of the appearance of a subject such as a sprout and its lack of true existence, and *proponents of thorough nonabiding* are those who assert ultimate truth to be a complete elimination—that is, appearances' mere elimination of the elaborations.[137] The first of these [224] were asserted to be masters such as Śāntarakṣita and Kamalaśīla. Some Indians also used the designations *illusion-like* and *thoroughly nonabiding*.

The great translator Loden Sherab[138] says, "Positing these as two groups from the point of view of how they assert the ultimate is a presentation that only impresses idiots." With regard to this, Master Yeshé Dé explains,

> The Madhyamaka treatises by the noble father, Nāgārjuna, and his spiritual son, Āryadeva, do not clarify whether external objects exist or not. After them Master Bhāviveka refuted the system of Consciousness Only[139] and established a system in which external objects conventionally exist. Then Master Śāntarakṣita made a different Madhyamaka system based on

Yogācāra scriptures and taught that external objects do not conventionally exist and that ultimately the mind is without inherent existence. Thereby two kinds of Mādhyamikas emerged. The former were called Sautrāntika-Mādhyamikas, the latter Yogācāra-Mādhyamikas.

This chronology of elucidation through great treatises is correct.

However, although Master Candrakīrti asserts that external objects conventionally exist, it is inappropriate to call him a Sautrāntika because he does not conform to other proponents of the tenet system. To assert that he accords with the Vaibhāṣika is also incorrect. The scholars of the later propagation of teachings in the land of snowy mountains created two designations for Mādhyamikas: Svātantrika and Prāsaṅgika.[140] This accords with Candrakīrti's *Clear Words* (*Prasannapadā*). Therefore the Mādhyamikas are specified as two types: those who conventionally assert external objects and those who do not. When the names are applied from the point of view of how the view that ascertains emptiness is generated within the mindstream, they are also specified as two types, Prāsaṅgika and Svātantrika.

Yet who did those masters follow to seek the intentions of the noble father and his spiritual son? The past gurus of these instructions held to this system as the main one by following the Great Elder, Atiśa, who made Master Candrakīrti's system the main Madhyamaka system. Master Candrakīrti saw that among the commentators on *Fundamental Treatise on the Middle Way* (*Mūlamadhyamakakārikā*), Buddhapālita had completely elucidated the noble one's intentions. He elucidated the noble one's intentions basing himself on Buddhapālita's system; he also took many good explanations from Master Bhāviveka, refuting those that seemed slightly incorrect. Since the commentaries by Buddhapālita and Candrakīrti [225] are seen to be very outstanding with regard to explaining the texts of the noble father Nāgārjuna, and his spiritual son, Āryadeva, their intentions will be determined here following in the footsteps of the former two masters.

HOW TO DETERMINE THE VIEW IN PARTICULAR

This has three points: identifying afflicted ignorance, demonstrating that it is the root of revolving in cyclic existence, and the need to seek the view of selflessness if you wish to eliminate the apprehension of a self.

IDENTIFYING AFFLICTED IGNORANCE

Among the antidotes taught by the Victor, those countering the mental afflictions of attachment and the like are partial antidotes, whereas the antidote to ignorance he taught is an antidote to all of them. Therefore ignorance is the basis of all errors and faults. *Clear Words* says:

> The nine divisions of the buddhas' teachings based on the two
> truths,
> such as the sets of sūtras, are perfectly proclaimed to meet the exten-
> sive behaviors of worldly beings.
> Among them, those taught in order to remove attachment will not
> eliminate hatred,
> those taught in order to remove hatred will not eliminate
> attachment,
> and those taught in order to exhaust pride will not overcome the
> other defilements.
> Therefore they are not so pervasive; all those discourses are not of
> such great import.
> Those that were taught for the sake of exhausting ignorance, how-
> ever, overcome all the mental afflictions.
> The victors taught that all the mental afflictions are thoroughly
> based on ignorance.

That being so, you must meditate on suchness as the antidote to ignorance. Moreover, unless you have identified ignorance, you will not know how to cultivate its antidote. Therefore it is extremely important to identify ignorance.

Ignorance is the opposite of knowledge, but this knowledge should not be understood as just any knowledge. Rather, it is the wisdom knowing the suchness of selflessness. Its opposite cannot be merely absence of that wisdom or merely something else; it must be its antagonist. It is the superimposition[141] of a self and, more specifically, the two superimpositions of a self of phenomena and of persons. So both the apprehension of a self of phenomena and the apprehension of a self of persons are ignorance. [226] The manner of superimposition is to apprehend that phenomena exist established by way of their intrinsic nature, by way of their intrinsic characteristics, or inherently. In this regard the *Questions of Upāli Sūtra* (*Upāliparipṛcchāsūtra*) says that phenomena are posited by the power of conceptuality:

> The various flowers that gladden the mind,
> the golden, resplendent, attractive mansions:
> both completely lack a creator—
> they are posited by conceptuality.
> The world is imputed by conceptuality.

Sixty Stanzas of Reasoning (*Yuktiṣaṣṭikā*, v. 37) also says:

> Since the perfect Buddha said
> the world had ignorance as its cause,
> how could it be invalid to say
> this world is due to conceptuality?

The commentary on the meaning of this statement explains that the worlds are not established by way of their intrinsic natures but are merely imputed by conceptuality.

Four Hundred Stanzas (8.3) also says:

> If, without conceptuality,
> desire and so forth do not exist,
> what intelligent person would uphold
> both intrinsic reality and conceptuality?

And [Candrakīrti's] commentary on this says, "Things that exist only through the existence of conceptuality and do not exist without conceptuality are, like a snake imputed to a rope, undoubtedly not established by way of their intrinsic nature." This statement explains that in terms of being imputed and not established by way of their intrinsic natures, attachment and so forth are like a snake imputed to a rope. Yet the latter is unlike attachment and so forth in terms of whether they conventionally exist.

For those reasons the manner of apprehending things as truly existent, which is to be negated, is to apprehend them not as posited by the power of beginningless conceptuality but as established by way of their intrinsic natures on top of objects. Its conceived object is called *self* or *inherent existence.* The selflessness of a person is taught as the nonexistence of this with a person as the basis for the attribute, and the selflessness of phenomena is taught as the nonexistence of this with a phenomenon such as an eye or a nose as the basis. [227] Therefore the apprehension of that inherent existence as present in persons and phenomena is implicitly understood as the apprehension of the two selves.

Commentary on Four Hundred Stanzas says:

> In this regard the so-called *self* is an essence of things that does not depend on anything else. Its nonexistence is selflessness. Owing to the division of phenomena and persons, it is understood as twofold, a *selflessness of phenomena* and a *selflessness of persons*.

It is like that.

With respect to the observed object of the apprehension of a self of persons, *Entering the Middle Way* explains that some Saṃmatīyas assert all the five aggregates and some assert only the mind to be the basis or observed object of the view of a self.[142] As for the mind, again, Cittamātrins and certain Mādhyamikas who assert a foundational consciousness (*ālayavijñāna*) assert that the foundational consciousness is the observed object. Some Mādhyamikas who do not assert [a foundational consciousness], such as Bhāviveka, and many śrāvaka schools assert that [the observed object] is the mental consciousness. However, with these systems, when it comes to the meaning invested in the term *person*, the one cultivating the paths, the one revolving in cyclic existence, and so forth, you need to distinguish these two modes: positing a mere I and positing something like a foundational consciousness as the basis of that I's characteristics.

With respect to the innate view of the transitory collection,[143] which is an apprehension of a self, *Entering the Middle Way* refutes that the aggregates are its observed object, and its autocommentary says it has the dependently imputed self as its observed object. It is said that even the mere collection of aggregates is not the conventional self, so neither the collection of aggregates at one time nor the collection that is the continuum of the aggregates from an earlier to a later moment is its observed object. Rather, the mere I that is the observed object of the mere thought "I" arising, or the mere person, should be taken as its observed object. Neither an individual aggregate nor their collection is posited as the basis of characteristics of that I.

Elsewhere, I have explained in detail that this point is an unsurpassed distinctive feature of this system.[144]

The mind thinking "I" that arises toward the observed object of the innate view of the transitory collection must arise naturally. Therefore the innate apprehension of the self of a person that apprehends the person associated with someone else's mindstream to be established by way of their intrinsic characteristics is innate, but it is not the innate view of the transitory collection of that person. The observed object of the innate view of the transitory collection apprehending a mine is the "mine" itself,[145] the observed object of the innate mind thinking "mine." [228] It should not be held that one's own eyes and so forth are the observed object. Its subjective aspect is to observe that object of observation and to apprehend the "mine" to be established by way of its intrinsic characteristic.[146]

The objects of the innate apprehension of a self of phenomena are the form aggregate and so forth; the eyes, ears, and so forth associated with one's own or someone else's mindstream; and the environment and so forth that is not included in a mindstream. Its subjective aspect is as explained above. *Entering the Middle Way Autocommentary* says:

> Ignorance (*moha*) is the ignorance (*avidyā*) that superimposes a nonexistent nature of things. It essentially obstructs the view of their nature; it obscures (*saṃvṛti*).

And:

> Thus [objects are posited as truly existent] through the power of the afflicted ignorance included in the links of existence.

This statement asserts that the apprehension of objects as truly existent is ignorance and that it is an afflicted ignorance. Therefore there are two ways of positing the apprehension of a self of phenomena, as a mental affliction and as an obstruction to omniscience; this accords with the former. This was also taught by the noble father and son. *Seventy Stanzas on Emptiness* (*Śūnyatāsaptati*) says:

> The Teacher said that ignorance is
> that which conceives things born from causes

and conditions to be real.
The twelve links arise from that.

When it is known well that things are empty,
since reality is seen, there is no ignorance.
That is the cessation of ignorance
whereby the twelve links cease to exist.

To "conceive things . . . to be real" is to apprehend them as established in
reality or truly. This is similar in meaning to a statement from *Precious Garland* (1.35):

As long as one apprehends the aggregates,
one apprehends an "I" in them.

This says that until you stop apprehending the aggregates as real, you will
not stop the view of the transitory collection.
Four Hundred Stanzas (6.10–11) also says:

Like the body sense in the body,
ignorance pervades them all.
That is why by conquering ignorance,
all the mental afflictions are conquered.

Ignorance will no longer arise
if dependent arising is seen.
Therefore, with all my effort here, [229]
I will only talk about that.

As regards the ignorance presented like this, the context is an identification
of the ignorance that is one of the three poisons and that is therefore afflicted
ignorance. In order to stop this ignorance, it is said to be necessary to realize
the profound meaning of interdependence in such a way that the meaning
of emptiness appears as the meaning of dependent arising. In accordance
with the explanation in [Candrakīrti's] commentary on this text, afflicted
ignorance should therefore be taken as a superimposition of true existence
onto things. This manner of understanding was set forth clearly by the ven-

erable Candrakīrti following the example of Buddhapālita's commentary on the noble Nāgārjuna's intention.

DEMONSTRATING THAT IT IS THE ROOT OF REVOLVING IN CYCLIC EXISTENCE

That being so, the ignorance apprehending the two selves explained above is not the apprehension of intellectually acquired selves of persons and phenomena that are thoroughly imputed by the unique assertions of non-Buddhist and Buddhist tenet systems, [including beliefs in] (1) a permanent, unitary, and self-powered person, (2) external objects of apprehension, which are either partless particles that lack an eastern side[147] or coarse composites of them, (3) an internal apprehending consciousness that is either moments of awareness without parts such as earlier and later or a continuum of awareness joining such partless moments together, and (4) self-consciousness that is nondual in that it is empty of such objects and subjects. Rather, it is the two innate apprehensions of a self shared by all, whether or not their minds are influenced by tenets. They have operated beginninglessly without depending on the minds' being affected by tenets. Here, just that is held to be the root of cyclic existence, because *Entering the Middle Way* (6.125) says:

> The apprehension of "I" is still seen to operate
> in those who have spent numerous eons as animals
> and do not conceive of some unborn permanent entity.

Through this reasoning it can be understood that what binds all sentient beings in cyclic existence is innate ignorance, and since intellectually acquired ignorance is only present in proponents of tenets, it is illogical for it be the root of cyclic existence.

It is extremely important to gain discriminating certainty about this. If you do not understand that, then, while ascertaining emptiness by means of the view, [230] you will not know how to hold as the main thing the ascertainment of the absence of real existence as apprehended by innate ignorance or how to negate the objects of intellectually acquired apprehensions subsidiary to that. If you negate the two types of self but do not refute the way they are apprehended by innate ignorance, you will ascertain just the selflessness that negates only imputations by the proponents of tenets mentioned above. Therefore, since the ascertainment by means of the view is for the purpose of meditation, when you meditate, you will necessarily only meditate on that.

Therefore, when you meditate on that selflessness and it becomes manifest, even if you perfect that cultivation, there will be nothing more to it than just that. Thus it is quite absurd to assert that the innate mental afflictions are reversed through seeing the nonexistence of the two selves merely as imputed by intellectual apprehensions. *Entering the Middle Way* (6.140) says:

> [You claim that] when one realizes selflessness, one abandons
> the eternal self, yet you assert that that self
> is not the basis of apprehending an I. Hence it is odd
> to claim that knowing such selflessness casts out the self-view.

And the autocommentary also says:

> For clarification, this point, the absence of a mutual relation
> [between seeing the absence of a permanent self and eliminating
> beginningless grasping at a self], is explained by way of analogy:
>
> > Say you see a snake in a hole in a wall of your house.
> > The idea that you could eliminate your fear of the snake
> > by saying, "There is no elephant here!" to clear up doubts
> > would, alas! only be laughable to others.

Although this is said with regard to the selflessness of persons, one could say the same with regard to the selflessness of phenomena, like this:

> When one realizes selflessness, one abandons
> the acquired self, yet you assert that that self
> is not the basis of ignorance. Hence it is odd
> to claim that knowing such selflessness casts out ignorance.

Someone might object and say, "Well, *Precious Garland* (1.35) says that the apprehension of a self of phenomena that apprehends the aggregates as truly existent is explained as the root of cyclic existence. It says:

As long as one apprehends the aggregates,
one apprehends an "I" in them.[148]
If one apprehends an "I," there is karma,
and from karma there is rebirth. [231]

Whereas *Entering the Middle Way* says that the view of the transitory collection is explained as the root of cyclic existence. It says (6.120):

Seeing with his wisdom that all faults and afflictions
arise from the view of the transitory collection . . .[149]

These two explanations are contradictory because it is illogical to have two different roots of cyclic existence."

We would answer that there is no fault in this. This system distinguishes the two apprehensions of a self by their distinct observed objects, but there is no difference in their mode of apprehension because both apprehend the object as established by way of its intrinsic characteristics. The contradiction of two roots of cyclic existence is understood to arise only when positing two modes of apprehension that do not accord in their way of engaging in their objects as the roots of cyclic existence. Therefore, when the apprehension of a self of phenomena is taught as the cause of the view of the transitory collection, the two subdivisions of ignorance are being described as cause and effect.[150] When the two are taught as the root of the mental afflictions, they are described as the root of all the mental afflictions with other modes of apprehension. Since this is the same for both of them, there is no contradiction [in saying both are the root of cyclic existence], just as there is no contradiction in saying both earlier and later moments of the same kind of ignorance are roots of cyclic existence.[151]

Although the venerable Candrakīrti does not appear to clearly explain the view of the transitory collection specifically as ignorance, he generally says that the apprehension of things as truly existent is afflicted ignorance, without differentiating between persons and phenomena. He also asserts that the apprehension of a self of persons is the apprehension of persons as established by way of their intrinsic characteristics. Moreover, he frequently explains the innate view of the transitory collection as the root of cyclic existence. If he asserted it to be different in meaning from the ignorance that is the apprehension of true existence, he would be positing two roots

342 | THE MIDDLE-LENGTH STAGES OF THE PATH

of cyclic existence with discordant modes of apprehension, which would be contradictory. Therefore both of them should be understood as ignorance.

All the other innate and intellectually acquired afflictions, as they operate, apprehend features of that very object that have been superimposed by the innate ignorance explained above. Therefore, just as the other four sense powers of eyes and so forth abide in reliance upon the body sense power rather than abiding independently in a separate place, all the other mental afflictions also operate depending on innate ignorance, [232] which is why ignorance is said to be primary. *Four Hundred Stanzas* (6.10) says:

> Like the body sense in the body,
> ignorance pervades them all.[152]

Commentary on Four Hundred Stanzas says:

> Attachment and so forth also operate by superimposing features such as attractiveness and repulsiveness on the mere inherent existence of things thoroughly imputed by ignorance, and as such, they operate in a manner that is not different from ignorance and even depend on it, for ignorance is primary.

After that, once ignorance has apprehended the objects as established by way of their intrinsic characteristics, if an object is agreeable to one's own mind, attachment arises when it is observed, and if it appears disagreeable to one's own mind, anger arises toward it. If the object does not appear agreeable or disagreeable to one's mind and remains as an ordinary thing in between, neither arises when the object is observed, but further ignorance of the same kind does arise. *Sixty Stanzas of Reasoning* (v. 52) says:

> Why would the great venom, afflictions, not
> arise in those whose minds have a basis for it?
> Even when it is an ordinary [object],
> they are seized by the snake of the mental afflictions.

In the commentary these lines are explained as above.

The intended meaning of *Precious Garland* also appears to be that the view of the transitory collection arises from apprehending the aggregates as truly existent. The way the remaining mental afflictions arise should be inferred and understood from the explanations in the context of persons of medium capacity. Also, *Commentary on Compendium of Valid Cognition* (2.218–19) says:

> He who sees a self will always
> adhere to what he refers to as "I."
> Through that adherence there's craving for happiness;
> through that craving faults are obscured.
>
> There is strong craving when excellence is seen.
> The "mine" is grasped as that which achieves it.
> As long as there is attachment to self,
> one will thus revolve in cyclic existence.

You should come to understand it that way. [233]

Although this system differs from the way the above explanation posits the two apprehensions of a self, you should come to understand the stages of how the mental afflictions arise depending on it. Initially, attachment to the self arises once the observed object of the thought "I" is apprehended as established by way of its intrinsic characteristic. That generates craving for the self's happiness. However, since there is no independent happiness for the self that does not depend on what is mine, there is craving for mine. That obscures the faults [in what is identified as mine] and causes one to see excellent qualities in it. Consequently, "mine" is grasped as something that achieves the self's happiness. Karma is committed owing to the mental afflictions that arise like this; through that karma, one is again reborn in cyclic existence. *Seventy Stanzas on Emptiness* says:

> Karma has mental afflictions as its cause;
> karmic formations derive from the afflictions.
> The body has karma as its cause.
> Those three are empty of a nature.

You should train in this manner to gain certainty regarding the stages of revolving in cyclic existence.

THE NEED TO SEEK THE VIEW OF SELFLESSNESS IF YOU WISH TO ELIMINATE THE APPREHENSION OF A SELF

This has two points: the reason you need to seek the view that realizes self-lessness if you wish to eliminate that ignorance, and how to generate the view that realizes selflessness.

THE REASON YOU NEED TO SEEK THE VIEW THAT REALIZES SELFLESSNESS IF YOU WISH TO ELIMINATE THAT IGNORANCE

It is necessary to want the extinction wherein the ignorance explained above as the twofold apprehension of a self has been eliminated. One may deem it necessary and even appear to want it, but one who wants to but does not put effort into understanding how apprehending a self becomes the root of cyclic existence has very dull faculties. So does someone who does not put effort into generating the pure view of selflessness in his mindstream despite partial insight into this, having thoroughly refuted the object grasped by the apprehension of a self with scriptures of definitive meaning as well as reasonings. That is because he has lost the vital essence of the path that leads to liberation and omniscience and yet remains indifferent about that.

This is why the glorious Dharmakīrti said [in his *Commentary on Compendium of Valid Cognition* 2.222–23]:

> Without their objects being disproven
> they cannot possibly be abandoned.
> Abandoning desire, hatred, and so forth
> connected with excellent qualities and faults
> requires not seeing these in objects
> and not some external approach. [234]

When removing an external object of elimination such as a thorn that has pierced your skin, you can completely remove it by means of something like a needle, independently of negating the object caught in this manner. When eliminating an internal mental object of abandonment, however, you cannot do it like this. Rather, you must eliminate it by seeing the nonexistence in the object of the meaning apprehended—the apprehension, for instance, of a self.

The glorious Candrakīrti also taught that once all the afflictions, such as attachment, and all the faults, such as birth, aging, and so forth, are seen to arise from the apprehension of a self, the desire to negate and eliminate it will arise. At that point the yogi negates with reasonings the object superimposed by the apprehension of a self, the self of a person. *Entering the Middle Way* (6.120) clearly says:

> Seeing with his wisdom that all faults and afflictions
> arise from the view of the transitory collection,
> a yogi knows the self to be its object
> and performs the negation of the self.

In fact that is what someone who meditates on suchness must do; that is why it says "a yogi."

This approach is also the excellent thought of the protector Nāgārjuna. He says in *Sixty Stanzas of Reasoning* (vv. 47 and 48):

> That is the cause of all the views;
> without it afflictions do not arise.
> Therefore, if you thoroughly know this,
> views and afflictions are thoroughly purified.
>
> If you wonder how this is known,
> it is by seeing dependent arising.
> The supreme knower of suchness taught
> that things born dependently are unborn.

He is pointing out that the apprehension of true existence called "asserting as things," which is the cause of all afflicted views and all other mental afflictions, is eliminated through realizing the suchness of things: that they are not inherently arisen because they are dependently arisen. The insight that there is no such inherent existence does not arise without negating the object of the apprehension of things as inherently established. A statement by Āryadeva that accords with this was already quoted above.[153] In *Four Hundred Stanzas* (14.25) he also says: [235]

> If selflessness is seen in objects,
> the seed of existence will cease.

That means the root of existence, ignorance, is cut by seeing that the object of observation grasped by the apprehension of a self lacks a self. The venerable Śāntideva also says [in his *Compendium of Trainings*]:

> Thus the emptiness of persons is thoroughly established, and since their root has been cut, all the mental afflictions do not arise at all. It is as the *Tathāgata's Secrets Sūtra* (*Tathāgataguhya-kasūtra*) says:
>
>> Śāntimati, it is like this. When a tree is cut at the root, all the branches, leaves, and twigs dry up. Likewise, Śāntimati, when you fully pacify the view of the transitory collection, you also fully pacify all the mental afflictions and secondary mental afflictions.

This means that the view of the transitory collection is reversed through cultivating the realization of emptiness that sees the person as empty of inherent establishment. Once it is reversed, all other mental afflictions are also reversed. Furthermore, the realization of selflessness is impossible without negating the object of the apprehension of a self of persons.

The sūtra passage points out that the view of the transitory collection is the root of all other mental afflictions. If it were different in meaning from ignorance, there would be two different roots of cyclic existence. Therefore it should also be understood as ignorance.

In brief, when the many supreme scholars who commented on the meaning of the profound scriptures determined the meaning of suchness, they carried out a thorough analysis by means of numerous scriptures and reasonings. They did so having perceived that it is impossible to realize selflessness and emptiness without seeing that the self grasped by the erroneous apprehension does not exist and without seeing that it is empty of that self. It is essential to gain certainty with regard to this.

If you do not meditate like this on the meaning of the negation of the erroneous object that is the root of being bound in cyclic existence, then even if you meditate on something else that you claim is profound, it will not harm the apprehension of a self at all. For unless the mind enters the suchness of selflessness and emptiness, the apprehension of a self cannot possibly be reversed. [236] Also, if you do not negate the object of the apprehension of a self, you might hinder your mind from going toward its object, but that cannot be posited as entering selflessness.

The reason why is that when the mind engages an object, there are three possible apprehensions: an apprehension of that observed object as truly existent, an apprehension of it as not truly existent, and an apprehension that does not qualify it as either of those two. Therefore, simply not apprehending something as truly existent does not entail that you apprehend it as not truly existent; likewise, a mere lack of involvement in the two selves does not entail that you are involved in the two selflessnesses. There are countless mental states in the third category.

The two apprehensions of a self mainly operate while something, a person or a phenomenon, is being observed. Therefore you must determine that the very bases for misapprehension do not exist in the way they are apprehended. Otherwise it would be like searching for a thief in a meadow after he has fled to the forest. Consequently, since you remove the mistake by meditating on the determined meaning, such an emptiness is the supreme meaning of suchness. If you determine something apart from the meaning of suchness that eliminates that [mistake], then the only thing that will cease is something imputed by your own assertions. Therefore remember that this deviates from the meaning of the scriptures.

That being so, the ignorance that apprehends the elaborations of persons, such as men and women, and of phenomena, such as forms and feelings, to be truly existent is stopped by gaining the view that realizes their emptiness, selflessness, and meditating on it. Once that ignorance has stopped, you stop discursive thought, which is the improper mental attention that superimposes qualities such as attractiveness and repulsiveness while observing the object of the apprehension of true existence. Once that has stopped, the other mental afflictions that have the view of the transitory collection as their root, such as attachment, also stop. Once they have stopped, karma motivated by them stops. Once that has stopped, rebirth in cyclic existence propelled by karma without control stops, and liberation is thereby achieved. With this in mind, generate strong certainty and then decisively seek the view of suchness. The *Root Text on Wisdom* (18.5) says:

> There is freedom when karma and afflictions are spent.
> Karma and afflictions arise from thoughts,
> and those arise from elaborations.
> Elaborations are stopped by emptiness. [237]

You must understand those stages of entering into and turning away from cyclic existence and greatly cherish the realization of the meaning of suchness. However, it will not come through a vague involvement that fails to distinguish well the objects of observation.

HOW TO GENERATE THE VIEW THAT REALIZES SELFLESSNESS

This has three points: the stages of generating the two views of selflessness, the actual progressive generation of the two views of selflessness, and presenting conventional and ultimate truths.

THE STAGES OF GENERATING THE TWO VIEWS OF SELFLESSNESS

As for the stages in which the two apprehensions of a self arise, the apprehension of a self of phenomena generates the apprehension of a self of persons. Still, when you engage in the suchness of selflessness, you must first generate the view of the selflessness of persons and then, after that, generate the view that realizes the selflessness of phenomena. *Precious Garland* (1.80–81) says:

> If persons are not earth, not water,
> not fire, not wind, not space,
> not consciousness, and not all of them together,
> then what else could persons be?
>
> Since beings are composites of the six elements,
> they are not real, and in that same way,
> each element is also a composite
> and therefore is not real either.

He explains lack of inherent existence first in terms of the person and then in terms of the basis it is imputed on, the elements such as earth. Candra-kīrti's *Clear Words* and Buddhapālita also explain that when entering into suchness, one first enters by way of the selflessness of persons. Śāntideva also says that.

It must be done like this because although the selflessnesses ascertained on the basis of persons and phenomena do not differ in terms of being more subtle or coarse, it is easier to ascertain selflessness on the basis of persons and more difficult to ascertain it on the basis of phenomena owing to attributes of the bases. Likewise it is more difficult, for example, to ascertain the selflessness of phenomena on the basis of eyes, ears, and so forth and easier to ascertain it on the basis of reflected images and the like, which is why these latter are taken as illustrations for determining the selflessness of the former. This is the intended meaning of the *King of Concentrations Sūtra* when it says:

> Just as you know the perception of self,
> apply it to everything mentally.
> The nature of all phenomena [238]
> is completely pure like space.
> All of them are known through one,
> and all of them are seen through one.

This says that once you know well the way the "I" abides with regard to which the perception of a self, thinking "I," operates, you should then apply its reasoning to all internal phenomena like eyes and ears and external phenomena like pots, knowing that they are similar to it. Thus, through knowing and seeing the natural disposition of one phenomenon, you are thus able to know and see the natural state of all other phenomena.

23 | The Selflessness of Persons

THE ACTUAL PROGRESSIVE GENERATION OF THE TWO VIEWS OF SELFLESSNESS

THIS HAS TWO POINTS: determining the selflessness of persons and determining the selflessness of phenomena.

DETERMINING THE SELFLESSNESS OF PERSONS

This has two points: identifying persons and determining them to not exist inherently.

IDENTIFYING PERSONS

Persons are persons of the six classes—gods and so forth—and persons who are ordinary beings, āryas, and so forth. They are also the accumulators of virtuous and nonvirtuous karma, the experiencers of the effects of those, revolvers in cyclic existence, cultivators of paths for the sake of liberation, attainers of liberation, and so forth. A sūtra quoted in works such as the *Entering the Middle Way Autocommentary* (*Madhyamakāvatārabhāṣya*) says:

> The so-called self is Māra's thought,
> and you have come to hold this view.
> The composition of aggregates is empty;
> there is no sentient being in it.
>
> Just as people speak of chariots
> based on collections of chariot parts,

they conventionally say "sentient beings"
based on the aggregates of beings.[154]

The first verse teaches the selflessness of persons, which is that ultimately persons do not exist. The first line says that the apprehension of a self of persons is a fiendish mind, the second one says that those who apprehend in this manner are under the power of bad views, and the third and fourth say that the aggregates are empty of a self of persons. The second verse indicates that persons exist conventionally. More specifically, the first and second lines present an analogy, and the last two connect it to the meaning, indicating that persons are merely imputed on the basis of the aggregates.

The sūtra passage is saying that the collection of aggregates is the basis of imputation of the person, and it is not logical for the basis of imputation [239] to be the imputed phenomenon. The collection of aggregates must be understood as both the collection of aggregates at a given moment and the collection of aggregates across earlier and later moments. Therefore it is illogical to posit the continuum of the collection of aggregates as the person.[155] When the collection is posited as the basis of imputation, the possessor of the collection is also posited as the basis of imputation, and therefore it is unreasonable for both to be the person. *Entering the Middle Way* (6.135) says:

> The sūtras say that since it depends on the aggregates,
> the mere collection of aggregates is not the self.

And (6.132):

> The Teacher said, "The aggregates are the self."
> If that's why you posit the aggregates as the self,
> it only refutes a self apart from the aggregates,
> for other sūtras make statements like "form is not self."

Therefore even the statement "The view of 'I' and 'mine' by some ascetics or brahmins is only a view of these five aggregates"[156] refutes, by means of the word "only," that a self with a different nature from the aggregates exists as the observed object of one's innate apprehension of an "I." However, that is refuted, and the aggregates are shown to not be the observed object of the apprehension of an "I." If they were, that would contradict the statements in other sūtras that the five aggregates are not the self. The reason for this is that, out of the two [dimensions of the view of the transitory collection], the observed object and the aspect of the apprehension of an "I," if the aggregates were the observed object, they would have to be posited as the self. Therefore the meaning of the sūtra statement about a view of the aggregates must be explained as referring to the observation of the self that is imputed to the aggregates.

That is why you should distinguish between statements that the mere I, referred to as *self*, conventionally exists and statements that an inherently established person, also referred to as *self*, does not exist even conventionally. Still, you should not say that this system asserts the self of persons to be conventionally existent.[157] Such an identification of persons is a distinctive feature of this unsurpassed system. Ascertaining this well is an excellent means of realizing the uncommon selflessness of persons.

DETERMINING THEM TO NOT EXIST INHERENTLY

This has three points: determining that the "I" does not inherently exist, determining that "mine" does not inherently exist, and showing how persons appear like illusions in dependence on that. [240]

DETERMINING THAT THE "I" DOES NOT INHERENTLY EXIST

The first of four essential points with regard to this is to examine one's own mindstream so as to identify the manner of apprehending a self of persons. That was explained previously.[158] The second is the decision that if the person is inherently established,[159] it must be established as either the same or different in nature from the aggregates and that there is no means of establishment other than these two. In general it is established through experience that, when you determine something to be plural, thinking something like "pot and pillar," you eliminate that it is singular, and when you determine something to be singular, thinking something like "pot," you eliminate that it is plural. A third alternative, something that is neither one nor many, does therefore not exist. Consequently you are made to ascertain that to be neither one nature nor different natures is also impossible. The third is to see the damage to the position that the person and the aggregates are one inherently established nature. The fourth is to see well the damage to the position that the two are established as inherently different. When the four are complete in that manner, this produces the pure view realizing the suchness that is the selflessness of persons.

In this regard, if the self and the aggregates had one inherently established nature, there would be three faults to refute this position. First, it would be pointless to assert a self. If the oneness of nature of the two were inherently established, they would be a completely indivisible one. This is because if their sameness of nature were ultimately established, then whatever mind those two appeared to, they would necessarily not appear distinct. Among falsities, or conventions, it is not contradictory for the way they appear and the way they abide to be discordant, but in something truly established, those two are necessarily contradictory, because something truly established that appears to a mind must appear just the way it is. A self established by its intrinsic nature is asserted to establish an agent who discards and adopts aggregates, because if he were one with the aggregates, this would be impossible. This is also set forth in the *Root Text on Wisdom* (27.5):

> Once you agree that apart from the aggregates
> that you appropriate, there is no self,
> then the self is nothing but the aggregates.
> In that case, your self does not exist.

Second, it follows that the self would be many. There would be the fault that if the self were established as one with the aggregates, then just as one person has many aggregates, so one person [241] would also have many selves, and just as there is no more than one self, so the aggregates would only be one. *Entering the Middle Way* (6.127) says:

> The aggregates are many; if they were the self,
> there would then be many selves.

Third, the self would arise and disintegrate. The *Root Text on Wisdom* (18.1) says:

If the aggregates were the self,
it would arise and disintegrate.

Just as the aggregates arise and disintegrate, so the self would also arise and disintegrate because the two would be one.

You may think, "It is asserted that the self or person arises and disintegrates in each moment." There is no fault in merely asserting this conventionally. However, an opponent who asserts that persons are established by way of their intrinsic characteristics thereby necessarily asserts that persons arise and disintegrate inherently. In this regard the *Entering the Middle Way Autocommentary* sets forth three faults. The first one is set forth in *Entering the Middle Way* (6.61):

For things to be distinct by their character
but included in one continuum is illogical.

With respect to something earlier and something later established as distinct by way of their intrinsic natures, a relationship of dependence between what is later and what is earlier is illogical. Since they are established with their own power as capable of setting themselves up, they cannot depend on anything else. If a single mental continuum is therefore illogical, it would be unreasonable to have a memory of former lives, "In that life, at that time, I was such and such." It is like with Devadatta when he remembers a former life. He does not remember "I was Yajñadatta" whose mindstream is distinct from his.

In our system a single mindstream of earlier and later moments is not contradictory even though it disintegrates in each moment.[160] Therefore the memory of former lives is valid. In people who have not realized the meaning of this, the frequent statement in sūtras "In the past I was this person" generates the first wrong view out of four bad views that were taught and that are based on an extreme associated with the past: "The two, the person at the time of buddhahood and the person at an earlier time, are one. Moreover, if they were compounded phenomena, they would disintegrate moment by moment and therefore could not be one. [242] Therefore the two are permanent." To avoid that view, you need to understand well the particular manner of remembering in which, as you remember, you remember the "I" in general, without making a distinction in terms of the specific country, time, and nature of a life.

The fault that karma that has been created would be wasted is that both the agent of an action and the experiencer of its effect could not be grouped together on the single basis of the mere I. The fault of meeting with actions one has not done is the absurd consequence that the effects of actions accumulated in some distinct mindstream would always be experienced by a different mindstream. These two faults are associated with the essential point explained above in *Entering the Middle Way* that if the person were established by way of its nature, its earlier and later moments could not be the same mindstream. The *Root Text on Wisdom* (27.16) also says:

> If a god and future human were discrete,
> their continuum would not be valid.

But what fault is there if you assert the self and the aggregates to be inherently different? The fault is set forth in the *Root Text on Wisdom* (18.1):

> If [the self] were other than the aggregates,
> it would not have their characteristics.

In this regard, if the self were different from the aggregates, and thus established by way of its distinct nature, it would not have the characteristics that characterize the aggregates as compounded phenomena: production, abidance, and disintegration. It would be like a horse, for example, which does not have the characteristics of an ox because it is established as an object other than an ox. You may insist, "It is indeed like that but . . ." Well then, it would be unacceptable as the observed object that is the basis of one's innate apprehension designating the verbal convention "self" because it is an uncompounded phenomenon—like, for instance, a flower in the sky or nirvāṇa.[161] Moreover, if it existed as inherently different from the characteristics of the aggregates, suitability as form and so forth, it would have to be observed as such, just as, for instance, form and mind are observed as different. Since there is no such apprehension, though, the self does not exist as something factually other. The *Root Text on Wisdom* (27.7) says:

> It is illogical for the self to be
> other than the appropriated aggregates. [243]
> If it were other, you could apprehend it
> in their absence. But you cannot.

And *Entering the Middle Way* says (6.124):

> Thus there is no self other than the aggregates,
> for, besides those, apprehending it is not established.

You should train in order to gain the firm certainty that sees that such reasonings damage the position that a self exists as a different nature from the aggregates. This is because if you have not induced pure certainty with respect to the two sides of sameness and difference, the conclusion that persons do not inherently exist will be a mere thesis, and you will not gain the pure view.

DETERMINING THAT "MINE" DOES NOT INHERENTLY EXIST

When you have thus sought with reasoning whether the self is or is not inherently established, you negate the inherent existence of the self by failing to find it to be either one or many. At that point, through the reasoning that analyzes suchness, you will not find an inherently established "mine," just as, when you do not observe a barren woman's son, you do not observe his "mine," such as his eyes. The *Root Verses on Wisdom* (18.2) says:

> If the "I" does not exist,
> how possibly could "mine" exist?

And *Entering the Middle Way* (6.165) says:

> Since no actions exist without an agent,
> there is no "mine" without a self.
> Therefore, by seeing the "I" and "mine" as empty,
> the yogi is completely liberated.

Thus those reasonings determine that the "I" of your own apprehending mindstream thinking "I" or self or person does not exist by way of its intrinsic nature. Through them you should also realize the entire meaning of the suchness that is the selflessness of persons: that all persons from hell beings through buddhas, and all their "mine," are not inherently established as the same nature or a different nature from their bases of designation, their contaminated or uncontaminated aggregates. Through those reasonings, you should also know how all their "mine" is likewise established as lacking inherent existence. [244]

SHOWING HOW PERSONS APPEAR LIKE AN ILLUSION IN DEPENDENCE ON THAT

This has two points: the meaning of the expression "like an illusion" and the method through which things appear like an illusion.

THE MEANING OF THE EXPRESSION "LIKE AN ILLUSION"

This has two points: the unmistaken manner of appearing like an illusion and the fallacious manner of appearing like an illusion.

THE UNMISTAKEN MANNER OF APPEARING LIKE AN ILLUSION

The *King of Concentrations Sūtra* says:

> Meditate on signs as empty of nature,
> like a mirage, a gandharva city,[162]
> like an illusion, or a dream.
> Know all phenomena to be like that.

The *Mother of the Victors*[163] also teaches that all phenomena, from form through omniscience, are like illusions and dreams. There are two meanings of being like illusions described in this way. First, there are things like ultimate truth, which is said to be illusion-like, and although it is established as merely existent, its true existence is understood to be negated.

And, second, there are things like the illusion-like appearance of that which appears while being empty. In this context, we are discussing the latter of these two. For this, both its appearance and its emptiness of truly existing in the way it appears are necessary. So if an object seems utterly nonexistent even as a mere appearance, like the horn of a rabbit or the son of a barren woman, and does not arise as "appearing yet empty of existing in the way it appears," then you have not understood the meaning of being an illusion-like appearance.

Hence you should understand other phenomena as resembling an illusion like this. Illusions conjured by a magician are from the start empty of being horses and elephants, and yet their appearances as horses and elephants undeniably arise. Likewise, phenomena such as persons are from the start empty of inherent existence, of being established by way of their intrinsic natures on top of the objects, and yet it is undeniable that they appear as if established that way.

That being so, the appearances as a god, a human, and so forth are posited as persons, and the objects that appear as form, sound, and so forth are posited as phenomena. Therefore, although persons and phenomena have not even a particle of inherent existence established by way of their intrinsic characteristics, nevertheless accumulators of karma and so forth, the actions of seeing and hearing and so forth, and all the interdependent actions and agents are valid. And since all actions and agents are valid, emptiness is not nihilistic. Primordially phenomena have always been empty like that and are understood merely as empty, [245] and so it is not a mentally fabricated emptiness, and since all objects of knowledge are asserted in this manner, neither is it a limited emptiness. That is why, when it is meditated on, it becomes the antidote to all attachment associated with the apprehension of true existence.

This profound meaning is not unsuitable to become the object of any mind whatsoever. It can be determined by means of pure view, and it can be made the object by means of meditation on the pure meaning. Therefore it is also not an emptiness that cannot be practiced at the time of the path or one that has nothing to see or realize.

Someone might object, "Well then, if the ascertainment that mirror reflections and so forth are empty of what they appear to be were the realization of their lack of inherent existence, the absence of inherent existence would be realized by the direct perception of normal beings; so the latter would be āryas. Otherwise, how could these be suitable analogies for the absence of inherent existence?"

Four Hundred Stanzas (8.16) says:

> It is explained that a seer of one thing
> is a seer of everything.
> The emptiness of one thing
> is the emptiness of all.

It explains that the seer or realizer of the emptiness of one thing can realize the emptiness of other things. The realization that the reflection of a face is empty of being a face does not in any way damage the object of one's apprehension of true existence that apprehends the reflection to be established by way of its intrinsic nature. Without the negation of its object, the emptiness of inherent establishment of the reflection cannot be realized. Therefore that mind does not realize the suchness of the reflection. Even if you realize that illusions are empty of being horses and elephants, and that the appearances in dreams are empty of what they appear to be, you have not found the Madhyamaka view that realizes that objects are like illusions and dreams.

The reason for taking them as analogies is because it is easier to realize that they do not inherently exist compared to other phenomena like forms and sounds. That they are empty of inherent existence established by way of their intrinsic natures is proven by showing the contradiction between the way they actually abide and the way they appear to the mind. For if an object were established as real, those two could not have different aspects. [246]

You need to first allow yourself to realize that these examples that are well known in the world to be false lack inherent existence, and then generate the realization that other phenomena that are *not* well known in the world to be false also lack inherent existence. The significance of having a sequence wherein one of these two comes first and the other follows is not that by realizing the emptiness of a single phenomenon, the emptiness of every other phenomenon is explicitly realized. Rather, the significance is that when the mind turns to another phenomenon to consider the way it exists, it can realize it.

That being so, to know that one is in a dream and to realize that the appearances of men, women, and so forth are empty of being [actual men, women, and so forth] is not the same as viewing in dreams all phenomena to be dreamlike. As said in the *Ornament for Clear Knowledge* (5.1):

> Even in your dreams, view all
> phenomena like dreams and so forth.

Likewise, the realization, in visions of meditative experience during concentration meditation, that appearances like pots and woolen cloth are empty of what they appear to be, does not have the same meaning as the realization that they are like illusions and dreams that are not inherently established. Therefore you should investigate well the uncommon manner in which things appear like an illusion set forth in scriptures and treatises of definitive meaning that say something should be known to be like an illusion and a dream.

Having said this, the following are similar to each other: a preverbal child who apprehends a reflection in the mirror as a face; a spectator who does not know about illusions and apprehends illusory appearances as horses, elephants, and so forth; and someone in a dream who is unaware of it and therefore apprehends the appearances of mountains, houses, and so forth as real. On the other hand, a more mature person, a magician, and a lucid dreamer are also similar in that they know their particular appearances to be untrue. Neither group has found the view of suchness.

THE FALLACIOUS MANNER OF APPEARING LIKE AN ILLUSION

If the measure of the object of negation explained above has not been grasped well and the object is analyzed by means of reasoning and broken down, the thought will first arise that "That object does not exist." Then, the analyzer is also seen to be like that. And since the ascertainer of his nonexistence is also nonexistent, any [247] ascertainment in terms of "It is this and not that" becomes impossible. Then the vague appearances that arise do so depending on the failure to differentiate inherent existence and nonexistence on the one hand from mere existence and nonexistence on the other. Therefore such an emptiness is an emptiness that also destroys dependent arising. Hence, even though the vague appearances arise induced by that realization, this is not at all the meaning of being like an illusion.[164]

That is why it is not difficult, upon reasoned analysis, to conclude that "Persons and so forth do not in the least have a mode of subsistence established by way of their intrinsic natures on top of the objects" and for appearances to simply arise vaguely depending on that. Something like that occurs to everyone with an interest in Madhyamaka tenets who has heard a little bit of Dharma being taught about how there is no inherent existence. However, the difficult point is to achieve certainty, from the depths of one's heart, about both negating all inherent existence established by way of an intrinsic nature and positing those inherently nonexistent persons and so forth as accumulators of karma, experiencers of effects, and so forth. Since that combination of two that enables one to posit both is next to impossible, it is extremely difficult to find the Madhyamaka view.

Therefore, as you analyze suchness with analytical reasoning, you find no production, and thereby you negate inherent production, but you do not negate every kind of production, cessation, and so forth. It is taught that, if you did, they would become empty of performing any function, like the horns of a rabbit or the son of a barren woman, and it would be untenable to have any interdependent actions and agents within that mere illusion-like appearance that is left over. *Four Hundred Stanzas* (15.10) says:

> If that is so, how would existence
> not resemble an illusion?

And [Candrakīrti's] commentary says:

> Once that which is dependently arisen is seen as what it is, it becomes like an illusory creation but not like the son of a barren woman. If one were to assert that production is negated in every way through this analysis and that therefore it demonstrates the nonproduction of compounded phenomena, then they would not be like illusions; they would be something to be examined in terms of the son of a barren woman and the like. For fear of someone concluding that the dependently arisen does not exist, [248] we do not compare phenomena with those but rather with illusions and the like, which do not contradict the dependently arisen.

And:

> Therefore, upon such thorough analysis, since the inherent exis-
> tence of things is not established, that illusion-like appearance
> itself will be left as a remnant for each thing.

Therefore the apprehension of dependent arisings as illusion-like appearances that are merely existent is not a mistaken apprehension of illusions,
but it would be mistaken if illusion-like appearances were apprehended as
established by way of their nature as truly existent.

The *King of Concentrations Sūtra* also says:

> Going through cyclic existence is like a dream.
> No one is born here, nor does anyone die.
>
> No sentient beings, humans, or life can be found.
> These phenomena are like foam, plantain trees,
> like illusions, lightning in the sky,
> like the moon in water, a mirage.
>
> Even after one dies here in this world,
> one does not move on to another world.
> Nevertheless, actions done are not lost;
> their white and black fruit ripen in cyclic existence.

There is no contradiction. Persons and the like who are born, die, and transmigrate and who bear analysis are not found, not even a particle, when
sought with the reasonings that analyze suchness. Nevertheless, positive
and negative effects occur relative to illusion-like phenomena. You need to
arrive at an understanding of such statements.

Moreover, some do not place and maintain the mind within the view
that has solved, in meditative equipoise, the ultimate mode of being but
just gain a stable single-pointedness in which the mind does not apprehend
anything at all. Through its power, when they arise from it, appearances
such as a mountain that previously appeared hard and obstructive now
appear insubstantial like a rainbow or thin smoke. This is also not the
illusion-like appearance explained in the scriptures; it is an appearance of

objects as empty of coarse obstructiveness rather than the appearance of objects as empty of inherent establishment. Emptiness is the absence of inherent existence; it cannot possibly be the lack of obstructive hardness. [249] Otherwise there would be the fault that it would be impossible for an apprehension of true existence to arise on the basis of apprehending rainbows and the like, and it would be impossible to generate a consciousness realizing the absence of true existence on the basis of apprehending obstructive objects.

THE METHOD THROUGH WHICH THINGS APPEAR LIKE AN ILLUSION

Well then, what do you do so that illusory objects appear without mistake? You see illusory horses and elephants, for example, with your eye consciousness and ascertain, with your mental consciousness, that no horses or elephants that accord with the appearance exist; in reliance upon that, the ascertainment arises that this appearance of horses and elephants is an illusory or false appearance. Likewise, persons and so forth undeniably appear to your conventional mind while you ascertain, by means of a reasoning consciousness, that they are empty of inherent existence established by way of their intrinsic natures; in reliance upon these two, the ascertainment arises that the persons are illusory or false appearances.

Owing to that essential point, the meditation in equipoise on space-like emptiness is on the nonexistence of even a mere particle of the referent object for apprehending characteristics. If this hits home, an illusion-like emptiness will appear as you look at the appearance of objects in postmeditation after you have risen from that meditation. Thus you analyze phenomena many times with the reasoning that analyzes whether they are established by way of their intrinsic natures, and you generate a very strong certainty that they lack inherent existence. Subsequently, when you look at the appearances that arise, they will appear like illusions. There is no separate method for determining illusion-like emptiness.

Therefore, even when engaging in active practices like prostrations and circumambulations, be governed by the ascertainment of your analysis as explained above. Train thereby in illusion-like appearance, and perform them from within that. Once you have trained thus, they will appear like illusions even through the mere recollection of the view.

Put simply and easy to understand, the method for seeking this ascertainment is as follows. As explained above, while engaging in the clear appearance of the generality that is the object of negation of rational analysis and carefully contemplating this inherent nature as fabricated by the ignorance within your own mindstream, you should identify it. Then you should contemplate how, if there were such inherent existence, it would not be beyond oneness and difference, and how there are flaws in any assertion of it as either. You should induce the ascertainment of seeing the flaws and finally stabilize the ascertainment by thinking, "A person [250] has not the least inherent establishment." You should train extensively in the factor of emptiness like that.

Then you should let the undeniable appearances of what are designated as persons arise as objects of your mind, attend to the interdependent factors of positing them as accumulators of karma and experiencers of effects, and gain certainty about how dependent arising is valid in the absence of inherent existence. When these two appear to contradict each other, take the analogy of a mirror image and the like and consider how they are noncontradictory. Although the reflection of a face is empty of whatever appears—the eyes, ears, and so forth—it nevertheless arises depending on a face and a mirror, and it disintegrates when either of those conditions is gone. These two [emptiness and arising] are undeniably contained in the common locus. You should train in the thought that likewise, although persons also do not have even a particle of inherent establishment, this does not contradict that they accumulate karma, experience effects, and are born depending on previous karma, afflictions, and so forth. This you should know in all such circumstances.

24 | The Selflessness of Phenomena

DETERMINING THE SELFLESSNESS OF PHENOMENA

THE BASIS OF DESIGNATION of a person, the five aggregates, the six elements such as the earth element, and the six sense fields such as the eye are phenomena, and the selflessness of those phenomena is their emptiness of an inherent existence established by way of their intrinsic natures. There are two ways to determine it: refutation using the reasoning explained above and refutation using another reasoning not explained above.

REFUTATION USING THE REASONING EXPLAINED ABOVE

Among the things that are aggregates, elements, and sense bases, there are two types. With physical phenomena, you investigate their parts in the various cardinal directions such as east as well as that which possesses the parts; with consciousnesses, you investigate their time segments such as earlier and later as well as that which possesses the segments. You refute them in the above fashion after investigating whether they are established by way of their natures as the same or different. That is the meaning of a sūtra statement quoted above:[165]

> Just as you know the perception of self,
> apply it to everything mentally.

REFUTATION USING ANOTHER REASONING NOT EXPLAINED ABOVE

This has two points: the logical proof of dependent arising and the way uncompounded phenomena are also established as not truly existent through this and earlier reasonings. [251]

THE LOGICAL PROOF OF DEPENDENT ARISING

With regard to the logical proof of dependent arising, the *Questions of Sāgaramati Sūtra* says:

> Those that originate interdependently
> do not exist by way of their nature.

Inherent establishment is clearly refuted with the reason of dependent arising. The *Questions of the Nāga King Anavatapta Sūtra* (*Anavataptanāgarā-japaripṛcchāsūtra*) also clearly says:

> Whatever is born from conditions is not born;
> it is not born by way of its intrinsic nature.
> Whatever depends on conditions is said to be empty;
> whoever has realized emptiness is heedful.

This is said very frequently in the precious scriptures. The meaning of what the first line refers to as "not born" is explained by the second line, "not born by way of its intrinsic nature." Therefore, in the refutation of birth, the object of negation is qualified. Candrakīrti's *Clear Words* quotes the *Descent to Laṅkā Sūtra* (*Laṅkāvatārasūtra*) as saying:

> Thinking that they are not born inherently, I said, "All phenomena are unborn."

The Teacher himself addressed the intention of the sūtras by explaining their meaning to be the nonexistence of *inherent* birth out of concern that without such a qualification, his statements that birth does not exist would be interpreted as meaning that all birth whatsoever is nonexistent.

Then, the third line says that dependence and reliance on conditions is the meaning of being empty of establishment by way of one's intrinsic nature. This teaches that emptiness of inherent establishment is the meaning of dependent arising, whereas an emptiness of performing functions, which would negate mere birth, is not.

The *Root Text on Wisdom* (7.16) also says:

That which arises in dependence
is free of intrinsic nature.

Because it arises dependently, it is pacified or empty of establishment by way of its nature. Whatever obscure fabrications have been propounded— that because of dependent arising itself, the Madhyamaka system must propound nonarising and so forth—are thereby cleared away. The logical proof of dependent arising that is like that is praised very much. The *Questions of the Nāga King Anavatapta Sūtra* says:

> Experts see that phenomena arise in dependence [252]
> and do not rely at all on extreme views.

In realizing dependent arising as it is, one does not depend on views holding to extremes. The meaning of this is set forth in *Entering the Middle Way* (6.115):

> Since things arise utterly through dependence,
> these conceptions cannot withstand analysis.
> Thus this reasoning of dependent arising
> shreds the net of all bad views.

This is the unexcelled distinctive feature of Mahātma Nāgārjuna, the father, and his spiritual son [Āryadeva]. That is why, from among various reasonings, I will explain that of dependent arising here.

Here, there are two main mistakes that obstruct pure view. The first is the view of permanence and superimposition that has as its referent object the apprehension of true existence; that is, it apprehends phenomena as truly existent. The second is the view of annihilation and denial, in which the scope of the object of negation is not delimited and becomes excessive. This makes it impossible to induce the ascertainment of dependently arising causes and effects in one's own system; there is no way of identifying that something is this and not that.

When inherent establishment is negated with a logical proof inducing the ascertainment that from such and such causes and conditions such and such effects arise, those two mistakes are abandoned without remainder. This is because through ascertaining the logical proof, the view of annihilation is radically negated, and through ascertaining the meaning of the thesis, the view of permanence is negated.[166]

Therefore external things such as sprouts and internal things such as karmic formations originate depending, respectively, on seeds and so forth and on ignorance and so forth.

If that is so, then establishment through their intrinsic characteristics is illogical. For if they were established through their intrinsic natures, they would necessarily be established for themselves, through their own-powered, self-sustaining inherent existence; so this would contradict their being dependent on causes and conditions. *Four Hundred Stanzas* (14.23) says:

> That which has a dependent origin
> does not exist autonomously.
> All these are not autonomous;
> hence, they do not have a self.

Through this you should understand that since persons and pots and the like are also imputed in reliance upon their own collections of parts, [253] they do not have inherent establishment. Those are the two presentations of the logical proof of dependent arising.

If something arises dependently and is imputed dependently, it does not exist as something established by way of its intrinsic nature as one with whatever it depends on. If it did exist as one, all actions and agents would be one. The two are also not established by way of their natures as different, because if they were, one could refute their relation, and this would contradict their being dependent.

The *Root Text on Wisdom* says (18.10):

> Whatever arises dependent on something
> is not identical with that thing,
> but neither is it different from it. Hence
> it is neither annihilated nor eternal.

And *Praise of the World-Transcending One* (*Lokātītastava*) says:

> Logicians claim that suffering is created by itself,
> by other, by both itself and other,

or without any cause.
You said that it arises dependently.

That which arises dependently
is asserted by you to be empty.
"Things do not exist independently!"
is your matchless lion's roar.

The logical proof of dependent arising is thus said to refute the apprehensions of oneness and difference, the extremes of eternalism and annihilation, and the four extremes of origination.[167]

Having thus induced certainty through the emptiness that is empty of all referent objects for apprehending signs, one does not eliminate one's ascertainment of the relation between actions and their effects. Discarding nonvirtues and adopting virtues while relying on that is highly praised. The *Essay on the Mind of Enlightenment* (*Bodhicittavivaraṇa*) says:

To rely on actions and their effects
while knowing this emptiness of phenomena
is more wonderful still than the wonderful
and more marvelous still than the marvelous.

For that to happen it is necessary to differentiate among inherent existence, mere existence, nonexistence by way of an intrinsic characteristic, and nonexistence. It is as stated in the *Entering the Middle Way Autocommentary*:

Knowing the presentation of cause and effect even in relation to a mirror's reflection without inherent existence, what wise person would determine forms, feelings, and so forth—which do not exist other than as causes and effects—to have an intrinsic nature based on observing them as merely existing? [254] Therefore although they are observed to exist, they are without inherent production.

If you do not differentiate among those four, things will exist by way of their intrinsic nature as soon as they exist, and they will be nonexistent as long as they do not exist by way of their intrinsic nature. You will not move beyond the two extremes of superimposition and denial. *Commentary on Four Hundred Stanzas* says:

> Those who propound that real substantial things exist think that as long as a thing exists, so long will it possess intrinsic nature, whereas the moment it is rid of its intrinsic nature, then the thing will no longer exist in any way and will therefore be like a donkey's horn. Therefore, since they do not pass beyond this duality, all their assertions only coordinate with difficulty.

This being so, you are freed from all extremes of existence through the absence of existence by way of an intrinsic nature and, within that, from all extremes of nonexistence through the ability to posit causes and effects without resorting to inherent existence.

With regard to extremes, *Principles of Exegesis* (*Vyākhyāyukti*) says:

> *Extreme* (*anta*) means "finish," "end,"
> "nearness," "direction," and "the lower."[168]

Such extremes are indeed asserted in our system as well. However, as for the extremes that are places where the so-called "view free from extremes" goes wrong, *Illumination of the Middle Way* (*Madhyamakāloka*) says:

> If in the Madhyamaka the mind were to exist as an ultimate thing with its intrinsic nature, then since it would exist for that system, how could clinging to it, thinking, "It is permanent" or "It is impermanent," be an extreme? It is illogical to refer to proper attention that corresponds to the suchness of a thing as a "position one stumbles over."

As stated here, attention that corresponds with how an object actually exists is not a position one would stumble over, so it does not constitute holding to an extreme. In the world the precipice of an abyss is called an *extreme* or an *edge* (*mtha'*), and stumbling off it is called "falling off the edge." Likewise the apprehension of phenomena as truly existent [255] and the apprehension that nothing at all is established or exists constitute, respectively, the falling to the extremes of permanence and annihilation, which are opposites of reality. On the other hand, the apprehensions that phenomena do not ultimately exist, that causes and effects conventionally exist, and so forth do not constitute holding to extremes because the objects abide in the way they are apprehended.

The reason is stated in *Refuting Objections* (*Vigrahavyāvartanī*, v. 26), which says:

> If lack of inherent existence is inverted,
> it's something established by its intrinsic nature.

That is, if something is not ultimately nonexistent, it ultimately exists. Also:

> We do not make explanations
> without asserting conventionalities.

Seventy Stanzas on Emptiness says:

> We do not refute this worldly mode:
> "depending on this that arises."

Therefore the difference made between "that thing is not existent" and "it exists" as opposed to "it does not exist" and "it is not nonexistent" is nothing more than a difference in the way of expressing it.[169] There is no difference whatsoever in the manner the two appear to the mind, however much you analyze. Therefore it is nothing more than a fixation on mere words to propound that one falls or does not fall to extremes through that manner of expression.

THE WAY UNCOMPOUNDED PHENOMENA ARE ALSO ESTABLISHED AS NOT TRULY EXISTENT THROUGH THIS AND EARLIER REASONINGS

Once compounded phenomena, persons and phenomena, have thus been established as not truly existent by way of the reasonings explained above, it is established with little difficulty that uncompounded phenomena such as space, analytical cessations, nonanalytical cessations, and reality do not truly exist.[170] With that intention the *Root Text on Wisdom* (7.33) says:

> Compounded phenomena are not established,
> so how could the uncompounded be?

An easy method for establishing this is as follows. When inherently established compounded phenomena have been negated as above, even though they are not inherently established, one may still posit [the functions of] agents and actions, bondage and liberation, causes and effects, and objects of comprehension and those who comprehend them. When that is established, even though non-products like ultimate natures and analytical cessations are not established as truly existent, one can still speak about them in terms of objects of attainment on the path, objects of comprehension, the Jewel of Dharma as refuge for disciples, and so forth. [256] If they are not asserted to truly exist, it cannot be claimed that this presentation that must posit them is illogical. Therefore it would be pointless to assert them as truly existent.

Even those who assert them to truly exist must and do indeed also accept functions such as their definitions and definienda, their causes and effects of separation,[171] their comprehension by such and such valid cognitions, and so forth. At that point, if they do not relate them to their respective objects of attainment, definitions, comprehenders, and so forth, they cannot refute that all unrelated things become definitions and definienda of each other and the like. If they assert relations, they cannot posit them since something truly existent, inherently established, cannot depend on something else.

Similarly, you should also investigate whether uncompounded phenomena are one with or different from their bases of designation and then negate their inherent existence.[172] If by this reasoned analysis you cannot refute the assertion that they are truly established, you cannot negate true existence even in the slightest because it is the same in all respects for compounded phenomena. Someone might think that if the meaning of "Compounded phenomena are empty of inherently established natures" is that those phenomena do not have such natures, that it is thereby a nihilistic emptiness, but suchness truly exists because it has its intrinsic nature. That is the furthest you can err in determining compounded phenomena as empty of inherent establishment, a view that denies the interdependence of compounded phenomena. The latter [view of suchness] is a terrible view of permanence that superimposes true existence if something has its intrinsic nature. Therefore you would be entering the meaning of perfect emptiness wrongly.[173]

If the emptiness of an inherently established nature were the absence of it in itself, the absence would mean that nothing at all could possibly exist, so the holder of the thesis that certain phenomena truly exist, the scriptures and reasonings proving this, and so forth would also be empty of an inherently established nature. Therefore the basis would not be established, and therefore positing the tenet that some phenomena are truly established is a random statement without investigation.

With good insight into the implications of this way of reasoning, all the Buddhist schools of the noble land of India that propound the true existence of phenomena are called proponents of things since they certainly propound that things are established as truly existent. [257] Propounding that things are without true existence and no more asserting any phenomena whatsoever to be established as truly existent would seem to indicate a distinct superiority over those who propound the nonsense of this faction.

With the above explanations you should also come to a good understanding of those who advocate two discordant positions with regard to suchness and of how they approach the debate on whether the ultimate is ultimately established, having agreed on the above kind of emptiness of an inherently established nature with regard to conventional phenomena. This is because these two are dissimilar in all respects: first, refuting true existence with regard to phenomena by reasoning and not asserting true existence with regard to any things or phenomena, and second, propounding that all things and phenomena are without true existence in reliance upon a nihilistic emptiness that is a mistaken manner of understanding emptiness.

Someone might object, if the meaning of "Compounded phenomena are not established, so how could the uncompounded be?"[174] were as explained above, wouldn't this contradict other statements by Nāgārjuna? *Sixty Stanzas of Reasoning* (v. 35) says:

> When the victors teach nirvāṇa
> as the one and only truth,

what scholar would conceive
that the rest is not untrue?

Only nirvāṇa is said to be real while everything else is said to be unreal.
Praise of the Sphere of Reality (Dharmadhātustotra) also says:

All the sūtras teaching emptiness
set forth by the Victor,
counteract the mental afflictions;
they do not diminish this sphere.

That is, the purpose of the sūtras that teach emptiness, the absence of inherent existence, is to eliminate mental afflictions; they do not teach that the sphere of natural purity (*dharmadhātu*) does not exist.

[Response:] Those who think that way approach the meaning of the scriptures incorrectly. The above statement means the same as the following statement by the Victor:

Monks, this ultimate truth is unique; it is nirvāṇa, that which is nondeceptive. All compounded things have the quality of being false and deceptive. [258]

This sūtra also says that nirvāṇa is true and that all compounded things are false. The first part of the sūtra quote very clearly explains that *true* means nondeceptive, and the latter part very clearly explains that *false* means deceptive. Moreover, the *Commentary on Sixty Stanzas of Reasoning (Yuktiṣaṣṭikāvṛtti)* explains nirvāṇa[175] as an ultimate truth, which it is. Therefore a mind looking at it with direct perception will see in it no deceptiveness of appearing inherently established while not being inherently established. A mind directly perceiving all other phenomena, compounded things, will see in them the deceptiveness of appearing inherently established while not being inherently established. That is why they do not turn out to be established as truths that withstand analysis when you examine them with the reasoning that analyzes whether they are truly established. What then is the point of being attached to mere words without thinking deeply about their meaning?

Sixty Stanzas of Reasoning (v. 6) also says:

> Cyclic existence and nirvāṇa—
> neither of these exists.
> Perfect knowledge of cyclic existence
> is what is called *nirvāṇa*.

This is an explanation that both existence and peace do not inherently exist and that nirvāṇa is posited as the very knowledge that an inherently established existence does not exist. So how could this be a position that asserts emptiness, the nontrue existence of cyclic existence, as a nihilistic emptiness?

The meaning of the scriptural passage from *Praise of the Sphere of Reality*, too, is this: To avert the apprehension of things as truly existent, the root of all other mental afflictions, the sūtras teaching emptiness, the absence of inherent establishment, teach that the object conceived by that apprehension does not exist. They do not teach that emptiness does not exist—the sphere of natural purity that negates the object of that apprehension of true existence, the two types of self. Although emptiness exists, it is not truly established. That is why this scriptural passage serves as a source for refuting the assertions "The emptiness that negates the object of negation, true existence, does not exist either" and "In order to eliminate all the mental afflictions, it is not necessary to realize emptiness, the ultimate suchness." In fact that very *Praise* says:

> These three purify the mind:
> "impermanence, emptiness, and suffering."
> What purifies it best is
> the absence of inherent existence.

And: [259]

> Phenomena have no inherent existence;
> meditate on this as the sphere of reality.

The fact that these phenomena lack an inherently established nature is said to be the sphere of reality (*dharmadhātu*), which is the object of meditation, and just meditation on that is said to be the mind's best purifier. Therefore how could it be suitable to interpret these quotes as supporting the position

that the emptiness that is the absence of inherent establishment of phenomena appearing inherently established is a nihilistic emptiness and that,
therefore, a truly established emptiness separate from it should be posited
as the emptiness that is the object of meditation?

That is like propounding that when it comes to eliminating the suffering
of fear arising from apprehending a snake in the east even though there is
none, showing that there is no snake in the east will not serve as an antidote
and one needs to show, rather, that there is a tree in the west. This is because
one would propound that when it comes to eliminating the suffering of
sentient beings as they adhere to true existence with regard to what appears
truly existent, the realization that the basis for the apprehension of true
existence lacks true existence will not serve as an antidote and instead one
needs to show some other useless basis to be truly existent.

25 | The Two Truths

PRESENTING CONVENTIONAL AND ULTIMATE TRUTHS

THIS HAS FOUR POINTS: the basis on which the two truths are divided, the number of divisions, the purpose of dividing them in that way, and the meaning of each division.

THE BASIS ON WHICH THE TWO TRUTHS ARE DIVIDED

Earlier scholars had many ways of asserting the basis of division of the two truths. However, here, objects of knowledge are the basis of division because the *Compendium of Trainings* says:

> Objects of knowledge are completely subsumed within these conventional and ultimate truths.

THE NUMBER OF DIVISIONS

Fundamental Treatise on the Middle Way states that objects of knowledge are divided into the two, conventional and ultimate truths, when it says "worldly conventional truths and ultimate truths."

THE PURPOSE OF DIVIDING THEM IN THAT WAY

Since dividing something into two must mean that the two are different, in what way are they different? Many earlier scholars propounded three types of difference. A pot and a woolen cloth, for instance, are different entities. Product and impermanence, for instance, are one entity but have different conceptual identities. In these two types of difference, the two things being differentiated are both functioning things. The [third] type of difference, when either thing is not a functioning thing,[176] is a difference that negates their being one. Among these three differences, the difference between the two truths was said to be one that negates their being one. [260] However, others asserted that the two are one entity and different conceptual identities.

It is acceptable to teach this according to *Illumination of the Middle Way*, which says that the relationship of same nature[177] is not contradictory even for nonfunctioning things. Therefore a oneness of entity does not contradict a difference of conceptual identities even if one or both things to be differentiated are nonfunctioning things. The *Entering the Middle Way Autocommentary* says:

> Two types of nature of all things are taught: conventional and ultimate.

Thus, with regard to the nature of each and every subject, there is both a conventional and an ultimate nature. If the two truths were not one entity, since it would also be very unreasonable for them to be different entities, they would be without entity and therefore nonexistent, because whatever exists necessarily exists as either one entity or many.[178]

Essay on the Mind of Enlightenment says:

> Conventions are explained as emptiness.
> Emptiness only is the conventional.
> For surely this does not occur without that,
> just like a product and impermanence.

If a sprout, for instance, were a different entity from its own ultimate nature, it would also be a different entity from its emptiness of true existence; so the sprout would be truly established. Therefore, since it is not a different entity, it is one entity. Although a sprout is empty of its own true existence, it is not its own ultimate truth.

A few texts set forth that the two truths are neither one nor different. Some of them are referring to inherently established oneness and difference, whereas others are referring to their not being either different entities or one conceptual identity.

THE MEANING OF EACH DIVISION

This has three points: conventional truths, ultimate truths, and teaching that the number of truths is definitely two.

CONVENTIONAL TRUTHS

This has three points: the meaning of the words *conventional* and *truth*, the characteristics of conventional truths, and divisions of conventionalities.

THE MEANING OF THE WORDS *CONVENTIONAL* AND *TRUTH*

Clear Words explains three meanings for the *conventional*: "concealers of suchness," "mutually dependent objects," and "worldly designations." The latter are said to be defined as objects of expression and means of expression, knowers and objects of knowledge, and so forth, [261] so they are not just designations by subjects—that is, by consciousnesses and expressions. Also, not all objects of knowledge and objects of expression should be held to be conventional truths.

The first of the three is the convention that is the concealing consciousness from whose perspective form and the like are posited as truly existent. It is the ignorance that superimposes onto phenomena that they have their own inherently established nature which in fact does not exist. This is because true establishment is actually impossible, which is why the positing of objects as truly existent is from the perspective of the mind. It is not possible for objects to be posited as truly existent from the perspective of a mind that does not apprehend true existence. That being so, *Entering the Middle Way* (6.28) says:

> Ignorance is a concealer, for it obscures the true nature.
> Its fabrications that seem truly existent
> were called *conventional truths* by the Sage,
> and fabricated things are mere conventions.

The *Entering the Middle Way Autocommentary* says:

> In this way, conventional truths are posited under the power

of afflictive ignorance, one of the links of cyclic existence. For śrāvakas, pratyekabuddhas, and bodhisattvas who have abandoned afflictive ignorance and who see compounded things as resembling the existence of mirror images and the like, these are fabricated natures rather than truths because such beings do not exaggerate them as truly existent. To the childish they are deceptive, but to others they are mere conventionalities owing to their arising dependently similar to illusions and the like.

This statement does not indicate that whenever conventional truths are posited as existent, they are posited as existent because of ignorance; nor does it indicate that conventional truths are never posited from the perspective of the minds of śrāvakas, pratyekabuddhas, and bodhisattvas who have abandoned afflictive ignorance. The reason for the first point is that, as explained above, afflictive ignorance is the apprehension of true existence, which is why the object it apprehends does not even exist conventionally. Whatever is a conventional truth necessarily exists conventionally. Therefore, if something is conventional in the sense of being a basis for positing phenomena as conventionally existent, it must be something that is not taken as conventional with regard to afflicted ignorance. [262]

The reason for the second point is that those who have abandoned the conventionality of afflicted ignorance do not have the conventionality of adherence to true existence from whose perspective true existence is posited. That is the reason why compounded things are established as untrue from their perspective, but this does not establish that they are not conventional truths. Consequently the statement that, from their perspective, compounded things are mere conventions means that for them, from among the two components *conventional* and *truth*, truth cannot be posited. So the word *mere* eliminates *truth* but not *conventional truth*. This is how to understand the intention of teaching both mere conventions and conventional truths.

Clear Words says:

That which is a truth for the world in a concealing manner is a worldly conventional truth.

This is explained in the *Entering the Middle Way Autocommentary*:

That which a concealer perceives to be truly existent and is individually perceived as a nature while not existing by nature is true for a worldly erroneous concealer. Therefore it is a worldly conventional truth.

In accordance with this clear statement, worldly conventional truths should be understood as truths for the concealer that is the ignorance explained above. They should not be understood as truly established conventionally, because that would contradict the system in which establishment by way of an intrinsic characteristic is impossible even conventionally. Also, the refutation of true existence and the proofs of the lack of true existence are performed conventionally. The explanation by the master Jñānagarbha of abidance as conventionally true should also be understood in this manner.

Now, one may think that the apprehension of the true existence of reality and the two selves is true from the perspective of a concealer and therefore are truths for a concealer. If that which is merely true for a concealer apprehending true existence were posited as a truth for a concealer, such would indeed be the case. However, that has not been propounded. All that was explained was that the truth of conventional truth is a true convention for a certain concealer and the way it is true for it.

THE DEFINITION OF A CONVENTIONAL TRUTH

Each and every external and internal thing has both a conventional and an ultimate nature. More specifically, if this is illustrated with regard to a sprout, for example, the two are (1) the sprout's nature found by a reasoning consciousness[179] that perceives the meaning of suchness, a true object of knowledge, [263] and (2) the sprout's nature found by a conventional consciousness that comprehends a deceptive object, a false object of knowledge. The former is the sprout's nature in terms of ultimate truth, and the latter is the sprout's nature in terms of conventional truth. In accordance with that, *Entering the Middle Way* (6.23) says:

Two natures of all things are apprehended
by seeing what is real and what is false.
The objects of seeing the real were taught to be suchness;
objects seen that are false are conventional truths.

This indicates that the sprout has two natures: the two truths. The ultimate one is found by the former consciousness and the conventional one is found by the latter. This does not teach that one single nature of the sprout is the two truths in reliance upon the former and latter consciousness. The *Entering the Middle Way Autocommentary* says:

> Two aspects of the nature of all things have been taught. They are conventional and ultimate.

This is saying that the natures of each and every thing are divided into two: the ultimate ones are found by consciousnesses that perceive reality, and the conventional ones are found by consciousnesses that see what is false.

Conventional truths in fact are not true but merely true from the perspective of the apprehension of true existence. Therefore, in order to ascertain their distinct meaning, it is necessary to ascertain them as false. In order to ascertain a basis of characteristics—for instance, a pot—as a false object of knowledge, a deceptive object, it is necessary to acquire a view, with regard to that basis, that negates the conceived object apprehended as true by a reasoning consciousness. This is because a falsity is not established by valid cognition without its truth having been refuted by reasoning.

Although a pot, a woolen cloth, and so forth are conventional truths, when they are established by a mind, the mind does not also need to establish the meaning of conventional truth. Likewise, although pots, woolen cloths, and so forth are not inherently existent and are accordingly illusion-like in their appearance, the minds that establish them need not establish their illusoriness.

That is why in this [Prāsaṅgika-Madhyamaka] system it is unreasonable to propound that pots, woolen cloths, and so forth are posited as conventional truths relative to the perspective of the minds of ordinary beings who lack the Madhyamaka view and that they are posited as ultimate truths relative to an ārya's experience. That would contradict what is set forth in the *Entering the Middle Way Autocommentary*:

> That is to say, something that is ultimate for ordinary beings [264] is a mere conventionality for āryas, who possess a sphere of experience that involves appearances. For them any emptiness of inherent existence is ultimate.

Ordinary beings apprehend pots and the like as truly existent, and precisely that is the apprehension of ultimate existence. In relation to their consciousness, pots and the like are therefore ultimately established rather than being conventional objects. The bases that for them are ultimately established, pots and the like, are conventionalities in relation to the vision of exalted wisdom in the mindstream of an ārya, who comprehends appearances as illusion-like. Since they cannot be posited as true in relation to that consciousness, they are known as *mere conventionalities*.

Since their nature is thus said to be an ultimate truth, you should discriminate and say that for āryas pots and the like are conventionalities and their nature is ultimate. You should not propound that pots and the like are ultimates for āryas. This is because their reasoning consciousness seeing reality does not find pots and the like, and because that which is found by a reasoning consciousness seeing reality is said to be the meaning of an ultimate truth.

Divisions of conventionalities

Svātantrika-Mādhyamikas ascertain that consciousness that appears to be established by way of its intrinsic characteristics[180] exists just as it appears. Therefore they do not differentiate between true and false subjects but instead differentiate whether what appears as an object does or does not exist by way of its intrinsic characteristics in accordance with how it appears. They assert this in accordance with the following statement in Jñānagarbha's *Distinguishing the Two Truths* (*Satyadvayavibaṅgha*):

> They seem the same, but since some can
> and some cannot fulfill a function,
> a distinction is made between real
> and unreal conventionalities.

Our [Prāsaṅgika] system asserts that whatever appears to the ignorant as established by way of its intrinsic characteristics is an appearance of that consciousness polluted by ignorance. Therefore conventional objects are not differentiated as two, true and false.

Now, the *Entering the Middle Way Autocommentary* says:

Whatever is false even conventionally is not a conventional truth. [265]

To the worldly conventional consciousness of someone conversant with words, it is not true that the reflection of a face, for example, is a face. Hence it is not conventionally true from that perspective. While this is so, it is still the object found by a consciousness seeing a false object of knowledge, a deceptive object; so it is a conventional truth. The consciousness that the reflection appears to is mistaken about its appearing object, and likewise those with ignorance to whom something blue and the like appears to be established by way of its intrinsic characteristics are mistaken about their appearing object. When a true object of comprehension is posited, it would be contradictory to claim that it is posited by a consciousness mistaken in that way. However, precisely that is helpful for positing false objects of comprehension. Otherwise something could not be posited as a conventional truth if it had not been established as conventionally true; so when illusion-like falsities are posited conventionally, they could not be posited as conventional truths.

The Prāsaṅgika system posits six consciousnesses unaffected by temporary causes of deception, six consciousnesses that are the opposite of those, six objects apprehended by the former six consciousnesses, and six objects apprehended by the latter six. The false objects and subjects are posited as false conventionalities, whereas the objects and subjects that are not false are posited as true conventionalities. Furthermore, it posits them as true and false conventionalities in relation to worldly or conventional valid cognition rather than in relation to a reasoning consciousness that accords with an ārya's perspective. In our Madhyamaka system, for someone with ignorance, the appearances of reflections and the like and the appearances of blue and the like do not differ with regard to whether they are mistaken in relation to the appearing object. That is why true and false conventionalities are not differentiated. *Entering the Middle Way* (6.25) says:

Whatever the worldly apprehend and perceive
by means of the six nondefective senses
is true only from the worldly perspective.
The rest is posited as false from that perspective.

Regarding the two types [innate and intellectually acquired] of apprehensions of persons and phenomena established by way of their intrinsic
characteristics, conventional valid cognition does not establish the opposite of the [intellectually acquired] mode of apprehension that arises, for
example, from the mind being temporarily polluted by one's own bad
tenets. [266] This is an exception.[181]

Moreover, although dualistic appearances occur for the exalted wisdom
knowing things in their variety free from all causes of pollution by predispositions of ignorance, it is not mistaken with regard to its appearing
objects. The reason is explained elsewhere.[182]

ULTIMATE TRUTHS

This has three points: explaining the meaning of *ultimate* and *truth*, the
definition of an ultimate truth, and divisions of ultimate truths.

EXPLAINING THE MEANING OF *ULTIMATE* AND *TRUTH*

Clear Words says:

> Since it is an object and it is ultimate, it is the ultimate object.
> Since it is nondeceptive, it is the truth.

This asserts that both *ultimate* and *object* apply to the *ultimate object truth*.
The way in which an ultimate truth is true is that it is nondeceptive. Specifically, it does not deceive the world by abiding in one way and appearing in a different way. The *Commentary on Sixty Stanzas of Reasoning* says
that an ultimate truth is merely posited as existent by the power of worldly
conventions.[183]

That being so, the meaning of the word *truth* in *conventional truth*,
which is a truth from the perspective of the apprehension of true existence,
and the meaning of the word *truth* in *ultimate truth* are not the same.

THE DEFINITION OF AN ULTIMATE TRUTH

This has two points: the actual definition and refuting an objection.

THE ACTUAL DEFINITION

As explained above in *Entering the Middle Way,* the definition of an ultimate truth is that which is found by seeing the meaning of a real object of knowledge. The commentary on that says:

> That is to say, the ultimate gains its own self-nature through being the object of a particular wisdom of those who perceive reality; it is not established intrinsically. This is one nature.

This means that it is found by the uncontaminated exalted wisdom comprehending suchness and not established by way of its intrinsic nature, so this negates the proposition that something is truly established if found by uncontaminated meditative equipoise. The words "a particular wisdom" mean that what is found by any wisdom of āryas is not sufficient and that instead ultimate truth is only what is found by a particular wisdom, [267] the wisdom that knows the ultimate mode of being. *Found* means that it is established as such by that consciousness, the same as with conventionalities.

Yet how does it find it? While the eyes of someone with an eye disorder see floating hairs in the space before them, healthy eyes do not see even an appearance of floating hairs in that space. Likewise, those who are damaged by the eye disorder of ignorance observe an intrinsic nature of aggregates and the like. The uncontaminated exalted wisdom of meditative equipoise of those who have exhausted all the imprints of ignorance and of āryas on the paths of learning, when perceiving suchness, does not perceive even subtle dualistic appearance, like eyes without a disorder. The nature perceived through this type of perception is an ultimate truth. *Entering the Middle Way* (6.29) says:

> Where false entities such as floating hairs
> are imputed because of an eye disorder,
> one with clear eyes sees things as they are.
> Suchness should be known here in like manner.

Its commentary also says:

The buddhas' ultimate truth is whatever reality of the aggregates
and so on that they, who are free from the imprints of ignorance,
perceive in the manner of those free of eye disorder who see no
floating hairs.

The ultimate perceived in this manner is the ultimate nature of two
natures that each and every subject has. More specifically, it is both the
naturally pure nirvāṇa, which is the emptiness of inherent establishment of
subjects, and the nirvāṇa that is a true cessation, which is reality free from
all the various seeds of defilements.

The meaning of the statements in the *Commentary on Sixty Stanzas of
Reasoning* "Is a nirvāṇa also a conventional truth? It is so" and "Therefore
a nirvāṇa is only designated as a conventional truth" [268] is that positing
a nirvāṇa, an ultimate truth, as existent also implies positing it as merely
existent from the perspective of a conventional consciousness, a conventional truth. They do not mean that this system asserts that nirvāṇa is a
conventional truth, for that same commentary also explains that the other
three truths are conventional truths but nirvāṇa is an ultimate truth.[184] The
Entering the Middle Way Autocommentary also sets forth the other three
truths as conventional truths and true cessation as an ultimate truth. Some
protest that if a nirvāṇa were posited as conventionally existent, this would
contradict the statement that it is an ultimate truth. In response to that,
it says that it was taught as an ultimate truth only by worldly conventions.

Therefore everything posited as existent is posited by the power of
worldly conventions. The *Perfection of Wisdom Sūtra in a Hundred Thousand Lines* (*Śatasāhasrikāprajñāpāramitāsūtra*) says:

All these phenomena are labeled in reliance upon worldly designations; they are not ultimate.

And *Seventy Stanzas on Emptiness* also says:

The Buddha taught abiding, arising, and disintegrating,
existence and nonexistence, and inferior, equal, and superior
by the power of worldly conventions
and not by the power of final reality.

In other words all the various presentations that the Victor taught about arising, disintegrating, and abiding; inferior, superior, and equal; and "This exists and this does not exist" were posited merely by the power of worldly designation. He said that they were not posited by the power of a pure mode of subsistence that is not merely posited by the power of designation.

Master Jñānagarbha states:

> Since it is a truth for an ultimate consciousness, it is an ultimate truth.

Here he explains that a reasoning consciousness is ultimate as well. The meaning here is to explain that what is nondeceptive from the perspective of such a cognition is truth. However, he does not mean that such a cognition is *truly existent* in terms of being able to withstand analysis, because in that text he refutes the true establishment of all phenomena.

Therefore, if it is asserted that "If the ultimate does not exist truly as ultimate, then conventional truth wouldn't exist truly as conventional," then we concur. On the other hand, if the assertion is that "If the first [the ultimate] does not exist ultimately, then the second [the conventional] would not exist conventionally," this would be tantamount to saying, "If the negation of true existence [269] does not exist truly, then the basis upon which it is negated would possess true existence." This is because ultimate truth is defined in terms of the mere negation of the true existence of a given basis, and to imply that such bases would have no conventional existence is to imply that they do not exist as deceptive realities. If that is what is being asserted, that would be absurd, for it is only by understanding the perceived things as devoid of true existence that the bases upon which true existence is being negated come to be established as deceptive.

Therefore for something to be posited as conventionally existent, it need not be established by a reasoning consciousness of suchness, but it also cannot be damaged by any valid cognition—that is, by a conventional or reasoning consciousness. The *Commentary on Sixty Stanzas of Reasoning* explains that since the appropriated aggregates conventionally have the four qualities of being impermanent and so forth,[185] the apprehension of those four is correct for that [mind], and since the aggregates do not abide even conventionally as [the opposite of] those four, permanent and so forth, the apprehension of these [latter] four is erroneous for that [mind].

Entering the Middle Way (6.26) says:

> Like the self imputed by non-Buddhists,
> who are overcome by the sleep of ignorance,
> what is imputed to magic, mirages, and such like
> does not even exist from the worldly perspective.

This is saying that the self, the fundamental nature, and so forth imputed by non-Buddhists (*tīrthika*), as well as magically emanated horses, elephants, and the like, do not exist even conventionally. Therefore the proposition that it is the Prāsaṅgika approach to posit as conventionally existent what only exists from the perspective of a mistaken mind is meaningless babble. None of the other great Mādhyamikas assert this either.

In *Entering the Middle Way*, objects and subjects are taken to be equal in terms of existence and nonexistence but not in terms of *mere* existence and nonexistence. Rather, the two are taken to be equal in terms of inherent existence and nonexistence.[186] That being so, whatever is posited as conventionally existent is posited as existent by the power of nominal conventions, but not everything posited by the power of these is asserted to be conventionally existent. Although phenomena are asserted to exist merely by the power of conventions, the word *mere* precludes the meaning that they are not conventions of subjects. It does not at all preclude that the objects posited are established by valid cognition.

This [Prāsaṅgika] system is not dissatisfied with such a way of positing phenomena by the power of conventional imputation. [270] What it does not do is search for an imputed object that is not merely posited like that but that exists in accordance with its meaning, and if it is found, posit it as existent, and if not, posit it as nonexistent. Rather, it asserts that if something findable were to emerge as one searches with this method, it would be truly established. Therefore it does not assert even conventionally that anything is found to exist upon such analysis. That is where the dividing line between analyzing and not analyzing suchness is drawn.

So one can see that if something established by way of its intrinsic characteristics existed, it would have to exist by way of its intrinsic nature as an object not merely posited by the power of a subject's designations. Having seen that, one does not even conventionally assert inherent existence, existence by way of an intrinsic characteristic, or existence by way of an intrinsic nature. This has already been explained in detail elsewhere.

REFUTING AN OBJECTION

Someone might object, if the Buddha's wisdom that knows the ultimate mode of being of phenomena finds ultimate truths, then what about the following statement from the *Entering the Middle Way Autocommentary*?[187]

> "Isn't such a nature not actually visible? So how do they see it?"
> "That is indeed true, but it is said that they see it by means of not seeing."

This explains that to not see anything at all is to see suchness. As a source for that, Candrakīrti quotes an explanation that ultimate truths are beyond even the objects of omniscient wisdom. He also explains that at the level of buddhahood, the movement of the mind and mental factors has permanently stopped and that at the time of the ten powers, when a buddha does not see aggregates and so forth, he knows all phenomena. How can these explanations not be contradictory?

We would answer that the statement "They see it by means of not seeing" does not refer to not seeing any objects at all. Rather, it teaches that if these objects, which are observed owing to the eye defect of ignorance, existed in reality, they would have to be observed by the uncontaminated wisdom of an ārya's meditative equipoise. So their suchness is seen by way of their not seeing anything at all. This is because, if the object of negation existed, it would be observable. The realization of the negation of the object of negation is posited because [the object] is not observed. The meaning of "Seeing without seeing is most excellent"[188] should also be understood in this way. [271]

Thus the *Verse Summary of the Perfection of Wisdom* (12.9) also says:

> "Those who do not see forms and do not see sensations,
> do not see perceptions and do not see intentions,
> do not see consciousness, mentality, nor mind,
> they see reality," the Tathāgata teaches.

Beings express themselves in words like "I see space,"
but in what way is space seen? Investigate this!
The Tathāgata teaches this as how reality is seen.
Such seeing cannot be expressed through other analogies.

What is not seen are said to be the five aggregates, and what is seen is reality. That is the meaning of suchness, just as in the statement "He who sees dependent arising sees reality."[189] More specifically, in the analogy, space is the mere elimination of obstructive tangible objects, and seeing or realizing it is like not seeing the obscuring obstructive objects of negation that would be observable if they were present. What is seen is space and what is not seen are obscuring obstructions. The last two lines negate that suchness is seen the way you might see blue rather than in accordance with the analogy. The statement that the five aggregates are not seen indicates that possessors of qualities are not seen from the perspective of uncontaminated meditative equipoise seeing suchness.

The *Engaging in the Two Truths Sūtra* (*Saṃvṛtiparamārthasatyanirdeśa-sūtra*) says:

> Divine child, this ultimate truth, possessing all supreme qualities, transcends all objects up to and including the objects of omniscient wisdom; it is not like what is expressed by saying, "It is an ultimate truth."

This explains that when you say, "This is an ultimate truth," it means object and subject are not seen as separate appearances for the mind. Therefore the quotation is a source supporting that dualistic appearances stop rather than that the Buddha does not realize the ultimate.

The *Entering the Middle Way Autocommentary* also says:

> He fully realizes true nature by directly perceiving that reality without touching produced things. That is why he is called "Buddha."

From the perspective of seeing suchness with a buddha's wisdom that knows the ultimate mode, [272] only reality is said to be realized without touching[190] that which is other powered.

The movement of the mind and mental factors[191] coming to an end means that when suchness becomes manifest, the movement of conceptualization comes to an end. It does not indicate that the mind or mental factors do not exist. *Clear Words* says:

> Conceptualization is movement of the mind. Because suchness is the absence of conceptualization, it is free from that [movement]. As is set forth in a sūtra, "What is ultimate truth? If there is not even movement of the mind in it, what need is there to mention words?"

The statement that there is no movement of the mind is explained to mean the absence of conceptual thought. Moreover, the *Entering the Middle Way Autocommentary* sets forth that at the time of an ārya's meditative equipoise on a learning path, it has not come to a permanent end, whereas at the time of buddhahood it has.

Apart from that, the *Entering the Middle Way Autocommentary* establishes with an accompanying source that if that true nature did not exist, it would be pointless for bodhisattvas to accomplish and experience their difficult conduct for the sake of realizing it. It says,

> Someone might ask, "What is their nature?" That which is unfabricated about them and which does not depend on anything else: their intrinsic nature that is realized by a consciousness free from the eye defect of ignorance. To those who ask, "Does it exist or not?" we would answer, if it did not exist, then for what purpose would bodhisattvas cultivate the path of the perfections? Why would bodhisattvas exert hundredfold effort in order to realize reality?

He then quotes the following [from the *Cloud of Jewels Sūtra*]:

> Child of the lineage, if the ultimate did not exist, pure conduct would be meaningless, and it would be pointless for tathāgatas to come forth. Since the ultimate exists, bodhisattvas are called "those skilled in the ultimate."

If ultimate truths did not exist, it would be pointless to engage in conduct for the sake of the purity of final nirvāṇa, it would be impossible for disciples to realize it, it would be pointless for a buddha to come to the world in order to make them realize it, [273] and the great children of the victors would not be skilled in ultimate truths. This is why he quotes a sūtra that establishes that ultimate truths exist. Therefore it is simply wrong to say that the great master's system propounds that ultimate truths are not objects of knowledge and that the wisdom realizing suchness does not exist in an ārya's meditative equipoise.

Furthermore the *Entering the Middle Way Autocommentary* says:

> Therefore it is posited through imputation that "suchness is realized," but actually it is not that something is known by something else because both the knower and the object of knowledge are unarisen.

The first part means that to posit the realization of suchness by taking wisdom and suchness separately as subject and object is to posit it merely from the perspective of conventional consciousness rather than positing it from the perspective of that wisdom. "The knower is unarisen" means that in relation to its object, which is not inherently arisen, it is like water poured into water.

Candrakīrti's *Entering the Middle Way Autocommentary* says further:

> Since mind and mental factors do not operate with respect to suchness, which is the object of wisdom, it is actualized only by the body.

In this statement, the object to be actualized is suchness; the subject, wisdom, is that which actualizes it; and the complete enjoyment body is the agent of the actualization, the exalted knower.[192] The manner in which it is thereby actualized is by way of stopping conceptual movement of minds and mental factors as explained above. It should be known from the explanation in the *Autocommentary* that the body by means of which suchness is actualized has the nature of peace because it is free from minds and mental factors. If a buddha did not perceive the aggregates and the like, this would deny his knowledge of things in their variety as well as the diversity of all objects, because to exist and to not be known by a buddha contradict each other.

Therefore the varieties of objects must appear to the exalted knower of things in their variety, and aspects appear to it because this system is not one that propounds an exalted knower without aspects. Yet the varieties of appearing objects are both that which is unpolluted by the imprints of ignorance, such as the signs and marks of a buddha, [274] and that which is polluted by the imprints of ignorance, such as the impure inanimate and animate world. As for the first of these, it would be nonsense if they came to an end at the buddha level, whereas the latter come to an end at that level because their causes come to an end.

The way they appear is as follows. When a buddha's signs and marks appear to a person who has not abandoned ignorance, they appear to be established by way of their intrinsic characteristics, but they are not. The reason for this is not that those objects arise owing to the imprints of ignorance. Rather, they appear like that because the subject is polluted by the imprints of ignorance. This is not because they appear to that subject merely from the perspective of appearing that way to other persons but because they appear that way from the subject's own perspective. Forms, sounds, and the like, objects that are not established by way of their intrinsic characteristics but still appear that way from the perspective of someone who has not abandoned ignorance, appear to a buddha's wisdom that knows things in their variety only by means of their appearance to persons with the pollution of ignorance. They do not appear from a buddha's own perspective, independently of their appearing that way to others. Therefore a buddha knows forms and the like, which are not inherently established but still appear to be, yet it is from the perspective of their appearing that way to those with ignorance. A buddha does not know them in the manner of their appearing that way from his own perspective, independently of their appearing that way to those persons. Hence, there is no sense in which he is deceived by appearances because they do not appear from pollution existing within the wisdom but because of the essential point that the wisdom necessarily knows all objects of knowledge. That being so, from the perspective of an exalted knower of things in their variety, all things appear to be selfless and lack inherently existent natures. Thus they appear as illusion-like falsities and do not appear as truths. When they appear to that wisdom in terms of their appearance to those with ignorance, they merely arise as that which appears true to other persons.[193]

Sixty Stanzas of Reasoning (v. 25) also says:

> Those who are skilled with respect to things
> see things as impermanent, deceptive phenomena
> that are made up, empty, and selfless
> and as what is referred to as "devoid."

[Candrakīrti's] commentary on this says that those who have completed the deeds see things in that way. [275] Thus *Distinguishing the Two Truths* says:

> Omniscient knowers directly see
> all that arises dependently,
> everything just as it appears,
> devoid of any imputed natures.

This says that [omniscient buddhas] see all things in their variety directly and vividly. Also:

> When consciousness, objects of consciousness,
> and the self are not perceived,
> since there is no appearance of signs,
> they do not arise, for they firmly abide.

This explains that omniscient knowers never rise from the concentration in which dualistic appearance has been completely pacified.

Although there are these two explanations, to someone who does not understand the modes of [perception within] both explanations correctly, it may seem contradictory to assert both and not just one of the two, but there is no contradiction. The wisdom seeing suchness and the wisdom seeing things in their variety are one in nature, but that does not in the least contradict the fact that in relation to individual objects, they become, respectively, a reasoning consciousness and a conventional consciousness. This depends on knowing well that there is not the slightest contradiction in there being two different modes of finding objects by means of a reasoning consciousness and a conventional valid cognition, based on a single object in the context of the ground when establishing the view.[194] If you know well not only this about the occasion of the result, when the two wisdoms comprehend their objects, but also which of the two valid cognitions is active, then you will also be able to know that the two subjects do not become one and the same[195] even though they do not ascertain their objects separately. Through this you will also understand fine details of the definitions of the two truths.

DIVISIONS OF ULTIMATE TRUTHS

Ultimate truths are enumerated in accordance with the *Entering the Middle Way Autocommentary*, which sets forth sixteen emptinesses when emptiness is divided in detail, four in the intermediate division (the emptiness of things, nonthings, self nature, and other nature), and two when summarized (the selflessness of persons and phenomena).[196] Other texts set forth two: actual ultimates and concordant ultimates. *Illumination of the Middle Way* says:

> Nonproduction accords with the ultimate and is therefore called an "ultimate," but it is actually not because in reality the ultimate is beyond all elaborations. [276]

And *Ornament for the Middle Way* (*Madhyamakālaṃkāra*) also says:

> This is referred to as an "ultimate"
> for it is compatible with the ultimate.
> If it really were [ultimate], it would be
> free from all number of elaborations.

Distinguishing the Two Truths states this similarly, and the *Distinguishing the Two Truths Autocommentary* (*Satyadvayāvibaṅghavṛtti*) and *Ornament for the Middle Way* explain that the negation of ultimate production and the like is conventional.

With respect to the meaning of those statements, many earlier masters differentiate two ultimate truths: enumerated and unenumerated ones. They assert that the emptiness that negates ultimate production and so forth with regard to form and the like is the former (an imputed ultimate truth yet fully qualified conventional truth) and that the latter cannot be made the object of any mind whatsoever, so it is not an object of knowledge. Since that is not the meaning of those texts, they should be explained like this: the object, reality, must indeed be taken as an ultimate, but the subject, a reasoning consciousness, is also often explained as such. *Distinguishing the Two Truths* says:

> Since it is without deception, a reasoning consciousness is an ultimate.

It is just as stated in *Illumination of the Middle Way* as well:

> The meaning [of *ultimate*] in propositions such as "Ultimately there is no production whatsoever" is asserted to be that all consciousnesses arisen from correct studying, contemplating, and meditating are subjects without error and therefore called "ultimate," because of being the ultimate among those [subjects].

Of the two types of reasoning consciousness, the nonconceptual wisdom of an ārya's meditative equipoise is without conceptions, whereas the conceptual reasoning consciousness comprehending suchness is based on signs and so forth. The explanation in *Blaze of Reasoning* that the ultimate includes both a nonconceptual wisdom and a concordant wisdom has the same intention as the explanation of two ultimates in *Illumination of the Middle Way*. Therefore the meaning of the texts is not that the explanation of two ultimates should only be applied to ultimate objects and not subjects. In this regard the first is an actual ultimate because when engaging in suchness, it is able to eliminate simultaneously the elaborations of true existence and dualistic appearance with respect to its object. [277] That is also what is meant by "beyond all elaborations."[197] A conceptual reasoning consciousness is able to negate the elaboration of true existence with respect to its object, but it cannot eliminate the elaborations of dualistic appearance. Therefore it is an ultimate that is concordant in aspect with the supramundane ultimate.

It is necessary to explain two modes also with respect to ultimate objects such as the negation of ultimate production and so forth for forms and the like. For a nonconceptual reasoning consciousness, that object's emptiness is the actual ultimate always free from the two elaborations. For a conceptual reasoning consciousness, on the other hand, it is not an actual ultimate always free from the two elaborations because it is only free from one type of them. Still, this is not to say that in general it is not an actual ultimate truth. So, except for some minds from whose perspective all the elaborations of dualistic appearance are gone, the emptiness of true existence cannot be free from all elaborations of appearance. Therefore the meaning of the texts is not that if something is an ultimate truth, it must be free from all elaborations of dualistic appearance. This being so, those who propound the establishment of illusions by a reasoning consciousness assert that the composite of two appearances (a basis such as an aggregate and its emptiness of true existence), being a mere object established by an inferential reasoning consciousness, is an ultimate truth. It is concordant with the ultimate, but it is not an ultimate truth.

Also, there is no benefit to proving that sprouts and the like appear to lack true existence because they appear to be free from being one or many to an intelligent person who has not eliminated doubt as to whether that basis truly exists. And for those who have eliminated that doubt, that reason is not a valid reason.[198] *Illumination of the Middle Way* says that both the reason "free from being one or many" and the predicate[199] are mere eliminations and that it is the same whether the reason is "It is neither one nor many" or "It does not exist as one or many." From those very examples, you can tell that the statements do not refer to affirming negations.[200] Therefore this is not at all the assertion of Master Śāntarakṣita, his spiritual son Kamalaśīla, or Master Haribhadra.

With respect to the elimination of the object of negation—the conceptual elaboration [of true existence]—in relation to appearances, a distinction can be made between two aspects: a negative determination and a positive determination. But there is not a single great Mādhyamika who would assert that the second, what is merely cognized by inferential cognition, constitutes ultimate truth. The explanation of their presentations in my longer *Stages of the Path* should be understood in detail along these lines.[201] [278]

In the course of explaining the negation of production and so forth as concordant with ultimate truth, Jñānagarbha says in his *Distinguishing the Two Truths Autocommentary*:

Others hold it to be only real. Therefore "also"[202] has the meaning of "and." In fact, if analyzed with reasoning, it is only conventional. Why? Since the object to be negated does not exist, it is clear that, in reality, its negation does not exist.

He is saying that others, Cittamātrins, assert that the emptiness negating a self of phenomena in the basis of negation is established in reality whereas his own system teaches that since the object of negation, the self of phenomena, does not exist, the negation that negates it is not established in reality. Therefore the explanation that the negation of ultimate production and so forth is conventional means that it *exists* conventionally rather than indicating that it *is* conventional.

The same commentary also says:

> [Objection:] "Since real production and the like does not appear when a thing appears, it is an unreal conventionality. Likewise, the negation of real production and the like is an unreal conventionality: when the thing, the basis of negation, appears, it does not appear."
>
> Reply: "It is not the case that it does not appear because it is not different from the nature of the thing."

The explanation that whenever something like blue appears its emptiness of true existence also appears does not imply that a mere elimination, the negation of true existence, appears to the eye consciousness and so forth. Rather, what is implied here is an affirming negation. Therefore something like that is a fully qualified conventionality, yet this does not contradict that an emptiness, the mere elimination of true existence, is an ultimate truth.

Ornament for the Middle Way explains that although the negation of ultimate production and the like is included among real conventionalities, it is a concordant ultimate because it accords with the ultimate. In the statement that the ultimate is the elimination of the entire web of elaborations such as the existence and nonexistence of things, "web of elaborations" accords with the *Distinguishing the Two Truths Autocommentary*, which explains the web of conceptuality as a web of elaborations. It says:

Thus the Blessed One taught,
"It is not empty, not nonempty,
not existent nor nonexistent,
neither produced nor nonproduced."

And:

Why is that? It is without elaborations. Suchness is free from the
entire web of conceptuality.²⁰³ [279]

That is the actual ultimate because those [elaborations] cease from the perspective of the direct realization of suchness. A reasoning consciousness
along with its object, which are not like that, are concordant with the former, and so forth, as explained above. There are also two components to
the negation of real production and the like: the reasoning consciousness
that negates it and its object of comprehension. So the way in which it is
included among real conventions should also be understood on that basis.
This manner of explaining the freedom from the web of all elaborations
with respect to the two truths is needed on many occasions.

TEACHING THAT THE NUMBER OF TRUTHS IS DEFINITELY TWO

If a given basis is determined to be a false deceptive object, its being a nondeceptive object is necessarily eliminated. Therefore deceptive and nondeceptive are mutually exclusive; their presence is contradictory. Since they
pervade all objects of knowledge in a mutually exclusive manner, they also
exclude the possibility of a third category. For that reason you should know
that the enumeration of truths is definitely two with respect to objects of
knowledge. The *Meeting of Father and Son Sūtra* (*Pitāputrasamāgamasūtra*)
says that objects of knowledge of the two truths are exhaustive. It says:

In this manner the Tathāgata realizes the two truths, conventional and ultimate. Objects of knowledge of these conventional
and ultimate truths are exhaustive.

The *Concentration Definitely Showing Suchness* (*Tattvanirdeśasamādhi*) also clearly enumerates the truths as definitely two:

> Everything is a convention or an ultimate;
> a third truth does not exist.

It is said that if you know the division between the two truths, you will not be confused about the words of the Sage, whereas if you do not know it, you will not know the essence of his teachings. Moreover, you need to know it in accordance with how the protector Nāgārjuna determined it. *Entering the Middle Way* (6.79–80) says:

> Methods for pacification do not exist
> for those outside Lord Nāgārjuna's path.
> They have strayed from the truths of conventions and suchness,
> and through their corruption, they cannot attain liberation.
>
> Conventional truths become the methods,
> and ultimate truths arise from those methods.
> Those who don't know the distinction between the two [280]
> enter bad paths because of flawed conceptualization.

Therefore it is extremely important for those who want liberation to be skilled in the two truths.

DIVISIONS OF SPECIAL INSIGHT

You should cultivate special insight once you have gained the view that realizes the two types of selflessness after attending to the prerequisites of special insight as explained above. Now how many types of special insights are there? Here, I will mainly teach the special insights you should cultivate while still an ordinary being and not the special insights of exalted levels. If you carry out a complete division of these special insights, there are the special insights of the four natures, the three doors, and the six modes of inquiry.

The four are differentiation and so forth mentioned in the *Unraveling the Intent Sūtra*. In this regard, *differentiation* observes things in their variety, and *thorough differentiation* observes their ultimate mode of being. The first has two types, full investigation and full analysis, and the second also has two types, [full] investigation and [full] analysis, which differentiate coarse and subtle objects. The identification of those four is set forth in *Śrāvaka Levels*, *Instructions on the Perfection of Wisdom*, and other scriptures.

The *Unraveling the Intent Sūtra* states the three doors as arisen from a sign, arisen from thorough searching, and arisen from fine investigative analysis. To illustrate them with respect to the meaning of selflessness, for example, those three are identified as follows. The first observes the self-lessness already ascertained and attends to its signs but does not determine very much. The second makes determinations for the sake of ascertaining that which has not been ascertained previously. The third carries out an analysis, as was done before, of the meaning already ascertained.

The six modes of inquiry carry out a thorough search into the meanings, things, characteristics, categories, times, and principles and, having sought them, also individually analyze them. With regard to those six, the inquiry into *meanings* is the search "The meaning of this word is this." The inquiry into *things* is the search "This is an internal thing, and that is an external thing." There are two modes of inquiry into *characteristics*: "This is the defining characteristic of something, and that is a general characteristic," [281] or "This is unique, and that is shared." The inquiry into *categories* looks at the category of nonvirtue in terms of faults and shortcomings and the category of virtue in terms of excellent qualities and benefits. The inquiry into *time* is the search "This thing occurred in the past, that thing will occur in the future, and this thing is presently occurring."

The inquiry into *principles* is of four types. First, the principle of dependence is that the occurrence of effects depends on causes and conditions. It is also an inquiry in terms of the conventional, the ultimate, and their bases taken individually. Second, the principle of the function is that phenomena perform their own functions, such as fire performing the function of burning. It is a search in terms of "This is the phenomenon, and that is the function; this phenomenon performs that function." The principle of evidence is to establish a meaning without contradicting valid cognition. It is a search that reflects on whether direct perceptions, inferences, or reliable scriptures (the three types of valid cognition) exist with regard to a given object. The principle of nature is to examine (1) natures that are well known in the world, such as heat being the nature of fire, moisture being the nature of water, and so forth, (2) inconceivable natures, and (3) abiding natures.[204] They are sought without searching for further reasons for their being as they are.

Through the sixfold presentation in this way, there are three objects to be known by a yogi: the meanings of expressions, the varieties of objects of knowledge, and their ultimate mode of being. The first inquiry is posited in terms of the first object. The inquiry into things and the inquiry into defining characteristics is posited in terms of the second one. The remaining three and the inquiry into general characteristics are posited in terms of the third one. The four special insights explained first have three gates and six modes of examination. Thus the three doors and the six search modes are included in the initial four.

Śrāvaka Levels teaches that the four types of attention that were explained above, tight engagement and so forth,[205] are common to both śamatha and special insight. Therefore the four attentions are also present in special insight.

26 | Uniting Śamatha and Special Insight

HOW TO CULTIVATE SPECIAL INSIGHT

THIS HAS THREE POINTS: the meaning of the statement that special insight is cultivated in reliance upon śamatha; the paths of which vehicle, Hīnayāna or Mahāyāna, this system relates to; and the actual way to cultivate special insight in reliance upon śamatha. [282]

THE MEANING OF THE STATEMENT THAT SPECIAL INSIGHT IS CULTIVATED IN RELIANCE UPON ŚAMATHA

The *Unraveling the Intent Sūtra* says that special insight should be cultivated later, after śamatha has first been accomplished. This is also stated similarly in many other instructions, such as those by the venerable Maitreya, Asaṅga's *Bodhisattva Levels* and *Śrāvaka Levels*, those of Bhāviveka and Śāntideva, Kamalaśīla's three volumes of *Stages of Meditation*, and Ratnākaraśānti's *Instructions on the Perfection of Wisdom*.

The intended meaning of these texts is not that special insight is understood as just maintaining the observation of selflessness after previously generating the śamatha that observes any object without observing the meaning of selflessness. This is because śamatha and special insight are not differentiated by way of their object. *Instructions on the Perfection of Wisdom* also explains that after observing suchness (the emptiness of duality between subject and object) and upon generating śamatha, you generate special insight through analytical meditation observing that same object. Ārya Asaṅga also discusses a special insight that observes things in their variety, saying that after śamatha has been generated, a special insight with peaceful and coarse aspects[206] is cultivated in reliance upon it. Moreover, he says that it is a path common to both non-Buddhists and Buddhists as well as to ordinary beings and āryas.

That being so, it is inappropriate for someone who has not attained śamatha and who is newly accomplishing it to not practice placing the mind single-pointedly on whatever object of observation it may be and to instead practice analyzing diverse aspects of his object of observation. The reason for this is that śamatha is achieved by the former method and is unachievable in the latter manner. If instead of extending your earlier habituation to mere placement meditation, you use the śamatha you achieved previously to carry out analytical meditation that, with wisdom, individually distinguishes whichever object is appropriate to the occasion—the ultimate mode of being or things in their variety—you can eventually induce a special single-pointed concentration. Since the extremely powerful kind of single-pointed concentration achieved through that cannot be achieved through the former method of mere placement, analytical concentration is praised.

The way to accomplish it is to first seek śamatha and then afterward cultivate special insight in reliance upon it. So that is the general reason why there are the two different ways of maintaining śamatha and special insight even if the object of observation—for instance, selflessness—is the same. In particular, the requirements for the arising of a strong and stable ascertainment are the cultivation of the special insight that has the peaceful and coarse aspects of individually distinguishing the faults and excellent qualities of higher and lower realms, [283] and the cultivation of the special insight that has the aspect of selflessness in which the meaning of selflessness is investigated and then maintained by means of fine investigative wisdom. Therefore they have great power with respect to eliminating their individual objects of elimination.

The special insight that observes things in their variety is not merely the meditation that has the peaceful and coarse aspects for the sake of eliminating manifest mental afflictions. According to the explanation in *Instructions on the Perfection of Wisdom*, it is also the analytical meditation that thoroughly differentiates the characteristics of the eighteen elements (*dhātu*). From that illustration, you should know that there are still other special insights, meditations that differentiate objects associated with things in their variety.

Instructions on the Perfection of Wisdom explains that before you generate śamatha and special insight that observe the ultimate mode of being, you must first generate śamatha and special insight on the level of the yoga that observes things in their variety. However, here, following the assertions of Śāntideva, Kamalaśīla, and so forth, some kind of śamatha is developed first and then special insight is developed. In fact, just that special insight that observes the ultimate mode of being will be taught here.

THE PATHS OF WHICH VEHICLE, MAHĀYĀNA OR HĪNAYĀNA, THIS SYSTEM RELATES TO

Now, does this sequential approach to the generation of śamatha and special insight relate to Mahāyāna or Hīnayāna, sūtra or mantra? It is common to the vehicles of śrāvakas and pratyekabuddhas, to the vehicle of the perfections, and in fact to each of the four tenet systems. In my *Great Treatise on the Stages of Mantra*, I have already explained the assertions of individual tantras and their great commentators to the effect that it is similar for the three lower classes of tantras of secret mantra.

With regard to highest yoga tantra, *Instructions on the Perfection of Wisdom* quotes the *Guhyasamāja Tantra* as saying:

> When you examine your own mind,
> all phenomena dwell in the mind.
> Phenomena dwell in that vajra of space.
> They do not exist, and nor does reality.

Also, the *Descent to Laṅkā Sūtra* says:

> Relying upon mind only,
> external things are not conceived.[207]
> Relying on nonappearance,
> One transcends mind only.
>
> Relying on observing suchness,
> one transcends nonappearance.
> If yogis stay in nonappearance,
> they do not see the Mahāyāna.

With these and other statements, Ratnākaraśānti explains that the three levels of yoga are taught to be observing mind only, observing suchness, and nonappearance. It appears that he is explaining that the way of attaining śamatha and special insight on the first two levels is through placement and analytical meditation as explained above. [284] Therefore he maintains that the way they are generated in a mindstream that focuses on the ultimate mode of being is similar [in both highest yoga tantra and the Perfection Vehicle].

Our own position is that, even in the context of highest yoga tantra, one's method for developing an understanding of the view must be compatible with what appears in the Madhyamaka texts. As for how it is maintained, there is analysis of and then mental attention to suchness during some post-meditation phases of the generation and completion stages. However, those practicing the completion stage who have attained the ability to penetrate vital points of the body[208] certainly must meditate placing the mind within the view when maintaining the meditative equipoise on suchness; nevertheless they do not perform the analytical meditation of special insight the way it is presented in other texts. Therefore, at that point, do not stop your single-pointed meditation on suchness within the view when you stop analytical meditation. Since this is not the right context to clarify the reasons why proceeding like that is sufficient [in highest yoga tantra], I will explain here the reasons for proceeding like that on the other paths.

THE ACTUAL WAY TO CULTIVATE SPECIAL INSIGHT IN RELIANCE UPON ŚAMATHA

If you have not found the view of selflessness, then no matter what system of meditation you perform, that meditation will not abide in the meaning of suchness. That is why it is necessary to find the view.

If you have an understanding of the view but are not mindful of it and do not place the mind upon it during meditation on suchness, the latter will not be a meditation on suchness. Therefore placing the mind without reflecting on anything at the end of some little preparatory analysis of the view does not constitute maintaining suchness either. Becoming mindful of the view and familiar with it by merely placing the mind within it also amounts to nothing more than the above method for maintaining śamatha.

Hence, that is not the meaning of the texts explaining a distinct method for maintaining special insight.

That is why you should individually analyze the meaning of selflessness by means of wisdom as explained above and then maintain it. If you only do analytical meditation, however, your previously developed śamatha will deteriorate. Therefore you should mount the horse of śamatha, maintain analysis, and occasionally alternate it with placement meditation.

More specifically, if the stability lessens because of too much analytical meditation, do more placement meditation and refresh the stability. If you do not really want to analyze because of too much placement meditation, or if despite analysis your mind is not fit to go anywhere and becomes engrossed in stillness, you should do more analytical meditation. Since it is very powerful if you cultivate both śamatha and special insight in continuous equality, [285] you should do it that way. The third *Stages of Meditation* says:

> Śamatha weakens when cultivating special insight causes wisdom to predominate. Therefore, since the mind will flicker like a butter lamp in the breeze, it will not perceive suchness very clearly. That is why you should cultivate śamatha at those times. Likewise, whenever śamatha predominates, you are like a sleeping person and do not see suchness clearly, so at those times, you should cultivate wisdom.

Like that, it is inappropriate to stop any and all conceptuality when sustaining analysis because you consider it to be apprehension of true existence. This is because, as I demonstrated several times above, conceptions that are apprehensions of true existence are only one category of conceptions. The view that anything apprehended by conceptuality is damaged by reasoning is a denial with an excessive object of negation; it has been proven that this is not the meaning of the scriptures either. You might say, I do not assert this in relation to all phenomena, but whatever is conceived by the mind in relation to suchness is necessarily an apprehension of true existence. But here, too, the fault arises from the manner in which it is apprehended, not from apprehension in and of itself. For it has been stated, ordinary people who aspire for liberation need to inquire into suchness by way of multiple avenues of scripture and reasoning.

412 | THE MIDDLE-LENGTH STAGES OF THE PATH

Someone might object that if meditation on suchness is for the sake of generating nonconceptuality, it will not arise from fine investigative analysis, for cause and effect must accord with each other. The Blessed One himself gave a clear answer to that. He says in the *Kāśyapa Chapter*:

> Kāśyapa, it is like this. Fire springs up from two trees rubbed together by the wind, and once it has sprung up, both trees are consumed by it. Likewise, Kāśyapa, when there is correct fine investigative analysis, an ārya's wisdom faculty develops, and that fine investigative analysis itself is consumed through its development.

Thus he is saying that an ārya's wisdom arises from fine investigative analysis. The second *Stages of Meditation* also says:

> That is how they [286] analyze with wisdom. When yogis definitely do not apprehend any nature of things as an ultimate, they enter the concentration of complete nonconceptuality. They also realize that the natures of all phenomena are nonexistent. Those who fail to individually analyze the nature of things with wisdom and to meditate on that, who instead cultivate just the mere elimination of attention, will never stop conceptualization. Neither will they ever realize the nonexistence of a nature because they will lack the light of wisdom. The Blessed One said, "When the fire of knowing reality just as it is thus springs from correct fine investigative analysis, it consumes the wood of conceptuality, like the fire that springs from wood rubbed together."

If it were not like that, the uncontaminated could not possibly arise from the contaminated, nor the supramundane from the mundane, nor a buddha from a sentient being, nor an ārya from an ordinary being, and so forth because the causes and their effects are not alike.

Essay on the Mind of Enlightenment says:

> Where conceptualization appears,
> how could there be emptiness?

Tathāgatas do not see minds
in terms of agents and objects of investigation.
Where there are agents and objects of investigation,
enlightenment does not exist.

What is being pointed out is that someone who apprehends agents and objects of investigation as truly existent has not attained enlightenment. If fine investigative wisdom were refuted and if the mere agents and objects of investigation were refuted, this would contradict this text's determination of suchness through many avenues of analysis associated with fine investigation. Also, if those two were not seen by buddhas, they would be nonexistent.[209]

That same text says:

To meditate on emptiness by
calling it "nonproduction," "emptiness,"
or "selflessness" is meditation
on what is a lesser truth.

This does not refute the meditation that observes selflessness, the emptiness that is the nonexistence of inherent production. Rather, it refutes the meditation on an emptiness that is a lesser nature, one apprehended as truly existent. [287]

Praise of the World-Transcending One says:

When you teach the nectar of emptiness
to clear away conceptual thinking,
whosoever adheres to it
is very much reproved by you.

In the same way *Precious Garland* (2.3) says:

Accordingly, self and selflessness
are not observed to be reality as it is.
Therefore the Great Sage rejected
the views of a self and selflessness.

Since neither self nor selflessness are established in reality, the Buddha rejected the view that the two exist in reality but did not refute the view of selflessness. This is because according to the above quotation from *Refuting Objections*, if phenomena did not lack the inherent existence of inherent establishment, they would exist as inherently established.

The *Verse Summary of the Perfection of Wisdom* (1.9) says:

> Although the bodhisattva thinks, "This aggregate is empty,"
> he employs signs and still distrusts the basis of nonproduction.

And the *Perfection of Wisdom in One Hundred Thousand Lines* says:

> One employs signs when using what is called "empty and selfless form" but does not employ the perfection of wisdom.

The meaning of these statements refers to the apprehension of emptiness and so forth as truly existent. Otherwise the phrase "distrusts the basis of nonproduction" would also be unreasonable, for to trust it would also be to employ signs.

The same sūtra says:

> Whoever perfectly knows that phenomena lack inherent existence employs the supreme perfection of wisdom.

And:

> When wisdom shatters uncompounded, compounded,
> virtuous, and nonvirtuous phenomena,
> and not even dust remains to be seen,
> the world counts this as the perfection of wisdom.

The *King of Concentrations Sūtra* also says:

> If phenomena are analyzed to be selfless [288]
> and are meditated on after being analyzed,
> that is the cause for attaining the fruit, nirvāṇa.
> You won't find peace through any other cause.

Also, in *Essence of the Perfection of Wisdom,* Śāriputra asks how a bodhisattva who wishes to engage in the profound perfection of wisdom should train, and Avalokiteśvara replies that he should thoroughly and correctly view even these five aggregates to be empty of their intrinsic nature. There are many statements like these that would otherwise be contradicted. That is why *Praise of the Sphere of Reality* says:

> The Dharma that supremely purifies the mind
> is the lack of inherent existence.

And:

> As long as one apprehends "I" and "mine,"
> one externally imputes aspects.
> The seeds of existence cease to be
> when you see the two aspects of selflessness.

Entering the Middle Way (6.165) also says:

> Therefore, by viewing "I" and "mine" as empty,
> the yogi is completely liberated.

You should understand this in accordance with the statements and maintain a continuous ascertainment of selflessness and the absence of inherent existence.

Here the first *Stages of Meditation* says:

> The *Dhāraṇī of Entering Nonperception* (*Avikalpapraveśa-dhāraṇī*) says that the signs of form and so forth are abandoned by not attending to them. This teaches that if you examine with wisdom, you do not mentally attend to what is not observed. It does not imply the mere absence of attention. It is not an elimination through merely eliminating the attention that is the beginningless adherence to form and so forth, like in the absorption of nonperception.[210]

These excellent passages are saying that the apprehension of signs should be eliminated through a meditation in which the mind does not attend to anything. Yet the intended meaning set forth is that you correctly examine with analytical wisdom and then establish meditative equipoise on the meaning of your realization that not even a particle of the referent object, the apprehension of true existence, is observed.

The second *Stages of Meditation* says: [289]

> It is said, "When you investigate what the mind is, you realize that it is empty. When you thoroughly search for the mind realizing that, its nature, you realize that it is empty. Through such a realization you enter the yoga of signlessness." This indicates that preparatory reflection is necessary to enter signlessness. It very clearly indicates that it is impossible to enter into complete nonconceptuality by merely eliminating mental attention altogether, without analyzing the nature of things by means of wisdom.

That statement from the *Cloud of Jewels of Sūtra* means if you have not found the view of suchness through correct prior analysis, you will not be able to engage in the meaning of suchness nonconceptually.

The third *Stages of Meditation* says that in order to refute the presumptuous claim that you can realize what is said to be inconceivable, beyond mind, and so forth by merely hearing and reflecting on the profound meaning, it was taught that these are objects known by individual āryas themselves and thus inconceivable by others and so on. This was also set forth to refute the improper reflection that apprehends the profound meaning as truly existent. However, it does not refute correct analysis by means of fine investigative wisdom. It is said that many reasonings and scriptures would be contradicted if that were refuted. Although [fine investigative wisdom] is considered conceptualization, nonconceptual wisdom arises from it because it is correct mental attention. Therefore those who want that wisdom should rely on it.

It is very important to understand the way in which these statements refute the Chinese master's [Heshang's] proposition that the view that determines suchness is not found in reliance upon scripture and reasoning and rather suchness is realized by meditative equipoise without any mental attention whatsoever.

These methods of meditation also appear in earlier instructions on the stages of the path. Potowa's *Jewel Box*[211] says: [290]

> Some say when you study and contemplate, you determine
> through logic that there is no inherent existence,
> but during meditation you cultivate nonthought.
> Yet if you do that, this unconnected emptiness,
> cultivated separately, will not become an antidote.
> Thus, even while you meditate, you must finely investigate
> by means of the reasonings you are familiar with:
> not one nor many, dependent arising, and so forth.
> Also briefly abide in nonconceptuality.
> Meditation like that is an antidote for the afflictions.
> For those who wish to follow the one lord [Atiśa]
> and wish to practice the way of the perfections,
> that is the way to cultivate wisdom.
> Having become familiar with the selflessness of persons,
> you should train in it accordingly.

The Elder, Atiśa, also said this [in *Entering the Two Truths*]:

> If you ask: who realized emptiness?
> Nāgārjuna, who saw the truth of reality
> and was prophesied by the Tathāgata,
> and his student Candrakīrti.
> Through oral instructions transmitted from them,
> the truth of reality will be realized.

Here I have expanded those instructions set forth by Atiśa as well as Master Kamalaśīla's considerations, which appear to be the same.

In order to maintain special insight in that manner, you should know how to observe the six preparatory practices[212] and how to act during the actual meditation session, afterward, and in between sessions. In particular, you should know the above methods for maintaining it free from laxity and excitement.

THE MEASURE OF HAVING ACCOMPLISHED SPECIAL
INSIGHT THROUGH MEDITATION

Until the pliancy explained above arises in your meditation while analyzing with fine investigative wisdom, it is a similitude of special insight. It is fully qualified special insight after pliancy arises. The nature of pliancy and the way it arises are as explained above. Yet since the śamatha already accomplished has not deteriorated and also induces pliancy, the presence of pliancy alone is not the measure of having accomplished special insight. Well then, what is it? When the power of analytical meditation itself is able to induce pliancy, then it has become special insight. It is the same for both the special insight observing things in their variety and the special insight observing the ultimate mode of being. [291]

In accordance with that, the *Unraveling the Intent Sūtra* also says:

> "Blessed One, before a bodhisattva achieves physical and mental pliancy, what do you call his mental attention that mentally attends to internal images, to the objects of concentration relative to phenomena he has properly thought about?"
>
> "Maitreya, it is not special insight. It should be described as possessing a type of attention that is similar to special insight."

And *Instructions on the Perfection of Wisdom* also says:

> Thereby he abides in that physical and mental pliancy he has attained. He should finely investigate with special belief the meaning of precisely what he has reflected on, the object that is the internal image of his concentration. It is a mental attention in accordance with special insight before physical and mental pliancy have arisen. When they have arisen, at that point it is special insight.

When [analysis] is able to induce pliancy by its own power, it is also able to induce single-pointedness of mind. Therefore inducing śamatha like this through the power of analytical meditation that finely investigates is an excellent quality of having already accomplished śamatha.

For someone well accomplished in śamatha, analytical meditation practice makes śamatha even more excellent. That is why you should not believe that the stability of your meditation will lessen if you practice the analytical meditation of fine investigative analysis.

HOW ŚAMATHA AND SPECIAL INSIGHT UNITE

If śamatha and special insight have not been achieved as explained in the context of the measure for their accomplishment, there will be nothing to unify. That is why, to be unified, both must have definitely been achieved. Now, from the point where special insight is first achieved, the unity is also achieved. The method for that is as follows. They are unified when, by the power of having done analytical meditation in reliance on earlier śamatha, you have attained mental application that operates naturally without fabrications and according to the explanation of śamatha above.

Śrāvaka Levels says:

> At what point do śamatha and special insight mix and unite evenly, and why is it called the "path where they enter into union"? [292] From the nine mental abidings, it proceeds like this. One attains that which constitutes the ninth abiding associated with meditative equipoise, and in reliance upon that full accomplishment of concentration, one puts great effort into superior wisdom, the thorough differentiation of phenomena. At that point, the path of that thorough differentiation of phenomena will operate naturally and effortlessly. Since it is without fabrication, just like the path of śamatha, the special insight will be completely pure and completely refined; it will follow śamatha and will be completely conjoined with a sense of bliss. This is why śamatha and special insight mix and operate evenly and why it is called "the path where śamatha and special insight enter into union."

The third *Stages of Meditation* also says:

> When the mind is balanced owing to freedom from laxity and excitement and becomes extremely clear with respect to suchness because it operates naturally, at that point you should establish

equanimity by relaxing and giving up effort. You should know that at that point, you have accomplished the path of the union of śamatha and special insight.

It is as stated before: from the juncture where fully qualified special insight has been achieved, there is union.

Instructions on the Perfection of Wisdom also says:

> Then you observe that very image connected with conceptualization. When you experience both of them in your mind through continuous uninterrupted and unobstructed attention, it is called the path of union of śamatha and special insight. That is to say, śamatha and special insight are a pair, and their relation is one of conjunction; they operate bound to each other.

"Unobstructed" means that there is no need to stop the process of analytical meditation and place the mind in nonconceptuality. Nonconceptuality is induced by that analytical meditation itself. To "experience both" is to experience both the śamatha that observes the nonconceptual image and the special insight that observes the image connected with conceptualization. [293] "Through continuous" should be understood from the point of view that the analytical special insight and the śamatha at the end of the analysis do not arise simultaneously. However, when there is actual śamatha induced by the power of analysis, both special insight, the discernment of phenomena that observes the ultimate mode of being, and śamatha, the concentration that firmly and single-pointedly abides on the ultimate mode of being, operate in association. At such time śamatha and special insight are mixed and operate equally. For that, it is necessary to gain a realization arisen from meditation. Therefore a collection of the two that allows one to finely investigate the meaning of selflessness from within a nonconceptual state of firm stability, like a little fish moving through water that remains still, may be posited as a similitude of śamatha and special insight. Yet this is not the meaning of the actual union of śamatha and special insight.

You should understand this manner in which śamatha and special insight unite in accordance with what appears in those authentic texts rather than trusting explanations that fabricate it in some other way. Reasoned conclusions, scriptural source passages, and detailed methods for cultivating the stages of the path to enlightenment should be known from the *Great Treatise on the Stages of the Path.*

27 | Conclusion

Now I will present a brief summary of topics of the general path. First of all, the root of the path rests on the way you rely on a spiritual teacher, so be clear and decisive about that. Then, if an uncontrived desire to take the essence of your freedom has arisen, it will urge you from within to practice. Therefore, in order to generate it, you should meditate on the topics of the freedoms and endowments. Then, if your effort for things of this life is not countered, a serious effort for future lives will not arise. Therefore apply yourself to meditation on impermanence, the fact that the body you have obtained will not last long, and the way you will wander in the lower rebirths after death. Mindful of this, an attitude of genuine fear will arise, so you should sincerely develop certainty about the excellent qualities of the Three Refuges, abide by the vow of the common refuge, and train in its trainings. Then you should develop—from many angles—the faith of conviction in karma and its effects, the foundation of all virtuous Dharma. Having made it firm, earnestly work to engage in virtue and desist from nonvirtue, always entering the path of the four powers. [294]

Once you have thus garnered the Dharma cycle of persons of lesser capacity, you should think extensively about the general and specific faults of cyclic existence and turn your mind away as much as you can from cyclic existence in general. Then identify the causes from which cyclic existence arises, karma and mental afflictions, and develop the uncontrived desire to eliminate them. Apply yourself to the three trainings in general, the path of liberation from cyclic existence, and in particular to the prātimokṣa vow that you yourself have undertaken.

Once you have thus firmly established the cycle of training of persons of medium capacity, contemplate the many others just like you who have fallen into the ocean of existence. Train in bodhicitta, which has its root in love and compassion. You must try as hard as you can for it to arise;

without it, the six perfections, the two stages [of tantra], and so forth are like a roof without supports. When you have had some small experience of it, adopt it through the ritual and put effort into its trainings so that you make your aspiring bodhicitta as stable as you can. Then explore the great waves of bodhisattva conduct. As you get to know the boundary between what you should desist from and what you should engage in, generate the desire to train in it. When that has arisen, take the vow of engaging bodhicitta through the ritual. Train in the six perfections that ripen your own mindstream and in the four ways of gathering disciples and so forth that ripen the minds of others. In particular, avoid a root downfall even at the risk your life. Try hard not to be tainted by small and medium transgressions or misdeeds either. If you are, try hard to restore your vow.

Then you need to train in the last two perfections in particular. Therefore become skilled in the method for maintaining meditative stabilization and accomplish concentration. Do everything you can for the pure view of the two selflessnesses to arise in your mindstream. Having gained it, understand how to maintain it by placing the mind in the view and maintain it. Such meditative stabilization and wisdom are designated with the names *śamatha* and *special insight*, but they are not different from the last two perfections, and so they are subsumed within the training in the bodhisattva precepts after taking the vow.

Also, cultivating the lower paths, you should grow more and more keen on attaining the higher ones, and hearing about the higher ones, you should increasingly wish to accomplish the lower ones. When you meditate on them, you also need to purify your thoughts and balance your mind. Thus, if your respect for the spiritual teacher who guides you on the path appears to be low, put effort into your manner of relying on him, for the root of your collection of goodness would otherwise be cut off. Likewise, if your enthusiasm for practice is weak, emphasize meditation on the topic of freedoms and endowments, [295] whereas if your clinging to this life increases, meditate mainly on the topics of impermanence and the faults of the lower rebirths. If you tend to neglect the ethical boundaries you have accepted, meditate mainly on karma and its effects. If your disenchantment with cyclic existence is weak, your effort for liberation will be nothing but words, so you should reflect on the faults of cyclic existence. If you do not seem to have the great strength of mind to make everything you do into something for the benefit of sentient beings, the root of the Mahāyāna will be cut off, so train in aspiring bodhicitta along with its causes. In the event you have taken the vow of the victors' children and are training in their conduct, then if the bondage that is the apprehension of signs appears to be very strong, break down the referent object of that apprehension with a reasoning consciousness and train in space-like and illusion-like emptiness. If your mind does not stay on its object and appears to become a slave to distraction, train mainly in the stability of your single-pointed meditation. This is what the masters of the past have taught.

From these examples you should also understand situations that have not been explained. In brief, you should not become imbalanced. Your mindstream should be serviceable for all virtuous initiatives.

HOW TO TRAIN IN THE VAJRAYĀNA IN PARTICULAR

Having thus trained in the paths that sūtra and mantra share in common, you should no doubt become engaged in mantra because that path is extremely rare compared with other Dharma and makes you complete the two accumulations quickly. When you engage in it, as described in *Lamp for the Path to Enlightenment*, you should first please your guru beyond what was explained above. It should be someone who has at least all the characteristics explained there.[213]

Then you should first have your mindstream ripened by means of an initiation explained in the authentic tantras. Then listen to and understand the commitments and vows taken on that occasion and guard them. If a root downfall occurs, even if the vow can be renewed, the development of excellent qualities of the path in your mindstream will be greatly delayed, so endeavor not to be tainted by that. Try not to be stained by the serious infractions, but if you are stained nevertheless, apply the means of restoring your commitments because they are the root for cultivating the paths. Without them it will be like a decrepit house whose support walls are collapsing.

The *Root Tantra of Mañjuśrī* says, "The King of Sages did not teach mantra attainments for those of loose ethics." [296] Statements such as this are saying that there will be no great, medium, or small accomplishments whatsoever. The highest yoga tantras also say that those who do not guard their commitments, those who have an inferior empowerment,[214] and those who do not understand suchness will not accomplish anything despite their practice. Therefore someone who claims to cultivate the path but does not keep the commitments and vows is straying far from the principles of mantra.

That being so, those who guard their commitments and vows should train in stages in the yogas with and without signs according to the three lower tantra classes and in the two stages of yoga according to the highest one in order to cultivate the paths of mantra.

Here the topic of becoming engaged in mantra is presented just nominally, so you must get to know these in detail in works on the stages of the mantra path. If you train in such a way, you will be training in a perfectly complete body of a path that includes all the essential points of sūtra and tantra, and you will make the opportunities you have achieved in this life meaningful through your training. You will be able to make the Victor's precious teachings flourish in your own mindstream and in that of others.

DEDICATION

Of the two paths—sūtra and tantra—taught by the Victor,
a fearless confidence in all the sūtra paths
of scripture and treatises ensures that
they effortlessly arise as direct instructions.

The shared Mahāyāna paths, as explained in the tantras,
are all made clear, which makes this the supreme purifier of the
    mindstream.

The concentrations common to Buddhists and non-Buddhists,
the Great and Lesser Vehicles, both kinds of Mahāyāna,[215]
the higher and lower tantras, and the two stages
are correctly explained according to very clear texts by many scholars,
allowing yogis to realize well the errors of paths they seek.[216]

Therefore for those who seek liberation,
I have arranged this abridged work on the stages of the path,
the path of the profound view and vast conduct
passed on from the regent Maitreya and the noble Mañjuśrī,
transmitted by the protector Nāgārjuna, Asaṅga,

and Śāntideva, three rivers merged as one
in the supreme instructions of the glorious Atiśa. [297]

Through the virtue gained here by my effort,
may the Victor's teachings, root of welfare for all beings,
prosper, uncorrupted, for a long time.

COLOPHON

This was a summary of essential points of all the scriptures of the Buddha, the tradition of the great trailblazers Nāgārjuna and Asaṅga, the Dharma system of supreme beings who progress toward the level of omniscience. It was a presentation of the stages of the path to enlightenment that teaches in full all the stages to be practiced by the three types of persons, the meaning of instructions that I have received and that were transmitted to Neusurpa from both Gönpawa and Chengawa, to Sharawa from Potowa, and to Dölpa from Potowa. This additional distillation of an extensive presentation of the stages of the path was composed by the learned and renounced fully ordained monk Tsongkhapa Losang Drakpai Pal on Mount Geden.

Notes

1. The *Eighty Stanzas of Praise* by Naktso Lotsāwa Tsultrim Gyalwa (1011–64). Naktso was among the envoys who invited Atiśa to Tibet and acted as his translator and companion for many years.
2. A principality in eastern India.
3. Tib. *dge slong,* usually translated in this work as "fully ordained monk."
4. The Kadampa master of Sangphu Monastery, Drolungpa Lodrö Jungné (b. eleventh century), met Atiśa when he was young, and his *Great Treatise on the Stages of the Teaching* was an inspiration for Tsongkhapa's works on the stages of the path.
5. Tib. *mu stegs,* Skt. *tīrthika,* sometimes translated literally as "forders." According to one etymology, the proponents of six principal Indian tenet systems at the time of the Buddha were *forders* because they claimed to point out fords for crossing the river of suffering—paths to liberation.
6. After the Buddha's passing, his teachings were organized into three groups according to topic or manner of presentation: Vinaya, Sūtra, and Abhidharma. These three are collectively known as the Tripiṭaka, the "three baskets." The higher Tripiṭaka includes texts of the Mahāyāna tradition, such as the Perfection of Wisdom Sūtras, while the lower Tripiṭaka includes texts of the Hīnayāna tradition.
7. The Mahāsāṃghika, Sarvāstivāda, Sthaviravāda, and Saṃmatīya schools.
8. That is, the contents of the three baskets (*piṭaka*) of scripture (Vinaya, Sūtra, and Abhidharma) correspond to the three trainings (*śikṣā*) in ethics (*śīla*), concentration (*samādhi*), and wisdom (*prajñā*).
9. "The one from the golden land," Dharmakīrti of Suvarṇadvīpa, where Atiśa traveled to receive instructions on bodhicitta. The precise location of Suvarṇadvīpa is not known. Though it has become common to identify it with the Indonesian island of Sumatra, it could be anywhere in Southeast Asia.
10. In this work, "common" generally means "shared in common," as in common to both Hīnayāna and Mahāyāna, or, as here, common to both sūtra and tantra. It can also mean common to both Buddhist and non-Buddhist paths. "Uncommon" then means "pertaining only to the higher or more esoteric level."
11. Different biographical sources provide different accounts.
12. Lha Lama Yeshé Ö, tenth–eleventh century king of Gugé, succeeded by his nephew, Lha Lama Jangchup Ö.
13. The five areas of knowledge (*pañcavidyā*) are the four mentioned above—languages, logical reasoning, medicine, and crafts—as well as the Buddhadharma.
14. The Pāramitāyāna, "the Perfection Vehicle," which includes the practice of the six bodhisattva perfections, refers to the non-esoteric practices of the Mahāyāna. The esoteric, or tantric, practices of the Mahāyāna are called variously the Mantra Vehicle (Mantrayāna) or the Diamond Vehicle (Vajrayāna).

15. This refers to the general lineage of all the tantric teachings, the lineage of Guhyasa-māja, the lineage of mother tantras such as Cakrasaṃvara, the lineage of action and yoga tantras, and the lineage of Vajrabhairava.

16. Khutön Tsöndrü Yungdrung (1011–75), Ngok Lepai Sherap (eleventh century), and Drom Gyalwai Jungné (1004–64).

17. Here and elsewhere, Tsongkhapa refers to Atiśa not by his name but as "the Elder" or "the Great Elder" (*gnas brtan chen po*).

18. The two masters are Serlingpa, expert in the system of Asaṅga, and the younger Vidyākokila, also known as Avadhūtipa, expert in the system of Nāgārjuna.

19. Tib. *sems skyed*, a very common ellipsis for *byang chub mchog tu sems skyed*, meaning "generation of the mind (aiming) for supreme enlightenment"—that is, the mind of *bodhicitta*.

20. This means that Atiśa carried all the teachings evenly, as when lifting a table by all four corners, without bias or preference.

21. Naljorpa Chenpo, "the great yogi," Amé Jangchup Rinchen (1015–78) succeeded Dromtönpa as the abbot of Radreng in 1065.

22. The Tibetan word *thos pa*, often rendered as "hearing" or "listening," refers to receiving teachings more generally, which encompasses reading as well. For instance, *thos pa mang po*, literally "having heard a lot," means "well read" or "educated." For this reason, *thos pa* is sometimes rendered as "study."

23. "Verses about Listening" (*Śrutivarga*) is chapter 22 of the *Collection of Indicative Verses*; this is verse 4 of that chapter.

24. *Suchness* (Tib. *de bzhin nyid*, Skt. *tathatā*) is the ultimate reality of phenomena, often a synonym for *emptiness*.

25. Tib. *legs par rab tu nyon la yid la zungs shig*. This is a quote from the *Perfection of Wisdom Sūtras*.

26. Kamapa Sherab Ö (1057–1131), a student of Gönpawa and the founder of Kam Monastery.

27. Also known as Prince Sutasoma.

28. "Mother of the Buddhas" is a common epithet for the discourses on the Perfection of Wisdom. The Buddha arranged his own seat as a sign of respect for the Dharma.

29. One *yojana* (Tib. *dpag tshad*) is usually considered equivalent to about four and a half miles (just over seven kilometers).

30. Tib. *rgyas gdab par bya'o*, literally "planted to thrive."

31. Tib. *mig rten*, literally "eye support"—something to rest one's eyes on. Radreng is the monastery north of Lhasa founded by Dromtönpa. The identity of Thashi (Mtha' bzhi) is not certain.

32. A place name, possibly in Tsang.

33. *Commentary on Four Hundred Stanzas* (*Catuḥśatakaṭīkā*).

34. Tib. *dam tshig*, the Tibetan equivalent of the Sanskrit word *samaya*. A master of one's commitments is the guru seen as indivisible from the body, speech, and mind of one's special meditative deity.

35. Tib. *mnar med*, "without respite," the lowest of the hells.

36. Tib. *'phags pa*, "āryas," who have gained direct insight into emptiness, the nature of reality, and thereby reached the path of seeing, which makes them highly realized beings.

37. Here and below, Tsongkhapa is referring to the well-known prayer from the *Gaṇḍavyūha Sūtra* called the *Prayer of Good Conduct*, mentioned above. Tibetans

typically refer to it as the *Prayer of Samantabhadra*, or the *King of Prayers*. It begins by laying out the preliminary practices for making the mind ready for meditation. Tsongkhapa only gives the first words of each verse, but the full text for these verses has been supplied by relying mainly on Sopa and Patt, *Steps on the Path to Enlightenment: A Commentary on Tsongkhapa's "Lamrim Chenmo,"* volume 1: *The Foundation Practices* (Boston: Wisdom Publications, 2004).

38. The five types of persons are buddhas, bodhisattvas, pratyekabuddhas, śrāvakas, and ordinary beings.

39. Generally speaking, in meditation practice, the observed object is a mental image, and the subjective aspect is the way that the object is held by the mind to which it appears. For example, when meditating on compassion, the object is sentient beings and the subjective aspect is any of three: sentient beings as suffering, sentient beings as impermanent, and sentient beings as empty of inherent nature.

40. Buddhist psychology understands perception to rely on three components: an object, a sense power, and a sense consciousness. These are each sixfold, one for each of the five senses, plus the mental sense. After an object appears to one of the six consciousnesses through any of the six sense powers, the mental consciousness may develop attachment to pleasant objects and aversion toward unpleasant ones.

41. A day is divided into six four-hour periods, three in the day and three at night.

42. The five hindrances are sensual desire, ill will, lethargy, agitation, and doubt.

43. Another name for the path of preparation.

44. Tib. *khams gong*, the form and formless realms, as opposed to the fortunate rebirths (Tib. *bde 'gro*) more generally.

45. The northern continent in the classical Buddhist representation of the world with four continents centered on Mount Meru.

46. Of the four continents in Buddhist cosmology, Jambudvīpa, in the south, is the one that we inhabit.

47. "Higher status" refers to birth as a human or a deity.

48. Lha Drigangpa relates this story from the Kadam master Potowa in his *Commentary on the Blue Compendium*.

49. "Maintaining a connection" between lives so that the next life builds on the virtues created in the present life without allowing them to become lost for a long time.

50. That is, the freedoms complemented by the endowments.

51. Kadam Geshe Dölpa Sherab Gyatso (1059–1131) was a student of Potowa and author of the *Blue Compendium* (*Be'u bum sngon po*).

52. According to the cosmogony alluded to here, everything physical will be destroyed by fire at the end of a cycle of eons.

53. See note 29.

54. The *Story of Saṅgharakṣita* is found within the *Chapters of the Vinaya*. Its parallel in the *Divyāvadāna* is translated in Rotman 2017, 135–66.

55. The Tibetan expression, which is consistently translated here as "well-being," consists of a combination of the two syllables *bde* and *legs*, *bde* referring to the happiness of happy (i.e., "higher") realms, and *legs* referring to definite goodness (i.e., liberation from cyclic existence, or enlightenment). Thus "well-being" implies both temporary and ultimate happiness.

56. Tib. *dkon mchog*, "rare (and) precious," is the word used for Jewel in the context of going for refuge.

57. Skt. *āmalaka*, a fruit with a somewhat transparent skin that allows for the veins, seeds, and pulp to shine through.

58. This verse from *Entering the Bodhisattva Way* (2.7) is commonly recited during offering ceremonies.

59. A god about to be reborn as a pig takes refuge in the Three Jewels on the advice of Śakra, king of the gods, and is reborn in a heaven higher than Śakra himself. The *Story of a Wretched Pig (Sūkarikāvadāna)* is story 14 in the *Divyāvadāna*. See translation in Rotman 2008, 325–28.

60. In Tibetan, the word for "action" and "karma" is the same (*las*). It will be useful to keep this in mind throughout the following explanations on karma. The word *karma* has been chosen in cases where the word *action* failed to put across the implied relation with an effect, e.g., "karma that is definitely experienced" or "accumulate karma."

61. Geshe Thubten Ngawang (Tibetan Center Hamburg) offered the following explanation for this passage: Buddha Śākyamuni, apart from accumulating the collections of merit necessary for attaining buddhahood, also spent some time accumulating further merit that he dedicated to the goal that his followers may have all necessary conditions for life. However, according to the law of karma, they can only experience the corresponding results if they themselves have accumulated a sufficient measure of the causes.

62. Those born from his speech are śrāvakas, those established for self-enlightenment are pratyekabuddhas, and the children of the victors are bodhisattvas.

63. In this context, the term "basis" (*gzhi*) refers to the object of the action.

64. Tib. *chung ma*, "wife," "mate," "consort," "partner."

65. The four opposites are that which one has not seen with the eye consciousness; that which one has not heard with the ear consciousness; that which one has not differentiated with the nose, tongue, or body consciousness; and that which one has not understood with the mental consciousness.

66. Geshe Thubten Soepa explains that all these aspects of denying activity are associated with the problem of nihilism, the refusal to accept certain conventional truths. In this context each of them has its special significance.

67. Despite the precise distinction drawn here, the general expression "ten nonvirtuous actions" has become common in English. Tibetan texts also frequently refer to *actions* in less-specific contexts even though, according to the definition proposed here, the last three of the ten nonvirtues do not constitute actions. Thus *action* should be understood as a term that requires specification only in certain contexts.

68. In this context, the difference in the strength of the support is the difference made by the sets of vows one holds, whether prātimokṣa, bodhisattva, or tantric.

69. Synonym for monastic robes.

70. Tsongkhapa enumerates these ten in his *Great Treatise on the Stages of the Path to Enlightenment*: actions carried out (1) in a dream, (2) unknowingly, (3) unconsciously, (4) without intensity or long duration, (5) mistakenly, (6) forgetfully, and (7) unintentionally, and actions (8) that are naturally neutral, (9) that have been purified through regret, or (10) that have been purified through antidotes.

71. This sūtra consists of numerous stories of past lives illustrating the karmic causes of present consequences.

72. The dhāraṇī of the goddess Cundā is *Namaḥ saptānāṃ samyaksambuddha koṭīnāṃ tadyathā oṃ cale cule cundī svāhā*. The text of the *Cundadevīdhāraṇī* lists some

of these dream visions, but this particular listing is drawn from *Compendium of Trainings*.

73. The unusual term *chos kyi sgrib pa* is not clear. According to Geshe Thubten Soepa's oral commentary, it is either a synonym for *shes sgrib*, "obstructions to omniscience," or *chos spong gi sgrib pa*, "obstructions (caused) through abandoning the Dharma."

74. The rebirths are counted as either five or six depending on whether gods and demigods are listed separately or grouped together. The four birthplaces are a womb, an egg, moisture, or spontaneous birth.

75. Geshe Thubten Ngawang describes the Tibetan term here for "threshold" (*'gag bsdoms*, literally "stop-bind") as the place in a central station where all the various tracks come together and where they can be connected or disconnected by means of switches.

76. The suffering of meeting with the unpleasant, the separation from what is pleasant, and seeking what you desire and not getting it could be added here.

77. Vasubandhu discusses immovable (*āniñjya*) karma in verse 4.46 of the *Treasury of Abhidharma*. Contaminated virtuous karma in the form and formless realms is called "immovable" or "immutable" because the level of existence that the results are experienced at is fixed. Unlike karma created in the desire realm, the destination cannot be modulated by prayers, intervening afflictions, and the like.

78. These nine are overeating, eating something indigestible, eating without having digested previous food, not passing undigested food, having a blocked intestine, not taking specific medicines for specific illnesses, not differentiating between appropriate and inappropriate activities, having a fatal accident, and sex.

79. Though not explicit, this must refer to gods of the form and formless realms and perhaps to denizens of the pure lands, who are also sometimes referred to as gods (*lha*). For as Tsongkhapa noted above, gods of the desire realm experience acute end-of-life agony.

80. The special ability to see through matter and over long distances without obstruction.

81. "Birth" here signifies one's entry into the mother's womb rather than one's exit from it.

82. Actions can either become a cause for determining a rebirth or they can merely determine some aspect of that rebirth. Someone "devoted to wrongdoing" (*sdom min*) is literally "contrary to the vows" in that they not only perform negative acts, they also hold the habit in the manner of a vow.

83. The nāga king Elāpatra in a past life as a monk under Buddha Kāśyapa broke a precept by cutting down a cardamom (*elāpatra*) tree in anger. As a consequence, he was reborn at the time of Śākyamuni Buddha as a giant serpent with a cardamom tree growing on his head.

84. That of śrāvaka arhats, pratyekabuddha arhats, and buddhas.

85. This verse is from the *Praise in One Hundred and Fifty Verses*, which is attributed variously to Mātṛceṭa or Aśvaghoṣa, both second-century poets at the court of King Kaniṣka.

86. The text says *sems skye* (mind generation) here, rather than *jang chub kyi sems* (bodhicitta), but the meaning is the same.

87. In this passage, the Buddha contrasts the response of those who merely grieve and lament when a beloved son falls into a pit of filth to one who actually jumps in to save him. The commentary in question is likely that of Asaṅga, the *Uttaratantraśāstravyākhyā*.

88. This is from Śāntideva's *Entering the Bodhisattva Way* 8.99.

89. The five cow substances are urine, dung, butter, milk, and yogurt. According to an oral explanation by Geshe Thubten Soepa, the five cow substances must come from a cow that has lived in remote mountain areas for a certain period of time feeding only on pure grass and herbs.

90. Tsongkhapa is here addressing a claim made by Sakya Paṇḍita and others that there is a distinction between the Madhyamaka (descending from Mañjuśrī via Nāgārjuna and Śāntideva) and Yogācāra (descending from Maitreya via Asaṅga and Candragomin) as to who is qualified to take the bodhisattva precepts and in the vow ceremony itself. Sakya Paṇḍita speaks of a "Madhyamaka tradition of bodhicitta" (*dbu ma lugs kyi sems bskyed*), but Tsongkhapa insists there is no distinction between the two Mahāyāna schools when it comes to bodhicitta. See Sakya Paṇḍita, *Clarifying the Sage's Intent*, 401, and note 46 on that page for relevant Sakya sources on this topic.

91. Such a passage is not found in the sūtra of this name found in the canon. Kamalaśīla was likely referring to a different discourse not translated into Tibetan.

92. On page 192.

93. Śāntideva's *Entering the Bodhisattva Way* 2.9.

94. The four activies (*las bzhi*) of pacifying, increasing, controlling, and destroying gained through tantric practice are used to remove obstacles and hindrances for self and others.

95. The story of the two celestial women in the sky appears in Jinpa, *Mind Training*, 207.

96. Tsongkhapa's commentary is called the *Highway to Enlightenment* (*Byang chub gzhung lam*).

97. These four are, respectively, the products of having practiced the perfections of generosity, ethics, patience, and joyous effort.

98. In other words, the six perfections exhaust the means for securing our own welfare, but to thoroughly secure the welfare of others, more is needed, such as the four ways of gathering disciples.

99. That is, as indicated above, one is not discouraged in the practices of both patience and joyous effort.

100. Natural misdeeds, such as killing and stealing, are negative by nature and thus negative for everybody, whereas proscribed misdeeds are negative only if one has taken a vow to desist from certain behaviors, such as the many proscriptions upheld by monks and nuns.

101. According to Abhidharma, there is a layer of gold underground that serves as a foundation for the earth.

102. The entire verse is "As for the karma that produces cyclic existence, some is heavy, / some is near, some is habitual, / and some you have done earliest. / The first within this list will ripen first."

103. This was discussed above on page 147. For the quote from Bhāviveka, see Tsongkhapa, *Great Treatise*, 1:255.

104. According to the *Ornament for Clear Knowledge*, among the many qualities that result from meditative concentration, there are six types of clairvoyance, eight faculties of mastery over forms and other objects, eight liberations from various realms, and ten faculties of totality, which have control over colors and elements.

105. The *Ornament for Clear Knowledge* (4.27–28) lists the eleven activities that benefit sentient beings: working for beings' benefit, working for their happiness, protecting

them, being a refuge for them, being their place of rest, being their final resort, being an island for them, being a leader, being effortlessly present, not realizing the fruit [as ultimately real], and being a perfect resource. The last three are special activities that allow beings to realize the mind of a buddha.

106. These eight are (1) magic tricks, (2) dreams, (3) mirages, (4) mirror reflections, (5) shadows, (6) echoes, (7) reflections in water, and (8) emanations.

107. That is, a practitioner distills the words of scripture to a single word or impression and focuses on that in meditation, e.g., "impermanence." See Tsongkhapa, *Great Treatise*, 3:17 and note 15.

108. The implication here is that analytical meditation generates a level of pliancy exceeding that of śamatha, which, however, does not come about without the latter. Cf. Wallace, *Bridge of Quiescence*, 125.

109. In *Ornament of Mahāyāna Sūtras* 16.14. This was cited above on page 246.

110. The śamatha in the preliminary stage is the culmination of the ninefold practice of single-pointed concentration in the desire realm. It is a precondition for entering the first of the four meditative stabilizations (*dhyāna*), the form-realm concentrations. As Tsongkhapa goes on to say, the first of these four is induced by a direct realization of the four noble truths, which takes place during the meditative equipoise that signals the onset of the path of seeing. After traversing through these four dhyānas, the meditator progresses to the four formless-realm meditative attainments (*samāpatti*).

111. These are the four cited from the *Unraveling the Intent Sūtra* and discussed at the beginning of the chapter: differentiation, thorough differentiation, investigation, and analysis.

112. According to note 51 in Tsongkhapa, *Great Treatise*, 3:396, the thirteen are (1) the chief prerequisites—i.e., familiarity with the teaching and inner discipline and, additionally, (2) excellence of one's own aims, (3) excellence of others' aims, (4) desire for the teaching, (5) renunciation, (6) vows of ethical discipline, (7) restraint of the senses, (8) moderation in eating, (9) the practice of wakefulness, (10) dwelling vigilantly, (11) solitude, (12) cleansing of obscurations, and (13) proper basis of concentration.

113. These are presented at the end of this chapter.

114. The sixteen aspects of the four noble truths are (regarding the truth of suffering) impermanence, suffering, emptiness, selflessness, (regarding the truth of the origin) origination, production, cause, conditions, (regarding the truth of cessation) cessation, serenity, subliminity, deliverance, and (regarding the truth of the path) path, correctness, achievement, and release.

115. As Tsongkhapa just enumerated above when explaining the five objects that purify conduct.

116. Yeshé Dé (eighth–ninth century) was one of the chief translators in the early imperial effort to translate the Buddhist canon into Tibetan. A student of Padmasambhava, he was also in the transmission line of the *Compendium of Abhidharma* dating back to Asaṅga.

117. That is, the first and second stages of śamatha. Cf. below, "The actual stages of mental abiding that arise."

118. The process of developing śamatha is divided up into nine stages associated with four types of attention. The first two stages, known as *placement* and *continuous placement*, are associated with the attention of tight engagement mentioned here. See page 315 below.

119. The Tibetan term *chu tshod*, translated here as "twenty-four minutes," is a unit of traditional Indian time measurement and used in the Abhidharma. It is equivalent to one sixtieth of a day—i.e., twenty-four minutes. What is translated here as "an hour and a half" (Tib. *thun phyed*) is literally "half a night watch," while "three hours" (Tib. *thun gcig*) is literally "one night watch," a common measure for a full meditation session.

120. This does not mean distraction is a totally pure state without any mental affliction but rather that, because there are also wholesome varieties, it is not necessarily included among the twenty secondary afflictions (from oral explanation by Geshe Thubten Soepa).

121. Geshe Thubten Soepa explains that a neutral obstruction is not nonvirtuous, but it is nevertheless a mental affliction. Another example of such a neutral mental affliction is attachment in beings in fortunate rebirths. It also belongs to the afflictive obscurations, but it is not classified as unwholesome.

122. Among the eight antidotes, "the basis" corresponds to aspiration, "that which it is based on" is effort, "the cause" is faith, and "the effect" is pliancy. These two lines are also explained above in the section "What to do before focusing the mind on the object."

123. That is, the "vehicle of characteristics" (Tib. *mtshan nyid theg*), indicating the approach of the nontantric teachings.

124. Unless identified otherwise, all the following quotations are taken from *Ornament for the Mahāyāna Sūtras* 14.11–14.

125. The states of equipoise are the four meditative stabilizations of the form realm and the four of the formless realm. As Tsongkhapa introduced briefly on page 319 above and elaborates here, whereas the attainment of śamatha is generally what launches one into the form-realm stabilizations, śamatha without complete pliancy—the similitude of śamatha—remains in the desire realm.

126. Negative mental tendencies and the development of the antidote are in direct opposition to each other: the more you have of one, the less the other will be present. Otherwise the obvious question would be why the antidote develops if you are already rid of negative states. The relationship should rather be understood in these terms: at the point where the negative states have come to an end, the antidote is fully developed. According to Geshe Thubten Soepa, they are "like hot and cold. One comes as the other one goes away."

127. A so-called mundane special insight, not exclusive to Buddhism, that consists in comparing the variety of samsaric states, seeing the courseness of the lower ones and the relative peacefulness of the higher ones (cf. p. 328 below).

128. Geshe Thubten Soepa explains that in this context "pure" means that the path has transcended the desire realm.

129. The Tibetan text has a different sentence order, so these indicators have been modified to match the English translation.

130. The "three signs and so forth" here is the becoming free from signs, free from conceptualization, and absolutely calm in the quote above.

131. Geshe Thubten Soepa explains that at this point, a given meditation does not need to have this view as its main object to remain linked with this view; it derives its particular taste from the view.

132. A mundane path is one that does not liberate from cyclic existence. "Nothingness" refers to the third of the four formless-realm meditative attainments (*samāpatti*).

They are called, in succession, infinite space, infinite consciousness, nothingness, and neither perception nor nonperception. The names of these attainments are both the object of meditative equipoise of the being in that realm and the name of the realm itself.

133. Selflessness is one of the sixeen aspects of the four noble truths enumerated in note 114 above.

134. One out of six attentions taught in the context of the access stage to the first meditative stabilization. See note 135.

135. Those six attentions are not equivalent to the four attentions described above. Rather, they are another set of attentions associated with special contemplations that Jé Tsongkhapa does not elaborate on here: (1) attention that knows the characteristics, (2) attention of firm resolution, (3) attention of solitude, (4) attention of withdrawing from sense pleasures, (5) attention of investigation, and (6) attention intent on final application. For a detailed account, see the explanation by Lati Rinpoche in Zahler et al., *Meditative States*, 85–102.

136. The three levels are underground, above ground, and on the ground.

137. These two philosophical positions will be taken up when the divisions of ultimate truths are presented on pages 398–402 below.

138. Ngok Loden Sherab (1059–1109), an early Kadampa master and the founder of Sangphu Monastery, was often known by his moniker Lochen, or "great translator." The scholastic tradition there with its rigorous philosophical approach set the stage for later masters like Tsongkhapa.

139. The system of Consciousness Only (Tib. *rnam rig [tsam]*, Skt. *vijñāpti[mātra]*), like Yogācāra, is a synonym for Cittamātra (Tib. *sems tsam*), the philosophical school of Mind Only, so called because its proponents maintain that all phenomena are of the same nature as the mind cognizing them.

140. "The land of snowy mountains" is an epithet for Tibet. Traditional Tibetan history divides the period of dissemination and translation of scripture and exegesis, court patronage of Indian monastic scholars, and compilation of Buddhist canons from India to Tibet into two parts: the early and later propagations. The early propagation begins with the conversion of Emperor Songtsen Gampo in the seventh century, and the later propagation begins with the patronage of Buddhism by the ruler Yeshe Ö in the eleventh century. This division into Svātantrika and Prāsaṅgika is thought to have originated with Patsab Lotsāwa (b. 1055), a Kadampa exegete of Sangphu Monastery whose translations of Candrakīrti's philosophical works are contained in the Tibetan canon.

141. The Tibetan word translated here as "superimposition" (Tib. *sgro 'dogs*) literally means "attach feathers." It is also rendered as "imputation" or "exaggeration."

142. Tsongkhapa is referring to verse 126 of chapter 6 of Candrakīrti's text. The Saṃmatīyas were an Indian Buddhist sect widespread at the time of Candrakīrti that appeared to assert a self or person. They are closely related to the Vātsīputrīya.

143. Skt. *satkāyadṛṣṭi*. Geshe Thubten Soepa explains that according to the Prāsaṅgika system, although the view of the transitory collection consists in regarding one's aggregates as self or as possessions of the self, the aggregates themselves are not its observed object. The statement that this view is directed at the aggregates should be understood as a gloss of the term *view of the transitory collection* and not as an identification of its observed object, which is instead a self.

144. Tsongkhapa addresses this in his commentary on Candrakīrti's *Entering the Middle Way*. See *Illuminating the Intent*, 421–23.

145. The Tibetan expression *nga yi ba nyid* literally means "mine-ness."

146. Cf. *Illuminating the Intent*, 186, where Tsongkhapa gives the same explanation, and the relevant note 344 by Thupten Jinpa, which says, "Tsongkhapa is here making an important psychological point concerning how our innate identity-view operates. He states that while our psychophysical aggregates as well as our personal possessions are instances of what we call 'mine'—my body, my mind, my house, and so on—when identity view in the form of the thought 'mine' occurs, it is in fact the notion of 'mine' itself that is the object of our innate grasping, not the specific objects that serve as the basis for the arising of that thought 'mine.'"

147. For particles to be truly partless, it must be impossible to divide them up into any portions at all, including front and back sides, or eastern and western sides. The same holds true for partless moments in the following line; if they were truly partless, they could not be divided into an earlier part of the moment and a later part.

148. Tsongkhapa cited these first two lines above on page 338.

149. Tsongkhapa cites the full stanza below on page 345.

150. This means that the apprehension of a self of persons is the cause and the apprehension of a self of phenomena is its effect.

151. This same discussion appears in Tsongkhapa, *Illuminating the Intent*, 422–23.

152. The full stanza was also cited above on page 338.

153. Cf. verse 6.11 on page 338 above.

154. Tsongkhapa quotes these same verses in *Illuminating the Intent*, 444–45. Though the source sūtra is not in the Tibetan canon, Vasubandhu quotes the verses in chapter 9 of his *Treasury of Abhidharma Autocommentary*, and parallel verses appear in the Pali *Saṃyutta-nikāya* I.5.10.

155. This is because one can neither say that it consists in the aggregates at a given point of time nor at an earlier or later point. Where else in the continuum would it be found?

156. This is a paraphrase of a line from a sūtra quoted but not identified in Candrakīrti's *Entering the Middle Way*.

157. In other words, the self is not conventionally existent in that an *inherently existent* person does not exist even conventionally, let alone ultimately. However, the mere I, which is a dependent arising, does exist conventionally.

158. In order to get a real sense of this manner by which we apprehend our own selves, the teachings suggest imagining one is unjustly blamed for something. One then observes the sense of "I" that emerges, which is considered a particularly tangible apprehension of "I."

159. "Inherently" (Tib. *rang bzhin gyis*), "by its intrinsic nature" (Tib. *ngo bo nyid kyis*, also rendered as "essentially"), and "through its intrinsic characteristics" (Tib. *rang gi mtshan nyid kyis*) are used synonymously here.

160. Since it is *conventional* disintegration, which is dependently arisen rather than inherently existent, there is the possibility for both transformation and continuity across moments of a single mental continuum.

161. Jé Tsongkhapa is giving two common examples for uncompounded phenomena: the flower in the sky for something nonexistent and nirvāṇa for a conventionally existent phenomenon. This syllogism is a paraphrase of Candrakīrti's *Clear Words*.

162. Gandharvas are deities from the ancient Indian Vedic scriptures who reveal celestial

secrets and prepare the divine potion *soma*. In the Tibetan tradition, they are treated as a type of spirit.

163. This is an epithet for the Perfection of Wisdom Sūtras.

164. "Vague appearances" (*snang ba ban bun*) is a post-meditative experience of things appearing as evanescent and indistinct. This is not necessarily a negative experience, but Tsongkhapa is stressing that such a dissolution of solidity and demarcation is not a realization of emptiness.

165. See page 349 above.

166. The logical proof is dependent arising; the thesis is "There is no self that inherently exists."

167. These four are origination from self, from other, from both, or from neither—i.e., without cause.

168. This occurs in a passage in chapter 1 where Vasubandhu gives thirteen examples of words whose meaning in the sūtras differs depending on the context, illustrating that it is easy to misread the sūtras if one has not heard many teachings.

169. In Tibetan like in many other languages such as Spanish, a distinction is made between "to be" in assignments of temporary characteristics (e.g., "to be happy," "*estar* feliz," *yin*) and "to be" as an existential verb (e.g., "to be or not to be," "*ser* o no ser," *yod*). However, in this particular case where the two are combined to make *yod pa yin* ("to be existent") as opposed to *yod pa* ("to exist"), there is no difference in meaning.

170. Cessations are not compounded phenomena because they consist in the absence of something. An analytical cessation is the freedom from mental afflictions that arises through methods such as investigation and meditation. A nonanalytical cessation is the mere discontinuation of something and is not free of the afflictions.

171. *Bral rgyu* and *bral 'bras*, that which causes separation from the afflictions and the fruits of that separation.

172. According to Geshe Thubten Soepa, in the case of a non-product, one investigates in detail whether it is the same as or different from its definition and definiendum, from its basis of designation and imputed phenomenon, from its essence and its characteristics, and so forth.

173. There is an important distinction here between "intrinsic nature" (something that does indeed exist conventionally) and "inherently existent nature" (something that is not possible even conventionally according to the Madhyamaka position).

174. Nāgārjuna's *Root Text on Wisdom* 7.33, quoted above.

175. The term *nirvāṇa* is used here as explained on page 377 below.

176. A functioning thing, something capable of performing a function, is by definition also impermanent and a product. So here this means that either of the two is a non-product, a permanent phenomenon.

177. Tib. *bdag gcig*, "same nature," and *ngo bo gcig*, "one entity," are synonyms in this context.

178. Everything that exists has its intrinsic nature; however, none subsists only through its intrinsic nature. In that respect the statement does not contradict the argument presented in the previous paragraphs as it does not refer to a nature that is self-established independently of anything else.

179. This does not refer to a conceptional consciousnesses only. Direct knowledge of suchness may also be called a "reasoning consciousness" (*rigs shes*), presumably because such knowledge is also based on reasoning, having arisen from logical investigation.

(Tibetan-Sanskrit-English Dictionary, A project of the Tibetan Studies Institute, Boonesville, Virginia, and the University of Virginia Tibetan Studies Program, © Jeffrey Hopkins, 1992). Cf. page 399 below.

180. The Svātantrika-Mādhyamikas assert that all phenomena exist conventionally, but not ultimately, through their *intrinsic characteristics* (*svalakṣaṇa*; Tib. *rang gi mtshan nyid*). It is important to understand that the same term has different usages in the context of Abhidharma and epistemology, where it is not connected to the discourse on the nature of the ultimate. It can mean a thing's *defining characteristics*, as, say, heat is a defining characteristic of fire. Or it can refer to Dharmakīrti's presentation of *unique particulars* as opposed to general properties. Here in his critique of Svātantrika, however, Tsongkhapa takes it to be a fixed, definitive essence of an object, one that he equates with *svabhāva* (Tib. *rang bzhin*), or inherent existence. Svātantrikas themselves reject inherent existence but distinguish that from existing conventionally by way of intrinsic characteristics. Cf. Thupten Jinpa's introduction to Tsongkhapa, *Illuminating the Intent*, 20–21.

181. This is a departure from the foregoing and an exception in that here, bad tenets are a source of deception that is not detected as wrong by one's everyday experience.

182. In other words, a buddha can still perceive duality, despite having eliminated distorted perception. The topic is taken up on page 396 below. It is explained in detail in Tsongkhapa's *Illuminating the Intent*, his commentary on Candrakīrti's *Entering the Middle Way*. There it says (p. 250), "Since an indirect knowing—knowing but not directly perceiving it—cannot be posited in relation to a buddha, conventional realities must be known by a buddha on the basis of directly perceiving them. So within the perspective of a buddha's gnosis perceiving things in their diversity, the buddha perceives conventional realities in a manner where the subject and its object do appear as distinct." Cf. Newland, *Two Truths*, 199.

183. "Without relying on conventions, the ultimate cannot be taught" (Nāgārjuna, *Root Text on Wisdom*, 24.10).

184. In other words, the third noble truth of cessation, or nirvāṇa, is an ultimate truth, whereas the three remaining truths are conventional.

185. The four qualities of the aggregates are impermanence, suffering, impurity, and selflessness.

186. In other words, nothing whatsoever exists inherently, but conventionally we can speak of the mere existence and nonexistence of things.

187. Tsongkhapa elaborates on this same objection with a similar discussion in *Illuminating the Intent*, 251–54.

188. This line, and variations of it, appears in several texts in both the Kangyur and Tengyur, including the *Compendium of the Teachings Sūtra*, which Bhāviveka cites in his *Blaze of Reasoning*.

189. In such sūtras as the *Dependent Arising Sūtra* (*Pratītyasamutpādasūtra*).

190. According to an explanation by Geshe Thubten Soepa, "without touching" (Tib. *ma reg par*) should be understood metaphorically, "the way you can take an egg from underneath a brooding hen without touching her."

191. The expression is taken up from a statement by Candrakīrti above that at the level of buddhahood, the movement of the mind and mental factors has permanently stopped. See page 392.

192. Geshe Thubten Soepa explains this passage as meaning "*How* is it manifested?

Through wisdom. *Who* manifests it? The sambhogakāya. That is a description of realization and embodiment at the time of buddhahood."

193. See note 182.

194. The "ground" (*gzhi*) here is the ground in the context of the threefold presentation of ground, path, and result.

195. Tib. *gzhi mthun mong ba*, literally "sharing a common locus."

196. Candrakīrti derives the sixteenfold and fourfold enumerations from the *Perfection of Wisdom Sūtra in Twenty-Five Thousand Lines.* Cf. Tsongkhapa, *Illuminating the Intent,* 487–513.

197. In, for instance, the quote from *Illumination of the Middle Way* on page 398 above.

198. Geshe Thubten Soepa explains that according to the Tibetan theory of debate, the question as to whether something is a reason, or a logical sign, also depends on whether it is suited to the opponent—i.e., whether, given his or her level of understanding, the argument may bring about fresh insight. In the former case the reason is given prematurely, since the person is lacking certain conditions that would make it meaningful and thus worthwhile. In the latter case the reason is given too late to spur new realizations.

199. In the syllogism "Sprouts and the like appear to lack true existence because they appear to be free from being one or many," the predicate is "appear to lack true existence."

200. Affirming negations are negations that do not just negate something but also imply or affirmatively establish something else. Geshe Thubten Soepa explains this as an example of a correct reason according to the Prāsaṅgika Madhyamaka system: "The subject, a sprout, is without true existence because it is free from being one or many." In contrast, the reason advanced as part of the position criticized here is "The subject, a sprout, appears to be without true existence because it appears to be free from being one or many." This is not a mere negation because of the manner of appearing. The exponents of complete nonabiding mentioned in the next section also accept an understanding that is tied up with appearances and that does not realize a mere negation.

201. See *Great Treatise,* 3:115–16. Tsongkhapa is stating that no great Madhyamaka master, including Śāntarakṣita and Haribhadra, would assert that emptiness is simply the object of inferential cognition—namely, the mere elimination of elaboration.

202. The "also" here is a word from Jñānagarbha's root verses.

203. Contrary to our common understanding of *conceptuality,* the Tibetan equivalent *rtog pa* is not restricted to conscious thought but also refers to unconscious mental construction. It includes any meaning that the mind imputes on its object and that a conventional consciousness would then take to be present in the object by its intrinsic nature.

204. Inconceivable natures are things or events that appear supernatural, including the Buddha's miraculous powers. An odd stock example of an inconceivable nature that comes from Indian tradition is that of a pigeon landing on a thatch roof and leaving an imprint on yogurt inside the house below. Abiding natures include a phenomenon's lack of inherent existence.

205. See pages 317–18 above, where the nine stages of śamatha were grouped into four levels of attention.

206. See note 127 above.

207. Tsongkhapa says only "and so on" here after the first two lines. The rest has been supplied for the convenience of the reader.
208. Geshe Thubten Soepa explains this as practitioners of completion stage yoga who can cause their energies to enter the central channel.
209. See page 395 above.
210. The absorption of nonperception (*asaṃjñisamāpatti*) is a state in the fourth level of the formless realm wherein beings only have mental activity at the times of birth and death and are otherwise unconscious. Vasubandhu discusses this at *Treasury of Abhidharma* 2.42.
211. *Be'u bum*—that is, the *Blue Compendium*, Dölpa's record of the lamrim teachings of Potowa. Geshe Thubten Soepa explains that a *be'u bum* is a round container that Tibetan Buddhist practitioners use to stow and transport texts as well as other precious items.
212. See pages 45–50 above.
213. See pages 32–35 above.
214. Geshe Thubten Soepa explains an inferior empowerment as one in which either the one giving it or the one receiving it does not meet all the necessary requirements.
215. That is, both the Perfection Vehicle and the Vajra Vehicle.
216. In these first three stanzas, Tsongkhapa is praising the virtues of Atiśa's lamrim tradition.

Bibliography

P The Peking edition of the Tibetan canon of Buddhist scriptures (Kangyur) and classical treatises (Tengyur). The Tengyur works listed below generally include an author name; the Kangyur works do not.

Sūtras, Tantras, and Indian Treatises

Abhidharma Sūtra. Abhidharmasūtra. This work is not extant.

Advice to the King Sūtra. Rājāvavādakasūtra. P887.

Application of Mindfulness Sūtra. Saddharmasmṛtyupasthānasūtra. P953.

Array of Qualities in Mañjuśrī's Buddhafield. Mañjuśrībuddhakṣetraguṇavyūha. P760.15.

Aspiration in Seventy Verses. Praṇidhānasaptati. Parahitaghoṣa Āraṇyaka. P5430 and P5936.

Blaze of Reasoning. Tarkajvālā. Bhāviveka. P5256.

Bodhisattva Levels. Bodhisattvabhūmi. Asaṅga, P5538.

Bodhisattva Prātimokṣa. Bodhisattvaprātimokṣa. P914.

Chapters of Scriptural Transmission. Āgamavastu. Refers here to the *Chapters on Finer Points of the Vinaya,* which preserves many stories from the early scriptures.

Chapters on Finer Points of the Vinaya. Vinayakṣudrakavastu. P1035.

Chapters on the Vinaya. Vinayavastu. P1030.

Clear Words. Prasannapadā. Candrakīrti. P5260.

Cloud of Jewels of Sūtra. Ratnameghasūtra. P897.

Collection of Indicative Verses. Udānavarga. P992.

Commentary on Compendium of Valid Cognition. Pramāṇavārttika. Dharmakīrti. P5709.

Commentary on Difficult Points of Kṛṣṇayamāri. Kṛṣṇayamāripañjikā. Ratnākaraśānti, P2782.

Commentary on Difficult Points of Lamp for the Path. Bodhimārgapradīpapañjikā. Atiśa. P5344.

Commentary on Four Hundred Stanzas. Catuḥśatakaṭīkā. Candrakīrti. P5266.

Commentary on Letter to a Friend. Vyaktapadāsuhṛllekaṭīkā. Mahāmati. P5690.

Commentary on Ornament for the Mahāyāna Sūtras. Mahāyānasūtrālaṃkāra-bhāṣya. Vasubandhu. P5527.

Commentary on the Perfection of Wisdom in Eight Thousand Lines. Aṣṭasāhasri-kāprajñāpāramitāvyākhyāna-Abhisamayālaṃkārāloka. Haribhadra, P5189.

Commentary on Sixty Stanzas of Reasoning. Yuktiṣaṣṭikāvṛtti. Candrakīrti. P5265.

Commentary on Thirty Verses. Triṃśikābhāṣya. Sthiramati. P5565.

Commentary on the Vinaya Sūtra. Vinayasūtraṭīkā. Dharmamitra. P5622.

Compendium of Abhidharma. Abhidharmasamuccaya. Asaṅga. P5550.

Compendium of Ascertainments. Viniścayasaṃgrahaṇī. Asaṅga. P5539.

Compendium of the Perfections. Pāramitāsamāsa. Āryaśūra. P5340.

Compendium of the Sūtras. Sūtrasamuccaya. Nāgārjuna. P5330.

Compendium of the Teachings Sūtra. Dharmasaṅgītisūtra. P904.

Compendium of Trainings. Śikṣāsamuccaya. Śāntideva. P5336.

Compendium of Trainings in Verse. Śikṣāsamuccayakārikā. Śāntideva. P5335.

Concentration Definitely Showing Suchness. Tattvanirdeśasamādhi. A sūtra quoted in the *Compendium of Trainings.* Not extant.

Concise Method for Accomplishing the Mahāyāna Path. Mahāyānapathasādhana varṇasaṃgraha. Atiśa. P5351 (and P5392).

Dependent Arising Sūtra. Pratītyasamutpādasūtra. P878.

Descent into the Womb Sūtra. Garbhāvakrāntisūtra. P760.14.

Descent to Laṅkā Sūtra. Laṅkāvatārasūtra. P775.

Dhāraṇī of Entering Nonperception. Avikalpapraveśadhāraṇī. P810.

Dhāraṇī of the Goddess Cunda. Cundadevīdhāraṇī. P188.

Discourse Explaining Seven Qualities. Saptaguṇaparivarṇanānākathā. Vasubandhu. P5663.

Discourse on the Collections. Sambhāraparikathā. Vasubandhu. P5422 (and P5666).

Discourse on the Eight Unfree States. Aṣṭākṣaṇakathā. Aśvaghoṣa. P5423 (and P5667).

Distinguishing the Middle from the Extremes. Madhyāntavibhāga. Maitreya. P5522.

Distinguishing the Two Truths. Satyadvayavibaṅgha. Jñānagarbha. Dergé 3881 (not in Peking Tengyur).

Distinguishing the Two Truths Autocommentary. Satyadvayāvibaṅghavṛtti. Jñānagarbha. Dergé 3882 (not in Peking Tengyur).

Drop of Reasoning. Nyāyabindu. Dharmakīrti. P5711.

Engaging in the Two Truths Sūtra. Saṃvṛtiparamārthasatyanirdeśasūtra. P846.

Entering the Bodhisattva Way. Bodhicaryāvatāra. Śāntideva. P5272.

Entering the Middle Way. Madhyamakāvatāra. Candrakīrti. P5262.

Entering the Middle Way Autocommentary. Madhyamakāvatārabhāṣya. Candrakīrti. P5263.

Entering the Two Truths. Satyadvayāvatāra. Atiśa. P5380 (and P5298).

Essay on the Mind of Enlightenment. Bodhicittavivaraṇa. Nāgārjuna. P2666.

Essence of the Middle Way. Madhyamakahṛdaya. Bhāviveka. P5255.

Essence of the Perfection of Wisdom (Heart Sūtra). Prajñāpāramitāhṛdaya. P160, vol 6.

Exegesis of the Vinaya. Vinayavibaṅgha. P1032.

Exhortation to the Extraordinary Attitude. Adhyāśayasaṃcodanasūtra. P760.25.

Explanation of Distinguishing the Middle from the Extremes. Madhyānta-vibhāgaṭīkā. Sthiramati, P5528.

Explanation of Entering the Middle Way. Madhyamakāvatāraṭīkā. Jayānanda. P5271.

Explanation of the Five Aggregates. Pañcaskandhaprakaraṇa. Vasubandhu, P5560.

Fifty Verses on the Guru. Gurupañcāśikā. Aśvaghoṣa. P4544.

Four Hundred Stanzas. Catuḥśataka. Āryadeva. P5246.

Fundamental Treatise on the Middle Way / Root Text on Wisdom. Mūlamadhya-makakārikā. Nāgārjuna, P5224.

Garland of Birth Stories. Jātakamālā. P5650.

Gathering All the Threads Sūtra. Sarvavaidalyasaṃgrahasūtra. P893.

Gayāśīrṣa Hill Sūtra. Gayāśīrṣasūtra. P777.

Golden Light Sūtra. Suvarṇaprabāsasūtra. P176.

Good Eon Sūtra. Bhadrakalpikasūtra. P762.

Great Detailed Explanation. Mahāvibhāṣā.

Great Final Nirvāṇa Sūtra. Mahāparinirvāṇasūtra. P787.

Guhyasamāja Tantra. Guhyasamājatantra. P28.

Heap of Jewels Sūtra. Ratnarāśisūtra. P760.45

Heart Summary. Hṛdayanikṣepa. Atiśa. P5346 (and P5383).

Hundred Verses on Wisdom. Prajñāśataka. Nāgārjuna. P5820.

Illumination of the Middle Way. Madhyamakāloka. Kamalaśīla. P5287.

Instructions on the Perfection of Wisdom. Prajñāpāramitopadeśa. Ratnākaraśānti. P5579.

Jewels' Blaze Dhāraṇī. Ratnolkādhāraṇī. P472.

Kāśyapa Chapter. Kāśyapaparivarta. P760.43.

King of Concentrations Sūtra. Samādhirājasūtra. P795.

Kṣitigarbha Sūtra. Kṣitigarbhasūtra. P905.

Lamp for the Path to Enlightenment. Bodhipathapradīpa. Atiśa. P5353.

Lamp That Combines the Practices. Caryāmelāpakapradīpa. Āryadeva. P2668.

Letter to a Friend. Suhṛllekha. Nāgārjuna. P5682.

Letter to a Student. Śiṣyalekha. Candragomin. P5410.

Letter to King Candra. Candrarājalekha. Mitrayogin. P5689.

Levels of Yogic Practice. Yogacaryābhūmi. Asaṅga. P5536–5543. A collection of eight texts, but references to this title typically refer to the first one, *Many Levels (Bahubhūmika)*.

Life of Maitreya. Maitreyavimokṣa. Part of the *Avataṃsaka Sūtra.* P761.

Lotus Sūtra. Saddharmapuṇḍarīkasūtra. P781.

Madhyamaka Instructions. Madhyamakopadeśa. Atiśa. P5324 (and P5326).

Magic of the Complete Certainty of Total Peace Sūtra Praśāntaviniścayaprāti-hāryasūtra. P797.

Many Levels. Bahubhūmika. The first section of *Levels of Yogic Practice.* P5536.

Marvelous Array Sūtra. Gaṇḍavyūhasūtra. P761. Part of the *Avataṃsaka Sūtra.*

Meeting of Father and Son Sūtra. Pitāputrasamāgamasūtra. P760.16.

Mind Generation Ritual. Cittotpādasaṃvaravidhi. Atiśa. P5364 (and P5403).

Moon Lamp Sūtra. Candrapradīpasūtra. AKA *King of Concentrations Sūtra.*

Ornament for Clear Knowledge. Abhisamayālaṃkāra. Maitreya. P5184.

Ornament for the Mahāyāna Sūtras. Mahāyānasūtrālaṃkāra. Maitreya, P5521.

Ornament for the Middle Way. Madhyamakālaṃkāra. Śāntarakṣita. P5282.

Overcoming Faulty Ethical Discipline Sūtra. Duḥśīlanigrahasūtra. P886.

Perfection of Wisdom Sūtra in One Hundred Thousand Lines. Śatasāhasrikāpra-jñāpāramitāsūtra. P730.

Perfection of Wisdom Sūtra in Twenty-Five Thousand Lines. Pañcaviṃśatisāhasri-kāprajñāpāramitāsūtra, P731.

Play of Mañjuśrī Sūtra. Mañjuśrīvikrīḍitasūtra. P764.

Praise in Analogies. Upamastava. A chapter within the *Praise of the One Worthy of Praise.*

Praise in One Hundred and Fifty Verses. Śatapañcaśatakastotra. Mātṛceṭa/Aśva-ghoṣa. P2038.

Praise of Confession. Deśanāstava. Candragomin. P2048.

Praise of Infinite Qualities. Guṇāparyantastotra. Triratnadāsa. P2044.

Praise of the Exalted One. Viśeṣastava. Udbhaṭasiddhasvāmin. P2001.

Praise of the One Worthy of Praise. Varṇāhavarṇestotra. Āryaśūra/Mātṛceṭa. P2029.

Praise of the Sphere of Reality. Dharmadhātustotra. Nāgārjuna. P2010.

Praise of the World-Transcending One. Lokātītastava. Nāgārjuna. P2012.

Praise to the Perfection of Wisdom. Prajñāpāramitāstotra. Nāgārjuna. P2018.

Prātimokṣa Sūtra. Prātimokṣasūtra. P1031.

Prayer of Good Conduct. Bhadracaryāpraṇidhāna. P716, vol 11.

Precious Garland. Ratnāvalī. Nāgārjuna. P5658.

Principles of Exegesis. Vyākhyāyukti. Vasubandhu. P5562.

Questions of a Lion Sūtra. Siṃhaparipṛcchāsūtra. P760.37.

Questions of Brahma Sūtra. Brahmaparipṛcchāsūtra. P825.

Questions of Householder Ugra Sūtra. Gṛhapatyugraparipṛcchā. P760.19.

Questions of King Dhāraṇīśvara Sūtra. Dhāraṇīśvararājaparipṛcchāsūtra. P814.

Questions of Ratnacūḍa Sūtra. Ratnacūḍaparipṛcchāsūtra. P760.47.

Questions of Revata Sūtra. Sūtra is no longer extant but is quoted by Asaṅga in the *Śrāvaka Levels.*

Questions of Sāgaramati Sūtra. Sāgaramatiparipṛcchāsūtra. P819.

Questions of Subāhu Tantra. Subāhuparipṛcchātantra. P428.

Questions of the Daughter Candrottara Sūtra. Candrottaradārikāparipṛcchāsūtra. P858.

Questions of the Householder Vīradatta Sūtra. Vīradattagṛhapatiparipṛcchāsūtra. P760.28.

Questions of the Nāga King Anavatapta Sūtra. Anavataptanāgarājaparipṛcchāsūtra. P823.

Questions of the Nāga King Sāgara Sūtra. Sāgaranāgarājaparipṛcchāsūtra. P820.

Questions of Upāli Sūtra. Upāliparipṛcchāsūtra. P760.24.

Refuting Objections. Vigrahavyāvartanī. Nāgārjuna. P5228.

Root Tantra of Mañjuśrī. Mañjuśrīmūlatantra. P162.

Root Text on Wisdom. See *Fundamental Treatise on the Middle Way.*

Satyaka Chapter. Satyakaparivarta. Otherwise known as the *Range of the Bodhisattva Sūtra (Bodhisattvagocaropāyaviṣayavikurvāṇanirdeśasūtra),* P813.

Seal Enhancing the Power of Faith Sūtra. Śraddhābalādhānāvatāramudrāsūtra. P867.

Seal of Engaging in Certain and Uncertain Destinies Sūtra. Niyatāniyatamudrāvatārasūtra. P868.

Seventy Stanzas on Emptiness. Śūnyatāsaptati. Nāgārjuna. P5227.

Seventy Verses on Going for Refuge. Triśaraṇasaptati. Candrakīrti. P5478.

Six Aspects of Going for Refuge. Ṣaḍaṅgaśaraṇa. Vimalamitra. P5367.

Sixty Stanzas of Reasoning. Yuktiṣaṣṭikā. Nāgārjuna. P5225.

Śrāvaka Levels. Śrāvakabhūmi. Asaṅga. P5537.

Stages of Meditation (3 works sharing the same title). *Bhāvanākrama.* Kamalaśīla. P5310–P5312. Pd Tengyur 62–64.

Story of Saṅgharakṣita. Saṅgharakṣitāvadāna. Included in the *Chapters on the Vinaya,* P1030 (*khe,* folios 99–114).

Sublime Continuum. Uttaratantra. Maitreya. P5525.

Sun Essence Sūtra. Sūryagarbhasūtra. P923, vol 36.

Sūtra of Cultivating Faith in the Mahāyāna. Mahāyānaprasādaprabhāvanāsūtra. P812.

Sūtra of Extensive Play. Lalitavistarasūtra. P763.

Sūtra of the Wise and the Foolish. Damamūkasūtra. P1008.

Sūtra on Cherishing Monks. Bhikṣuparejusūtra. P968.

Sūtra on the Concentration That Perceives the Buddha of the Present Face to Face. *Pratyutpannabuddhasaṃmukhāvasthitasamādhisūtra.* P801.
Sūtra Teaching the Tathāgata's Inconceivable Secret. Tathāgatācintyaguhyanirdeśa-sūtra. P760.3.
Tantra Bestowing the Initiation of Vajrapāṇi. Vajrapāṇyabhiṣekamahātantra. P130.
Tathāgata's Secrets Sūtra. Tathāgataguhyakasūtra. See *Sūtra Teaching the Tathā-gata's Inconceivable Secret.*
Teaching of Vimalakīrti. Vimalakīrtinirdeśasūtra. P843.
Teachings of Akṣayamati Sūtra. Akṣayamatinirdeśasūtra. P842. vol. 34.
Ten Dharmas Sūtra. Daśadharmakasūtra. P760.9.
Ten Grounds Sūtra. Daśabhūmikasūtra. P761.
Three Heaps Sūtra. Triskandhakasūtra. P950.
Treasury of Abhidharma. Abhidharmakośa. Vasubandhu. P5590. Pd Tengyur 79.
Treasury of Abhidharma Autocommentary. Abhidharmakośabhāṣya. Vasubandhu. P5591.
Unraveling the Intent Sūtra. Saṃdhinirmocanasūtra. P774.
Vairocana's Manifest Enlightenment. Vairocanābhisaṃbodhi. P126.
Vajra Peak Tantra. Vajraśikharatantra. P113. Pd Kangyur 84.
Verse Summary of the Perfection of Wisdom. Prajñāpāramitāsañcayagāthā. P735.
Verses about Listening. Śrutivarga. This is chapter 22 of the *Collection of Indicative Verses.*
Vinaya Sūtra. Vinayasūtra. Guṇaprabha. P5619.

Tibetan Works

Dölpa, Geshe. *The Blue Compendium. Be'u bum sngon po.* Translated by Ulrike Roesler in *Stages of the Buddha's Teachings.* The Library of Tibetan Classics 10. Boston: Wisdom Publications, 2015.
Drolungpa Lodrö Jungné. *Great Treatise on the Stages of the Teaching. Bstan rim chen mo.*
Je Yabse Sungbum (The Collected Works of Jé Rinpoche [Tsongkhapa] and His Two Disciples). Mundgod: Drepung Loseling Pethub Kangtsen, 2019.
Lha Drigangpa. *Commentary on the Blue Compendium. Be'u bum sngon po'i 'grel pa.*
Naktso Lotsāwa Tsultrim Gyalwa. *Eighty Stanzas of Praise [of Atiśa]. Bstod pa brgya bcu pa.*
Sakya Paṇḍita. *Clarifying the Sage's Intent. Thub pa'i dgongs pa rab tu gsal ba.* Translated by David Jackson in *Stages of the Buddha's Teachings.* The Library of Tibetan Classics 10. Boston: Wisdom Publications, 2015.
Tsongkhapa. *Great Treatise on the Stages of Mantra. Sngags rim chem mo.*

Tsongkhapa. *Great Treatise on the Stages of the Path to Enlightenment. Lam rim chen mo.* Translated by the Lamrim Chenmo Translation Committee in three volumes. Ithaca, NY: Snow Lion Publications, 2000, 2002, and 2004.

Tsongkhapa. *Highway to Enlightenment: An Exposition of Bodhisattva Ethics. Byang chub sems dpa'i tshul khrims kyi rnam bshad byang chub gzhung lam.* Translated by Mark Tatz in *Asaṅga's Chapter on Ethics with the Commentary of Tsong-Kha-Pa: The Basic Path to Awakening, the Complete Bodhisattva.* Lewiston, NY: Edwin Mellen Press, 1986.

Tsongkhapa. *Illuminating the Intent. Dgongs pa rab gsal.* Translated by Thupten Jinpa in *Illuminating the Intent: An Exposition of Candrakīrti's Entering the Middle Way.* The Library of Tibetan Classics 19. Boston: Wisdom Publications, 2020.

OTHER WORKS

Hopkins, Jeffrey. *Tsong-kha-pa's Final Exposition of Wisdom.* Ithaca, NY: Snow Lion Publications, 2008.

Jinpa, Thupten, trans. *Mind Training: The Great Collection.* The Library of Tibetan Classics 1. Boston: Wisdom Publications, 2006.

Jinpa, Thupten. *Tsongkhapa: A Buddha in the Land of Snows.* Boulder, CO: Shambhala Publications, 2019.

Krause, Cornelia, trans. *Der Mittlere Stufenweg (Lam rim 'bring ba) von Dsche Tsongkhapa.* Munich: Diamant Verlag, 2007.

Newland, Guy. *The Two Truths.* Ithaca, NY: Snow Lion Publications, 1992.

Rotman, Andy, trans. *Divine Stories: Divyāvadāna, Part 1.* Boston: Wisdom Publications, 2008.

Rotman, Andy, trans. *Divine Stories: Divyāvadāna, Part 2.* Somerville, MA: Wisdom Publications, 2017.

Sopa, Geshe Lhundub, et al. *Steps on the Path to Enlightenment: A Commentary on Tsongkhapa's Lamrim Chenmo,* 5 vols. Boston: Wisdom Publications, 2004, 2005, 2008, 2015, and 2017.

Thuman, Robert A. F., ed. *The Life and Teachings of Tsongkhapa.* Somerville, MA: Wisdom Publications, 2018.

Wallace, B. Alan. *The Bridge of Quiescence: Experiencing Tibetan Buddhist Meditation.* Chicago: Open Court, 1998.

Wayman, Alex. *Ethics of Tibet: Bodhisattva Section of Tsong-Kha-Pa's Lam rim chen mo.* Albany: State University of New York Press, 1991.

Zahler, Leah, et al. *Meditative States in Tibetan Buddhism.* Boston: Wisdom Publications, 1997.

Index

Root Tantra of Mañjuśrī (*Mañjuśrīmūlatantra*), 182
on Vajrayāna, 425
Root Text on Wisdom, 347–48
on dependent arising, 368–69, 370
on selflessness of persons, 354–55,
356–57
on selflessness of phenomena, 374
See also *Fundamental Treatise on the
Middle Way*

S
Sadāprarudita, 43
Sakya Paṇḍita, 434n90
śamatha, 9, 16, 33, 52, 55, 72, 158, 277–86,
319–30, 435nn117–18
determining length of sessions, 301–2
eliminating faulty approaches to,
299–301, 326–27
nine stages of, 313–15
objects of, 291–92, 293–96
obstructions to, 303–10
preparation for, 288
prerequisites of, 287–88
and special insight, union of, 10
See also four types of attention; meditation; mindfulness; placement meditation; six powers; union: of śamatha and
special insight
saṃsāra. See cyclic existence
Saṅgha, 110–11
excellent qualities of, 106
and merit, 216
See also Three Jewels
Śāntarakṣita, 332–33
Śāntideva, 9, 209. See also *individual works*
Satyaka Chapter (*Satyakaparivarta*), 17,
103, 105, 144
Sautrāntika-Madhyamaka, 332–33
scholars, and meditation, 55
scriptural knowledge, 33
excellent qualities of, 7–8
as personal instruction, 16–17
self
of phenomena, 341
as superimposition, 334–35
See also *under* ignorance
self-cherishing, 213

selflessness, 20, 33, 437n133, 438n157
establishing through investigative analysis, 410–17
of persons, 328, 336, 351–65
of phenomena, 367–78
suchness of, 334–35
view of, 333, 344–49
senses, restraining, 52
sentient beings
equanimity regarding, 200–201
as one's mother, 201–4
See also six classes of beings
Serlingpa, 9, 38
seven-limb practice, 46–50, 70, 71
See also confession; dedication; offering;
prostrations; rejoicing; spiritual
teachers: requesting to turn wheel of
Dharma; supplication
Seventy Stanzas on Emptiness (*Śūnyatāsaptati*, Nāgārjuna), 337–38, 343, 389
on dependent arising, 373
Seventy Verses on Going for Refuge
(*Triśaraṇagamanasaptati*, Candrakīrti), 100, 115
Sharawa, 184–85
siddhis, 38
Śīlarakṣita, 8
single-pointed focus, on ultimate reality, 8
six classes of beings, 351. See also rebirth
six consciousnesses, 52, 386
six modes of inquiry, 404–5
six perceptions, 22–26. See also senses,
restraining
six perfections, 233, 234, 240–46, 424,
429n14, 434n98. See also *individual
perfections*
six powers, 315–17
six preparatory practices, 45–46
Sixty Stanzas of Reasoning (*Yuktiṣaṣṭikā*,
Nāgārjuna)
on conceptuality, 335
on illusion-like appearances, 397
on mental afflictions, 342
on nirvāṇa, 375–76; 377
on self, 345
skillful means, 20, 190
sleeping, correct practice of, 53–54

About the Authors

TSONGKHAPA LOSANG DRAKPA (1357–1419) was renowned as a scholar, a tantric master, and a monastic reformer. He studied widely among the traditions of his day, and his many works have left an indelible imprint on Tibetan Buddhism. These include his *Great Treatise on the Stages of the Path to Enlightenment*; his Madhyamaka masterwork, *Illuminating the Intent*; and his explanation of the completion stage of highest yoga tantra, *A Lamp to Illuminate the Five Stages*. He founded Ganden Monastery at the end of his life and the Geluk school, which went on to produce the lineage of the Dalai Lamas.

PHILIP QUARCOO began studying Tibetan Buddhism in London in the late 1990s. He earned his first degree in modern European languages at the University of Durham, UK, and in 2007 graduated with a master's degree in Tibetan studies from the University of Munich, Germany, where he is currently researching nineteenth-century Tibetan and Mongolian devotional poetry.

What to Read Next from Wisdom Publications

Illuminating the Intent
An Exposition of Candrakīrti's Entering the Middle Way
Tsongkhapa
Translated by Thupten Jinpa

The Dalai Lama's translator and author of the definitive biography of Tsongkhapa here presents the first translation of one of that master's seminal and best-known works.

Steps on the Path to Enlightenment
A Commentary on Tsongkhapa's Lamrim Chenmo
Geshe Lhundub Sopa with David Patt
Foreword by His Holiness the Dalai Lama
    Vol. 1: The Foundation Practices
    Vol. 2: Karma
    Vol. 3: The Way of the Bodhisattva
    Vol. 4: Śamatha
    Vol. 5: Insight

"This should be carefully studied and practiced by all those who wish to proceed along the Buddhist path to enlightenment."
—B. Alan Wallace, author of *Stilling the Mind*

Mastering Meditation
Instructions on Calm Abiding and Mahāmudrā
His Eminence Chöden Rinpoché
Foreword by His Holiness the Dalai Lama
Translated by Tenzin Gache

"Kyabjé Chöden Rinpoché was more kind to me than all the three times' buddhas. His teachings are not just words but come from a learned mind— and from experience." —Lama Zopa Rinpoche

Ornament of Precious Liberation
Gampopa
Foreword by His Holiness the Karmapa
Translated by Ken Holmes
Edited by Thupten Jinpa

"This text has the power of a direct transmission from master to student . . .
Though there are several earlier translations of *Ornament of Precious Liberation*, this translation is the most readable and faithful."
—His Holiness the Karmapa, Ogyen Trinley Dorje

The Library of Wisdom and Compassion **series**
His Holiness the Dalai Lama with Venerable Thubten Chodron

Vol. 1. Approaching the Buddhist Path
Vol. 2. The Foundation of Buddhist Practice
Vol. 3. Saṃsāra, Nirvāṇa, and Buddha Nature
Vol. 4. Following in the Buddha's Footsteps
Vol. 5. In Praise of Great Compassion
Vol. 6. Courageous Compassion

"It's truly wonderful that His Holiness and Thubten Chodron are collaborating to produce this much-needed series of books on the Lam Rim designed for a modern audience. These books will be highly beneficial for teachers and students alike!"
—Kathleen McDonald, author of *How to Meditate*

Tsongkhapa's Praise for Dependent Relativity
Commentary by Lobsang Gyatso
Translated by Geshe Graham Woodhouse

"In this elegant text, the Ven. Geshe Graham Woodhouse translates Tsongkhapa's jewel-like masterpiece. The radiance of Tsongkhapa's poetry is refracted and enhanced by the brilliant and lucid commentary of the late Gen Losang Gyatso."
—Dr. Jay Garfield, Dorris Silbert Professor in Humanities and Professor of Philosophy at Smith College

Liberation in the Palm of Your Hand
A Concise Discourse on the Path to Enlightenment
Pabongka Rinpoche
Edited by Trijang Rinpoche
Translated by Michael Richards

"The richest and most enjoyable volume from the lamrim tradition . . . published to date."
—*Golden Drum*

Nāgārjuna's Middle Way
Mūlamadhyamakakārikā
Mark Siderits and Shōryū Katsura

"Authoritative, vivid, and illuminating."
—Graham Priest, author of *Logic: A Very Short Introduction*

About Wisdom Publications

Wisdom Publications is the leading publisher of classic and contemporary Buddhist books and practical works on mindfulness. To learn more about us or to explore our other books, please visit our website at wisdomexperience.org or contact us at the address below.

Wisdom Publications
199 Elm Street
Somerville, MA 02144 USA

We are a 501(c)(3) organization, and donations in support of our mission are tax deductible.

Wisdom Publications is affiliated with the Foundation for the Preservation of the Mahayana Tradition (FPMT).